WITHDRAWN FROM
MACALESTER COLLEGE
LIBRARY

Politics/Sense/Experience

Politics/Sense/Experience

A Pragmatic Inquiry into the Promise of Democracy

Timothy V. Kaufman-Osborn

Cornell University Press

ITHACA AND LONDON

CORNELL UNIVERSITY PRESS IS GRATEFUL FOR THE SUPPORT RECEIVED FROM THE
PRESIDENT'S CONTINGENCY FUND OF WHITMAN COLLEGE IN PUBLISHING THIS BOOK.

Copyright © 1991 by Cornell University

All rights reserved. Except for brief quotations in a review, this book,
or parts thereof, must not be reproduced in any form without
permission in writing from the publisher. For information, address
Cornell University Press, 124 Roberts Place, Ithaca, New York 14850.

First published 1991 by Cornell University Press.

International Standard Book Number 0-8014-2504-2
Library of Congress Catalog Card Number 91-6325

Printed in the United States of America

*Librarians: Library of Congress cataloging information
appears on the last page of the book.*

∞ The paper in this book meets the minimum requirements
   of the American National Standard for Information Sciences—
   Permanence of Paper for Printed Library Materials, ANSI Z39.48-1984.

Contents

Preface

Eloquent in its silence, the rubble of the Berlin Wall demonstrates that political identities and oppositions fashioned during the Cold War are no longer equal to late–twentieth-century actualities. No longer can we so neatly divide the world into free and unfree regimes, and so no longer can we determine who we are simply by pointing to who we are not. As events outstrip mind's accustomed resources, we are reminded that the aim of thinking is not to mirror a finished reality but to anticipate the possibilities disclosed by affairs still very much in the making.

Witnessing the emergence (and sometimes the suppression) of popular reform movements in China, the Soviet Union, South Korea, the Philippines, Poland, and other unexpected places, we may be tempted to discount the novelty of the present moment by assimilating it to the past. We may be inclined, following Francis Fukuyama, to conclude that what we now behold is "the end point of mankind's ideological evolution and the universalization of Western liberal democracy as the final form of human government."[1] Yet is it possible that this self-congratulatory conclusion prematurely resolves the import of our cur-

---

1. Francis Fukuyama, "The End of History?" *National Interest* 16 (Summer 1989), 4.

rent situation? If we were to check our desire to fix the meaning of the present, might we secure a richer apprehension of its ambiguous admixture of promise and peril? Might we, for example, speculate that adequate appreciation of the claims of democracy becomes most difficult when parliamentary institutions and civil liberties are (at least formally) endorsed without exception? Might it be that the term "democracy" loses its power to question what is when we all come to call ourselves democrats?

When the sense of the past slips away but the contours of the new remain equivocal, the time is ripe for fresh demarcation of the meanings in terms of which future conflicts will be fought. This book is animated by the perhaps naïve hope that we are now entering a crucial period of struggle over what democracy means. Those who identify democracy's import with specified institutional forms, as does Fukuyama, forget that their existence is compatible with that of profoundly antidemocratic cultures. The defining structures of contemporary Western societies—the corporation, the research university, the bureaucratic state, the mass media, and so forth—are to a greater or lesser extent inegalitarian, unaccountable, and exploitative. Consequently, the task for the democrat today is to inquire into the meaning of that paradoxical situation in which the superficial triumph of democracy excuses our failure to attend to its deeper bidding.

For reasons I explain in this book, I do not think that such an inquiry can be accomplished without at the same time engaging in a genealogical examination of the complex history out of which our received account of reason has emerged. The adjective "democratic" refers to a qualitatively unique form of specifically political experience. Any effort to foster such experience presupposes an exploration into what frustrates its realization; what chiefly does so now are the institutionalized embodiments of what I call a teleocratic conception of reason. That conception, whose roots I trace to the city-state of classical Greece, holds that everyday experience must be deemed insufficient or unreal as long as it remains insubordinate in the face of reason's rule. Redemption of the cause of ordinary embodied experience is indispensable, therefore, if the term "democracy" is to be available for purposes other than describing accomplished fact.

I was initially persuaded to ask whether the claims of democracy and those of a teleocratic conception of reason might stand in inverse relationship to each other by reading the work of John Dewey, and, although my thinking has been shaped by many others, Dewey stands as the principal source of inspiration for this book. Yet aside from this preface and the introductory chapter that follows, I make very few explicit references to Dewey or to the philosophical school to which he putatively belongs. Why?

This book is not *about* Dewey, and it is not *about* pragmatism. I am persuaded that Dewey's writings suggest original ways of thinking about the relationship between reason and experience, and that these ways are worthy of exploration by those who deem it important to reflect on the current state of democratic politics. I do not, however, believe that Dewey's work furnishes a set of determinate meanings that we can know without at the same time transforming what is known. To hold otherwise is, wittingly or no, to endorse one of the key dualisms against which those calling themselves "pragmatists" have long railed. Specifically, it is to affirm the existence of an unequivocal disjunction between reader and that which is read; and it is to construe reading as an activity through which the precisely demarcated subject that is the reader secures an equally precise representation of its circumscribed object.

For reasons I explicate throughout this work, this formulation does not do justice to the experience of fashioning sense from what at first appears unfamiliar. In an autobiographical statement composed in 1930, Dewey wrote: "I seem to be unstable, chameleon-like, yielding one after another to many diverse and even incompatible influences; struggling to assimilate something from each and yet striving to carry it forward in a way that is logically consistent with what has been learned from its predecessors."[2] Although the activity of making sense can be decomposed into its constitutive elements for analytic purposes, its experienced reality is always one in which knower and known are continuously engaged in creation and re-creation of each other. To forget that meaning is engendered *within* the mutual relationship between these two essentially ambiguous creatures is to forget, quoting Dewey again, that "all discourse, oral or written, which is more than a routine unrolling of vocal habits, says things that surprise the one that says them."[3] Thus any reader who seeks to craft sense from texts that caught their author off-guard is sure to beget meanings that are startling to both. To deny this possibility is to make certain that neither will pass beyond the superficial and so realize the significances of which each is capable.

Criticism of this work's arguments should therefore be predicated

---

2. Dewey, "From Absolutism to Experimentalism," in *ENF*, p. 13.
3. Dewey, *EN*, p. 194.

on grounds other than those of infidelity to a "Dewey" whose alleged existence is symptomatic of the rationalism Dewey sought to undermine. To forestall such criticism, however, is not to claim that what follows is simply the unsubstantiated invention of an autonomous ego. To counter any objectivist account of interpretation, it is best to emphasize the reader's contribution to the enterprise of making sense. But to counter its subjectivist counterpart, it is best to stress the contribution of what is to be read. Having already done the former, let me now do the latter.

Although I believe this book will prove comprehensible to those unfamiliar with Dewey's work, I will nonetheless offer a brief overview of the texts from which I have principally drawn. Just before World War I, Dewey became ever more disgruntled with the increasingly arcane questions vexing the increasingly professionalized discipline of philosophy. That dissatisfaction was given compressed expression in a 1917 essay titled "The Need for a Recovery of Philosophy." There, Dewey asserted that his aim was to "forward the emancipation of philosophy from too intimate and exclusive attachment to traditional problems. It is not in intent a criticism of various solutions that have been offered, but raises a question *as to the genuineness, under the present conditions of science and social life, of the problems*."[4] To question the "genuineness" of philosophy's conventional problems is, by implication, to label those preoccupations "artificial" and so, by extension, to contest their appearance of reality. To make clear the sense in which such problems are insignificant, Dewey set to work articulating an ontology whose paradoxical purpose was to check philosophy's felt need for a theory of reality. Refusing to supply what all previous ontology had taken to be its essential end, Dewey declined the tradition's invitation to draw an invidious distinction between pure objects whose existence is guaranteed by being certainly known and those mundane things of everyday experience that cannot be so redeemed. "The chief characteristic trait of the pragmatic notion of reality is precisely that no theory of Reality in general, *überhaupt*, is possible or needed. It [pragmatism] occupies the position of an emancipated empiricism or a thoroughgoing naïve realism. It finds that 'reality' is a *denotative* term, a word used to designate indifferently everything that happens. Lies, dreams, insanities, deceptions, myths, theories are all of them just the events which they specifically are. Pragmatism takes

4. Dewey, "The Need for a Recovery of Philosophy," in *ENF*, p. 21.

its stand with daily life, which finds that such things really have to be reckoned with as they occur interwoven in the texture of events. The only way in which the term reality can become more than a blanket denotative term is through recourse to specific events in all their diversity and thatness."[5]

To restore some sense of the import of ordinary events, Dewey wrote his occasionally poetic and often obscure *Experience and Nature* (1929). That work sketched the outlines of what might be called a naturalized Hegelian historicism. Its largest aspiration was to rescue the category of experience, construed as an existential site of potential meaning, from denigration at the hands of a rationalistic philosophic tradition whose contempt for this world relegates its affairs to a shadowy realm of partial being. To this end, Dewey asked what shape the relationship between nature, experience, and meaning might assume if thinking were to take its cues not from received doctrine, but rather from the characteristic qualities of experience in gross, that is, from life as it is immediately lived by those unblessed with philosophic insight. "As against this common identification of reality with what is sure, regular and finished, experience in unsophisticated forms gives evidence of a different world and points to a different metaphysics."[6]

To explore the genesis of the philosopher's turn away from unrefined experience, Dewey sometimes, as in *Reconstruction in Philosophy* (1920), trained his sights on the ancient Greek city-state. For the most part, however, his abiding concern was seventeenth- and eighteenth-century reformulations of this classical inheritance. Within early epistemological writings, Dewey located sophisticated explications of the cultural forms coming to mark the condition of collective unhappiness known as modernity. Defined by its institutionalization of the tradition's oppressive disjunctions between mind and body, means and ends, art and labor, and the like, that condition was quickly eroding the capacity of ordinary undertakings to retain any sense of their unrationalized reality. In *The Public and Its Problems* (1927), accordingly, Dewey argued that recovery from the malady of pernicious dualism requires animation of the cause of democratic association. For only that mode of human relatedness adequately respects and celebrates the meaning-bearing possibilities of everyday life. (This work, I might note in passing, does not succeed very well in developing the specifi-

5. Ibid., p. 59.
6. Dewey, *EN*, p. 47.

cally political dimensions of the ontology articulated in *Experience and Nature*. Hence, on one level, the present book might be read as an attempt to do what Dewey never quite managed to do, that is, to state the politics appropriate to a world that has at last abandoned *The Quest for Certainty* [1929].)

Finally, in *Art as Experience* (1934), Dewey described the form of conduct he thought most responsive to experience's capacity to nurture and bring forth the fruits of meaning. Premised on a denial of reason's special access to what is real, that account effectively brought his critique of the Western philosophical tradition to a close. That conclusion, although marking the end of Dewey's journey, cannot be ours. For, as I suggest in these pages, Dewey's critique implicitly raises a question he himself could never quite pose: Does a commitment to the cause of significant experience now entail repudiation of our inveterate Enlightenment conviction that knowledge is the sine qua non of emancipation from the fetters of the present?

Although this artificially simplified exposition of Dewey's mature writings may suggest otherwise, I do not think it possible to extricate an untarnished and trouble-free philosophical system from beneath the accumulated weight of nearly a century's (mis)reading. His assessment of Francis Bacon is easily turned back on himself: "Like many another prophet, he suffers from confused intermingling of old and new."[7] Dewey did not always adequately appreciate the demands placed on anyone seeking to remap from within the recalcitrant complex of meanings defined by our collective conceptual inheritance.[8] This shortcoming is most apparent when, falling prey to the rationalism he wanted to criticize, he defined his project as an explication of the meaning of modern science. In his *Logic* (1938), for example, Dewey asserted that the "demand for reform of logic is the demand for a unified theory of inquiry through which the authentic pattern of experimental and operational inquiry of science shall become available for regulation of the habitual methods by which inquiries in the field of common sense are carried on."[9] In his *Theory of Valuation* (1939), he compounded the problematic import of these claims by writing: "Not

7. Dewey, *RP*, p. 28.
8. On this point, see Dewey's essay "The Objects of Valuation," *Journal of Philosophy* 15 (1918), 258: "I console myself with a belief that while my own inexpertness in statement is largely responsible for my failure to make myself understood, some of the difficulty lies with the immensely difficult transformation in methods of thinking about all social matters which the theory implies."
9. Dewey, *LTI*, p. 98.

only is science *a* value (since it is the expression and fulfillment of a special human desire and interest) but it is the supreme means of the valid determination of all valuations in all aspects of human and social life."[10] These quotations, although they may be interpreted in more or less charitable ways, make all but irresistible the positivist temptation to regard modern science as the final solution to philosophy's quest for an ahistorical tribunal whose privileged relation to the real justifies condemnation of all practice that does not bow before it. Encouraged by the Enlightenment's illusion that sufficient reconstruction of established forms of collective order can produce perfect concord among purely rational agents, Dewey too often identified the cause of his pragmatism with that of a liberalism whose state-centered order proves intolerant of all that resists extension of its finely textured web of (self-)disciplinary controls.

To refashion Dewey's project in ways that extend its soundest impulses while leaving its scientistic excesses behind, I have relocated his distinctive vocabulary within a political present that bears some elements of continuity and some of discontinuity with that out of which it originally emerged. How that transplantation has additionally altered the meaning of his words is a matter over which I have at best partial control. My hope is that whatever sense grows from such recultivation effectively contests previous accounts of the political bearing of pragmatism and at the same time contributes to ongoing debates about the possibilities of democratic politics in a scientific age.

Because the account of experience explicated in these pages renders highly problematic the notion of speaking in one's own voice, I have made Dewey a participant in this book's narrative rather than its object. It is unjust to ascribe the fruit of this exploratory dialogue either to myself or to Dewey. Consequently, I have employed a compositional form that, to the degree it is successful, exemplifies this book's substantive argument regarding the need to recover some sense of what experience might tender were it less completely subjected to the eviscerating categories of imperious reason. Braiding together Dewey's words and mine wherever I thought a paraphrase would diminish the former's punch, I have blurred but not effaced the distinction between my contribution and that of my collaborator.

With more than an ounce of misgiving, I have observed the scholarly convention of furnishing citations for quotations taken from

10. Dewey, *TV*, p. 66.

Dewey's texts. But I have rejected other conventions that visually intimate that his words are independent matter awaiting objective representation rather than pregnant offerings whose potentialities have yet to be fully explored. I have, for example, dispensed with the custom of indenting and single-spacing longer quotations, with the use of ellipses to indicate when language from different texts has been merged within a single claim, and with the employment of colons to introduce quotations appropriated from Dewey's texts. Also, I have occasionally hyphenated words and phrases in order to accentuate the always tense relationship between how we *think* about experience and what it is to *have* such experience. Whether these stylistic peculiarities alleviate or aggravate the disabilities of Dewey's prose, which, Oliver Wendell Holmes once claimed, sounded much as "God would have spoken had He been inarticulate but keenly desirous to tell you how it was,"[11] is not for me to say.

I thank the Center for Dewey Studies, Southern Illinois University, Carbondale, for permission to quote from the Southern Illinois edition of Dewey's previously unpublished works. Portions of this book have been published elsewhere, and I thank the journals and their publishers for permission to make use of this material. A portion of Chapter 2 appeared as "Politics and the Invention of Reason," *Polity* 21 (Summer 1989). Portions of Chapter 4 appeared as "John Dewey and the Liberal Science of Community," *Journal of Politics* 46 (November 1984), published by the University of Texas Press, and as "Modernity's Myth of Facts: Émile Durkheim on Political Education," *Theory and Society* 17 (1988), 121–145, copyright Kluwer Academic Publishers, reprinted by permission of Kluwer Academic Publishers. A portion of Chapter 6 appeared as "Pragmatism, Policy Science, and the State," *American Journal of Political Science* 29 (November 1985), published by the University of Texas Press.

For reasons only partly clear to me, this project took longer than anticipated to complete. Hence the matter of acknowledging my debts proves more than ordinarily complicated. To my siblings, my parents, and my children, I owe thanks for their toleration of my more than occasional crankiness. I am indebted to the National Endowment for the Humanities, the John Dewey Research Fund, and the Earhart

11. Oliver Wendell Holmes, quoted in James Kloppenberg, *Uncertain Victory: Social Democracy and Progressivism in European and American Thought, 1870–1920* (New York: Oxford University Press, 1986), p. 375.

Foundation for financial support at various stages of this project. To several of my teachers, including Harlan Wilson, the late John Lewis, Patrick Riley, Charles Anderson, Sheldon Wolin, and Dennis Thompson, I owe much of my sense of how to go about thinking theoretically about political matters. I am grateful to my colleagues at Whitman College, especially Mary Hanna, Dave Schmitz, Ed Foster, and David Deal, for their always patient encouragement. To Shirley Muse, I owe thanks for her unflagging willingness to print draft after draft of this manuscript. Both Holly Bailey and my anonymous readers deserve acknowledgment for their confidence in a manuscript whose idiosyncratic features gave others pause. I owe a special thanks to Dennis Wakefield for his relentlessly good-natured criticism of my every intellectual move. Finally, I am most deeply indebted to Sharon Kaufman-Osborn, for her example has shown me why it is that an argument of the sort advanced here is never merely an intellectual concern.

TIMOTHY V. KAUFMAN-OSBORN

Walla Walla, Washington

Abbreviations

While this manuscript was in preparation, Southern Illinois University Press had not yet finished its publication of Dewey's complete works. Whenever possible, therefore, citations refer to editions more commonly found in circulation. I have used the Southern Illinois edition of previously unpublished works; and these have been abbreviated, with the appropriate volume number, as follows: *EW* (*Early Works*), *MW* (*Middle Works*), and *LW* (*Later Works*). References to other works of Dewey are abbreviated as follows:

AE	*Art as Experience.* New York: Capricorn Books, 1958.
CE1	*Characters and Events* vol. 1 New York: Octagon Books, 1970.
CE2	*Characters and Events* vol. 2 New York: Octagon Books, 1970.
CF	*A Common Faith.* New Haven: Yale University Press, 1934.
DE	*Democracy and Education.* New York: Macmillan, 1961.
EEL	*Essays in Experimental Logic.* New York: Dover, n.d.
EN	*Experience and Nature.* New York: Dover, 1958.
ENF	*On Experience, Nature, and Freedom.* Ed. Richard Bernstein. Indianapolis: Bobbs-Merrill, 1960.
FC	*Freedom and Culture.* New York: Capricorn Books, 1962.
HNC	*Human Nature and Conduct.* New York: Modern Library, 1930.
HWT	*How We Think.* Chicago: Henry Regnery, 1971.
IDP	*The Influence of Darwin on Philosophy.* New York: Peter Smith, 1951.

KK	*Knowing and the Known*. With Arthur Bentley. Boston: Beacon Press, 1949.
LSA	*Liberalism and Social Action*. New York: Capricorn Books, 1963.
LTI	*Logic: The Theory of Inquiry*. New York: Henry Holt, 1938.
PC	*Philosophy and Civilization*. New York: Minton, Balch, 1931.
PM	*Problems of Men*. New York: Philosophical Library, 1946.
PP	*The Public and Its Problems*. Chicago: Swallow Press, 1954.
QC	*The Quest for Certainty*. New York: Capricorn Books, 1960.
RP	*Reconstruction in Philosophy*. Boston: Beacon Press, 1957.
SS	*The School and Society*. Chicago: University of Chicago Press, 1899.
TV	*Theory of Valuation*. Chicago: University of Chicago Press, 1939.

Numerical citations (for example, 61/17) refer to the cataloging system employed by the Morris Library of the University of Southern Illinois to organize Dewey's unpublished manuscripts.

Politics/Sense/Experience

1 /
Relocating the Pragmata
of Pragmatism

I

What is the quality of our present political experience? To contemporary ears, this question sounds a bit odd. To answer it, we are likely to make reference to the percentage of eligible voters casting ballots in any given election, to the results of polls asking about the degree of public confidence in major political and economic institutions, to the capacity of the contemporary state to ensure that most of its citizens do not fall below a prescribed poverty level, and so on.

That we are inclined to respond in this fashion is revealing. Each of these answers effectively translates a question of quality into one of quantity. In place of detailed inquiry into our significant lives as citizens, we speak in terms of statistical abstractions. That language, in a way, is peculiarly appropriate. For it accurately expresses the sense in which political experience, for most, now assumes the character of a remote spectacle.[1] As so many bystanders, we witness but cannot quite grasp the global political events zipping past our mind's eye. We

1. For a penetrating analysis of the theatrics of contemporary politics, see Murray Edelman, *Constructing the Political Spectacle* (Chicago: University of Chicago Press, 1988).

are persuaded that what is reported to us are newsworthy matters; but these flitting appearances have little or no tangible presence and so bear little or no palpable quality.

The reduction of politics to a staged show produced by the mass media finds its corollary in the devaluation of everyday life and its distinctive concerns. To learn that the world is governed by the play of forces whose being is best articulated in measured terms is to learn that the loci of ordinary experience are essentially inconsequential. It is, additionally, to learn that all experience can be definitively tagged according to whether it fits into the public realm that is occupied by these untouchable fetishes, or into the private realm whose parochial affairs, although joyful and tragic, exasperating and fulfilling, confining and liberating, are in the last analysis not quite real. That bifurcation, in turn, reinforces our passivity in the face of things as they currently stand. For when our response to the anonymous objectivity of the political universe is confined to our merely "subjective" opinions, especially should they remain unpolled, the basic structures of collective life persist unchallenged.

In casting about for a symbol appropriate to the experience so described, I am drawn to the work of Max Weber and Michel Foucault. Through his haunting image of the iron cage, Weber gestures at the abstract imperatives that mock our hope for a less oppressive future. Recasting its bars as the concrete walls of Jeremy Bentham's Panopticon, Foucault explores this structure's interior by dissecting the finely meshed disciplinary techniques that fashion selves eager to embrace these cramped quarters as their own. So synthesized, Weber and Foucault offer a vision of modernity that is truthful not because it penetrates behind the veil of appearances, but rather because it gives partial form to our otherwise inarticulate feeling of complicitous entanglement within constellations of power from which there seems to be no escape.

This nihilistic vision is especially unnerving because it hints that modernity's scarcely visible but transparently exploitative confines represent the fulfillment of reason. In the second volume of his *Economy and Society*, Weber advances an uncanny anticipation of Foucault's central thesis in *Discipline and Punish*:

> No special proof is necessary to show that military discipline is the ideal model for the modern capitalist factory, as it was for the ancient plantation. However, organizational discipline in the factory has a completely rational basis. With the help of suitable methods of measurement, the

optimum profitability of the individual worker is calculated like that of any material means of production. On this basis, the American system of "scientific management" triumphantly proceeds with its rational conditioning and training of work performances, thus drawing the ultimate conclusions from the mechanization and discipline of the plant. The psycho-physical apparatus of man is completely adjusted to the demands of the outer world, the tools, the machines—in short, it is functionalized, and the individual is shorn of his natural rhythm as determined by his organism; in line with the demands of the work procedure, he is attuned to a new rhythm through the functional specialization of muscles and through the creation of an optimal economy of physical effort. The whole process of rationalization, in the factory as elsewhere, and especially in the bureaucratic state machine, parallels the centralization of the material implements of organization in the hands of the master. Thus, discipline inexorably takes over ever larger areas as the satisfaction of political and economic needs is increasingly rationalized.[2]

The dispassionate tone of this passage, taken from a work affirming its own value-free status, mimics the content it describes but can no longer find the words to condemn. Effectively silenced by his own ideal of objectivity, Weber is reduced to posing a question to which he can offer no adequate response: "The great question thus is . . . what we can set against this mechanization to preserve a certain section of humanity from this fragmentation of the soul, this complete ascendancy of the bureaucratic ideal of life?"[3] For those not fortunate enough to inhabit this "section," Weber can only tender the unfounded hope that habituation to routinized discipline will conceal the contradiction of an order that proclaims itself "democratic" in order to disguise its true character as a "dictatorship resting on the exploitation of mass emotionality."[4]

Read side by side, Weber and Foucault offer what I take to be the most compelling articulation of the situation now confronting those concerned about the fate of democratic politics. The hollowing out of public life is, as they insist, inextricably bound up with our notion of reason as well as the various institutional forms through which it is concretely objectified. Acknowledging this situation, the more influential strands of recent Continental political theory have exhibited an

2. Max Weber, *Economy and Society*, vol. 2 (Berkeley: University of California Press, 1978), p. 1156.

3. Weber, quoted in Anthony Giddens, *Capitalism and Modern Social Theory* (New York: Cambridge University Press, 1971), p. 236.

4. Max Weber, "Politics as a Vocation," in *From Max Weber*, ed. Hans Gerth and C. W. Mills (New York: Oxford University Press, 1946), p. 107.

unexpected measure of convergence. Emerging from the traditions of phenomenology, existentialism, hermeneutics, neo-Marxism, deconstructionism, and so on, that convergence's overall thrust is indicated in a rough way by the term "antifoundationalism." What joins these efforts together is skepticism toward the view, whether labeled representationalism, objectivism, scientism, logocentrism, realism, or something else, that the world guarantees the adequacy of reason's grasp of its antecedently existent and essential meaning. No more can we rest assured that there is a determinate fit between the cognizable properties of what is real and the cognizing powers of the human mind. For noncognitive experience is prior to human speculation in the sense that all knowing, whether scientific or commonsensical, is inescapably embedded in historically contextualized webs of practical activity that resist radical penetration or full disclosure by reason's insight. Hence besides finding suspect the cosmological and theological dogmas that once sustained faith in reason's access to the world's truth, we now find it necessary to question the form of foundationalism apparent in so much Enlightenment rationalism. No longer, that is, can we uncritically adhere to that utopia in which all autonomous subjects, uniformly purifying their minds of the errors sown by superstition, prejudice, and tradition, attain transparent insight into the nature of truth via the truth of nature.

To grant the general sense of contemporary Continental philosophy's antifoundationalist bent is, by extension, to review our felt need to ground politics in something more certain and steady than politics itself. In one way, it is intensely liberating to realize that the legitimation of specifically democratic politics need not be rooted in the fixed constitution of human nature, or the unalterable demands of reason, or even the necessary structure of human communication. Yet that emancipation contains within the seeds of its own ironical reformulation. For at the very moment when democracy's possibilities seem ripest for reexploration, we are becoming ever more tightly enmeshed within rationalized structures that, although disinclined to inquire into the conditions of their own authority, do all the labor once done by the past's more sublime sources of peremptory order.

It is this paradox that indicates why any effort to rethink the politics of democracy cannot be disjoined from a correlative effort to rethink the meaning of modern science. Although the roots of rationalization extend well past the age of Copernicus, Galileo, and Newton, it is only the development of modern science that has turned the West's recurrent fantasy of a world ruled by reason into a realizable ambition. In reflecting on the meaning of that development, however, we too often accept the familiar representation of science as either neutral instrumentality or as one-dimensional master; and we then lapse all too quickly into either cheerful relativism or cynical despair, neither of which offers an antidote to the power of reason in the present. Millenarian socialists, scanning the horizon for the ghost of Marx, pine for the revolution that will institute an unproblematic synthesis of democratic politics and technological instrumentalities; while romantic communitarians, seeking solace in Rousseau, hark back to a mythic past that escaped the need to grapple with the situation of science. Lovers of antiquity, resurrecting Aristotle's distinction between *technē* and *phronēsis*, cling to the hope that dialogic association will offer an effective counterthrust to the structural imperatives of a technocratic political economy; while friends of liberalism, recalling Francis Bacon's contention that a collective quest to master nature must now displace the struggle of each individual to dominate all others, persist in the faith that unremitting accumulation of scientific knowledge will overcome what has been irretrievably spoiled by the march of progress. Arch structuralists, unable to draw upon their absent selves, relegate the actors who might contest the present to the status of mythical placeholders whose reason is epiphenomenal; while unstable deconstructionists, full of Nietzschean *ressentiment*, reduce the art of politics to a fanciful game of arbitrary signifiers played exclusively among those who, to borrow a line from Dewey, are certain that if "we can only get as many shocks from words as we do from things and render the sequence of words as jumpy and blind as is the sequence of events, we shall have proved our competency to keep even, up-to-date."[5] As so many protests against forms of order cunning enough to recapture their critics no matter how much ironic distance they secure, the efflux of these genres does little to overcome the gulf between the frustrations we now experience and the ill-suited words we find available for their articulation.

To pass beyond these confines, let us return to my initial characterization of the contemporary political spectacle. What defines the experience of that spectacle, I suggested, is its abstraction, its absence of any significant measure of differentiated tangible quality. If we are to make sense of and perhaps even to contest the forces that systemati-

5. Dewey, "Events and Meanings," in *CE1*, p. 127.

cally reproduce such dessicated political experience, we must translate our ill-formed sense of discontent into more specific questions. Here then are two questions that, together, inform the present inquiry: First, how are we to account for the contemporary partitioning of ordinary experience into so many discrete domains (for instance, family, work, citizenship), each of which is increasingly subject to various forms of expert intervention grounded in instrumentalized forms of knowledge? And, second, how might we begin to recover our sense of the reality of peculiarly democratic experience and thereby enhance its capacity to resist the logic of what Weber calls "rationalization"?

In formulating my responses to these questions, I have turned to a suspect source. Weber was right to point to America as a hyperbolic exemplar of the fate soon to consume the remainder of the West. What he did not see was that it is also America that furnishes the inchoate materials out of which we can fashion an answer to rationalization's apparently inexorable march through history. It is the burden of this book to show that pragmatism (a term I reject for reasons explained below) has something of significance to say when permitted to enter debates that, for the most part, have been dominated by Continental thinkers.[6] Inviting us to recultivate the resources of specifically democratic experience, pragmatism suggests how we might limit that experience's susceptibility to expropriation in the service of antidemocratic ends.

II

In titling this chapter "Relocating the Pragmata of Pragmatism," I mean to signal my commitment to two interrelated beliefs. First, if we are to recover our sense of specifically democratic experience, we must step outside the boundaries of familiar linguistic usage. That usage falsifies the character of qualified experience by passing it through the reifying filters suggested by so many forms of misguided rationalism. Most significantly, its illicit importation of an antecedent disconnection between subject and object ensures that the temporally and spa-

6. I share the minority view, recently expressed by James Kloppenberg in his *Uncertain Victory: Social Democracy and Progressivism in European and American Thought, 1870–1920* (New York: Oxford University Press, 1986), that "Dewey and Weber are the two most significant social theorists America and Europe have produced in the twentieth century" (pp. 350–51).

tially qualified dimensions of lived experience will go unappreciated. The term "pragmata," by way of contrast, points toward aspects of experience about which rationalism cannot speak without endangering its claim to rule the conduct of ordinary life.

Second, if pragmatism is to help us speak more truthfully about the experience of experience, "it" must contest its own reification by recalling its original meaning. This book is well understood as a series of intertwining attempts not to define but to explicate the sense of the term "pragmata"; and that term may itself be understood as an abbreviation that, when interwoven with others such as "experience," "habit," "sense," and "art," provides a complex answer to the questions I posed at the close of the preceding section.

A first stab at articulating the qualitative dimensions of experience connoted by the term "pragmata" can be suggested by means of a brief etymological excursus. (In the following section, I will return to the issue of "pragmata-ism.") Standing before his accusers, Socrates uses the phrase *ta politika pragmata* to suggest the form of practice in which he has not, and will not, engage:

> It may seem curious that I should go round giving advice like this and busying myself in people's private affairs, and yet never venture publicly to address you as a whole and advise on matters of state. The reason for this is what you have often heard me say before on many other occasions—that I am subject to a divine or supernatural experience, which Meletus sought fit to travesty in his indictment. It began in my early childhood—a sort of voice which comes to me, and when it comes it always dissuades me from what I am proposing to do, and never urges me on. It is this that debars me from entering public life, and a very good thing too, in my opinion, because you may be quite sure, gentlemen, that if I had tried long ago to engage in politics, I should long ago have lost my life, without doing any good either to you or to myself.

To translate *ta politika pragmata* as "politics," as Hugh Tredennick does here,[7] is to reify the adjective *politika* and to disregard altogether the meaning of the plural noun *pragmata*. Of what sense are we thereby deprived?

Derived from the verb "to do" (*prassein*), the singular *pragma* is one of the most common words in the vocabulary of ancient Greece,

---

7. *The Apology*, in *The Collected Dialogues of Plato*, ed. Edith Hamilton and Huntington Cairns (Princeton: Princeton University Press, 1961), 31c–d. For another example of the translation of this phrase as "politics," see Harold Fowler, in his *Plato*, vol. 1, (Cambridge: Harvard University Press, 1982), p. 115.

furnishing the root for a complex array of compound verbs and nouns. Its range of meaning covers much more ground than I need specify in this context.[8] As the concrete of its cognate *praxis*, however, one of its most basic senses refers to a specific act or deed. Thus, in his "Against Aristogeiton" (1.57), Demosthenes explains how Aristogeiton sought to sell Zobia, his mistress, into slavery after she "did the act of a woman" (*gunaiou pragm' epoiei*). Here, *pragma* is appropriately used in the context of a circumscribed situation about which there is some to-do. The distinctive quality of that situation, as well as others like it, is suggested by the idiom *pragma esti moi*. Best translated as "it concerns me," this phrase conveys the adverbial sense that there is "something the matter," something unsettled, within a present state of affairs that summons the attentive response of those concretely implicated in its eventual issue.

The specific sense borne by such idiomatic usage varies in accordance with the urgency of a situation's imperatives. At one extreme, actors may be so wholly swept along by an ongoing course of events that they cannot appreciate its eventualities at the moment. Such, we may guess, was the situation of Harmodius and Aristogeiton when, according to legend, Hipparchus sought to intrude on what Aeschines calls their *pragma*, that is, their affair (1.132). The noble Aristogeiton had no clue at the time that his act of tyrannicide, provoked by jealous rage, would bring even greater political repression and so eventually engender the revolts that yielded a democratic Athens.[9]

By contrast, when the struggle to make sense of the unfamiliar is less immediately bound up with the demand that something be done right now, it sometimes proves possible to reflect on the connections sustained between the past from which that situation is emerging and the future into which it is passing. When an affair is thus considered *as* an affair—that is, when it becomes the subject of thinking *about* what is the matter—it loses a measure of its concrete imperiousness. But that in and of itself does not necessarily spell diminution of the concerned involvement suggested by the idiomatic *pragma esti moi*. To see this, consider Euthyphro, who in the Platonic dialogue bearing his name

8. For much of the etymological discussion that follows, I rely on the appropriate entries in Henry Liddell and Robert Scott, *Greek-English Lexicon* (Oxford: Clarendon Press, 1925). I also acknowledge Dana Burgess's assistance in working through the complexities of this term's various senses.

9. In his extended account of this affair (*The Peloponnesian War* 6.53–59), Thucydides suggests that "the conspiracy of Harmodios and Aristogeiton originated in the wounded feeling of a lover, and their reckless action resulted from a momentary failure of nerve."

chides his father for paying no attention to the hired worker who has been bound and thrown into a ditch, thinking "it did not matter" (*ouden on pragma*) whether he lived or died (4d). Euthyphro thereby implies that his father has failed to recognize that the urgency of this troublesome business is part and parcel of its full import.

The versatility of the term *pragma* stems from its capacity to convey meaning in situations whose temporal and spatial boundaries are still less clearly defined. Think in this regard of Cyrus, who, unsure how he should conduct war against the Massagetae, assembles "the chiefs among the Persians and lays the matter [*pragma*] before them, asking them to advise him what he should do" (Herodotus, 1.206). Similarly, to renew the Athenians' flagging confidence in the midst of the Peloponnesian War, Pericles reminds his listeners that the suffering produced by the plague is the "the only thing [*pragma*] which has happened that has transcended our foresight" (Thucydides, 2.64). In each of these instances, the speaker stands at some remove from the matter that prompts his speech, and so the term *pragma* carries the sense of a given but not static state of affairs whose implications for a collectivity's past hopes, present plight, and future projects are as yet very much unresolved.

This sense is retained in the opening scene of Aristophanes' *Lysistrata*. There the comedy's protagonist seeks to persuade her sisters to join her intrigue by insisting that *tes poleos ta pragmata*, which Liddell and Scott render as "the fortunes of the state," are now "anchored on us women" (32).[10] While off the mark as a literal translation, the term "fortunes" is quite apt, for it effectively captures the common association between the plural *pragmata* and the contingencies of human affairs. Never wholly responsive to the impress of purposive design, these uncertain matters are always subject to unanticipated twists of fate, and so pregnant with the possibility of suffering and sadness. That is surely Thucydides' implication in fashioning his account of the *pragmata*, the "circumstances" (1.89), that explain the emergence of Athens as an imperial power and so set the stage for the tragedy whose larger meaning he can decipher only because the Peloponnesian War is now completed.

10. For an interesting twist on accustomed usage, see Eteocles' opening speech in Aeschylus's *Seven against Thebes*: "Burghers of Cadmus, to say what the hour demands, is the part of him who guards the fortunes [*pragos*] of the State, guiding the helm upon the stern, his eyes not closed in slumber." If Liddell and Scott are correct, *pragos* is to be read here as a poetic rendering of *pragmata*.

It is this last sense that Socrates draws upon when, in the closing remarks of the *Apology* (41d), he insists that it is better for him "to die now and be freed from" what Fowler translates as his "troubles" (*apellachthai pragmaton*).[11] As his unresponsiveness to Crito's offer of escape will soon confirm, it is at just this moment that Socrates' patience in the face of this world's woes passes into a yearning to secure some final release from what Tredennick, translating the same phrase, calls his "distractions." When that longing becomes a consuming passion, as it does in Plato's *Republic*, it slips into a radical turning away from the transitory circumstances *in* which we are presently immersed but *about* which we ought to have no concern: "For surely, Adeimantus, the man whose mind is truly fixed on eternal realities has no leisure to turn his eyes downward upon the petty affairs [*pragmateias*] of men, and so engaging in strife with them to be filled with envy and hate, but he fixes his gaze upon the things of the eternal and unchanging order" (500c).

What sort of being, on Plato's account, is unable to recognize the immaterial nature of this world's insignificant affairs? A partial response is intimated when Socrates, in *Protagoras*, contemptuously asks Hippocrates if he knows what sort of "thing" (*pragmati*) a Sophist is (312c). In the *Gorgias*, that thing's character is revealed when Socrates ascribes to it the mean-spirited attributes of the *demos* it flatters: "In fact, for my own part, I always regarded public speakers and sophists as the only people who have no call to complain of the thing [*touto to pragmati*] that they themselves educate, for its wickedness towards them" (520b). Aristotle, for his part, simply extends this scornful sense when he employs the compound *pragmateuontai* to characterize the activities of those engaged in ignoble pursuits: "But the dicer and the foot pad or brigand are to be classed as mean, as showing sordid greed, for both 'ply their trade' and endure reproach for gain, the robber risking his life for plunder, and the dicer making gain out of his friends, to whom one ought to give" (*Nichomachean Ethics* 1122a9).

As the polis decays and the Roman Republic assumes its place, the

---

11. This is one of Plato's most characteristic uses of this term. This same sense is conveyed at 406e of the *Republic*. There Plato employs the plural to praise the craftsman who, when ill, spurns long courses of medical treatment and returns to work, either to regain health or, "if his body is not equal to the strain," to die and so be "freed from all his troubles." See also *Phaedo* 115a: "I think it is better to bathe before drinking the poison, that the women may not have the trouble of bathing the corpse."

term *pragma* comes to carry still more complex connotational freight. Reflecting a reconsideration of the skills appropriate to the profession of politics, Rome appropriates the abstract noun *pragmatikos* (rendered in Latin as *pragmaticus*), and employs it to designate "one skilled in the law, who furnishes orators and advocates with the principles on which they base their speeches" (Cicero, *Orations* 1, 59). This is the sense called upon by Cicero in using the phrase *pragmatici homines* to praise "men of affairs" (*Letters to Atticus* 2.20.I). Yet in spite of the considerable prestige attached to legal business in Rome, this characterization cannot quite shake loose the implication that such persons are too much preoccupied with the unworthy things of this world. That resonance is essential to Cicero's contemporary Philodemus when he deploys the epithetical *pragmatokopos* (*Rhetoric* 2.53) to taunt those unscrupulous "meddlers" and "busybodies" who cannot refrain from interfering in the affairs of their fellows.

The very shift from Socrates' *politika pragmata* to the Latin *res publica* says much about the new sense-making needs of those whose political affairs more and more take on the character of an objectified "public thing"; and the ever more frequent identification of that thing with power unilaterally exercised is suggested by the Justinian Code's use of the phrase *pragmatica sanctio* to signal the force of imperial decrees. Here power that had once assumed the character of a collaborative project cultivated among the city-state's engaged citizens reemerges as an exaction imposed on the empire's distanced subjects.

III

In his *Metaphysics*, Aristotle uses the term *pragmateia*, variously translated as "system" or "enterprise," to designate the philosophy of Plato (987a30). Here the original sense of *pragma*, its reference to a concrete deed or act, is turned on itself; it now becomes party to a noun designating a structure of interrelated concepts whose intolerance toward and distance from the realm of everyday affairs is implicit in the radicalism of its political ambitions. Such hypostatization achieves its consummate expression in English when an "ism" is grafted onto "pragmata," and when from this manufactured abstraction there arises a distinctive tradition of professional discourse devoted to explicating the meaning of this academic being. I have no desire to tell the complete story of the invention called "pragmatism." Because its history illustrates certain important dimensions of this work's larger argument about rationalism's deformation of experience, however, I offer a highly abbreviated outline of its most recent chapter.[12]

In the years following World War II, pragmatism suffered a fate not unlike that endured by "Marxism." Undeterred by Dewey's insistence that its "spirit is primarily a revolt against that habit of mind which disposes of anything by tucking it away in the pigeon holes of a filing cabinet,"[13] pragmatism's sense has been carved up, dispersed among, and assimilated to a variety of more or less self-contained forms of disciplinary discourse. Three are of special note for my purposes.

The first was anticipated by George Santayana in a sardonic essay published in 1939: "Dewey's pragmatism . . . is the pragmatism of the people, dumb and instinctive in them, and struggling in him to a labored but radical expression. . . . He is not interested in speculation at all, balks at it, and would avoid it if he could; his inspiration is sheer fidelity to the task in hand and sympathy with the movement afoot: a deliberate and happy participation in the attitude of the American people, with its omnivorous human interests and its simplicity of purpose. . . . He is the devoted spokesman of the spirit of enterprise, of experiment, of modern industry. To him, rather than to William James, might be applied the saying of the French pragmatist, Georges Sorel, that his philosophy is calculated to justify all the assumptions of American society."[14]

Santayana's representation, as refashioned by Daniel Boorstin in his *Genius of American Politics* and Louis Hartz in his *Liberal Tradition in America*, achieves preeminence in the immediate postwar decade.[15] In a reading subsequently endorsed by many others,[16] Hartz and

---

12. For a more encompassing account of its evolution, see Philip Wiener's entry "Pragmatism" in *Dictionary of the History of Ideas*, vol. 3, ed. Philip Wiener (New York: Scribner's, 1973), pp. 551–70.

13. Dewey, "Preface," in *IDP*, p. iv. On p. 16 of his *Necessity of Pragmatism* (New Haven: Yale University Press, 1986), Ralph Sleeper quotes from a letter in which Dewey states: "As I see it now, though not at the time, I've spent most of my years trying to get things together; my critics understand me only after they split me up again."

14. George Santayana, "Dewey's Naturalistic Metaphysics," in *The Philosophy of John Dewey*, ed. P. Schilpp (Chicago: Northwestern University Press, 1939), pp. 247–48.

15. Daniel Boorstin, *The Genius of American Politics* (Chicago: University of Chicago Press, 1953); Louis Hartz, *The Liberal Tradition in America* (New York: Harcourt Brace, 1955), passim.

16. For additional examples of this reading, see Morton White, *Social Thought in America* (Boston: Beacon Press, 1947); Henry Steel Commager, *The American Mind* (New Haven: Yale University Press, 1952); John Smith, *The Spirit of American Philosophy* (New York: Oxford University Press, 1963); Joseph Featherstone, "John Dewey and David

Boorstin suggested that pragmatism furnishes philosophical expression to a society united upon certain core values and hence free to dedicate its energies to their most efficient realization. As such, pragmatism discloses the ethos of a liberal culture that, because unmarred by fundamental conflict, is entitled to the illusion that nothing need disturb its incremental politics. That assurance, they continued, is the presupposition of pragmatism's identification of reason with science, and modern science in turn with technology. For the efficient application of method to the solution of discrete problems can proceed unproblematically only when there exists a substantial ground of homogeneous opinion regarding the ends toward which technique is to be directed.

Pragmatism's relationship to the culture out of which it first arose took a different tack in the second postwar decade. As the instrumental rationality that Hartz and Boorstin had identified with pragmatism increased in sophistication and power, its self-propagating tools began to shed their subordinate status as neutral means to the goals specified by America's liberalism. As the direction of that reason was ever less dictated by America's cultural ground, academic interest in pragmatism shifted away from the discipline of intellectual history (which could not so readily abandon its reference to concrete context) and on to that of philosophy.[17] The seeds of this appropriation had been planted early in the twentieth century in the turn from French to Austrian positivism; and its first significant fruit appeared in 1939 when Otto Neurath and Rudolf Carnap convinced a Dewey who should have known better to contribute an essay titled "Theory of Valuation" to the *International Encyclopedia of Unified Science*. This mar-

---

Riesman: From the Lost Individual to the Lonely Crowd," in *On the Making of Americans: Essays in Honor of David Riesman*, ed. Herbert J. Gans (Philadelphia: University of Pennsylvania Press, 1979), pp. 3–39; and Quentin Anderson, "John Dewey's American Democrat," *Daedalus* 108 (1979), 145–59. David Hollinger provides a useful overview of this literature in "The Problem of Pragmatism in American History," *Journal of American History* 57 (1980), 88–107.

17. For characteristic examples of the philosophical appropriation of pragmatism generally, and Dewey in particular, see H. S. Thayer, *Meaning and Action* (Indianapolis: Bobbs-Merrill, 1973); Israel Scheffler, *Four Pragmatists* (London: Routledge and Kegan Paul, 1974); and the essays in *John Dewey Reconsidered*, ed. R. S. Peters (London: Routledge and Kegan Paul, 1977). For a helpful overview of this literature, see Garry Brodsky, "Recent Philosophical Work on John Dewey," *Southern Journal of Philosophy* 14 (1976). For an account of contemporary philosophy's use and abuse of pragmatism which differs in important respects from that offered here, see Richard Rorty, "Professionalized Philosophy and Transcendental Culture," in his *Consequences of Pragmatism* (Minneapolis: University of Minnesota Press, 1982), pp. 60–71.

riage of convenience, however, could not be consummated until logical positivism, rescuing the method of science from the rubble of
transcendental philosophy, became sublimated within analytic philosophy. Only then could pragmatism be applauded for its early appreciation of the sterility of metaphysical disputes about the reality of
essence. That recognition, however muddleheaded its formulation,
helped till the soil necessary to professional philosophy's cultivation of
the rigorous procedures now tearing through the thickets of ordinary
language.

In its first reincarnation, pragmatism was read as the mirror image
of an unreflective culture that places technique at the disposal of
whatever values are currently regnant. In the second, it was read as a
step on the path to final formulation of a logic that would insure the
objectivity of its knowledge by guaranteeing its abstraction from that
same culture. Although for different reasons and in different ways,
each of these two postwar appropriations necessitated that its object of
concern disappear. Hartz's reading required that those dimensions of
pragmatism that did not fit neatly within the outlines of his caricature
be buried beneath what he called "America's absolutism: the somber
faith that its norms are self-evident."[18] Testifying to this nation's remarkable ability to declaw the disconcerting by rendering it common,
the image of pragmatism became as indistinct as the background into
which it faded so well.

By the same token, in order for analytic philosophy to complete its
disengagement from America, it had to turn its back on those whose
preparatory work had made its success possible. Pragmatism's founding texts (excluding those of Peirce) fared poorly when judged by the
standards set by philosophy's identification of reason with symbolic
logic. Hence, in the last analysis, those texts hindered the struggle to
overcome the past via a steady cumulation of piecemeal advances. As
Hans Reichenbach recognized as early as 1939, pragmatism "will occupy, without a doubt, a leading position in the history of modern
philosophy" by virtue of its "first approximation in the approach to an
empiricist theory of meaning." Yet, he continued, "the early period of
empiricism in which an all-round philosopher could dominate at the
same time the fields of scientific method, or history of philosophy, of
education and social philosophy has passed. We enter into the second
phase in which highly technical investigations form the indispensable

18. Hartz, *The Liberal Tradition in America*, p. 58.

instrument of research, splitting the philosophical campus into specialists of its various branches."[19] Tainted by its unrigorous focus on the less than tidy dilemmas of ordinary experience, pragmatism had to be left behind in the march toward that form of methodical discourse which would at last make it possible to distinguish conclusively between knowledge and opinion.

The absorption of pragmatism within America as a result of its capture by the disciplines of philosophy and intellectual history became problematic when the "glacierlike" substratum of "submerged conviction" that Hartz identified as the core of its native liberalism no longer appeared quite so solid. So in the third postwar decade it became necessary to remake pragmatism's meaning once more. Given its initial manifesto in Harold Lasswell's 1951 essay "The Policy Orientation," the breed of political science conventionally known as policy science did not truly begin to flourish until America's state, confronted by an unraveling social fabric, found thrust upon itself responsibility for securing the order its culture could no longer guarantee. Furnishing that state's complex of institutions with the problem-solving techniques it requires in order to stimulate and coordinate the material and human energies of a degrounded political economy, this wellspring of endless expertise has now assured its right to speak truth to power. And as Harold Lasswell, Charles Lindblom, Aaron Wildavsky, Heinz Eulau, and others have made apparent, the task of authorizing this union has fallen to pragmatism generally and to Dewey more particularly. As I show in some detail in Chapter 6, policy science thereby joins together the antipolitical and antihistorical thrust implicit in pragmatism's first and second postwar appropriations, and so effectively seals its identification with America's *raison d'état*.

These three appropriations of "pragmatism's" dissected remains are not especially significant in their own right. Considered in relation to one another, however, they offer clues to the advancing dynamic of modern science in its postwar colonization of America. Pragmatism has been manufactured and remanufactured in accordance with this nation's need to make sense of and to legitimate science's transformation from a tool whose use is dictated by the collective hand of the culture that grasps it, to a method whose claim to authority derives not from its cultural ground but rather from the neutrality it secures in

19. Hans Reichenbach, "Dewey's Theory of Science," in Schilpp, *The Philosophy of John Dewey*, pp. 175, 192.

virtue of its abstraction from America's soil, and finally to its incorporation within a rootless social engineering state whose techniques
fashion from society the regulated organization it requires.

That dynamic receives its most adequate account, as well as its most
persuasive defense, in Richard Rorty's *Philosophy and the Mirror of
Nature*.[20] Confirming Dewey's observation that academic philosophy,
"uneasy in its isolation, travels hastily to meet with compromise and
accommodation the actual situation in all its brute unrationality,"[21]
that work ingeniously synthesizes pragmatism's three major postwar
appropriations. It employs the argumentative forms of analytic philosophy to legitimate, under the cover of a Hartzean consensus, the
forms of order which assure that the reason of the managerial state will
remain secure. As such, it foreshadows not pragmatism's rejuvena-
tion, but rather consummation of the history through which it has
been rendered safe for America.[22]

Reflecting Hans-Georg Gadamer's hermeneutics in the light cast by
Michael Oakeshott's metaphor of the "conversation of mankind,"
Rorty represents the history of the West as an extended talk that is in
principle endless because its only substantive aim is to "keep pragmatic tolerance going as long as we can."[23] Although not teleological
in any more determinate sense, that conversation is nonetheless progressive. For on Rorty's account, "bourgeois liberalism" offers a paradigmatic articulation of the code of civility that best regulates this talk;
and the substantive content of that code is best exemplified by the
method of modern science which, to complete the circle, offers a
"particularly good example of the social virtues of the European bourgeoisie."[24] In sum, the mutually reinforcing practices of the liberal

20. Richard Rorty, *Philosophy and the Mirror of Nature* (Princeton: Princeton University
Press, 1979).

21. Dewey, "Intelligence and Morals," in *IDP*, pp. 75–76.

22. For criticisms of Rorty that focus on the specifically political dimension of his
work, see Christopher Norris, "Philosophy as a Kind of Narrative: Rorty on Post-
Modern Culture," in his *Contest of Faculties* (London: Methuen, 1986), pp. 139–66; Cornel
West, "Afterword: The Politics of American Neo-Pragmatism," in *Post-Analytic Philosophy*, ed. John Rajchman and Cornel West (New York: Columbia University Press, 1986),
pp. 260–75; Milton Fisk, "The Instability of Pragmatism," *New Literary History* 17 (1985),
23–30; Frank Lentricchia, "Rorty's Cultural Conversation," *Raritan* 3 (1983), 136–41;
Jeffrey Stout, "Liberal Society and the Languages of Morals," *Soundings* 69 (1986), 32–59;
and Rebecca Comay, "Interrupting the Conversation: Notes on Rorty," *Telos* 69 (1986),
119–30.

23. Rorty, *Consequences of Pragmatism*, p. 229.

24. Richard Rorty, "Habermas and Lyotard on Post-Modernity," *Praxis International* 4
(1984), 36.

state and modern science furnish the most adequate models of "solidarity we have yet achieved, and Deweyan pragmatism [their] best articulation."[25]

When Rorty goes on to argue that "we can hardly be too grateful" for the discoveries that furnish "the basis of modern technological civilization," he gives us cause to suspect that his "pragmatism" will not easily tolerate those who doubt this article of faith. And when he uses the phrase "social engineering" as a synonym for the "Deweyan attempt to make concrete concerns with the daily problems of one's community . . . the substitute for traditional religion,"[26] he gives us reason to suspect that he does not appreciate the power of the linguistic usages that now facilitate the reduction of all political issues to matters of bureaucratic management, and so mock his representation of democratic culture as discourse in ceaseless flux.

Rorty can sustain these blind spots because he takes for granted a vision of America resting on what William Connolly has aptly called a "species of social foundationalism."[27] Rerooting the quest for certainty in the myth of a consensual tradition, he speaks of "we inheritors of European civilization"[28] without inquiring too deeply into either the precise identity of that "we" or the ruptures that render this pronoun an obfuscation. Striking out at correspondence theories of truth, privileged representations, self-reflective transcendental subjects, and the like, Rorty forgets that criticism of the philosophical tradition is at best one way to discover how reason's conduct has depleted the substantial soil from which democratic culture must take its nutrition. Flattering the self-image of the nation that most perfectly exemplifies liberalism's desire to evade its own deficiencies by sweeping political conflict beneath the cover of progress, Rorty thereby reflects America (or is it "the West"?) in his image of pragmatism, and pragmatism in his image of "the West" (or is it America?). Once within this hall of mirrors, neither can any longer contest the other's appearance as truth.[29]

---

25. Rorty, *Consequences of Pragmatism*, p. 207.

26. Rorty, "Habermas and Lyotard on Post-Modernity," pp. 36, 42.

27. William Connolly, "Mirror of America," *Raritan* 3 (1983), 135.

28. Rorty, quoted in Richard Bernstein, "One Step Forward, Two Steps Backward: Richard Rorty on Liberal Democracy and Philosophy," *Political Theory* 15 (1987), 544.

29. The extent to which pragmatism and American culture have lost their ability to distinguish each from the other was first noted by C. E. Ayres. In a review of Dewey's *Logic* which appeared in the 18 January 1939 issue of the *New Republic*, Ayres wrote: "Veneration is a fatiguing exercise; and in the course of years Dewey's ideas have become commonplace" (p. 303). One decade later, in the 17 October 1949 issue of the *New Republic*, which celebrated Dewey's ninetieth birthday, George Boas suggested that

IV

"In the very degree in which a new movement is felt to be in a new orbit, to be revolutionary, it will of necessity be reported in terms which inject into the report habitudes and dispositions which are residues of bygone history. It may even be said that the more acute and more assured is the sense of revolutionary break, the more will it be necessary to make the intellectual reckoning under conditions that are going to be gradually, more or less insensibly, replaced. Not till a new movement is mature in development, until it is a fact, something done, can it be perceived in its own perspective."[30]

Must pragmatism be what it has now become, a textual gloss on the dominant practices of contemporary America? What if, with apologies to Marx, we were to entertain the hypothesis that the interpretations of the living weigh like a nightmare on the minds of the dead? Might we speculate that the import of pragmatism's tentative steps into an unknown future were destined to be retranslated onto the terrain they sought to escape, at least until the rationalistic tradition they trespassed had grown considerably weaker? If "anything that is at most but a hundred years old has hardly had time to disclose its meaning in the slow secular processes of human history," then perhaps only now can we appreciate what Dewey meant when he urged return to an age "when reflective thought was young and lusty, eager to engage in combat in the public arena, instead of living a sheltered and protected life."[31]

"It is dangerous to give names, especially in discourse that is far aloof from the things [read: *pragmata*] named."[32] Heeding Dewey's warning, at the close of the current section I will (almost entirely)

"there is no one of the present generation of Americans who can have escaped his influence," for pragmatism has become "a pervasive cultural force" (p. 26). Still another decade later, in his *John Dewey in Perspective* (New York: Oxford University Press, 1958), George Geiger wrote: "Dewey's contributions . . . have become commonplaces, and one doesn't get very excited about commonplaces" (p. 186). Most recently, John Diggins, in *The Lost Soul of American Politics* (New York: Basic Books, 1984), has shown that it is still very much possible to dismiss pragmatism while simultaneously arguing that "Dewey was the most important social philosopher in the first half of the twentieth century" (pp. 160–61). It would appear that because we are all Deweyans now, we can dispense with an examination of his texts.

30. Dewey, "Experience and Nature: A Re-introduction," in *LW*, vol. 1, p. 360.
31. Dewey, "Individualism Old and New," in *LW*, vol. 5, p. 53; "Philosophies of Freedom," in *PC*, p. 299.
32. Dewey, *EN*, p. 80.

banish the term "pragmatism" from this work.[33] My arguments do not vindicate a peculiarly American politics of hardheaded realism. Nor do they, following Kant, equate the pragmatic with the *pragmatische*, that body of means-ends maxims that assures technical efficacy. Nor do they ratify Dewey's contention that the term "pragmatic" designates "the function of consequences as necessary tests of the validity of propositions, *provided* these consequences are operationally instituted and are such as to resolve the specific problem evoking the operations."[34] If Santayana is right in seeing these latter two senses as merely intellectualized articulations of the first—that is, of an American mind unable to generate anything other than a vindication of its own crassness—then my aim is to deprive that mind's voice of its national accent.

To undermine the conventional caricature of pragmatism, which simply certifies Europe's native disposition to endorse the banal parody Americans have manufactured for purposes of domestic consumption,[35] we must first tear up its roots. But once removed from American soil, they must not be replanted with the aim of generating a more adequate *pragmateia*, yet another philosophical "system." As long as admirers of William James and John Dewey seek to best their rivals on the ground first mapped by Plato and his heirs, they assure only their own defeat. On that terrain, any revivified pragmatism cannot help but be, as James once remarked, "a trunk without a tag, a dog without a collar." Hence this book rejects "pragmatism" when that term is taken to refer to a self-contained doctrine whose raison d'être consists of preservation and extension of the terms of its own discourse. To the degree that such discourse forgets that its purpose is to light up so many paths back into significant experience, it remains

33. Here I follow Dewey's example in *LTI*. See pp. iii–iv: "The word 'Pragmatism' does not, I think, occur in the text. Perhaps the word lends itself to misconception. At all events, so much misunderstanding and relatively futile controversy have gathered about the word that it seemed advisable to avoid its use."

34. Dewey, *LTI*, p. iv.

35. For one of the many European expressions of this caricature, see Karl Jaspers, *Man in the Modern Age* (Garden City, N.Y.: Doubleday, 1957), p. 176: "Pragmatism seemed to be laying new foundations; but what it built thereon was . . . a mere expression of blind confidence in the extant confusion." For a more intriguing expression of this caricature, see Heidegger's dismissal, as quoted in Rorty's *Consequences of Pragmatism*: "Americanism is something European. It is an as-yet-uncomprehended species of the gigantic, the gigantic that is itself still inchoate and does not as yet originate at all out of the complete and gathered metaphysical essence of the modern age. The American interpretation of Americanism by means of pragmatism still remains outside the metaphysical realm" (p. 58).

abstractly disconnected from the things and affairs of this world. Accordingly, although Rorty's stimulation of renewed interest in the texts of Dewey, James, and Peirce is to be applauded in a way,[36] that interest is misdirected as long as it is *about* the reification called "pragmatism." As long as *that* is its subject, it cannot help but reinforce a rationalistic tradition that breeds contempt for and so hinders the recovery of this world's pragmata.

The branches of that tradition, trailing off along the diverse paths suggested by the names Aristotle, Augustine, Aquinas, Hobbes, Hume, share a common root. That root can be characterized by noting its offshoots' common commission of what James and Dewey, using shorthand labels for a complex thesis, designate the "rationalist" or the "psychological" or the "intellectualist" fallacy. In his lecture "The One and the Many," James invites his audience to perform the following thought experiment:

> Hold a tumbler of water a little above your eyes and look up through the water at its surface—or better still look similarly through the flat wall of an aquarium. You will then see an extraordinarily brilliant reflected image say of a candle-flame, or any other clear object, situated on the opposite side of the vessel. No ray, under these circumstances, gets beyond the water's surface: every ray is totally reflected back into the

36. Here I think of works such as Michael Weinstein, *The Wilderness and the City* (Amherst: University of Massachusetts Press, 1982); Joseph Kupfer, *Experience as Art* (Albany: State University of New York Press, 1983); Kloppenberg, *Uncertain Victory;* Eugene Rochberg-Halton, *Meaning and Modernity: Social Theory in the Pragmatic Attitude* (Chicago: University of Chicago Press, 1986); Sleeper, *The Necessity of Pragmatism;* Sandra Rosenthal, *Speculative Pragmatism* (Amherst: University of Massachusetts Press, 1986); Joseph Margolis, *Pragmatism without Method* (Oxford: Basil Blackwell, 1986); Thomas Alexander, *John Dewey's Theory of Art, Experience and Nature: The Horizons of Feeling* (Albany: State University of New York Press, 1987); C. G. Prado, *The Limits of Pragmatism* (Atlantic Highlands, N.J.: Humanities Press International, 1987); Raymond Boisvert, *Dewey's Metaphysics* (New York: Fordham University Press, 1988); J. E. Tiles, *Dewey* (New York: Routledge, 1988); and Cornel West, *The American Evasion of Philosophy* (Madison: University of Wisconsin Press, 1989). In tossing this blanket criticism over these various works, I do not mean to deny the debt I owe to each of them. In passing, I might also mention that the past three decades have produced, to the best of my knowledge, only three book-length discussions of pragmatism's specifically political dimensions. The first, Alfonso Damico's *Individuality and Community: The Social and Political Thought of John Dewey* (Gainesville: University Presses of Florida, 1978), is easily the best of the three, although my reservations about its central thesis will become clear later. The second, A. H. Somjee's *Political Theory of John Dewey* (New York: Teachers College Press, 1968), represents Dewey as the founder of behavioral political science, a view I contest as well. And the third, Gary Bullert's *Politics of John Dewey* (Buffalo: Prometheus Press, 1983), serves chiefly as a catalog of Dewey's changing views on international affairs. For a critique of Bullert's book, see my review in *Modern Age* 30 (1986), 304–7.

depths again. Now let the water represent the world of sensible facts, and let the air above it represent the world of abstract ideas. Both worlds are real, of course, and interact; but they interact only at their boundary, and the *locus* of everything that lives, and happens to us, so far as full experience goes, is the water. We are like fishes swimming in the sea of sense, bounded above by the superior element, but unable to breathe it pure or penetrate it. We get our oxygen from it, however, we touch it incessantly, now in this part, now in that, and every time we touch it, we turn back into the water with our course re-determined and re-energized. The abstract ideas of which the air consists are indispensable for life, but irrespirable by themselves, as it were, and only active in their re-directing function. All similes are halting, but this one rather takes my fancy.[37]

Prior to all occasions of knowing, we inhabit a world of qualitative experience. Before that world is known *as* a world, it is there; and we, as Jamesian fish, are within it. Always given to us in the context of particular situations, that world's diverse things must be *had*, suffered or enjoyed, before either they or the medium in which they subsist can be rendered an object of cognition. To acknowledge this truth is to practice humility. It is, to quote Dewey, "to come upon the mystery of things being just what they are. Their occurrence, their manifestation, may be accounted for in terms of other occurrences, but their own quality of existence is final and opaque. The mystery is that the world is as it is—a mystery that is the source of all joy and all sorrow, of all hope and fear, and the source of development both creative and degenerative."[38]

Although the world can never be transparently and completely grasped as an object of reflection, its things are not had as brute, insignificant entities. Our experience always bears some measure of sense, however partial, in virtue of its mediation and information by the meaning-sustaining habits we acquire as members of particular cultures and inheritors of specific traditions; and it is the cultivation of that sense, disclosing and vitalizing our various ways of being in the world, that gives human life its distinctive resonances and depths. Correlatively, it is this sense that furnishes the ground, the origin, the material, and the end of that peculiar form of mediated activity through which human beings deliberately fashion meaning from the

37. William James, "The One and the Many," in his *Pragmatism* (Cleveland: Meridian, 1955), pp. 89–90.
38. Dewey, "Time and Individuality," in *ENF*, p. 241.

ineliminable indeterminacy of what happens in qualitative experience. To think, in other words, is to take part in transforming the questionable pragmata of experience in ways such that their present ambiguity gives way to a more profound feel for their qualitative significances. For no matter how far removed from the welter of concrete matters, the conduct of thinking takes its cues from and remains deficient until re-fused within the unreduplicable contexts of noncognitive experience from which it is ultimately derived.

If we are to think like fishes swimming in a sea of sense, we must first unlearn what we now believe we know about the relationship between knowledge and the world's affairs. We must, that is, work our way round a philosophical tradition that disparages the reality of everyday experience. To speak much too broadly, from its classical origins to contemporary epistemology, Western rationalism is defined by its self-induced amnesia. In flight from the finitude and precariousness of human being, that tradition cannot acknowledge that we are able to say something about the knowledge relation only because, prior to any occasion of knowing, we stand in a multitude of nonepistemic relations to what is experienced. That tradition can uphold its claims to supremacy over things that are first and foremost matters of weal and woe rather than objects known only as long as it denies that a world of immediate experience is the precondition of all intellectual discourse, even though the former can never appear as such within the latter.

The philosophic tradition's denial of the dimly apprehended but dramatic medium within which all thinking is situated has achieved widely varying formal articulations. At rock bottom, though, all reduce to the contention that cognition's results possess a reality and a power superior to that characteristic of other less refined modes of experience. On this foundation, whose elementary building blocks are suggested by terms like "soul," "substance," "Geist," "nature," "transcendental subjectivity," the correlative conviction arises that there exists a complete and perfect correspondence between what is known and what is real. The cognitively true is thereby equated with what is real in being; and this, in turn, engenders the conclusion that epistemic objects furnish the ontological standards by which to measure the reality of that which appears in all other modes of experience. Having treated the features peculiar to a single form of experience as if they were paradigmatic of *all*, proponents of such rationalism can no longer admit that its power is limited by its situation within a medium that encompasses much more than what at any moment is known. With reason rendered groundless by its own vicious abstraction, we find it ever more difficult to consider credible its pretensions to authority. Leaving experience experientially unrecognizable, rationalism as it travels through history spawns ever deeper crises of skepticism and nihilism.

The present expression of these crises loses some measure of its immediacy and so becomes available for reflection about its meaning when we realize that thinking presupposes neither establishment of unquestionable points of departure nor correspondence of its representations with finished realities. Instead, what thinking's conduct requires is release and cultivation of whatever potencies prove able to show their truth by sustaining the forms of practical engagement constitutive of meaningful experience. "Meaning is wider in scope as well as more precious in value than is truth. Poetic meanings, moral meanings, [political meanings], a large part of the goods of life are matters of richness and freedom of meanings, rather than of truth; a large part of our life is carried on in a realm of meanings to which truth and falsity as such are irrelevant."[39] To acknowledge that knowing is a derivative way of taking part in and so helping to shape the affairs of other modes of experience is to learn that specifically critical thinking is a way of questioning whatever meaning-laden practices presently compromise the qualitatively complex sense of situated experience. In the present, the task of such thinking is to interrogate all forms of institutionalized power whose authority to rule over everyday conduct stems from a false equation of its truths with the completed reality of experienced affairs.

"One can only see from a certain standpoint, but this fact does not make all standpoints of equal value. A standpoint which is nowhere in particular and from which things are not seen at a special angle is an absurdity. But one may have affection for a standpoint which gives a rich and ordered landscape rather than for one from which things are seen confusedly and meagerly."[40] If we recall that the intricately entangled is what is ordinarily found in the concrete affairs of daily life, then we will remember that the aim of thinking is not to expunge life's uncertainty and mystery, but rather to indicate how we might better turn experience back on itself so as to intensify its immanent qualitative

---

39. Dewey, "Philosophy and Civilization," in *PC*, p. 4; *EN*, p. 411.
40. Dewey, "Context and Thought," in *ENF*, p. 102.

possibilities. Consequently, while I hope that the arguments presented
in the following pages persuade in their own right, their adequacy is
not a self-contained matter. "There are two kinds of demonstration:
that of logical reasoning from premises assumed to possess logical
completeness, and that of showing, pointing, coming upon a thing.
The latter method is that which the word experience sums up, general-
izes, makes universal and ulterior. To say that the right method is one
of pointing and showing, not of meeting intellectual requirements or
logical derivation from rational ideas, does not, although it is non-
rational, imply a preference for irrationality. For one of the things that
is pointed out, found and shown, is deduction, and the logic that
governs it. But these things have also to be found and shown, and their
authority rests upon the perceived outcome of this empirical denota-
tion. The utmost in rationality has a sanction and a position that,
according to taste, may be called sub-rational or supra-rational."[41]

This work therefore means to indicate, to point out, a series of
overlapping paths that, should they be followed, may eventuate in
situations that are less insignificant than those enforced by the various
objectifications of what we now take reason to be. What those situations might be experienced *as* can be intimated by the language of a
text, but its words can never supplant their consummatory immediacy. For perception is "more potent than reasoning; the deliverances
of intercourse more to be desired than the chains of discourse; the
surprise of reception more demonstrative than the conclusions of
intentional proof."[42] In the last analysis, this book can only invite its
readers to ask whether my genealogical recounting of reason's project
enables them to get a better feel for some of the constraints that now
hem experience in. "It places before others a map of the road that has
been travelled; they may accordingly, if they will, re-travel the road to
inspect the landscape for themselves."[43]

V

"Strange as it may sound to say it, the question which was formulated
by Kant as that of the possibility of knowledge, is the fundamental
political problem of modern life."[44] Struggles over the definition, sub-

41. Dewey, "Experience and Philosophic Method," in *LW*, vol. 1, p. 372.
42. Dewey, "Ralph Waldo Emerson," in *CE1*, p. 70.
43. Dewey, *EN*, p. 29.
44. Dewey, "The Significance of the Problem of Knowledge," in *EW*, vol. 5, p. 14. In

stance, and justification of knowledge, as contests over the disposition of a vital cultural resource, are always and at the same time struggles over the generation, distribution, and legitimation of power. Therefore, the conquest of qualitative experience by an imperious reason is in its primary signification a political rather than a philosophical problem.

When the pragmata of everyday life are taken to be forms of partial being incapable of sustaining their own meaningfulness, their capacity to bear significance is taken to be a function of their subsumption beneath knowledge's refined objects. A rationality that must deny its embeddedness in certain contingent features of human history in order to sustain its authority fulfills its aberration of experience's possibilities through the unplanned but relentless usurpation and rationalization of everyday affairs.[45] Rationalism thus assumes the character of a historical project that slowly erodes the integrity of whatever forms of conduct might otherwise check its drive to self-completion.

That project must prove antipolitical. To seek to root politics in stable foundations by grounding its practice in something less corrigible and contingent than its own conduct is to violate the qualitative dimensions that preserve it as what it is and not something else. Fashioned out of what is engendered by the interweaving of ongoing collective activities, and located within the situated spaces sustained by those same activities, the reality of distinctively political affairs is compromised, if not denied altogether, when reason's antecedently formulated truths are imposed on its emergent realities.

If we reject the reductionist thrust of such rationalism, we may then be reminded that the term "politics" designates not an object awaiting determinate conceptual specification, but rather a distinctive mode of experience. That mode is not to be identified with either a specific institutional configuration or the achievement of discriminated ends. Lacking either of these sources of antecedent definition and order, it is

---

this regard, see Dewey's "Experience, Knowledge, and Value: A Rejoinder," in Schilpp, ed., *The Philosophy of John Dewey*. There Dewey complains that his readers have ignored "the contextual problems by which my statements have their import determined" and, by implication, denied the subordination of his project to its governing political end: "If the urgency of these problems is ignored or slighted (urgent in philosophy because urgent in actual cultural life when the latter is submitted to analysis), the context of the larger part of what I have written will be so missed that what I have said will seem to be a strange, a gratuitously strange, intellectual adventure, redeemed—if at all—only by the presence of a certain technical skill" (pp. 524–25).

45. For a recent work whose central thesis is broadly congruent with this claim, see Benjamin Barber, *The Conquest of Politics* (Princeton: Princeton University Press, 1988).

a nonteleological way of crafting common sense from involvement in presently unsettled matters of general concern. As such, its "purpose" is simply to preserve and cultivate the ground of its own being, to sustain the forms of power that enable "politika pragmata" to be caught up within webs of significance fashioned and refashioned in time.

Political experience is a fragile form of being. Its possibilities must be reclaimed when endangered. If the relationship of thinking to politics is immanent in the sense that the former, depending on its character, can either nourish or starve the latter, then reaffirmation of political experience in the present requires a critique of knowledge's constitution qua instrumental rationality, and of scientific truth's claim to monopolistic jurisdiction over all experience. In short, the claims of thinking must now be turned against those asserted by a science that, as the contemporary heir of philosophical rationalism, defines itself in terms of its impiety toward the affairs of ordinary experience.

That reaffirmation also requires articulation of the conditions and form of a democratic culture. The term "democracy" designates a way of collective being which, although more comprehensive than political experience per se, is nonetheless a condition of its integrity. For the possibility of politics turns on the constitution of a culture composed of individuals who appreciate the need to resist whatever encroaches on their capacity to cultivate the significances offered to human being via nature, as the latter is caught up in webs of ongoing experience. "Democracy is neither a form of government, nor a social expediency, but a metaphysic of the relation of man and his experience to nature."[46] The question I ask, therefore, is not how might politics assume the form demanded by reason's truths, but rather how we might "essay our deepest political and social problems with a conviction that they are to a reasonable extent sanctioned and sustained by the nature of things."[47]

VI

"The subject matter which follows is that of a drama in three acts, of which the last is the unfinished one now being enacted in which we,

46. Dewey, "Maurice Maeterlinck," in CE1, p. 43.
47. Dewey, "Philosophy and Democracy," in CE2, p. 849.

now living, are the participants."[48] Taken as a single entity, the play of this text treats the unfolding of Western thinking about matters political as a clue to the formation, transformation, and deformation of lived experience. Its overarching purpose is to disclose the roots of experience's constitution as so much matter available for rationalization and, in time, for expert colonization by modernity's managerial state.

This drama's first act (Chapter 2) tells of the emergence of reason within the ancient Greek city-state; and its second (Chapter 3) tells of the Enlightenment's reconstruction of that invention via the enterprise called "epistemology." Chapters 4 through 6, tracing out certain subplots implicit within this second act, explore the dense legacy we inherit from our predecessors, which to a considerable extent constitutes the loosely bounded field upon which most specifically liberal political and social discourse proceeds today. These chapters scrutinize the unstable interplay of classical and Enlightenment fragments within characteristic examples of twentieth-century French, German, and American thought, each of which retains in some way the tradition's conviction that experience's worth turns on its rationalistic reconstruction.

Chapter 4, beginning from some broader claims about the characteristic dilemmas of social contract theory, examines Emile Durkheim's attempt to slow the erosion of liberalism's sociocultural foundations through public dissemination of sociology's *faits sociaux*. Chapter 5, taking its cues from the challenge to liberalism posed by "Critical Theory," examines Jürgen Habermas's effort to thwart the tyranny of "instrumental rationality" by securing the integrity of what he calls "communicative rationality." And the sixth chapter, informed by some broader claims regarding the academic study of politics in America, examines the policy sciences' provision of "usable" knowledge to the state of late modernity.

I choose the cosmopolitan but unlikely trio of Durkheim, Habermas, and American policy science for three reasons. First, collectively considered, this trio's membership shows that the damage done by the project of rationalism knows no national boundaries or favorites; each expresses democratic aspirations and yet, in retaining rationalism's ambitions, proves unable to show how the conditions of collective meaningfulness might be salvaged. Second, each self-consciously enters into a dialogue with pragmatism and so offers a convenient means

48. Dewey, *FC*, p. 104.

of indicating how the latter, denied its "ism," helps to elicit sense from our present political situation. Third, and most important, criticism of each intimates the character of critical conduct that might nurture rather than subvert democratic engagement with and embeddedness in political affairs.

Pursuit of those intimations is the subject of the third and final act of this play. Drawing together the strands left more or less disconnected in Chapters 4 through 6, I ask in Chapter 7 how we might think about and act within a present whose eventual shape is now so unsettled and uncertain. As I reiterate in this work's postscript, to answer that question is not to offer a "solution" to the "problem" to which Weber affixes the summary label "rationalization." Indeed, even if I were to think it appropriate in a work of this sort to recommend specific courses for action, I would not do so. That would simply tempt my readers to assimilate the cause of relocating pragmatism's pragmata to that of appreciating the cash-value of Yankee ingenuity.

2 /
Politics and the Emergence of Reason

I

What is gained by rooting the critique of contemporary politics in a return to the polis?[1] Wonderful in its plasticity, the city-state has assumed many forms and accommodated many purposes during the second half of this century. For Leo Strauss and Eric Voegelin, its privileged access to the truth of human order discloses the impoverishment of a civilization whose relativism leaves it internally incoherent and externally defenseless.[2] For Hannah Arendt and (more ambig-

1. The source of the polis's continuing appeal is given elegant formulation in the following passage from Michael Ignatieff's *Needs of Strangers* (New York: Penguin, 1984): "The *polis* would continue to beckon us forward out of the past even if no actual *polis* had ever existed. Its human dimensions beckon us still: small enough so that each person would know his neighbour and could play his part in the governance of the city, large enough so that the city could feed itself and defend itself; a place of intimate bonding in which the private sphere of the home and family and the public sphere of civic democracy would be but one easy step apart; a community of equals in which each would have enough and no one would want more than enough; a co-operative venture in which work would be a form of collaboration among equals. Small, co-operative, egalitarian, self-governing and autarkic: these are the conditions of belonging that the dream of the *polis* has bequeathed to us" (p. 107).

2. See especially Leo Strauss, "On Classical Political Philosophy," in his *What Is Political Philosophy?* (Glencoe, Ill.: Free Press, 1959), pp. 78–94; and Eric Voegelin, *The New Science of Politics* (Chicago: University of Chicago Press, 1952), especially pp. 1–3, 61–75.

uously) Sheldon Wolin, the city-state's celebration of debate among equals on a public stage recalls the forgetfulness of an era that no longer knows how to distinguish between the practice of politics and the efficient provision of welfare services.[3] For Hans-Georg Gadamer and Alasdair MacIntyre, its appreciation of the qualitative distinction between *technē* and *phronēsis* suggests a repudiation of the modern state's formulation of all political dilemmas as problems to be solved through the application of expert technique.[4]

Though all share a vague melancholia, each of these thinkers tells a somewhat different story about what it means to capture a more authentic appreciation of politics. Each, moreover, implicitly contends that it is in principle possible to recover certain dimensions of the ancient city-state's significance without at the same time carrying forward others that undermine or violate the contemporary purpose of that appropriation. Each, that is, elects to overlook or discount those features of the polis that very few are now eager to endorse. Strauss presupposes that we can disconnect classical philosophy's quest for "that political order which is best always and everywhere" from the cosmology that rendered this search a meaningful enterprise.[5] Arendt holds that we can dissociate the Greek concept of the political from its relationship to a culture that required the wholesale exclusion of those who inhabited but did not fully belong within the most inclusive form of human association. MacIntyre contends that we can abstract the ancient understanding of practical wisdom and so render contingent its dependence on the integrity of premodern forms of collective identity.

In this chapter, I do not mean to reject out of hand any effort to locate either solace or inspiration in the philosophy of the classical city-state. I do, however, wish to caution democrats who would do so without examining the ways in which that philosophy emerges out of and constructs its relationship to the affairs of ordinary experience. The

3. See Hannah Arendt, *The Human Condition* (New York: Doubleday, 1958), especially pp. 294–325; and Sheldon Wolin, *Politics and Vision* (Boston: Little, Brown, 1960), especially pp. 414–19. In identifying Wolin with Arendt, I do not mean to deny the former's gradual disengagement from the spell of the latter; nor do I mean to ignore his essentially Aristotelian criticism of Plato (pp. 57–63).

4. See Hans-Georg Gadamer, "Hermeneutics as Practical Philosophy," in his *Reason in the Age of Science* (Cambridge: MIT Press, 1981), pp. 88–112; and Alasdair MacIntyre, *After Virtue* (Notre Dame: University of Notre Dame Press, 1984), especially pp. 76–102, 137–53. For a related use of the polis, see Ronald Beiner, *Political Judgment* (Chicago: University of Chicago Press, 1983), especially pp. 88–138.

5. Strauss, "On Classical Political Philosophy," p. 87.

tale I relate here suggests that the tradition of classical philosophy is essentially tainted inasmuch as its core concepts, especially those circling around the idea of reason, owe their origin to metaphorical extrapolation and reification of understandings originally rooted in the know-how of specific crafts. As we shall see, once these understandings are refashioned into the hypostatized stuff of classical metaphysics, they are then turned upon the forms of practice from which they were initially derived and employed to call into question the self-sufficiency of all activity that has not yet been subjected to reason's commands.

If this be so, then any attempt to appropriate the city-state for specifically democratic purposes must prove self-defeating as long as it does not first explore the ways in which our conventional language of reason, in spite of its internal complexity, bears the marks of this birth. If we are to question the adequacy of our familiar habits of thinking to inform the sense of present experience, if we are to loosen the grip of certitudes whose immediacy otherwise blocks our apprehension of their power, we must first learn to detect the twisted remains of ancient categories of thought within a world that no longer shares antiquity's assurance of nature's teleological order. To do otherwise is to participate in reproducing the instrumentalities of domination.

The story that unfolds in this chapter presupposes and exemplifies the general account of the relationship between thinking and experience sketched in the previous chapter. Neither an idealist narrative, which neglects the cultural background out of which philosophy first emerged, nor a materialist account, which affirms a unilinear causal relationship between substratum and ideological epiphenomena, will suffice. For "reason" has a history that is neither distinct from nor intelligible apart from the rise and fall of specific forms of cultural life. More pointedly, because the refined questions that define philosophical inquiry find their ultimate origins in dislocations afflicting collective life, its constructions are best construed as second-order theorizations whose analytic decomposition and synthetic refashioning of the heterogeneous, meaning-laden context out of which they grow gives intellectualized voice to its unresolved dilemmas and persistent conflicts. As clues to forms of collective association that may be consolidated or undermined when reason's distilled meanings are reappropriated by their context, philosophy's texts always point beyond themselves. "It is no longer enough for a principle to be elevated,

noble, universal and hallowed by time. It must present its birth certifi-
cate, it must show under just what conditions of human experience it
was generated, and it must justify itself by its works, present and
potential."[6]

II

The stability of archaic Greece's quasi-feudal order presupposed un-
deviating fidelity to a body of custom whose ratification of the layered
rights and duties of the semiautonomous *oikos* legitimated the domination of its warrior aristocracy over the silent *demos*.[7] This mythopoetic
code endowed that culture's coincidence of class and political strat-
ification with divine significance; for the unchallengable relations of
dependence sustained between master and serf found their cosmic
reduplication in the *monarchia* of Zeus, as well as in the complex
hierarchy of powers his rule upheld. Transmitted across generational
lines via the poetry of Homer and given its most systematic expression
in Hesiod's *Theogony*, this web of communal conviction ensured that
individual particularities were swallowed up within the comprehensive imperatives of unity.

6. Dewey, *RP*, p. 48.
7. Prior to 1920, Dewey's treatment of ancient Greece was largely incidental. For
examples of this early work, see "The Ethics of Democracy" (1888) in *EW*, vol. 1, pp.
227–49, as well as "Intelligence and Morals" (1908) and "The Influence of Darwin on
Philosophy" (1909), which appear in *IDP*, pp. 1–19, 46–76. It is only with the publication
of *Reconstruction in Philosophy* (1920) and *Experience and Nature* (1925) that Dewey recognizes that a challenge to the presuppositional core of Western thought requires a careful
critique of Plato and Aristotle; however, in each of these works, his understanding of the
cultural material out of which ancient philosophy emerges is partial at best. Only during
the last decade of his life, in an unpublished and apparently unfinished manuscript
whose early chapters indicate considerable anthropological study, does Dewey begin
the project that might have fulfilled his own historicist ambitions. For the only published intimation of this account, see Dewey, "Syllabus: Types of Philosophic Thought,"
in *MW*, vol. 13, pp. 364–71. To the best of my knowledge, Dewey's reading of classical
philosophy has been subjected to close examination in only four articles. In reverse
chronological order, they are: Joseph Betz, "Dewey and Socrates," *Transactions of the
Charles S. Peirce Society*, 16 (1980), 329–56; Frederick Anderson, "Dewey's Experiment
with Greek Philosophy," *International Philosophical Quarterly* 7 (1967), 86–100; John Anton, "John Dewey and Ancient Philosophies," *Philosophy and Phenomenological Research*
25 (1965), 477–99; and Walter Veazie, "John Dewey and the Revival of Greek Philosophy," *University of Colorado Studies in Philosophy* 2 (1961), 1–10. Dewey's understanding
of the significance of the polis for the present has not received the attention it deserves
because we remain in the grip of a prejudice given typical expression by John Diggins in
his "Republicanism and Progressivism," *American Quarterly* 37 (1985), 572–98: "Dewey's
attitude towards the past was profoundly ambiguous, if not downright ahistorical" (p.
387).

This order began to unravel when its received resources of intelligibility proved insufficient to fashion unproblematic sense from the shifting parameters of collective experience. Here I need not do full justice to the why and how of this erosion. For my purposes, it is enough to note two interconnected developments. First, the seventh and eighth centuries B.C. witnessed settlement of the loosely confederated Ionian colonies along the coast of the Aegean Sea as well as the correlative resumption of maritime trade with the East. Unimpeded by the bureaucratized institutions that guaranteed ecclesiastical dominion in Egypt and Mesopotamia, the protoscientific speculations of Asia Minor fell on fertile soil within the Hellenic world.[8] Second, acceleration of artisanal accomplishment within the Ionian colonies effectively challenged myth's tacit assertion that the struggle to exert significant control over the material circumstances of collective existence was ultimately futile in virtue of the radical dependence of human projects on the intervention, whether for ill or good, of an omnipotent Zeus.[9] Implicitly questioning the justice of the woes imposed upon humankind as punishment for Prometheus's theft of fire, practitioners of the arts of medicine, drama, navigation, artisanship, gymnastics, war, speech making, and the like slowly emancipated themselves from the routines of ancestral custom and so asserted a claim to reflective attention.[10]

8. See Dewey, *LTI*, pp. 72–73; "Oriental cultures, especially the Assyrian, Babylonian and Egyptian, developed a division between 'lower' and 'higher' techniques and kinds of knowledge. The lower, roughly speaking, was in possession of those who did the daily practical work; carpentering, dyeing, weaving, making pottery, trading, etc. The higher came to be the possession of a special class, priests and the successors of primitive medicine men. Their knowledge and techniques were 'higher' because they were concerned with what were supposed to be matters of ultimate concern; the welfare of the people and especially its rulers—and this welfare involved transactions with the powers that ruled the universe. *Their* kind of practical activity was so different from that of artisans and traders, the objects involved were so different, the social status of the persons engaged in carrying on the activities in question was so enormously different, that the activity of the guardians and administrators of the higher knowledge and techniques was not 'practical' in the sense of practical that applied to the ordinary useful worker. These facts contained dualism in embryo, indeed in more or less mature form. This, when it was reflectively formulated, became the dualism of the empirical and rational, of theory and practice, and, in our own day, of common sense and science. The Greeks were much less subject to ecclesiastic and autocratic political control than were the peoples mentioned."

9. For the most well-known expression of the city's capacity to turn nature's powers to its own benefit, see Sophocles' *Antigone* 332ff.

10. Dewey's understanding of the pre-Socratics owes much to his reading of Benjamin Farrington's *Head and Hand in Ancient Greece* (London: Watts, 1947). Farrington argues that "if the early Greek philosopher was interested in the process of change, it was not simply because nature is so changeable . . . but because man himself had never before been so active and independent an agent of change" (p. 20). For a vigorous

Embedded in their flexible and discriminating habits, the skilled craftsmen who practiced these arts secured nature's cooperation by fashioning mutable resources in the service of concrete needs. Although ultimately rooted in palpable receptions of the body's diverse senses, these materials did not take shape as experience (in the sense suggested by the term *empeiria*) until the power of recollection detached common elements from the multiplicity of particular instances in which they were originally embedded and refashioned these into resources available for deft response to novel circumstances. Sufficiently articulated, that memory took shape as loosely integrated clusters of prosaic generalizations about how to answer the shifting demands of everyday experience, whether encountered in building a house, making a statue, or leading an army. Such knowledge, although fully contained and expressed within the habit-laden practice of specific agents, had "nothing merely personal or subjective about it; it was a consolidation, effected by nature, of particular natural occurrences into actualization of the forms of such things as are thus and so usually, now and then, upon the whole, but not necessarily and always."[11] Consummating possibilities intimated but only partly realized within experience's emergents, such skilled conduct secured the useful and, at the same time, responded to the senses' desire to fashion coherent wholes from informed materials. "The potter shapes his clay to make a bowl useful for holding grain; but he makes it in a way so regulated by the series of perceptions that sum up the serial acts of making, that the bowl is marked by enduring grace and charm."[12]

Only imperceptibly did *technai's* disclosure of nature's regularities and possibilities come to threaten the authority of archaic cultural traditions. Knowing fate to be the vehicle through which the gods might at any moment suspend or disrupt the familiar cycles of birth, growth, decay, and death, that order's collective sense of the human condition was governed by its presentiment of the arbitrary, the terrible, and the inexplicable. "There are two urns that stand on the doorsill of Zeus," Homer reminds his audience in the *Iliad* (24.525). "They are unlike for the gifts they bestow: an urn of evils, an urn of blessings.

---

objection to Farrington's (and, by implication, Dewey's) reading of the origins of philosophy, see Ludwig Edelstein, *Ancient Medicine* (Baltimore: Johns Hopkins University Press, 1967), pp. 415–29. For reasons that will become apparent in this chapter, I do not share Edelstein's more charitable vision of reason's birth.

11. Dewey, *EN*, pp. 230–31.
12. Dewey, *AE*, p. 50.

If Zeus who delights in thunder mingles these and bestows them on man, he shifts, and moves now in evil, again in good fortune." Nevertheless, each new expression of Prometheus's primal crime could not help but chip away at forms of collective consciousness that knew no distinction between the profane and the magical. Indicating acknowledgment of sequential bonds linking nature's recurrent events, the deployment of tools and other artifacts signified that what had once been accepted in its qualitative immediacy was now construed in terms of relational structures joining experience and nature via their reciprocal doing and suffering. "As long as men are content to enjoy and suffer fire when it happens, fire is just an objective entity which is what it is. That it may be taken as a deity to be adored or propitiated is evidence that its 'whatness' is all there is to it. But when men come to the point of *making* fire, fire is not an essence, but a mode of natural phenomena, an order of change, a 'how' of a historic sequence. Acumen, shrewdness, inventiveness, accumulation and transmission of information are products of the necessity under which man labors to turn away from absorption in direct having and enjoying, so as to consider things in their active connections as means and as signs."[13]

The disruptive possibilities implicit within this interruption of experience's qualitative immediacy were first grasped, albeit fragmentarily, when the Ionian *physiologoi* began to use analogies culled from the activities of the cook, the farmer, the potter, and the smith to render the cosmos's events intelligible without recourse to anthropomorphic or animistic agencies. "These early philosophies were stories of nature. As Homer told the story of the Trojan war and the wanderings of Odysseus, so Thales and others recounted the epic of nature, relating its movements to the elements that formed its *dramatis personae*."[14] Considered comprehensively, the plots of these early narratives are best grasped by considering how each appropriated and reconfigured the metaphorical content suggested by two overlapping but distinct domains of technical practice. Among the arts the most evident contrast was between those that cultivated things found growing in nature and those that withdrew nature's gifts from their original setting

13. Dewey, *EN*, pp. 234, 122. Cf. p. 128: "The very conception of cognitive meaning, intellectual significance, is that things in their immediacy are subordinated to what they portend and give evidence of."

14. Dewey, unpublished ms. (53/17). In passing, I should note that my understanding of Ionian "science" is essentially congruent with and much indebted to Gregory Vlastos, "Equality and Justice in Early Greek Cosmologies," *Classical Philology* 42 (1947), 156–78.

so as to transform them more completely in accordance with the designs of the imagination. As we shall see, the complex and interwoven history of the metaphorical clusters elicited from these domains of craft goes a long way toward explaining the peculiarities as well as the impasses of the philosophical tradition.

When ancient thinking about the cosmic drama located its inspiration in analogical extrapolation of meanings wrought from agrarian experience, the most salient categories used to explain the segregation of specific realms of being out of a primordial state of undifferentiated chaos took their cue from incidents of generation. So informed, as was uniformly the case with Milesian speculation, the material root underlying all change was rendered as a seminal agency endowed with the capacity for self-movement qua reproduction and growth; thus Anaximander interprets the formation of the world by referring to a germ, or *gonimon*, capable of begetting heat and cold. The process of change, on this account, was said to be ruled by the seasonal or rhythmic alteration of qualitatively opposed active and passive principles such as male and female, hot and cold, wet and dry; and the termini of change were discovered within mature consummations of such patterned transformations. Declining to draw an unambiguous distinction between the vital and the nonliving, the Milesians apportioned an originally inchoate reality by ordering things into kinds according to their organic derivation from the cosmos's primal seeds. The cosmos, in short, is alive, self-moving, and self-governing; it is a teleological order whose changes are uniformly directed toward fixed and predestined ends.

By way of contrast, when nature was read through analogical extrapolation of meanings fashioned from more recently developed forms of mechanical practice, as in Leucippus and Democritus, the material roots underlying all change were pictured not as qualitatively distinct elements, but rather as homogeneous structural units that lent themselves to reshaping in virtue of their capacity to be stretched, hammered, molded, and twisted. Consequently, processes of change were held to take shape not as generation and growth, but as quantitative separation and aggregation of compositional parts whose mechanical motion was conceived after the analogy of falling in space; and their termini were found to consist not of differentiated substances gifted with the power of self-action, but of matter's formation in accordance with antecedently existent designs. Whereas the first tale implicitly held that natural processes were spontaneously directed toward realization of the fruit that gives them meaning and value, the second regarded nature's offerings as comparatively indifferent and even recalcitrant. Thus its recitation more characteristically assumed the form of a prescription or a recipe whose instructions informed a physician, a cook, or a metal worker how much of each substance to select and how to compound it with others in order to secure the ends of human use and enjoyment.

How these epics of nature testify to the archaic world's decay is best illustrated by the speculations of Anaximander and Heraclitus. However unwittingly, Anaximander challenges divine prerogative, as well as its expression in omens, oracles, and marvels, when he draws his account of the sun's motion from observation of a familiar technical achievement—in this case, the chariot wheel—and its elaboration as an explanatory generalization capable of extension to a multiplicity of phenomena.[15] By the same token, Heraclitus undermines the representation of change as evidence of divine intervention when, after examining the conduct of taut bowstrings, he concludes that the appearance of rest in nature conceals an orderly cycle of transformation between dynamic powers turning in concurrent opposition to one another: "Cold things grow hot, hot things grow cold, the wet dries, the parched is moistened. . . . The latter [of each pair of opposites] having changed becomes the former, and this again having changed becomes the latter" (Frgs. 126, 88).

These imaginative extrapolations could not suspend altogether the anxiety of a human situation beyond its own command. But by locating its most fateful powers within a macrocosm whose motions generally appear to heed intelligible regularities, terror of the inexplicable and unanticipated is substantially checked. Anaximander, in this regard, argues that the triumph of the earth's stability over the motions of the cosmos is explained not by the *archē* of an external cause governing its motions, but rather by the situation of this well-rounded, free-floating, and motionless sphere, "like a stone column" (Frg. 5), at the center of an order whose harmony is a function of the dynamic equilibrium sustained by recurrent association among its reciprocal con-

15. See Aetius 2.20.1: "Anaximander says the sun is a circle 28 times the size of the earth, like a chariot wheel, with its felloe hollow and full of fire, and showing the fire at a certain point through an aperture as though through the nozzle of a bellows." Except where otherwise indicated, all pre-Socratic quotations, including this one, are taken from *The Worlds of the Early Greek Philosophers*, ed. J. B. Wilbur and H. J. Allen (Buffalo: Prometheus Books, 1979).

stituents. Because that order is invested with the directive capacities hitherto ascribed to the gods, it is capable of self-regulation and so does not require divine rule to insure its *dikē*. No longer is Zeus, to quote from Aeschylus's *Suppliant Maidens*, the "lord of lords, most blessed among the blessed, power most perfect among the perfect" (524–26), and no longer is his *dynasteia* over all things the condition of their unity. Indeed, in an important sense, his rule is incompatible with the claims of justice. For the rectitude of the cosmos's affairs can be guaranteed only as long as the original equality of its opposing powers is maintained, that is, only as long as no single power dominates the others.[16] Hence when injustice occurs, as it does on Anaximander's account of the seasons' alternation, compensation is exacted via a commensurate subjection dictated not by the gods, but by the cosmos's drive to sustain its tense balance of powers: "For they pay penalty and retribution to each other for their injustice according to the assessment of time" (Frg. 1). In sum, the very possibility of thinking the thought of "nature" presupposes subversion of the strict segregation between a higher and a lower grade of being, whether cast as divine and mortal or master and servant.

Be that as it may, the *physiologoi*'s departure from the mythopoetic construction of the cosmos, as well as its authorization of corresponding earthly hierarchies, should not be exaggerated. Although their cosmologies are not explicitly linked to acknowledged public cults, the ancient divinities persist, albeit in sublimated form. Unwilling to abandon wholly the past's assurance of cosmic order, the Ionians seek to reconcile the ethical standards embodied in the traditional code with the unsettling possibilities suggested by reflection on *technai*'s explanatory import. The result is an uneasy synthesis that extracts from inherited legends, myths, and tales an all-encompassing, singular principle of divine being and then subordinates these new explanatory forms to its imperatives. Thus Anaximander subsumes his more particular insights beneath the claims of the ungenerated, imperishable, and homogeneous *Apeiron* (Boundless Stuff); and this abstracted articulation of the hylozoistic substance identified by Thales effectively offers metaphysical comfort to those confused by disintegration of the

---

16. For another statement of the equality of the basic components of the cosmos, see Parmenides: "But since all things are named Light and Night, and names have been given to each class of things according to the power of one or the other [Light or Night], everything is full equally of Light and invisible Night, as both are equal, because to neither of them belongs any share [of the other]" (Frg. 9).

customs that hitherto had assured the meaningfulness of human existence. Similarly, revealing the unease called forth by his own contention that "this ordered universe was not created by any one of the gods
or of mankind" (Frg. 30), Heraclitus recasts the *archē* of Zeus as the
depersonalized and immanent rule of a divine Logos whose power
"steers all things through all things: . . . If we speak with intelligence,
we must base our strength on that which is common to all, as the city
on the Law and even more strongly. For all human laws are nourished
by one, which is divine" (Frgs. 41, 114). In each of these cases, the hint
of a cosmos whose immanent destiny is left unspecified by divine
pleasure is glimpsed; but that hint goes unfulfilled in the quest to
reinstate the reassuring subjection of experience to fate by conceiving
of causality as a primary and monistic substance whose unchanging
presence guarantees the surpassing unity and identity of that which
is. For water, air, fire, number, and the like are simply different ways of
naming the divine principle that encompasses all things, and so rules
their changes.

III

When these ambiguous narratives of nature were transported from
Asia Minor to the Greek mainland (where the transition from an
agrarian economy grounded in the *oikos* to a craft- and trade-based
economy centered in the polis was already well advanced), myth's
unreflective assurance that mere existence is the measure of its rightness became ever more problematic. No longer certain that the terms
of conventional speech are the natural vestments through which
things necessarily disclose their logos, the Sophists came to suspect
that every account of nature *is* an account and, as such, is subject to the
conditions of adequate discourse, that is, to logic. Making explicit the
Ionians' unspoken divorce of *physis* from *nomos*, the Sophists express
the speculation, welcome to some and deeply unsettling to others,
that human order is not the work of a nature whose divine compass
embraces all genuine goods, but rather something manufactured like a
pot or a house. To Antiphon, this suggests that "the edicts of the laws
are imposed artificially, but those of nature are compulsory. And the
edicts of the laws are arrived at by consent, not by natural growth,
whereas those of nature are not a matter of consent" (Frg. 44). To
Protagoras, secure in his conviction that "about the gods I am not able

to know whether they exist or do not exist, nor what they are like in form" (Frg. 4), this same premise signifies that what a given collectivity regards as right and good is, within its confines, right and good.

The dispute between Antiphon and Protagoras proves possible and intelligible only because its audience now finds problematic the archaic sense of experience's pragmata. Recall that the archaic age was defined by its strict hierarchical congruence between the exercise of economic privilege, the power of rule, and the rites through which this correspondence was grounded in the divine. For example, the righting of wrong, as when Odysseus slew Penelope's suitors, was an exclusive prerogative of an aristocratic nobility whose special connection with matters of sacred import legitimated its monopolistic jurisdiction over questions of justice. Within these confines, the emergence of affairs taken to be peculiarly common because they mutually implicate ruler and ruled is severely circumscribed by the special status of those who, replicating the role of Zeus, are the condition and source of order's possibility.

That hegemony is challenged when Solon, gleaning the import of changes long in the making, decrees that homicide is not a restricted matter to be settled between one *gene* and another in light of the claims of a divinely ordained ethos, but rather a common affair in which all, regardless of official status, have a shared stake.[17] By giving each title to intervene on behalf of anyone who has suffered an injury, Solon questions whether celestial signs are sufficient to resolve issues of justice, and so invites public appropriation of the prerogatives previously restricted to a few. Reweaving the web of everyday circumstance, Solon opens up a space within which matters of general concern and consequence, of qualitatively inclusive pragmata, can begin to emerge from those more delimited in significance. Decades later, that space expands as Cleisthenes, completing the transformation of Homer's assembly of the invisible *demos* into a deliberative body of the *demes*, formally identifies all free inhabitants of Attica as Athenian citizens. Substituting the distinction between citizen and noncitizen for that between noble and commoner, Cleisthenes effectively fixes the identification of the city as a political rather than a geographical entity.

17. On these questions, see Gregory Vlastos, "Solonian Justice," *Classical Philology* 41 (1946), 65–83; Jean-Pierre Vernant, *The Origins of Greek Thought* (Ithaca: Cornell University Press, 1982), passim; and J.A.O. Larsen, "Cleisthenes and the Development of the Theory of Democracy at Athens," in *Essays in Political Theory Presented to George Sabine* (Port Washington, N.Y.: Kennikat Press, 1972).

Just what this identification demands of citizens becomes apparent when, in his "Funeral Oration," Pericles insists that Athenians "regard the man who takes no part in public affairs [*pragmata*], not as one who minds his own business, but as good for nothing" (2.40.2). When that charge is no longer fulfilled, as it is not after Pericles' death, peculiarly political matters are eclipsed, as a lopsided distribution of power subverts the tense equilibrium that first made their appearance real. The continued disclosure of distinctively political pragmata, in sum, depends on (re)generating the power-laden media that sustain their emergence in the loosely bounded field wrought by an-archic collective association.

Ironically, the most revealing expression of the relationship between collective empowerment and the rise of specifically political concerns appears in Plato's *Protagoras*, where Protagoras retells the myth of Prometheus.[18] Protagoras explains how Prometheus provided for the necessities of human existence by stealing from Hephaestus and Athena "the gift of skill in the arts." But, he continues, this acquisition left human beings unable to live in peace with one another; "for they had not the art of politics. Zeus therefore, fearing the total destruction of our race, instructed Hermes to impart to men the qualities of respect for others and a sense of justice, so as to bring order into our cities and create a bond of friendship and union." This specifically *politike techne*, he further ordered, was not to be distributed as were the other *technai*, that is, in accordance with the necessities of specialized labor. Countering Plato's claim that "no large group of men is capable of acquiring any art, be it what you will" (*Statesman* 300c), Protagoras insists that political competence is not a natural legacy but a collective accomplishment. Moreover, precisely because the capacity for excellence in all other arts is unevenly distributed, "everyone must share in this kind of virtue; otherwise the state [the form of association whose end is to cultivate political pragmata] could not exist." Making explicit the political import of Empedocles' insistence that the elements composing the cosmos "are equal and of the same age in their creation, but each

18. See *Protagoras* 320d–27c, in *The Collected Dialogues of Plato*, ed. Edith Hamilton and Huntington Cairns (Princeton: Princeton University Press, 1961). All subsequent quotations from Plato are taken from this volume. For an interpretation of "Protagoras" that explores the idea of *politike techne*, see John Wallach, "Political Reason, Deliberation, and Democracy in Ancient Greek Political Theory" (Ph.D. diss., Princeton University, 1981). For an interpretation that links the "Great Speech" to the invention of politics, see Cynthia Farrar, *The Origins of Democratic Thinking* (New York: Cambridge University Press, 1988), especially chaps. 3 and 4.

presides over its own office, and each has its own character, and they prevail in turn in the course of Time" (Frg. 17), Protagoras acknowledges that *isonomia*, equal engagement in the fashioning and exercise of power, is an essential condition of the reality of peculiarly political phenomena.

The fragility of the Protagorean project becomes apparent when the Sophists' navigation of nature's tales toward more worldly contexts produces the enigmatic figure of Socrates; for his story contains within it the fleeting promise of a reason that is in no danger of being caught up within its own logical machinations as well as the germ of its own miscarriage. From one perspective, Socrates' lifework signifies final decomposition of the deferential ethos that for so long frustrated the transmutation of archaicism's unperceived inequalities into the fifth century's class-conscious conflicts between urban democratic and aristocratic-oligarchic factions.[19] Practicing a dialectic that acknowledges its own finitude but does not renounce its capacity to criticize that which is, Socrates' questioning reveals the transformation of knowledge into a common cultural possession that, because open to a plurality of readings, unveils the issue of truth. From another perspective, though, his work points toward a possible rehabilitation of that same ethos. When Socrates asks whether it is possible to discover intelligible concepts to which all necessarily refer even in disagreement, he shows how the conflict stimulated by the democratic challenge to noble *archē* might at last be overcome. Intimating that the virtues of a declining aristocracy might be cast not as attributes immanent within certain classes of action, but as transcendent universal ideals to which all conduct is related as approximation rather than as instance, Socrates foreshadows the paradox of a reason that owes its existence to *technē*'s devitalization of mythological doctrine, yet whose form as well as

---

19. On this point, see the detailed sociological investigation of transformations within the class structure of ancient Greece furnished by Ellen and Neal Wood in their *Class Ideology and Ancient Political Theory* (New York: Oxford University Press, 1978): "The old essentially agrarian class opposition principally between aristocratic and peasant landholders, which had been the motivating force of early political developments, had now been transformed into a new conflict focused on the *polis*: a conflict which expressed itself particularly in a political opposition between, on the one hand, rich citizens, who felt victimized by the democratic polis, the role it gave banausics, its redistributive function extracting funds from the rich and conferring public payments on the poor; and, on the other hand, poorer citizens who stood to gain from the institutions of democracy, its checks on the rich and its diversion of surplus product to subsidize the political judicial activities of the poor" (pp. 52–53). For a critique of the Woods' argument, see Peter Euben's review in *Political Theory* 8 (1980), 245–49.

content refortify a decaying order's customary creed. Poised between the enclosed mysteries of the wisdom cults and the exposed controversies of the agora, the ambiguity of Socrates is soon to be resolved in favor of an ever denser theoretical construct whose purified expression of traditional belief supplies some measure of compensation for its loss of practical efficacy. "To put it in a word, that which had rested upon custom was to be restored, resting no longer upon the habits of the past, but upon the very metaphysics of Being. Out of this situation emerged, if I mistake not, the entire tradition regarding the function and office of philosophy which till very recently has controlled the systematic and constructive philosophies of the western world."[20]

IV

"Greek philosophy converted not psychological conditions but positive institutional affairs into cosmic realities."[21] More specifically, the metaphysics of Plato and Aristotle are best read as intellectualized transmutations of *technē*'s unsystematized and flexible skills, as well as the products of that craft, into decontextualized and rigidified conceptual truths given in the nature of abstract things.[22] The distinction

20. Dewey, *RP*, pp. 17–18. In their conclusion to *Class Ideology and Ancient Political Theory*, the Woods argue that "Socrates, friend and associate of the aristocracy, founded a philosophical school with a pronounced aristocratic moral and social bias at a time when the traditional Athenian nobility was in the process of decay. His most important successors, the patricians Plato and Aristotle, developed, modified, and systematized his ideas, and maintained agrarian aristocratic ideals in a period of Athenian history marked on the one hand by the steady decline of the old landed gentry and peasantry and their agrarian economic base, and on the other by the growth of democracy more firmly grounded in the urban classes of craftsmen, shopkeepers, and labourers" (p. 259).

21. Dewey, *EN*, p. 215. In passing, I would note here the congruence of this reading of philosophy with that of Michel Foucault in "Nietzsche, Genealogy, History," reprinted in *Language, Counter-Memory, Practice*, ed. Donald Bouchard (Ithaca: Cornell University Press, 1977). Foucault writes: "The very question of truth, the right it appropriates to refute error and oppose itself to appearance, the manner in which it developed (initially made available to the wise, then withdrawn by men of piety to an unattainable world where it was given the double role of consolation and imperative, finally rejected as a useless notion, superfluous, and contradicted on all sides)—does this not form a history, the history of an error we call truth?" (p. 144).

22. See Dewey, *QC*, p. 16: "If one looks at the foundations of the philosophies of Plato and Aristotle as an anthropologist looks at his material, that is, as cultural subject-matter, it is clear that these philosophies were systematizations in rational form of the content of Greek religious and artistic beliefs." Dewey's interpretation of classical philosophy does not display as much scholarly rigor as does that of G.E.R. Lloyd, whose *Polarity and Analogy: Two Types of Argumentation in Early Greek Thought* (Cambridge: Cambridge University Press, 1966) carefully explores its dependence on analogies

between them turns on how each transforms the common stock of materials inherited from his predecessors within an order that now embraces the *polis* rather than the *oikos* as the principal unit of collective life, that is, that now defines its most comprehensive relationships in terms of citizenship rather than kinship.

Plato's synthesis of earlier philosophies of nature with the logicoethical ideas he derived from Socrates resolves the tension between the mechanical and agrarian epics of nature by elevating his teacher's dialogic into a metaphysic, and then fashioning the latter into a cosmology whose geometrically patterned order is imbued with living spirit by the skillful practice of a demiurge. At first, and conforming to Socrates' account of ethical form as that ingredient shared by all instances of a specified class of actions, Plato understands the intelligibility of a thing as its immanent organization when seen as an embodied whole. Before long, mistaking the structure of his discourse for the structure of things themselves, he refashions the conceptual materials left to him by his predecessors into an architectonic logical structure whose self-sufficiency demands the subordination of all change to its directly enjoyed fulfillments. Completing the expropriation of *technai*'s prosaic intelligence from its original embeddedness in ordinary practice, he resituates *craft*'s capacity to achieve form within a divine realm where its realization no longer requires material embodiment to prove either real or intelligible.

Arguing that the cosmos's fund of realized, objective, and impersonal designs furnishes the ideal standards that make possible judgment on its necessarily imperfect approximations, Plato defends the rule of craft's practice by rigidified caricatures of its own achievements. If the rational practice of any art presupposes the existence of fixed models, then the element of individual invention must be condemned as caprice. For the product of fabrication is real only to the extent that it bears the impress of form whose existence precedes any particular realization. Moreover, as Plato insists in the *Gorgias*, because *technē* makes no "pretense whatever to reason and practically no effort to classify" (501a), its skill can generate no knowledge of the ends to which its fruits are to be put. As such, the bearers of that skill con-

---

drawn from various realms of practice. Still, because he is sensitive to the political context of classical Greece, Dewey can offer an explanation for the conjunction of philosophy's contempt for craftsmen and its use of metaphors drawn from *technē* to describe the order of the cosmos. Lloyd, in contrast, can go no further than to find this fact "remarkable" (p. 293).

stitute a class that must be kept in order by laws imposed from above, since otherwise its intrinsically limitless action cannot help but destroy harmony in the name of liberty. Finding incredible Anaximander's contention that order is the fruit of a tense equilibrium sustained between dynamic parts, no one of which exercises permanent superiority over the others,[23] Plato resurrects archaicism's assurance that only absolute rule of the divine over the mundane, now cast as the governance of particulars by the disciplining power of incorruptible Form, can ward off the disruptive thrust of that which by nature is slave. "When soul and body are both in the same place," he insists in the *Phaedo*, "nature teaches the one to serve and be subject, the other to rule and govern" (79e–80a).[24]

The achievement of order, accordingly, must be the work of those who mimic craft's concrete accomplishment by returning a hypostatized rendering of its teleological practice to the arena of politics and thereby subjecting "arbitrary" custom to the impositions of a totalizing rationality. Recasting the virtues of a declining nobility as the specialized proficiencies of those skilled in the sovereign art, Plato offers the personification of *techne*'s alienated intelligence, disentangled from the world's flux, as the exclusive intermediary through which those bereft of logos may secure access, however partial, to the transcendent.[25] Representing the purified polis as the aristocratic *oikos* writ large, Plato offers the latter's hierarchy as an antidote to an Athens in which decomposition of that same household has at last disclosed a realm of distinctively political affairs.

Because Plato's thought, in tension with itself, metaphorically privileges the work of those artisans who "coerce" nature by subjecting it to an "artificial" yoke, his representation of philosophy's supreme reality can prove no more than an uncongenial heresy. Its power

---

23. See especially Plato, *Laws* 889b–90c.

24. See also *Timaeus* 44d: "First, then, the gods, imitating the spherical shape of the universe, enclosed the two divine courses in a spherical body, that, namely, which we now term the head, being the most divine part of us and the lord of all that is in us; to this the gods, when they put together the body, gave all the other members to be servants, considering that it must partake of every sort of motion."

25. On this point, see Wood and Wood, *Class Ideology and Ancient Political Theory*, pp. 124–25: "The aristocratic values that Plato propounds are clearly not those of the feudal house-hold and its warlord masters, but rather the values of a landed leisure class which is to occupy its rightful place *in the polis* as a modern ruling class. Plato sets himself the almost self-contradictory task of elaborating a polis-centred aristocratic morality, virtually free of the tribal, anti-political values that had persisted in the aristocratic code throughout the democratic age."

dwindles when challenged by a rival whose resolution of the *physis-nomos* dichotomy more persuasively promises to restore the harmony that was lost when myth's assurances were undermined and when the city, once the model of order and decorum, became a scene of factional strife and insecurity.[26] Aristotle's agrarian-based teleology is best read as a synthetic conjunction of Plato's Forms, understood as the ultimate goal of all absolute insight, with the material elements drawn from pre-Socratic philosophy. Regarding matter as indeterminate stuff not yet organized into specific form, Aristotle argues that realization in an organic body of the forms found in things constitutes mind as the end of nature. That, in turn, enables him to overcome Plato's difficulties in explaining the union of form and matter without falling prey to the errors of earlier materialist doctrines that, with the exception of the Pythagorean, were unable to account for the qualitative differentiation of natural phenomena out of a homogeneous universal root. Yet this achievement, I would argue, entails no significant departure from the overarching political bent of Platonic metaphysics.

Diffusing *technē*'s concrete capacities throughout a demythologized nature, Aristotle ascribes its powers to the spiritualized *nisus* of a mind that, although endowed with the animating force needed to arouse movement from potentiality to actuality, is emancipated from the degradation of intercourse with matter. Then, impious toward the practice that gives form and substance to his own theoretical constructs, he invests nature's consummatory ends with an intrinsic worth he denies to craft's actual creations. Having read the terms of late antiquity's class hierarchy into nature's teleology, Aristotle then deploys its sanctions to sustain the exclusion of artisans from the best political order. Furnishing reflective expression to the praxical disjunction between the causality of the master who utters orders and the efficacy of the servant who executes them,[27] his doctrine of the four causes recapitulates the fixed relations of rule that obtain when the labor of one class is justified through reference to the necessity of another's disembodied leisure; "one that can foresee with his mind,"

26. See Dewey, "Syllabus: Types of Philosophic Thought," in *MW*, vol. 13, p. 364: "While men had begun by thinking of social order as the type of all order, and nature outside as wild and irregular, they came to reverse the attitude and to seek in nature an order they did not find in factional and shifting political life."

27. On this point, see Aristotle, *Rhetoric*, trans. W. Rhys Roberts (New York: Modern Library, 1954), 1367a30: "Again, it is noble not to practise any sordid craft, since it is the mark of a free man not to live at another's beck and call."

Aristotle argues, "is naturally ruler and naturally master, and one that can do these things with his body is subject and naturally a slave."[28]

The form of Aristotelian logic surpasses the particularity of myth's heroic ethic, while reasserting the universality of its authority to regulate everyday affairs. As such, that logic offers rhetorical displays whose magnification of the signs of undeniable demonstration seek to compel its audience to acquiesce in truths they can no longer uncritically accept.[29] This attempt to eliminate the contestability of order's most basic presuppositions, however, ensures the disappearance of peculiarly political experience. The very possibility of such affairs requires a web of common involvements that can itself emerge only among human beings who are no longer convinced, quoting Aristotle's *Politics*, that "in every composite thing, where a plurality of parts . . . is combined to make a single common whole, there is always found a ruling and a subject factor" (1254a). Political pragmata can neither arise nor flourish when cosmic and earthly hierarchies, reciprocally reified through assimilation of each to the other, are jointly constituted as closed aristocracies consisting of a limited number of qualitatively distinct and eternal classes whose mutual exclusivity is the sine qua non of order's conservation.

Consequently, Aristotle is guilty of bad faith when, in the opening book of his *Metaphysics*, he insists that it was purely speculative "curiosity that first led men to philosophize and that still leads them." While it may be that the possibility of such discourse emerged only "after all the necessities for commodious and enjoyable living had

28. Aristotle, *The Politics*, trans. Ernest Barker (New York: Oxford University Press, 1958), 1252a. Cf. 1328a–29a: "In the state, as in other natural compounds, the conditions which are necessary for the existence of the whole are not organic parts of the whole system which they serve. . . . The *citizens* of our state must have a supply of property [in order to have leisure for goodness and political activities]; and it is these persons who are citizens—they, and they only. The class of mechanics has no share in the state; nor has any other class which is not a 'producer' of goodness."

29. On this point, see Wood and Wood, *Class Ideology and Ancient Political Theory*, p. 138: "The form of poetic ethic may be explained by the fact that in a society completely dominated by hero-nobles and their values, object lessons in the form of model hero-nobles might in themselves carry sufficient absoluteness and universality to serve as absolute and universal moral principles. In a society where they no longer reigned supreme such models must have appeared much too particular and relative. One could no longer take for granted that the values of the noble class were regarded as universal or that the audience being addressed shared them. If the values of that class were to be universalized, they had to be embodied in a more unassailably absolute form. The individual hero-models of Homer had to be transformed into universal philosophical moral principles."

become common," it is equally true that classical philosophy was conceived and begotten of the arts in the sense that its conceptual core presupposes the arduous history through which the intelligence implicit in *techné*'s purposeful engagements was abstracted from its accustomed sphere of reference and then employed analogically to make sense of change. Forgetting that the initial ascription of causal regularities to the totality of nature merely expressed in generalized form a vital prerequisite of crafts' skilled conduct, Aristotle cannot acknowledge that nature can appear as a system of ends only because human beings first acted as fabricators. To sustain his contention that a teleological metaphysics is "the most appropriate kind" of knowledge "for God to have,"[30] Aristotle must hide reason's ultimate origins in the partly articulated and partly unsaid know-how of those who reshape the offerings of nature-in-experience.

"This lack of piety concealed from" Plato and Aristotle alike "the poetic and religious character of their own constructions, and established in the classic Western philosophic tradition the notions that immediate grasp and incorporation of objects is knowledge; that things are placed in graded reality in accordance with their capacity to afford a cultivated mind such a grasp or beholding; and that the order of reality in Being is coincident with a predetermined rank of Ends."[31] Diverting thinking from concerns of collective life and toward more "noble" controversies about the conditions, organs, and objects of knowing, that tradition's conceptual distinctions between truth and falsity, knowledge and opinion, reality and appearance, depend in the last analysis on forms of conduct whose worth these dualisms deny. In this sense, domination is situated at the core of a discursive order whose abstracted reification of narratives' metaphors rule the powerless through the medium of a vocabulary they once spoke but never "knew."

At a still deeper level, the significance of classical philosophy's expropriation concerns its inability to relocate the experiential ground from which it grows ever more detached. Recall that the "Greeks were induced to philosophize by the increasing failure of their traditional customs and beliefs to regulate life. Thus they were led to criticize custom adversely and to look for some other source of authority in life

---

30. Aristotle, *Metaphysics*, trans. Richard Hope (Ann Arbor: University of Michigan Press, 1960), 982a10–b22.
31. Dewey, *EN*, p. 108.

and belief. Since they desired a rational standard for the latter, and had identified with experience the customs which had proved unsatisfactory supports, the struggle of reason for its legitimate supremacy could be won only by showing the inherently unstable and inadequate nature of experience."[32] As a manifestation of those realms of being that are infected by chance and change, *empeiria* is defined by two great disabilities. First, as we have seen, its intelligence cannot be other than opinion since it is unable to transcend its prosaic ground in the accumulation of so many instances of trial and error. Second, in contrast to the self-sufficiency of contemplative rationality, its dependence on mundane tools and materials signifies its unfreedom. Each of these defects is itself indicative of a metaphysic that confines embodied conduct to an ontologically inferior realm. Hence Plato in the *Timaeus*:

> If mind and true opinion are two distinct classes, then I say that there certainly are these self-existent ideas unperceived by sense, and apprehended only by mind; if, however, as some say, true opinion differs in no respect from mind, then everything that we perceive through the body is to be regarded as most real and certain. But we must affirm them to be distinct, for they have a distinct origin and are of a different nature; the one is implanted in us by instruction, the other by persuasion; the one is always accompanied by true reason, the other is without reason; the one cannot be overcome by persuasion, but the other can; and lastly, every man may be said to share in true opinion, but mind is the attribute of the gods and of very few men. Wherefore we must also acknowledge that one kind of being is the form which is always the same, uncreated and indestructible, never receiving anything into itself from without, nor itself going out to any other, but invisible and imperceptible by any sense, and of which the contemplation is granted to intelligence only. And there is another nature of the same name with it, and like to it, perceived by sense, created, always in motion, becoming in place and again vanishing out of place, which is apprehended by opinion jointly with sense. (51d–52a)

Establishment of a fixed distinction between two realms of existence is the condition of philosophy's precedence over *doxa* as well as the source of its inversion of the ontological relationship between reason and its prereflective ground. Dissolving experience's particularistic entities within its pure objects, the Platonic reading of reason presupposes that its refined noetic constructs exhaust the meaning of things,

32. Dewey, *DE*, pp. 275–76, 263.

and in doing so it renders the concrete fabric of matter-of-fact experience immaterial, unproblematic, and in time invisible. "Since thinkers claim to be concerned with knowledge of existence, rather than with imagination, they have to make good the pretention to knowledge. Hence they transmute the imaginative perception of the stably good object into a definition and description of true reality in contrast with lower and specious existence, which, being precarious and incomplete, alone involves us in the necessity of choice and active struggle. Thus they remove from actual existence the very traits which generate philosophic reflection and which give point and bearing to its conclusions. What is left over, (and since trouble, struggle, conflict, and error still empirically exist, something *is* left over) being excluded by definition from full reality is assigned to a grade or order of being which is asserted to be metaphysically inferior. Then the problem of metaphysics alters: it becomes an endeavor to adjust or reconcile to each other two separate realms of being."[33] So detached from the finite web of affairs, which are of consequence because they are of concern, reason thus conceived cannot help but violate the things emerging within experience; for its legitimate authority requires that the qualitative dimensionality of temporally qualified pragmata, the transient affairs of daily life, be grasped exclusively through the "self-sufficient" concepts generated by its misinformed ontology.

Identification of Becoming with indeterminate negation and of Being with the fully real is one of the defining presuppositions of most Western philosophical thinking after Plato. That premise, which is well represented as an effort to privilege the knower-known relationship over the doer-sufferer relationship, is characteristically expressed as a claim on behalf of reason's exclusive and nonmediated insight into the world's truth; and this representation of cognition as a kind of vision into essence is itself made possible by gradual semantic transformation of the terms *nous* and *physis*. With Homer, the verbal form of *nous* (*noein*), designates a distinctive way of being within an unfamiliar situation.[34] Presupposing no dissociation between an intellectual or-

33. Dewey, *EN*, pp. 53–54.
34. For the following remarks on evolution of the term *nous*, I am much indebted to Kurt von Fritz, "Noos and Noein in the Homeric Poems," *Classical Philology* 38 (1943), 79–93; "Nous, Noein and Their Derivatives in Pre-Socratic Philosophy (Excluding Anaxagoras), Part I," *Classical Philology* 40 (1945), 223–42; and "Nous, Noein and Their Derivatives in Pre-Socratic Philosophy (Excluding Anaxagoras), Part II," *Classical Philology* 41 (1946), 12–34. On this question, see also Bruno Snell, *The Discovery of the Mind*, trans. T. G. Rosenmeyer (Oxford: Basil Blackwell, 1953), pp. 191–245.

gan and its function, Homeric usage ordinarily denotes either the act of appreciating the "true" sense of a circumscribed and singular situation, as when Helen suddenly grasps that her visitor is not an old wool dresser, as she first appeared, but rather Aphrodite in disguise (*Iliad*, iii, 396ff.); or, alternatively, the act of crafting a course of action that responds to a situation's import for the present's movement into the future, as when Nestor urges the Achaians to consider how undoing the wrong done to Achilles by Agamemnon might restore the former's prowess to their cause (*Iliad*, ix, 102ff.). As such, *noein* may be taken to refer to a form of perception but only if we keep in mind, first, that it is always the verbal sense that is foremost and, second, that such perception always takes its bearings from the larger context of human doing and suffering in which it is firmly anchored. Accordingly, perception is a matter of appreciating unattained possibilities, of grasping the present in light of what it might become, of anticipating the issues now emerging out of relations sustained among immediate appearances. In sum, *noein* suggests a sort of posture, an attitude of expectant wariness regarding what is not yet but may be soon.

The possibility of overcoming the particularism of such usage was initially disclosed, as we have seen, by advances in the sphere of *technai*; "the first groping steps in defining spatial and temporal qualities, in transforming purely immediate qualities of local things into generic relationships were taken through the arts. The finger, the foot, the unity of walking were used to measure space; measurements of weight originated in the arts of commercial exchange and manufacture."[35] These steps were consolidated when the Ionians, in their appropriation of *technai*'s analogies, marginalized the role of the embodied senses by insisting that only the peculiarly intellectual sense of *nous*, which "is infinite and self-ruling and is mixed with nothing, but is alone itself by itself" (Anaxagoras, Frg. 12), can penetrate beyond the world as most take it to be.[36] Plato merely announces the logical terminus of this evolution when, in the *Republic*, he effects the disembodied reification of *theoria*'s truth as an autonomous epistemic reality

35. Dewey, *EN*, pp. 128–29.
36. On this point, consider Empedocles: "It is not possible to bring God near within reach of our eyes, nor to grasp him with our hands, by which route the broadest road of Persuasion runs into the human mind. For he is not equipped with a human head on his body, nor from his back do two branches start; [he has] no feet, no swift knees, no hairy genital organs; but he is Mind, holy and ineffable, and only Mind, which darts through the whole universe with its swift thoughts" (Frgs. 133, 134).

available to but a few:[37] "When he [the philosopher] had reached the stage of trying to look at the living creatures outside the Cave, then at the stars, and lastly at the Sun himself, he arrived at the highest object in the visible world. So here, the summit of the intelligible world is reached in philosophic discussion by one who aspires, through the discourse of reason unaided by any of the senses, to make his way in every case to the essential reality" (532a).

The Homeric act of perceiving thus becomes the Platonic acknowledgment of likeness, that is, of recognition. The sense of sight is thereby isolated from its sullied intercourse with the body's other openings onto the world. This is Plato's point in the *Timaeus*'s comprehensive discussion of the senses' creation (61d–68e), as well as in the *Republic*'s declaration that sight is peculiarly bound up with the creation of the rational soul and hence with the divine, as the latter is symbolized by sun's illumination: "As the good is in the intelligible region to reason and the objects of reason, so is this in the visible world to vision and the objects of vision. . . . When it [the soul] is firmly fixed on the domain where truth and reality shine resplendent it apprehends and knows them and appears to possess reason, but when it inclines to that region which is mingled with darkness, the world of becoming and passing away, it opines only and its edge is blunted, and it shifts its opinions hither and thither, and again seems as if it lacked reason" (508b–c). Likening the intellect to the eye and light to the medium of its perception, Plato dissociates the recognition of truth from the entangling dimensions of its mundane achievement, that is, from the sympathetic alliance of the body's various senses in the process of seeing.

This construction of truth from the objectified viewpoint of a disconnected center of reason, one who is expert at "being an onlooker," is paralleled by the constitution of knowing's knowns as self-contained objects whose *physis* is left untouched by that vision. Before myth gave way to philosophy, the familiarity of any ordinary thing—that is, acknowledgment of its participation within a meaningful situation— was rooted in an anticipatory sense of how that thing typically inter-

37. See Dewey, *QC*, p. 23: "The theory of knowing is modeled after what was supposed to take place in the act of vision. The object refracts light to the eye and is seen; it makes a difference to the eye and to the person having an optical apparatus, but none to the thing seen. The real object is the object so fixed in its regal aloofness that it is a king to any beholding mind that may gaze upon it. A spectator theory of knowledge is the inevitable outcome."

acts with others appearing within the shifting and overlapping contexts of everyday circumstances. The "nature" of a "thing" was thus taken as a clue to what it most often does, as when Homer uses the term *physis* to refer to the appearance of a plant whose present import stems from its capacity to yield magical effects (*Odyssey* 10.303). This reference to anticipated consequences starts to fall away as the *physiologoi* begin to picture knowing as a relationship between an object torn from its situatedness in everyday affairs and a solitary knower. Infusing that relationship with special power to reveal an object's governing principle, Heraclitus hails the capacity of *nous* to distinguish "each thing according to its *physis* [its not immediately visible structure] and so point out how it really is" (Frg. 1). This abstraction from the qualitative culminates, again, in Plato, for whom things and events as they appear to common sense are merely "shows," seductive shadows and seemings unable to defeat the press of the transitory. Supposing that the activity of apprehending is simple and singular, Plato determines that the essence of the object apprehended must be as well. Accordingly, as he concludes in the *Sophist*, "truth" is a property of statements that accurately express "the things that are as they are" (263b).

To grasp the explicitly political import of this impoverishment of experience's contents, it is important to see that *theoria*'s characterization of its unconditioned entities turns upon a synthetic assimilation of, on the one hand, its hypostatized rendition of the qualities that define craft's purposive productions (beauty, symmetry, and the like) and, on the other, its sublimated recapitulation of myth's conviction that the persistence of order requires the sustaining presence of a supreme source of power. When philosophy transforms *technai*'s fruits into the unambiguous and indubitable ends of its cognition, and then ascribes to those ends the authoritative imperatives once ascribed to Zeus, the result is a teleocratic view of knowledge, that is, a view of knowledge whose realization demands the rule of concrete experience by reason's determinate reifications. Certain that all particulars are real only to the degree they participate in eternally self-identical forms, reason's relationship to experienced pragmata, like myth's *monarchia*, necessarily assumes the character of monologic and unilinear command. To remain assured of its own truth, accordingly, philosophy must assimilate or subjugate all dimensions of experience that do not fit the refined terms specified by its incorruptible and sovereign abstractions.

V

The imperium of the purely conceived over the contextually lived is given its most obvious political exemplification in the class structure of Plato's *Republic*. It might appear, by way of contrast, that Aristotle rejects his mentor's subsumption of all experience beneath the categories of knowledge when he contends that the soul is the perfected entelechy of the body, and hence that experience offers a kind of cognitive ladder by means of which forms can be gradually elicited from their apparent submergence in matter. Certain, however, that the cosmos it has analogically contructed is the product of reason's original vision, Aristotelian knowing also culminates in immediate apprehension of abstracted form invisible to sense; and so each embodied and contingent particular, to which *nous* can have no direct access, proves intelligible only in virtue of its membership within the ungenerated and indestructible species of which it is a transient and partial specimen. Moreover, when he insists that all entities either move or are moved toward determinate ends given prior to that movement itself,[38] Aristotle completes transformation of the Milesians' understanding of *archē*, the principle whose dynamic rule brings about and limits the rhythms of nature, into the teleocratic abstraction of substance, the self-causing end whose ruling presence informs all change and so unambiguously determines things to be what they are and not something else. Plato's radical transcendentalism thus spawns its logical counterpart: affirmation of a world that, aside from mutations caused by obdurate matter that refuses to yield wholly to form, already manifests its full complement of Being.

Although inviting at first glance, Aristotle's appeal to *phronēsis*, a form of rationality that addresses those things that can be other than they are, is suspect because it is situated within and irreducibly informed by his hierarchical ontology. While ethical and political knowledge ranks higher than does that of the artisan, its concern with practical needs and their satisfaction renders it inferior to *epistēmē*. Moreover, inasmuch as the polis is an association of persons dependent on one another for the realization of *phronēsis*, it lacks self-sufficiency and so must in the last analysis serve an end beyond itself. Finally, because natural reason is a human attribute reflecting God's creation, contemplation's disdain for the mundane affairs of ordinary

38. See especially Aristotle, *Metaphysics* 1050a, 1070a.

experience is a condition of humanity's achievement of nobility. In sum, the location of Aristotelian *phronēsis* within the larger confines of his teleological ontology, which finds practical expression in his justifications of slavery, patriarchy, and aristocracy, renders problematic any attempt to salvage an untainted core from the integrated structure of his thought.

If the turn to the classical city-state aims to locate an account of reason which, although in need of considerable refashioning, intimates the character of thinking which might nourish rather than eviscerate the cause of democratic politics, then other less problematic resources are available. Specifically, the craft of medicine is worthy of attention if only because it alone among the arts offered significant resistance to classical philosophy's rationalistic dispossession and subjugation. Spared the scorn directed toward other *banausic* occupations because its concern was the body of the citizen rather than soulless matter, this *technē* emancipated its intelligence from mythopoetic constraints without falling prey, until the age of Galen, to their reimposition via Platonic Form/Matter and Aristotelian Cause/Substance talk. Developing an integrated body of interrelated precepts regarding the etiology and treatment of different classes of disease but refusing to sanction its hypostatization as self-subsistent theory,[39] the healing arts escaped the limitations of unintelligent practice without degenerating into unpractical intelligence. As such, they are justly celebrated by Aeschylus as Prometheus's greatest gift (*Prometheus Bound* 475–84).

Alcmaeon of Croton, an early fifth-century physician, unfolds an account of the body's structure which, in its fundamentals, recapitulates Anaximander's vision of the cosmos, absent the dogmatic dimension stemming from the latter's reduction of all that exists to a single principle of being. Unwilling to grant that the body's internal order requires the rule of its subordinate parts by an unambiguously differentiated source of governance, Alcmaeon represents health as a kind of egalitarian equilibrium sustained among its constituent powers: "Health is the equality of rights of the functions, wet-dry,

---

39. On the political purpose served by the subordination of medical practice to the imperatives of mythical tradition, see the Hippocratic treatise "The Sacred Disease," in Wilbur and Allen, *The Worlds of the Early Greek Philosophers*, p. 238: "My own view is that those who first attributed a sacred character to this malady were like the magicians, purifiers, charlatans, and quacks of our own day, men who claim great piety and supreme knowledge. Being at a loss, and having no treatment which would help, they concealed and sheltered themselves behind superstition, and called this illness sacred, in order that their utter ignorance might not be manifest."

cold-hot, bitter-sweet, and the rest; but single rule among them causes disease; the single rule of either pair is deleterious. . . . Health is the harmonious mixture of the qualities" (Frg. 4). Disease, then, is a sign of *monarchia*, a condition in which either one member from a single pair, or one among these various pairs, masters the others and so destroys the equipoise of an evenly matched contest. To speak of the body's *physis*, accordingly, is to refer to that organism's constitutional structure, the political body's blending of opposed forces within a balanced whole; and that in turn is the condition of its maturation.[40]

Later Hippocratic medicine, bound by an oath that guaranteed its subordination to the satisfaction of human need, joined an examination of symptoms with a search for ways to relate each to the others such that their otherwise disconnected details came to make sense. Taking the precepts implicit within inherited know-how as heuristic tools whose truth is merely potential until actualized in practice, the medical art's commitment to the particularity of the cognitively real permitted no distinction between its knowledge and its ability to heal. Granted, resolution of its crises entailed the construction of practical judgments that rendered its diagnoses intelligible in light of criteria that might become objects of rational discourse apart from the immediacies of concrete practice. But such generalized knowledge did not furnish the material of syllogisms whose major premises, codified as categorical formulae, contained unconditionally valid propositional content from which a determinate result might be mechanically deduced. Rather, and because the diversity and novelty of experienced situations precluded their unambiguous representation as instantiations of universal rules, this store of practical wisdom merely intimated traits to be on the lookout for in studying a particular case, and its worth rested exclusively in the assistance it offered in promoting individualized responses to specific situations. Ancient medicine was thus unburdened by the quest for an essence beyond experience because it was limited to attentive interpretation of issues whose full significance was contained within a present whose parameters extended forward and backward but not outside of time. By the same

40. On this point, consider also the following quotation from chapter 4 of the treatise *On the Nature of Man*, ascribed to Polybus, the son-in-law of Hippocrates: "The body of man contains blood and phlegm and yellow bile and black bile, and these are the nature [*physis*] of his body; and it is because of these that he suffers or enjoys health. He is most healthy when these are mingled in due proportion to one another in power and quantity; he suffers when there is too little or too much of one of these, or when one is separated in the body and not blended with the rest."

token, its conduct was unhindered by any strict segregation of theory from practice because it trusted that its knowing, conveyed by apprenticeship's composite memory of significant exemplars rather than didactic instruction in formalized statements, would advance through dialectical elaboration of the lessons of its own conduct.

Practiced in a domain where the imperative to act could not be evaded, the ancient practice of medicine never eliminated the inevitability of error, overcame the intervention of chance, or passed beyond the merely probable in its prescription. Because medicine dealt with questions whose issue had yet to be determined, a plurality of plausible interpretations was always possible, each of which might be affirmed on grounds presently but not necessarily always found reasonable. This falling short of philosophy's standard of universal validity and absolute certainty, though, did not impugn its value. As the author of the mid-fifth-century Hippocratic treatise "On Ancient Medicine" affirmed: "We ought not to reject the ancient art as non-existent . . . just because it has not attained exactness in every detail"; rather, we ought to praise it "because it has been able by reasoning to rise from deep ignorance to approximately perfect accuracy." Hence within this domain there could be no supreme specialists whose assertion of expert wisdom so transcended the limitations of ordinary intelligence that it justified disregard for the claims of common sense or obviated the need for personal acquaintance with the matter at hand: "If you miss being understood by laymen," "On Ancient Medicine" continued, "you will miss reality"; for the "subject of inquiry and discussion is simply and solely the sufferings of ordinary folk when they are sick or in pain."[41] Consequently, the truth of medicine, which entailed the ability to project oneself into the situation of another and so appreciate that other's suffering as potentially one's own, began and ended within the embodied experience of those who alone could testify to the adequacy of its resolutions.

Ancient medicine's knowledge was identified not with clear vision of antecedently existent realities but with the dynamic capacity to use unhypostatized metaphorical resources in grasping and negotiating the unfamiliar in an adroit manner (as when the fetus was compared to a grain and the healing of cuts to the gluing of surfaces). To know, accordingly, was to discern the needs and possibilities of a given situation, understood as a partly ordered and partly disordered whole

---

41. W.H.J. Jones, *Hippocrates*, vol. 1 (New York: Putnam's, 1923), pp. 15–17, 33.

unfolding in time; to select from among its diverse features those found significant because deemed pertinent to its possible resolution; to fill out one's sense of these phenomena by articulating the likely consequences of acting in ways that, if well informed, might reunify the sufferer's vital powers of action; and finally, because the full significance of a problematic situation could become apparent only through transformative conduct, to consummate its craft in navigating situated events to meanings capable of immediate enjoyment.

VI

How shall we now read those contemporary political theorists who locate their inspiration in the polis? Taking one from each of the three pairs of theorists cited at the beginning of this chapter, let us first consider Leo Strauss. While we may appreciate the brilliance of his exegetical skills, we need not take too seriously his effort to overcome "the crisis of our time, the crisis of the West" by resuscitating the polis's transhistorical wisdom about the "nature of political things."[42] If it is true that philosophy's original accomplishments constitute so many attempts to answer with equal authority but in alternative form the questions to which myth responded prior to its devitalization, then perhaps our interest in reason is best served if those questions are simply laid aside. No longer convinced that knowledge is derived from a higher source than practical activity, and no longer sure why politics requires extrapolitical warrant to ensure its authority, we may acknowledge the incompatibility between foundationalist proclivities and democratic sensibilities. The former, exemplified in Strauss's rehabilitation of natural law, derives from the desire to transcend the vicissitudes of precarious Becoming by placing certain cherished convictions beyond debate; the latter, eager to endorse Heraclitus's contention that the individual occurs within the strife sustained by tensely counterposed opposites, regards the will to extract the essence from experience as a partisan effort to evade politics by eliminating its contestability. To escape experience's sting by privileging the necessary, universal, and fixed over the changing and contingent is to condemn reason to ceaseless vacillation between, on the one hand, the

42. Leo Strauss, *The City and Man* (Chicago: Rand McNally, 1964), p. 1; *What Is Political Philosophy?*, p. 11.

quest to measure up to standards it ought to abandon and, on the other, the search for consolation when those standards go unmet. Only when we tire of compensating for our disappointments by fashioning hypostatized truths out of the objects of ordinary experience, with their flaws removed and their hints fulfilled, can we begin to ask why our accustomed ways of ordering collective existence continue to spawn so many failed efforts to recover the reassurances once furnished by custom. Only then can we entertain the hypothesis that ordinary experience, once freed from its subjection to a reason gone wrong, is adequately equipped to sustain a sense of its own legitimacy and to cultivate the resources of its own critical elaboration into an unknown future.

Second, recalling that the possibility of the city-state required the superimposition of a layer of cultured citizens upon a dense mass of artisans and laborers, we must find suspect Hannah Arendt's contention that the "general crisis that has overtaken the modern world" is rooted in reversal of the hierarchical order once sustained among the human condition's essential dimensions.[43] With Arendt, we may grant that philosophy is born out of a desire to "find a remedy for the frailty of human affairs" through discovery of truths whose imposition upon practice promises an escape from the perils of politics.[44] Recognizing, however, that the emergence of democratic politics within Athens depended on the empowerment of nondependent laborers which, in turn, made possible a dissociation of economic and civic status, we must call into question Arendt's uncritical embrace of philosophy's dissimulating representation of techné. The tale told here suggests that Arendt's triadic conception of the *vita activa* (labor, work, and action) bears significant traces of the aristocratic ethos that informs antiquity's invention of the *vita contemplativa*. Arguing for the wholesale exclusion of *homo faber* and *animal laborans* from a public realm in which men expose themselves to one another in unmediated purity, Arendt defends a dramaturgical vision of political action that is "theoretical" in the sense that its practice as a self-contained end-in-itself presupposes abstraction from the concrete drives and needs that enmesh actors in the immediate engagements of everyday living.

---

43. Hannah Arendt, *Between Past and Future* (New York: Viking, 1961), p. 173.
44. Arendt, *The Human Condition*, p. 174. Cf. Arendt, *Between Past and Future*, p. 18: "Political philosophy necessarily implies the attitude of the philosopher toward politics; its tradition began with the philosopher's turning away from politics and then returning in order to impose his standards on human affairs."

Unable to acknowledge that political performance is grounded in embodied experience, Arendt endorses the philosophical tradition's contempt toward sensuous involvement in transfiguring the forms of life
that either disclose or hide matters political. Consequently, she concludes that the chief threat to democratic politics is the inversion of
public and private realms rather than the persistence of institutional
structures that consolidate the domination of body's mind, practice's
theory, and democracy's aristocracy. The upshot, as articulated in *The
Human Condition*, is an argument that reconfigures as a division between decontextualized structures of experience the disjunction between means and ends fashioned by Aristotle from the city-state's
segregation of the superior from the inferior.

Finally, we must question Hans-Georg Gadamer's contention that if
we are to overcome the contemporary crisis we must first "enlighten
the modern attitude of making, producing, and constructing about the
necessary conditions to which it is subject."[45] Echoing Plato, Gadamer
urges us to recall *technē*'s inability to generate the standards that
govern use of its products, and so its need to be subordinated to the
authority of a qualitatively different kind of knowledge. The troublesome character of this appeal to *phronēsis*, replicating the more general
difficulties noted above, becomes apparent when Gadamer argues
that the correctness of moral and political reasoning is to be specified
in terms of its adequacy to the telos at which it aims. Should Gadamer,
on the one hand, take this to mean, as Aristotle suggests in his *Rhetoric*, that such reasoning simply discerns the most useful means to a
given end,[46] then he must forego the critical advantage he hopes to

45. Hans-Georg Gadamer, *Truth and Method* (New York: Crossroad, 1975), p. xxv. See
also Gadamer's essay "Notes on Planning for the Future," *Daedalus* 95 (1966), 572–89,
where he argues that "it is the essence of *technē* that it does not exist for its own sake or
for the perfectibility of the object, as though the latter existed for its own sake. What
pertains to the nature and appearance of the perfectible object is wholly dependent on
the use for which it is intended. But regarding the utility of the object, neither the
knowledge nor the skill of the craftsman is the master. The faculties of the craftsman do
not guarantee that the object will be used according to its requirements or, more
decisively, that it will be used for something which is right" (pp. 577–78). This, then, is
the presupposition of his argument in "Hermeneutics and Social Science," *Cultural
Hermeneutics* 2 (1975), 307–16, where he writes: "That is the point of philosophical
hermeneutics. It corrects the peculiar falsehood of modern consciousness: the idolatry
of scientific method and of the autonomous authority of the sciences and it vindicates
again the noblest task of the citizen—decision-making according to one's own responsibility—instead of conceding that task to the expert" (p. 316).
46. See Aristotle, *The Rhetoric* 1162a17–20: "Now the political or deliberative orator's
aim is utility: deliberation seeks to determine not ends but the means to ends, i.e., what
it is most useful to do."

derive from the idea of *phronēsis*. Should he, on the other hand, embrace the broader sense of deliberation offered in Book 6 of the *Ethics*, that of deliberation that incorporates consideration of the ends of a good life,[47] then he must acknowledge the untenability of the metaphysical foundations that sustained Aristotle's view, as well as the lack of any contemporary consensus about what counts as such a life. In either case, Gadamer's argument, whose intelligibility presupposes the existence of solidaristic traditional communities that have virtually disappeared in the West and could be reconstituted only through authoritarian measures, recapitulates the class-based premises of ancient philosophy in its anachronistic affirmation of the liberal over the vocational arts.

VII

Our experience of the present is thoroughly "saturated with the products of the reflection of past generations and by-gone ages. It is filled with interpretations, classifications, due to sophisticated thought, which have become incorporated into what seems to be fresh, naive empirical material. If we may for the moment call these materials prejudices (even if they are true, as long as their source and authority is unknown), then philosophy is a critique of prejudices."[48] That critique, whose aim is to explore the architectonic structure within which the furniture of our minds is so often arranged and rearranged without altering its overall dimensions, is intended to undermine the present's legitimacy by offering a critical recovery of and from the past. We may call this endeavor "philosophical," but only if we acknowledge that this compound term's etymology is more suggestive than Plato's usage indicates. Strictly speaking, "philosophy is a form of desire, of effort at action—a love, namely, of wisdom; but with the thorough proviso, not attached to the Platonic use of the word, that wisdom, whatever it is, is not a mode of science or knowledge."[49]

---

47. See Aristotle, *Nichomachean Ethics*, trans. Terence Irwin (Indianapolis: Hackett, 1985), 1142b28–33: "Further our deliberation may be unconditionally good or good only to the extent that it promotes some [limited] end. Hence unconditionally good deliberation is the sort that correctly promotes the unconditional end [the highest good], while the [limited] sort is the sort that correctly promotes some [limited] end."

48. Dewey, *EN*, p. 37.

49. Dewey, "Philosophy and Democracy," in *CE2*, p. 843.

Contra Strauss, such a project cannot claim "to understand the thinkers of the past exactly as they understood themselves."[50] With the passage of time, the past's possible meaningfulness becomes both greater and richer due to its involvement in ever more complex networks of events whose content enters vitally into the constitution of the present. As the present becomes past and the future present, there emerge qualitatively distinct epistemic relationships between that which has passed away and our current situation; and so the polis cannot help but alter its character as a possible object of knowledge. "Dis-membering is a positively necessary part of re-membering. But the resulting *disjecta membra* are in no sense experience as it was or is."[51] Moreover, just as the past's intelligibility stems from its incorporation within a story relating the emergence of a situation that was not until now, the present's significance stems from its presentation of signs pointing toward a future that is not yet. The purpose of this tale, consequently, is to fashion a narrative that discloses to us our complicity in an unfolding drama whose meaning gives point to our daily practice but whose plot we only partly comprehend. Its value is measured by its ability to quicken in us a sense of how accustomed meanings shape our experience in some ways but not in others, as well as its ability to designate a path whereby we might bring into existence ways of being intimated but not realized within the tradition that tale refashions.

What forms of experience might be disclosed if we were to think along the outside edge of a tradition that, fearful of the world's perplexities and pluralities, inflicts its monologic spectatorial ideals upon the concrete, the contingent, and the complex? To challenge the hyperrationalistic conviction that knowledge is concerned with revelation of antecedently real existences, and that the properties of value discovered therein provide determinate standards for the regulation of conduct, is not to dig beneath the core of teleocratic reason and so gain access to a plane of "pure experience," whatever that might mean. Our reflection upon the how of what we experience may be resculpted, but it will never penetrate to a secret realm of pure essence. Nor does it urge that we simply invert the polarities that give shape to that core by,

50. Strauss, *What Is Political Philosophy?*, p. 67.
51. Dewey, "Experience and Objective Idealism," in *IDP*, pp. 220–21. For an excellent explication of pragmatism's understanding of the past's intelligibility, see Sandra Rosenthal, *Speculative Pragmatism* (Amherst: University of Massachusetts Press, 1986), pp. 144–46, 165–66.

for example, elevating practice above theory and so rendering articulate presently marginalized or trivialized forms of activity; because that would mean remaining trapped within its governing confines. Rather, our reflection upon the how of what we experience suggests that if we work our way back to the spatiotemporal forms of meaningful experience from which the claims of reason were originally wrought, we may find ourselves in a position to consider how rationality can be regrounded in its contextualized moorings and thereby deterred from equating its abstracted parts with the whole from which it is derived; and that, in turn, may lead us to recollect the qualitative dimensionality of the distinctive form of emergent experience that Socrates, in the *Apology*, designated using the phrase *ta politika pragmata*.

Given that the words to be used in undertaking such a project owe much of their current connotational import to the very web of meaning from which we seek some release, one can only hope to occasion slight transformations in their present significations. But if our desire is to achieve a more nuanced immersion in political matters, we might begin by heeding Empedocles, who cautions that we ought not to "hold any [percept of] sight higher in credibility than [those] according to hearing, nor [set] the loud-sounding hearing above the evidence of the tongue [taste]; nor refuse credence at all to any of the other limbs where there exists a path for perception, but use whatever way of perception makes each thing clear" (Frg. 3).[52] To sustain its distance from and authority over *empeiria*, teleocratic reason denies that *nous'* access to *physis* is grounded in the actions of a moving body substantially involved in a world known through the media of other senses. Yet achievement of any perspective, including that hypostatized as classical contemplation, can emerge only because sight is already situated by dynamic kinesthetic activities that generate the dimensional coordinates through which the eye's envisionings are integrated into a sense of objects' corporeality and location.[53] "We do not believe a thing to be 'there' because we are directly cognizant of an external origin for our perception; we infer some external stimulation of our sensory apparatus because we are successfully engaged in motor response.

52. See also the quotation ascribed to Dewey by Herbert Schneider, in *Dialogue on John Dewey*, ed. Corliss Lamont (New York: Horizon, 1959), p. 95: "I think this whole problem of understanding should be approached not from the point of view of the eyes, but from the point of view of the hands. It's what we grasp that matters."

53. For an excellent discussion of the priority of touch over sight, see Hans Jonas, "The Nobility of Sight: A Study in the Phenomenology of the Senses," in his *Phenomenon of Life* (New York: Harper & Row, 1966), pp. 135–56.

Only when the latter fails, do we turn back and examine the matter of sensory stimulation."[54] Contrary to Aristotle, who contends that reason possesses no bodily organ, sight is but a single function of an organic agency whose knowings turn upon the interrelated engagement of many ways of grasping the world's pragmata.

To relocate knowing within the structures of embodied experience is to recall the link between politics and the verb *poiein* (doing something). Although too often forgotten, *poiein*'s conceptual relationship to the term *epistēmē* was once retained via the latter's derivation from a verb meaning "to be able." Its definitive segregation from *technē* such that the latter was denied all association with the arts of *poiēsis*, while *epistēmē* came to be considered sole heir of the mind's nobler pursuits, was not finally consummated until Aristotle determined that "the sciences which are cherished on their own account and in the interest of knowledge are closer to wisdom than those desired on account of their by-products."[55] To reconstruct the thinking that culminates in this assertion is to unearth earlier usage that, absent Aristotle's division of all entities into those produced by their own kind and those produced by other species of being,[56] situated techniculture's yields within a complex of meanings that drew no unambiguous ontological distinction between nature and art. It is, in other words, to see that the Platonic/Aristotelian syntheses of mechanical and agrarian metaphors are optional, and hence that it is possible to fashion hybrids that formulate anew the terms of reason, and so of reason's politics as well.

Let us re-member—that is, put back together—*physis* and *nous*, understood as overlapping manifestations of that larger life-giving dynamic through which experience's mutable offerings are shaped to form in time.[57] To that recollection, let us wed vernacular speech's recognition that experience is primarily a matter of undergoing or

54. Dewey, *EN*, p. 335.
55. Aristotle, *Metaphysics* 982a15. For Aristotle's broad use of the verb *poiein* for doing something or acting in general, see *Ethics* 1147a28 and 1136b29. For its more restricted use in reference to the form of action peculiar to production aiming at an end outside itself, see *Ethics* 1140b6.
56. See Aristotle, *Metaphysics* 1070a6–9: "We note that all primary beings (both those generated naturally and otherwise) come into being out of something with the same name. Things come into being by art or by nature, or else by fortune or by chance. When they are generated by art, their source is in something else; when by nature, their source is internal to them (thus, it is man that generates man); and when they become by fortune, they do so by privation of art; and when by chance, by privation of a natural factor."
57. On this matter, see Martin Heidegger, "The Question concerning Technology," in his *Question concerning Technology and Other Essays*, trans. William Lovitt (New York: Harper & Row, 1977), pp. 10–14.

suffering something. Should we do so, we may find ourselves guided toward forms of thinking whose integrity does not demand subsumption of the rich and complex textures of everyday life beneath teleocracy's determinate ends. So oriented, we may acknowledge that to know political pragmata, to recover those affairs that citizens discover to be of mutual concern, is to actualize existences that are resident as emergents within experience but are not yet shaped to common sense by critical explorations of their unborn potentialities. The "truth" of that sense, grounded not in a logical principle but rather in the supportive soil of everyday being, is an unfolding fruit that, depending on its fertility, will fare well or ill when planted alongside other truths at varying moments in their respective histories. Democratic experience, emerging from within this tangle, may thus become the subject of a tendance that gathers together its animating capacities, as impediments to a fuller flowering of its powers are winnowed from more familiar ways of fashioning experience's affairs.

As the following pages make only too clear, any effort to refashion our accustomed meanings in the fashion suggested here proves deficient at some points and unsuccessful at others. Still, reconstruction of the sort hinted at here is inseparable from the struggle to show how we might overcome the irony of a tradition that affirms the ultimacy of reason, yet denies the ground out of which it first emerged in order to stay its unsettling possibilities. "The more it is asserted that thought and understanding are 'ends in themselves,' the more imperative is it that thought should discover why they are realized only in a small and exclusive class. The ulterior problem of thought is to make thought prevail in experience, not just the results of thought by imposing them upon others, but the active process of thinking. The ultimate contradiction in the classic and genteel tradition is that while it made thought universal and necessary and the culminating good of nature, it was content to leave its distribution among men a thing of accident, dependent upon birth, economic, and civil status."[58] Thus the moral of this tale of reason's generation becomes apparent: the possibility of relocating the forms of democratic experience requires unlearning a present whose "truth" hinders recovery of "that which in the name of religion, of philosophy, of art and of morality, has been embezzled from the common store and appropriated to sectarian and class use."[59]

58. Dewey, *EN*, p. 120.
59. Dewey, "Ralph Waldo Emerson," in *CE1*, p. 75.

3 /
How the Enlightenment Went Awry

I

"The enlightenment, the *éclaircissement*, the *Aufklärung*—names which in the three most advanced countries of Europe testified to the widespread belief that at last light had dawned, that dissipation of the darkness of ignorance, superstition, and bigotry was at hand, and the triumph of reason was assured."[1] At the present time, it is no longer possible to endorse this simple faith. The movement designated by the term "Enlightenment" has itself become a target of accusations very much like those Enlightenment thinkers once directed against the priests and aristocrats of the ancien régime. Bentham's celebration of utilitarianism's capacity to slice through feudalism's web of invidious privilege is now read as a harbinger of modernity's egalitarian incarceration within Panopticon's cells. Condorcet's paean to progress is recast as a dirge justifying the sacrifice of present generations to a

---

1. Dewey, "Time and Individuality," in *ENF*, p. 227. For Dewey's explicit comparison of American pragmatism with "the French philosophy of the Enlightenment," see "The Development of American Pragmatism," in *PC*, p. 34; and for his claim that the "faith" of the Enlightenment "may have been pathetic but it has its own nobility," see "Time and Individuality," in *ENF*, p. 227.

future that will never materialize. And Kant's tale of escape from a state of self-incurred tutelage is retold as a tragedy whose conceit of radical autonomy bolsters the agencies of normalization.[2]

To a considerable degree, the Enlightenment invited such debunking by assimilating the cause of modern science to that of humanity's universal salvation. For at least two centuries, that identification helped to mask the ways in which scientific knowledge and its technological instrumentalities, encouraged by the modern state and deployed by modern capitalism, were becoming entangled in the constitution of institutional forms serving very specific political and class interests. Today, however, the ubiquity of cynicism furnishes a telling sign of the gap between the Enlightenment's promise of redemption and its actual complicity in fashioning new bonds of servitude.[3]

How are we to understand the Enlightenment's miscarriage? Within the confines of this chapter, it would be foolish and beside the point to attempt a comprehensive history of this complex period in European intellectual history. The diversity of the figures commonly grouped together under this label—from Hume to John Stuart Mill, from Montesquieu to Voltaire, from Leibniz to Kant—make generalization a hazardous enterprise at best. I do, however, argue that we gain an important clue to the project we call the "Enlightenment" when we construe its writings as so many diverse attempts to answer a common question: How is the experience of modern science to be assimilated to late medieval structures of thought that are themselves best read as the fruit of a synthesis of classical metaphysics and Catholic cosmology?

Gathered together, the various responses to this question demarcate the field of philosophical discourse commonly called "epistemology." In spite of its appearance of wide-ranging opposition, I argue that the debate that gives this terrain its distinctive topography is actually quite confined. For "empiricists" and "idealists" alike attempt to acknowledge the novelty of modern science without abandoning the presuppositions constitutive of what I labeled "teleocratic reason" in the previous chapter. Reworking without fundamentally questioning classical philosophy's mature conviction regarding the relationship be-

2. For a helpful review of this anti-Enlightenment literature, see Richard Bernstein, "The Rage against Reason," *Philosophy and Literature* 10 (1986), 186–210.
3. For a refreshingly irreverent examination of the growth of modern cynicism, see Peter Sloterdijk, *Critique of Cynical Reason*, trans. Michael Eldred (Minneapolis: University of Minnesota Press, 1987).

tween reason and experience, Enlightenment epistemology effectively insists that science serve as a nostalgic surrogate for premodern doctrines whose cosmological impulses are no longer deemed intellectually respectable but whose insinuation within modern philosophy of science indicates the continued power of collective longings for the attainment of securely grounded and self-enclosed unity. "The theological problem of attaining knowledge of God as ultimate reality was transformed in effect into the philosophical problem of the possibility of attaining knowledge of reality."[4]

To put this slightly differently, the burden of the present chapter is to show that we can begin to break the epistemological standoff, as well as its correlative complicity in denying dignity to the pragmata of everyday politics, only when we repudiate the Enlightenment's inherited conviction that practice has value only to the degree that it is subjected to theoretical reconstruction. Only when we acknowledge the ontological priority of noncognitive experience over rationalism's abstractions will it prove possible to begin anew an exploration of the ethical (in the sense of ethos) significance of modern science for our contemporary situation and so to fashion some measure of sense from the forms of experience in which science is now so deeply implicated.

II

Its internal complexity notwithstanding, Platonic/Aristotelian discourse represents the first of the three pivotal moments in the larger tale I tell about the historical evolution of our sense regarding the rightful character and claims of reason. The present's groping attempts to rework that heritage, whose destination no one can yet discern, is the third. The rise of modern science as a self-conscious enterprise in the seventeenth century inaugurates the second.

In structuring my account of reason's history in this way, I do not mean to deny the independent contribution of medieval Catholic theology to that evolution. But with qualifications to be noted below, that theology moves within the presuppositional confines established by

---

4. Dewey, "The Need for a Recovery of Philosophy," in *ENF*, p. 41. The "method" of analysis offered here bears some resemblance to that employed by Hans Blumenberg when he advances the notion of a "reoccupation of positions." For a clarification of his meaning, see *The Legitimacy of the Modern Age*, trans. Robert Wallace (Cambridge: MIT Press, 1983), especially pp. 63–75.

classical philosophy. This contention can be illustrated by turning briefly to Thomas Aquinas. The ontology of the *Summa Theologica* is irreducibly informed by Aristotle's *Metaphysics*, and hence by that work's hypostatization of the metaphors intimated by crafts' customary practice. At an elementary level, this is seen in Aquinas's contention that every entity is composed of matter shaped in a certain way, and that the substantial form responsible for that shape is the condition of its being: "For with regard to the infinite as applied to matter, it is manifest that everything actually existing possesses a form; and thus its matter is determined by form . . . since form is an act, and matter is being only in potentiality."[5]

These ontological commitments derive from Aristotle's qualified naturalism, which, as noted in the preceding chapter, located the physical at the lowest stratum in the hierarchical order of Being and the psychical at its apex. Not surprisingly, then, Aquinas endorses the classical tradition's belief that "the nobler a form is, the more it rises above corporeal matter, the less it is subject to matter," and so he recapitulates its disparagement of the forms of practical engagement from which that tradition's essential conceptual equipment was originally wrought. Although granting that "even in speculative matters there is something by way of work: e.g., the making of a syllogism or of a fitting speech, or the work of counting or measuring," Aquinas nevertheless insists that such practices "are appropriately designated *liberal* arts, in order to distinguish them from those arts that are ordained to works done by the body; for these arts are, in a fashion, servile, inasmuch as the body is in servile subjection to the soul."[6] In doing so, he recapitulates Aristotle's transformation of accustomed relations of domination and subordination into a legitimation of the epistemic hierarchy sustained among various forms of cognition. To wit: "In every art or science, those who can control others aright are more praiseworthy than those who merely carry out the directions of others with competence. . . . An architect is more esteemed and is paid more highly because he plans the house, compared with the builder who labors to construct what the architect has designed."[7]

The specifically ethical import of this ontology is revealed when

5. Thomas Aquinas, *Introduction to Saint Thomas Aquinas*, ed. Anton Pegis (New York: Modern Library, 1948), pp. 55, 292.
6. Ibid., pp. 295, 572.
7. Thomas Aquinas, "On Princely Government," in *Aquinas: Selected Political Writings*, trans. J. G. Dawson (Oxford: Basil Blackwell, 1978), p. 49.

Aquinas, responding to the dilemmas posed by the Hebraic tradition's ascription of free will to God's most noble creature, affirms reason's capacity to realize the inclusive human form, that is, its peculiar end: "Now the proper operation of man as man is to understand, for it is in this that he surpasses all animals. Whence Aristotle concludes that the ultimate happiness of man must consist in this operation as properly belonging to him. Man must therefore derive his species from that which is the principle of his operation. But the species of each thing is derived from its form. It follows therefore that the intellectual principle is the proper form of man."[8] Given this construction of what it means to live a distinctively human life, Aquinas of necessity embraces the teleocratic conception of action that arises out of classical philosophy's reification of *technē*'s skill and its issues. Consequently, asking whether right is the object of justice, Aquinas responds: "Just as there pre-exists in the mind of the craftsman an expression of the things to be made externally by his craft, which expression is called the rule of his craft, so too there pre-exists in the mind an expression of the particular just work which the reason determines, and which is a kind of rule of prudence."[9] Although acknowledging that cognition in the spheres of political and ethical conduct cannot secure the indubitability of theoretical knowledge, Aquinas nonetheless insists that the very possibility of rational conduct turns upon the existence of antecedent and unambiguous ends whose relationship to the action they inform is one of command: "A ship, for instance, will sail first on one course and then on another, according to the winds it encounters, and it would never reach its destination, but for the skill of the helmsman who steers it to port. In the same way man, who acts by intelligence, has a destiny to which all his life and activities are directed; for it is clearly the nature of intelligent beings to act with some end in view."[10]

The character of the politics that coheres with this model of action is suggested when Aquinas, disclosing the dependence of Scholastic metaphysics on mythological assurances ostensibly shed at the moment of reason's invention, contends that a king must assume "the duty of being to his kingdom what the soul is to the body and what God is to the universe." What it means to exercise that duty follows from Aquinas's conviction that the unity of any thing presupposes the

8. Thomas Aquinas, *Introduction to Saint Thomas Aquinas*, p. 295.

9. Thomas Aquinas, *Saint Thomas Aquinas: On Law, Morality, and Politics*, ed. William Baumgarth and Richard Regan (Indianapolis: Hackett, 1988), p. 138.

10. Aquinas, "On Princely Government," p. 3.

hierarchical organization and unidirectional flow of the powers that compose it: "Whenever there is an ordered unity arising out of a diversity of elements there is to be found some such controlling influence." Hence intermediate between the universe, which would collapse into an-archy were the hand of divine providence removed, and the human body, which "would disintegrate were there not in the body itself a single controlling force, sustaining the general vitality of all the members,"[11] there stands political order; and its capacity to secure the rule of unity over plurality, of Being over non-Being, turns upon the sustaining presence of an unambiguously demarcated source of order: "That is best which most nearly approaches a natural process, since nature always works in the best way. But in nature, government is always by one. . . . So, since the product of art is but an imitation of the work of nature, and since a work of art is the better for being a faithful representation of its natural pattern, it follows of necessity that the best form of government in human society is that which is exercised by one person."[12] In sum, just as "the plan of whatever is to be done by art flows from the chief craftsman to the undercraftsmen who work with their hands," so too "the plan of what is to be done in a political community flows from the king's command to his inferior administrators. . . . For those who are concerned with the subordinate ends of life must be subject to him who is concerned with the supreme end and be directed by his command."[13]

Much like archaic Greece prior to its disintegration, the essential outlines of the order refashioned in the thought of Aquinas appear unquestionably given to those who are its inhabitants. Its class divisions mirror those of a divinely created and pyramidal nature in which each discrete species holds an inviolable position that entitles it to press specified claims on those below and obligates it to perform certain services for those above. What distinguishes medieval culture from its classical counterpart, consequently, is not its reading of political relationships into nature, but rather its development of a more effective institutional apparatus with which to secure the identification of truth with unmediated apprehension of an immutable structure of Being. "We have only to refer to the way in which medieval life

---

11. Ibid., pp. 5, 67.
12. Ibid., p. 13. Cf. p. 67: "A king, then, should realize that he has assumed the duty of being to his kingdom what the soul is to the body and what God is to the universe."
13. Thomas Aquinas, *Saint Thomas Aquinas: On Law, Morality, and Politics*, p. 37; "On Princely Government," p. 77.

wrought the philosophy of an ultimate and supreme reality into the context of practical life to realize that for centuries political and moral interests were bound up with the distinction between the absolutely real and the relatively real. The difference was no matter of a remote technical philosophy, but one which controlled life from the cradle to the grave, from the grave to the endless life after death. By means of a vast institution, which in effect was state as well as church, the claims of ultimate reality were enforced."[14]

Much as mythical consciousness had once impeded the evolution of *technai*'s skill by insisting upon action's subjection to the contingencies of divine intervention, so too Christianized Aristotelianism discouraged any effort to turn the body of prosaic generalizations emerging from the unliberal arts to self-conscious regulation of natural phenomena. Given its endorsement of the doctrine of final causes, conduct aimed at the deliberate introduction of novelty could only produce deviation from the motions prescribed by immutable form. Elaborating the epistemic implications embedded in the Pauline doctrine regarding carnal flesh's radical corruption, high Scholasticism imposed severe constraints on all forms of embodied experience in the fashioning of knowledge; for even at their most exacting, the body and its senses could do no more than intimate the truth of a superior realm whose teleological objects escaped the deficiencies of all that is tainted by matter. Consequently, to the extent that action did in fact aim at harnessing knowledge in the service of human need, it characteristically took the form of magic and astrology, the attempt by the human soul to secure access to a nature whose energies and forces are, as in Greek cosmology, vitalistic and psychical.

The pillars of this order were shaken when the issue of the analogical import of forms of embodied engagement whose intelligence had been dispossessed and metaphysically reified within classical philosophy was reopened. The asking of that question, however, took on novel dimensions in the sixteenth and early seventeenth centuries in light of startling advances in the design and construction of machines. In spite of its proficiency in various crafts, the culture of antiquity was severely limited in its development of devices operating on distinctively mechanical principles. Although able to make catapults and water clocks, these did not impinge sufficiently upon the sense-bearing structures of everyday life to exert any appreciable influence on

14. Dewey, "The Need for a Recovery of Philosophy," in *ENF*, pp. 60–61.

classical cosmology. Hence Aristotle's metaphysical transformation of the forms of understanding implicit in received ways of cultivating things growing in the soil remained essentially uncontested.

With fabrication and widespread use of printing presses, windmills, pumps, clocks, and the like, however, generalized exploration of the analogical possibilities implicit in such feats began to erode Aristotle's organicist account of nature's ends. Robert Boyle's corpuscular metaphysics, for example, took as its governing premise the conviction that principles of mechanical operation could legitimately be extended to all things, whether seen or unseen:

> And though nature works with much finer materials, and employs more curious contrivances, than art; yet an artist, according to the quantity of the matter he employs, the exigency of the design he undertakes, and the magnitude and shape of the instruments he uses, is able to make pieces of work of the same nature or kind, of extremely different bulks where yet the like art, contrivance, and motion may be observed. Thus a smith who, with a hammer and other large instruments, can, out of masses of iron, forge great bars or wedges to make strong and ponderous chains to secure streets and gates may, with lesser instruments, makes smaller nails, and filings, almost as minute as dust; and with yet finer tools, make links wonderfully light and slender. And therefore, to say that though in natural bodies, whose bulk is manifest and their structure visible, the mechanical principles may be usefully admitted but are not to be extended to such portions of matter, whose parts and texture are invisible, is like allowing that the laws of mechanism may take place in a town-clock, and not in a pocket-watch.[15]

As the metaphorics of reason were so recast, the representation of *epistēmē* and *empeiria* as qualitatively distinct and hierarchically ordered forms of cognition became ever more problematic. The conduct of early modern science hinted that the classical tradition's strict isolation of those who make things with their hands from those who grasp truths with their intellects, as well as its scorn for the concrete and the mutable, might be without divine authorization. To pose this possibility is not to call God's existence into question. But it is to recast the action of God qua artificer in mechanical rather than organic terms. As Boyle suggests: "Thus the universe being once framed by God and the laws of motion settled and all upheld by his perpetual concourse and general providence; the same philosophy teaches, that the phenom-

---

15. Robert Boyle, quoted in *The Scientific Background to Modern Philosophy*, ed. Michael Matthews (Indianapolis: Hackett, 1989), p. 115.

ena of the world are physically produced by the mechanical properties of the parts of matter, and, that they operate upon one another according to mechanical laws."[16]

Given appropriate theological authorization, certain early modern thinkers began to associate the conduct of knowing not with contemplation or the resolution of dialectical puzzles, but rather with the capacity to engender certain kinds of change. The larger cultural import of this transformation was grasped by Francis Bacon, who a half century prior to Boyle complained of the "opinion or conceit, which though of long standing is vain and hurtful, namely, that the dignity of the human mind is impaired by long and close intercourse with experiments and particulars, subject to sense and bound in matter; especially as they are laborious to search, ignoble to meditate, harsh to deliver, illiberal to practice, infinite in number, and minute in subtlety. So that it has come at length to this, that the true way is not merely deserted, but shut out and stopped up; experience being, I do not say abandoned or badly managed, but rejected with disdain."[17]

When joined by the challenge of Copernicus's *De revolutionibus orbium coelestium* to Aristotle's geocentric cosmos, antiquity's distinction between high, sublime, and ideal forces operating in the heavens and those lower material forces that actuate terrestrial events no longer appeared self-evidently true. Consequently, and although Bacon himself could not acknowledge this implication, the form of early modern science's conduct intimated that Scholasticism's essentially feudal cosmology might be displaced by a democracy of individual events, no one of which was intrinsically superior to the others. Calling into question Aquinas's representation of embodied individuality as either the accidental qualification of determinate being or, less charitably, the failure of indwelling form to impress itself upon stubborn matter, early modern science's artful practice made it possible to speculate that each particular might not exist merely to illustrate a principle, or to realize a universal, or to embody a kind. Perhaps the capacity of any individual existent to take part in the generation of significance was not contingent on its antecedent subordination to the imperatives of eternal form.

16. Ibid., p. 111.
17. Francis Bacon, *The New Organon* (Indianapolis: Bobbs-Merrill, 1960), p. 80. Cf. p. 72: "Whereas in the mechanical arts, which are founded on nature and the light of experience, we see the contrary happen, for these (as long as they are popular) are continually thriving and growing, as having in them a breath of life, at the first rude, then convenient, afterwards adorned, and at all times advancing."

If the critical force of the scientific revolution consisted in its demystification of customary legitimations of socioeconomic privilege
and political domination, its prospective significance inhered in its
deliberate indifference to classical teleology. In explaining change
through reference to the efficient causality of material things already
fully existent at the moment of movement's initiation, Galileo envi-
sioned a nature that was mathematically explicable because the motions of its homogeneous matter were governed by strict mechanical
laws. Exploration of the meaning of that nature, as Galileo well understood, could not leave unchallenged antiquity's hypostatization of the
esthetic dimensions manifest in the products of antiquity's craft, and
so its identification of knowledge with unmediated apprehension of
transcendental substances. For when stripped of all that is immediate
and qualitative, of all that is final and self-sufficient, its objects were
effectively denied the sources of meaning that had sustained Aristotelian cosmology.

That loss, though, bore within it a sort of compensation. For as
emergent technical arts were deployed in the production of existential
effects that could never have been anticipated by either Aristotle or
Aquinas, early modern science cast doubt on any teleological cosmology that identified innovation with violation of nature's immanent
final causes. No longer, that is, could innovative action be condemned
on the grounds that it violated the immanent integrity of the order that
hitherto had bound individuals and their hopes within its tight confines. Stripped of its traditional teleological attributes, the experienced
world acquired a new sense of purposive possibility. In sum, by free-
ing all being from its fixed limits, the conduct of early modern science
gestured at "a world which is not in, and never will be, which in some
respects is incomplete and in the making, and which in these respects
may be made this way or that according as men judge, prize, love and
labor."[18]

III

Why is it that the emancipatory promise of science now appears so
hollow? This question may be answered by referring to institutionalized relations of power whose legitimacy is inseparable from early

18. Dewey, "Philosophy and Democracy," in CE2, p. 851.

modernity's failure to disentangle the more unsettling implications of the new science from more familiar ways of fashioning sense from experience. In its challenge to accustomed understandings, early modern science did not begin its career on unplowed ground. The effects of its maturation on an already well-cultivated field are most apparent in the sustained debate that goes by the general name of epistemology. That debate is well read as an effort to render intelligible the conceptions of cognition and nature intimated by scientific inquiry without abandoning either the presuppositional core of classical metaphysics or the theological baggage assimilated to it by medieval Christianity. "Wherever we look into the fundamentals of the new physical science we find inherited conceptions of immutability and universality retained as necessary support for revolutionary innovations which, if carried through, would utterly destroy the classic scheme."[19]

To grasp the essential contours of the epistemological problematic, it is necessary to recall the cultural dilemma that gives shape to its content and form. As the Church of late medievalism began to lose its authority over matters of cognition, interrogation of its authority in matters of conduct surfaced as well. Although the import of this challenge would not reveal its full political force until the French Revolution, its theoretical portent was grasped long before. For the scientific revolution signaled the need to furnish to agents ever farther removed from the confines of customary hierarchies an alternative code to regulate everyday conduct. While that code's precise content would only become clear when liberalism achieved hegemony, its form was effectively preordained. Just as classical philosophy had discovered that the struggle to supersede its rivals required that it affirm its ability to do all the work once done by mythologically sanctified custom, so too did the earliest expositors of modernity's reason find it imperative to claim for Enlightenment epistemology the same measure of universality and authority once claimed by Roman Catholic theo/teleology. The method of modern science was thus portrayed as the exclusive vehicle through which agents could conclusively adjudicate between rival courses of action in all realms of conduct. "Greek philosophy began when men doubted the authority of custom as a regulator of life; it sought in universal reason or in the immediate particular, in being or in flux, a rival source of authority, but one which as a rival was to be as certain and definite as custom had been.

19. Dewey, "Experience and Nature: A Re-Introduction," in *LW*, vol. 1, p. 347.

Medieval philosophy was frankly an attempt to reconcile authority with reason, and modern philosophy began when man, doubting the authority of revelation, began a search for some authority which should have all the weight, certainty and inerrancy previously ascribed to the will of God embodied in the divinely instituted church. The new claimant to the abode of objective truth prided itself upon wearing the mantle of the dispossessed occupant."[20]

Epistemological debate thus constitutes so many responses to a cultural crisis to which classical cosmology and medieval theology could no longer effectively respond. As such, the central dispute giving this debate its structure, that between rationalist and empiricist readings of early modern science, is a smokescreen that obscures the common ground on which this conflict takes place. Accordingly, although each party to this controversy is today showing unmistakable signs of exhaustion, neither can afford to take advantage of the other's weakness and so win a decisive victory. Each can assure its own preservation only by ensuring the continued existence of the opponent in terms of which it defines itself.

To show how the epistemological project sought to answer inherited questions it might have left unasked, I offer an abbreviated discussion of Descartes and Locke as well as a still more cursory reading of Kant. Establishing the basic terms of the epistemological debate, Descartes and Locke articulate recurrent themes and familiar moves that, cropping up repeatedly throughout its subsequent history, find their most elegant synthesis in the work of Kant. My aim in offering this abstracted reconstruction, which glosses over the discontinuities and uncertainties that dogged the lived experience of the Enlightenment, is to highlight only those dimensions that prove most illuminating in light of this work's larger aim. Were my purpose otherwise, these deliberately one-sided accounts could not remain so unqualified.

Despite manifest differences of style and substance, the texts of Descartes and Locke are commonly informed by three interlocking presuppositions, each of which is ultimately rooted in the Platonic/ Aristotelian synthesis described in the previous chapter. The first consists of the conviction that discursive conclusions depend for their status as knowledge on their necessary derivation from premises that are themselves self-certifying. In the *Republic*, the need for such certainties is made clear when, in his account of various forms of cogni-

20. Dewey, "Philosophy and Democracy," in *CE2*, p. 853; "The Problem of Truth," in *MW*, vol. 6, p. 55.

tion, Plato argues that reason must at first treat "its assumptions not as absolute beginnings but literally as hypotheses, underpinnings, footings, and springboards so to speak, to enable it to rise to that which requires no assumption and is the starting point of all, and after attaining to that again taking hold of the first dependencies from it, so to proceed downward to the conclusion, making no use whatever of any object of sense but only of pure ideas" (511b).

When epistemology relinquished the task of generating substantive bodies of knowledge to the new experimental sciences, philosophy could no longer sustain its self-representation as the Thomistic queen of the sciences. In response, it redefined itself as the metascientific source of their shared ground, what Descartes labeled "the firm and permanent structure" presupposed by and common to the practice of all. Composed of those "indubitable conception[s]" that, on Descartes's account, arise "from the light of reason alone,"[21] this structure is the sine qua non of knowledge of those things that "are known with certainty although they are not evident in themselves for the sole reason that they are deduced from true and known principles by a continuous and uninterrupted process of thought, in which each process of the thought is clearly intuited."[22] In sum, whether formulated as Cartesian universal truths achieved through a priori intuition or as Lockean sense data apprehended through simple ideas, epistemological discourse is certain that its very possibility turns on its ability to discover privileged starting points from which to derive all subordinate judgments. That quest, in turn, reveals the persistent power of the intellect's desire to know a self-confirming world whose most essential elements, received in a way such that the mind cannot help but take them just as they are, irrevocably excludes the possibility of doubt. Correlatively, the insistence that these elements be shared by all minds attests to the felt need to locate a politically viable simulacrum for a universalism that can no longer count on cosmological authorization.

The second premise of epistemological debate consists of belief in the inherent correspondence of knowledge with Being or Reality in toto. Here, too, the ancient premise is retained, although the sense of the term "correspondence" is considerably altered in response to epis-

---

21. René Descartes, "Rules for the Direction of the Mind," in *The Philosophical Works of Descartes*, vol. 1, ed. Elizabeth Haldane and G.R.T. Ross (London: Cambridge University Press, 1931), pp. 7–8.
22. Descartes, "Meditations on First Philosophy," in *The Philosophical Works of Descartes*, vol. 1, p. 144.

temology's reshaped account of that which is. On the classical understanding, the physical and the material were clearly distinguished; the
former was formed and the latter was without. Matter, accordingly,
was deemed unknowable until it received the form necessary to overcome its slip into non-Being. Early modern philosophy, however,
found it imperative to recast the physical as the material. Accom-
modating the Church's dogma regarding the omnipotence of God's
providential will and His creation of the world ex nihilo, Cartesian
science argued that only His external imposition, as expressed in
natural laws, can account for the patterned motions of all phenomena
as well as whatever connections they sustain with one another. Con-
ceptualizing reality in terms of the motion of inanimate, dumb, and
passive matter through uniform space and time, Descartes's science
discredited the Aristotelian understanding of *physis* as that which
determines the growth of seed to mature form and thereby establishes
the possibility of its intellectual apprehension. The unity of classical
cosmology, predicated upon the reality of hierarchical grades of existence and a corresponding hierarchy of grades of "mind," was thereby
sundered.

Recapitulating the logic implicit in the Milesians' effort to save traditional morality by identifying the singular source of all Being, Descartes expresses the ambiguous results engendered by this conceptual
reconstruction when he insists that "there is always one principal
property of substance which constitutes its nature and essence, and on
which all the others depend."[23] With this premise in place, he then
splits nature into two parts (although the term "part" seems inappropriate to two substances that, in principle, can have nothing in
common with each other). More precisely, Descartes contends that all
Being is either incorporeal substance whose essence is thought or
corporeal substance whose essence is extension.

That distinction, it should be clear, reveals the tenacity of antiquity's
belief that Being's unity through time requires the power supplied by
an identifiable source of *archē*, even as it rejects the teleology that
originally rendered this conviction intelligible. The tension between
the old and new is apparent when Descartes argues that the body, "as
a machine created by the hand of God,"[24] is incapable of ordering its
own movements. Like Plato in the *Timaeus*, Descartes must conclude

---

23. Descartes, "Principles of Philosophy," in *The Philosophical Works of Descartes*, vol. 1,
p. 240.
   24. Descartes, "Discourse on Method," in *The Philosophical Works of Descartes*, vol. 1, p.
116.

that the body's observable cycles, like all of nature's regularities, find their ultimate source in the external imposition of its divine ruler. But given his endorsement of spirit's radical disjunction from nature, he is unable to answer the question of how human thought, which is not an attribute of matter's substance, can cause motion in a body to which it bears only a contingent relationship, as well as how the latter can cause sensations to be registered in the former. Only God can save Descartes from the dilemma caused by this promiscuous mixing of ancient, medieval, and modern categories; and He can do so only because He, qua deus ex machina, is defined as the common creator of each of these two substances.

This ontological problem pales in difficulty, though, when compared with the epistemological question of how mind, understood as a kind of immaterial gaseous substance, can possibly sustain valid reference to something that is not mind. How, for example, is the "soul," now relocated within the abstract but substantial inner space known as "consciousness," to know anything about a human body that, like all other bodies in nature, is an entity whose external motions are scientifically explicable only because wholly subject to unalterable laws? How, more generally, can reason have legitimate epistemic access to a world outside itself once it has been denied the teleological grounds for thinking its knowing participates in a reality that is intelligible because the latter is itself suffused with *nous*?

In resolving this dilemma, Cartesian epistemology cannot embrace the classical conviction that knowledge consists of achievement of identity with the form that defines the essence of a thing. It cannot contend, as had Plato in *Cratylus*, "that things have names by nature, and that not every man is an artificer of names, but he only who looks to the name which each thing by nature has, and is able to express the true forms of things in letters and syllables" (390e). Rather, that epistemology must rethink the ocular metaphors that account for the traditional representation of knowledge as direct grasp and envisagement in a way that proves compatible with modernity's dualistic ontology. Accordingly, embracing Galileo's claim that "the sense of sight, most excellent and noble of all the senses, is like light itself,"[25] Descartes describes knowing as "looking with the eyes of the mind"; and on this basis, he elucidates the criteria to be employed in determining the worth of epistemic claims: "I term that clear which is present and

25. Galileo, quoted in Matthews, *The Scientific Background to Modern Philosophy*, p. 59.

apparent to an attentive mind, in the same way as we assert that we see objects clearly when, being present to the regarding eye, they operate upon it with sufficient strength. But the distinct is that which is so precise and different from other objects that it contains within itself nothing but what is clear."[26]

Here Descartes takes the watchful eye of the classical Greek *theoria*-ist—that is, the agency through which the *nous* of wisdom's lover is wedded to the cosmos's structure—and recasts it as a private inner stage on which distinctively mental activity casts its nonmaterial apprehensions. Characterizing mind as a form of immediately self-revealing activity, he is thereby drawn to a peculiarly modern definition of knowledge as the inherent transparency of ideas given without mediation to consciousness. But the term "idea" refers not to archetypes present within the divine intellect, as Aquinas's usage dictated, but rather to the necessary explanatory constituents of our internal mirroring: "I take the term idea to stand for whatever the mind directly perceives."[27] Descartes thus abandons antiquity's endeavor to locate the source of absolute certainty in the cosmos's design, as well as medievalism's effort to find it in heavenly revelation. He must define truth, accordingly, not as Platonic *homoiosis*, moral assimilation to the Good, nor as Thomistic *adequatio intellectus ad rem*, the consonance of a human concept with a thing,[28] but rather as mathematically certain intuition of representations impressed upon mind in literally the same way that a seal's figure is impressed upon wax.[29]

26. Descartes, "Principles of Philosophy," p. 237. Cf. Descartes, "Rules for the Direction of the Mind," pp. 28–29: "Truly we shall learn how to employ our mental intuition from comparing it with the way in which we employ our eyes. For he who attempts to view a multitude of objects with one and the same glance, sees none of them distinctly; and similarly the man who is wont to attend to many things at the same time by means of a single act of thought is confused in mind. But just as workmen, who are employed in very fine and delicate operations and are accustomed to direct their eyesight attentively to separate points, by practice have acquired a capacity for distinguishing objects of extreme minuteness and subtlety; so likewise do people who do not allow their thought to be distracted by various objects at the same time, but always concentrate it in attending to the simplest and easiest particulars, are clear-headed."

27. René Descartes, "Third Set of Objections," in *The Philosophical Works of Descartes*, vol. 2, ed. Elizabeth Haldane and G. R. T. Ross (London: Cambridge University Press, 1912), pp. 67–68.

28. See Thomas's claim in *Saint Thomas Aquinas: On Law, Morality, and Politics*, p. 35: "The types of the divine intellect do not stand in the same relation to things as the types of the human intellect. For the human intellect is measured by things, so that a human concept is not true by reason of itself but by reason of its being consonant with things, since an opinion is true or false depending on whether a thing is or is not."

29. See Descartes, "Rules for Direction of the Mind," p. 36: "Let us conceive of the matter as follows:—all our external senses, in so far as they are part of the body, and

Concluding that Descartes's doctrine of innate ideas must fall beneath the weight of its own absurdity, Locke's empiricist reformulation of this second element of the epistemological problematic reads the fundamental category of modern science, external or mechanical relation, into the philosophy of mind. This defection from his mentor, though, proves compatible with the Cartesian presupposition, to quote Locke, that "our idea of body is an extended solid substance, and our idea of soul is of a substance that thinks."[30] Built upon this dualistic foundation, his thinking about thinking differs only in form from its French foil.

Protected from what will eventually become Humean skepticism by his deep faith in nature's divinely instated order, Locke asks in his *Essay concerning Human Understanding* how it is that the mind, conceptualized as a blank tablet or an unwritten book, comes to have characters imprinted on it. To answer, he begins by endorsing the fundamental implication of Descartes's *cogito ergo sum*, that consciousness constitutes the essence of the substance that is the self-identical self: "When the Mind turns its view inwards upon it self, and contemplates its own Actions, *Thinking* is the first that occurs." This, in turn, is the premise of his Cartesian claim that our most basic ideas are unambiguous and irrefutable impressions: "These *simple Ideas* when offered to the mind, *the Understanding can* no more refuse to have, nor alter, when they are imprinted, nor blot them out, and make new ones in it self, than a mirror can refuse, alter, or obliterate the Images or *Ideas*, which, the Objects set before it, do therein produce." Accordingly, he represents "the clearest and most certain" knowledge "that humane Frailty is capable of" as a form of immediate perceptual consciousness—specifically, intellectual "perception of the connexion and agreement, or disagreement and repugnancy of any of our Ideas. . . . This part of Knowledge is irresistible, and like the bright Sun-shine, forces it self immediately to be perceived, as soon as ever the Mind turns its view that way; and leaves no room for Hesitation, Doubt, or

---

despite the fact that we direct them towards objects, so manifesting activity, viz. a movement in space, nevertheless properly speaking perceive in virtue of passivity alone, just in the way that wax receives an impression from a seal. And it should not be thought that all we mean to assert is an analogy between the two. We ought to believe that the way is entirely the same in which the exterior figure of the sentient body is really modified by the object, as that in which the shape of the surface of the wax is altered by the seal."

30. John Locke, quoted in Dewey, "Leibniz's New Essays," in *EW*, vol. 1, p. 373.

Examination, but the Mind is presently filled with the clear Light of it."[31] Finally, to round out this conceptual scheme, he contends that the truth of all compounded beliefs is to be determined through their reduction to these same "simple ideas." (If the truth be known, those ideas are really just convenient fictions predicated upon Locke's unacknowledged importation of Newton's atomic corpuscles into his theory of mind.)[32]

In sum, Locke is an epistemological "conformist" who, like his Continental counterpart, believes (a) that "reality" is already there in ready-made, fixed, and finished form; and (b) that knowing is a matter of passive reflection of this antecedent existence by the self-contained vessel that is consciousness. To both, nature as an object of knowledge is a book, while knowledge itself is the mind's realization of that text's singularly correct reading. For both, the demonstration that primary ideas and the fixed relations existing between them are immune to human refashioning is the clearest possible demonstration of reason's ultimate dependence on the benevolence of divine will.

The final shared premise of epistemological debate, which is entailed by its identification of presence in consciousness with knowledge, consists of belief in a knowing self, ego, or subject whose innate powers or structures render it peculiarly equipped to receive that knowledge. At its most refined, this belief finds expression in Kant's quest to isolate universal standards for all actual and possible cognitive endeavor. That venture, on the tale told here, must be interpreted as a forlorn attempt to compensate for the elimination of ideal forms from nature by reinstating the intrinsic rationality of the universe via an examination of the conditions under which knowledge is possible. As such, it unwittingly testifies to the much more pervasive subjectivism that infects virtually every version of the epistemological project in one way or another.

"The identification of the mind with the individual self and of the

31. John Locke, *An Essay concerning Human Understanding*, ed. Peter Nidditch (Oxford: Oxford University Press, 1975), pp. 118, 226, 525, 531.

32. See Newton, quoted in Matthews, *The Scientific Background to Modern Philosophy*, p. 155: "All these things being consider'd, it seems probable to me, that God in the Beginning form'd Matter in solid, massy, hard, impenetrable, moveable Particles, of such Sizes and Figures, and with such other Properties, and in such Proportion to Space, as most conduced to the End for which he form'd them; and that these primitive Particles being Solids, are incomparably harder than any porous Bodies compounded of them; even so very hard, as never to wear or break in pieces; no ordinary Power being able to divide what God himself made one in the first Creation."

latter with a private psychic consciousness is comparatively modern. In both the Greek and medieval periods, the rule was to regard the individual as a channel through which a universal and divine intelligence operated. The individual was in no true sense the knower; the knower was the 'Reason' which operated through him."[33] For example, late Scholastic ontology held that an entity exists subjectively—that is, as a subject—if it has spatiotemporal existence; and subjects, so construed, were assigned different grades of reality in accordance with their varying degrees of perfection and causal power, the intimacy of their relationship to divine Reason. The ontology of Galileo, by way of contrast, suggested that "primary" or intrinsic properties of objects—for example, their size, shape, and location—are "real" because describable in the language of Cartesian analytic geometry. "Secondary" properties such as color, which could not be so depicted, were discovered to have no reality apart from the mind upon which such effects are produced. As modifications produced in us by the operation of natural bodies upon our sense organs, they were disparaged as mere "subjective" appearances. Hence in The Assayer Galileo argues: "I think, therefore, that tastes, odors, colors, etc., so far as their objective existence is concerned, are nothing but mere names for something which resides exclusively in our sensitive body [corpo sensitivo], so that if the perceiving creatures were removed, all of these qualities would be annihilated and abolished from existence."[34]

We may readily recast Galileo's point in the terms suggested in Chapter 2. Philosophers of early modern science simply followed a course first charted by their ancient counterparts when they accorded ontological standing to the results achieved through employment of analogies drawn from observation of unsophisticated forms of machine production. Once completed, this reifying project necessarily implied the unreality of those qualitative traits of experience whose intelligibility turned, in the last analysis, on analogical elaboration of teleological and organic metaphors drawn from the domain of agrarian practice. For if science's object is a Galilean world, and if knowledge grasps what truly is, then qualities of experience that cannot be reduced to mathematical or mechanical form must not be real. "Immediate qualities, being extruded from the object of science, were left

33. Dewey, DE, p. 292.
34. Galileo, quoted in Matthews, The Scientific Background to Modern Philosophy, pp. 56–57.

thereby hanging loose from the 'real' object. Since their *existence* could not be denied, they were gathered together into a psychic realm of being, set over against the object of physics."[35] Once so relocated, they became purely subjective impressions in the mind or, failing that, inexplicable anomalies whose continued appearance mysteriously attested to the reality of a realm of being above the natural.

This transformation of nature into a despiritualized exhibition of mechanical forces punctured the illusion that the world is a variegated and soulful medium designed to furnish human beings metaphysical solace. It could not, however, eliminate the epistemological puzzle posed by the rich textures of everyday pragmata. The fact that human beings continued to fashion ends, to experience sounds and colors, to pass judgment on good and bad, was troublesome if not downright embarrassing. To account for the tenacity of such qualified experience in a disenchanted universe was the service performed by the Enlightenment's most novel invention—the individuated self. Answering the call for an author who might account for life's continued capacity to bear significance, the atomic individual was constructed as a mind standing somehow outside of nature. "When real objects are identified, point for point, with knowledge-objects, all affectional and volitional objects are inevitably excluded from the 'real' world, and are compelled to find refuge in the privacy of an experiencing subject or mind."[36] Lockean and Cartesian epistemology therefore signifies not a radical break with the past but rather an interiorization of its most cherished assumptions. Just as "Descartes' thought is the *nous* of classic tradition forced inwards because physical science had extruded it from its object, so Locke's simple idea is the classic Idea, Form or Species dislodged from nature and compelled to take refuge in mind."[37]

Paradoxically, this nonnatural center of individuated experience— whether called soul or spirit or mind or ego or consciousness or subject—was itself invested with the essentialist status ascribed by classical cosmology to the qualities (qua metaphysical forms) reason could no longer ascribe to nature. Hypostatizing the power of agency displayed by particular agents engaged in specific struggles to loosen the fetters of received custom, epistemology's creation came to look

35. Dewey, *EN*, p. 264.
36. Ibid., p. 24.
37. Ibid., p. 229.

suspiciously like a secularized version of Protestantism's soul. "The power and capacities which belong to human nature in its differentiation from cosmic nature were not just referred to 'individuals' in the sense in which *private* may be properly distinguished from public, and the socially singular from the socially incorporated; that which was called 'individual,' and thereby in effect the human generally, was interpreted and described in terms borrowed from the ancient theories of mind, which had been taken up into Christian theology and which through the Church had found their way into the popular culture of the western world. Because of this latter influence, the practical, the essentially moral and social, operation of this and that daring pioneer in breaking away from old customs and from accepted tradition, which was the legitimate heart of modern individualism as a *social* manifestation, was transformed into a metaphysical doctrine of the inherent constitution of human beings."[38] Moreover, as we have seen, that being's consciousness was deemed radically private, self-encased, and intrinsically independent of all others. As such, its bearer was condemned to become "not merely a pilgrim but an unnaturalized and unnaturalizable alien in the world."[39]

Not surprisingly, the politics appropriate to this self without determinate content proved to be that of liberalism. As I show in greater detail in Chapter 4, liberal political discourse presupposes the great divide between nature, construed as a self-enclosed world of objects in which the occurrence of all events is determined unequivocally, and the subject, identified as a container of consciousness whose freedom qua autonomy demands protection and consolidation of this rift. Confronted by anything other than itself, liberalism's aspiring sovereign can preserve its self-identity only by confirming its own autarchy or by arrogating the other to its self; so constituted, this disconnected subject wavers indeterminately between the twin poles of anarchy and despotism. Liberal political practice can dare to establish this subject as the final authority in all matters of practical judgment, therefore, only if its epistemologists prove able to articulate and legitimate a set of constitutional rules that enable those who see the world in very different ways to coexist in a relationship of mutual forebearance. That is the dilemma for which liberal political theory seeks a final solution.

38. Dewey, unpublished ms. (59/9).
39. Dewey, *EN*, p. 24.

IV

Exposure of epistemology's dependence on presuppositions surreptitiously imported from a past it claims to overcome is not an end in itself. One purpose of the previous chapter, recall, was to suggest certain of the complex and mediated ways in which philosophical reflection is linked to social and political crises. More precisely, the rarefied content of classical philosophy can be traced back to meanings intimated by specific forms of nonphilosophical experience; and the ways in which those meanings are deployed in larger philosophical constructions express the hopes and fears of those confronting a general breakdown of traditional forms of collective order. Correlatively, the questions whose repeated asking preserves the basic structure of epistemological debate are not self-contained; to grasp their full significance, we must also relocate them within the larger history of which they form a part. For epistemology's allegedly absolute and fixed distinctions are in fact contingent responses to a widespread cultural crisis; its dualistic distinctions between sensation and thought, subject and object, mind and matter, for example, are simply condensed formulae gesturing toward divisions present in the structure of early modern life. It follows, accordingly, that resolution of epistemology's apparently unanswerable questions is in the last analysis a political task. "As the philosopher has received his problem from the world of action, so he must return his account there for auditing and liquidation."[40]

So situated, epistemological debate is well read as an uncommon transcript of the inarticulate categories of self-interpretation employed by those caught between a decaying past and an unknown future. Those meanings first emerged as so many attempts to craft sense from a collective situation in which extension of the capitalist market was rapidly subverting the integrity of feudal mores; in which the rise of Protestant sectarianism betrayed the Catholic Church's ideal of a universal Christendom; in which the early modern state, mobilizing bureaucratized armies and revenue collection systems, began to expropriate the resources of more localized centers of political power. But inasmuch as we have yet to substantially reform the categories of

---

40. Dewey, "The Significance of the Problem of Knowledge," in *IDP*, p. 6.

thought engendered by these overlapping crises, these meanings are still very much our own.

To see this point, permit me to draw a deliberately one-sided caricature, an ideal type as it were, of the perplexities afflicting a modern self who no longer finds conventional religious faith a viable option, but who nonetheless finds that the structure of her daily experience makes it difficult to abandon the quest for certainty altogether. That done, I will indicate how that self's understanding of reason, incorporating the core presuppositions of the epistemological project, helps to reproduce and legitimate the institutional conditions that systematically undermine her capacity to fashion coherent sense from her situation.

Ensnared within an institutionalized web of dualistic oppositions, that self finds unavailable forms of experience that might otherwise temper the alienations of contemporary life. Vaguely sensing that encroachment of scientific knowledge has vitiated doctrines that once linked everyday affairs to a transcendent ground, that being either exhausts her energies in a frenzied pursuit of material gain whose achievement cannot overcome the confusion to which it attests or, alternatively, she retreats into an "inner life" in search of protection against the fragmentation of social existence into so many discrete spheres. Seeking an object of assurance to moderate her alternation between rigid dogmatism and radical nihilism, that ego eagerly presses on science the hopes and fears she once projected on another world. Credited with the certainty characteristic of unreflective faith, granted access to a more profound plane of reality than that grasped by ordinary experience, and ascribed an omnipotence that reaffirms the insignificance of the privatized self, science becomes the severe deity of a new monotheism. Although the spread of that cult hastens the decay of pre-Enlightenment authorities, its abstracted rationalism cannot satisfy the foundationalist urges that first called those authorities into being.

That the irrelevance of the individual in the face of this reified agency may become all but irremediable is a very real possibility contained within epistemology's reconstruction of the teleocratic account of reason left behind by Plato and Aristotle. That reconstruction, recapitulating philosophy's original inversion of the relationship between its creations and the forms of activity from which its metaphorics are derived, all the more completely denies dignity and significance to ordinary experience. "Philosophy, like all forms of reflective analysis, takes us away, for the time being, from the things had in primary experience, as they directly act and are acted upon, used and enjoyed. Now the standing temptation of philosophy, as its course abundantly demonstrates, is to regard the results of reflection as having, in and of themselves, a reality superior to that of the material of any other mode of experience. The commonest assumption of philosophies, common even to philosophies very different from one another, is the assumption of the identity of objects of knowledge and ultimately real objects. The assumption is so deep that it is usually not expressed; it is taken for granted as something so fundamental it does not need to be stated."[41] Obsessed with the distinctive form of conduct that is knowing, Western rationalism since the time of Plato has proven incapable of radically jettisoning its conviction that all experiencing is a mode of cognition, albeit a mode whose fruits are far inferior to those achieved through philosophical reflection.

Like its classical predecessor, the epistemological reading of science presupposes that the intelligibility of nature entails perception of the Being in Becoming,—that is, apprehension of the permanent reality that ensures the victory of *archē* over the particulars it rules. When the self-sufficient whole of Newtonian physics is interpreted in light of this presupposition, this geometrically formalized system of departicularized and law-abiding objects cannot help but occlude and in time supplant the contextualized experience from which its abstractions were originally wrought.[42] "Practically all epistemological discussion depends upon a sudden and unavowed shift to and fro from the universe of having to the universe of discourse. At the outset, ordinary empirical affairs, chairs, tables, stones, sticks, etc., are called physical objects—which is obviously a term of theoretical interpretation when it is applied, carrying within itself a complete metaphysical commitment. Then physical objects are defined as the objects of physics. . . . But such objects are clearly very different things from the plants, lamps, chairs, thunder and lightning, rocks etc. that were first called physical objects. So another transformation phantasmagoria in the tableau is staged. The original 'physical things,' ordinary empirical objects, not being the objects of physics, are not physical at all but mental. Then comes the grand dissolving climax in which objects of physics are shown as themselves hanging from empirical objects now

41. Dewey, *EN*, p. 19.
42. On this point, see Edmund Husserl, *The Crisis of the European Sciences*, trans. David Carr (Evanston: Northwestern University Press, 1970), passim.

dressed up as mental, and hence as themselves mental. Everything now being mental, and the term having lost its original contrasting or differential meaning, a new and different series of transformation scenes is exhibited. Immediate empirical things are resolved into hard sensory data, which are called the genuine physical things, while the objects of physical science are treated as are logical constructions; all that remains to constitute mental existence is images and feelings."[43] The scientific concept, epistemologically construed, thus levels experience's indeterminate things by deducing their existence from the superior reality of discrete inert objects causally coordinated upon a field whose movement through time does not, in and of itself, enter into the constitution of their being. A hypostatized theoretical interpretation, which must posit a "subjective" knower in order to account for the discrepancies between science's unchanging objects and the mutability of experience's contextualized pragmata, thereby absorbs the latter's affairs within the abstract categories of a mathematized reason claiming to grasp the totality of what is.

In this sense, modern epistemology recapitulates the logic of classical philosophy. By and large, however, it does so without fully acknowledging that the cosmology from which it was originally fashioned is now in tatters; and this explains why its articulation of the demands of teleocratic reason proves even more imperious than its ancient counterpart. Classical philosophy, distinguishing its theoretical wisdom from what Plato called "right opinion," defined experience as the habits and skills acquired through repeated efforts to shape the affairs of daily existence. The sense-making grid of Cartesian/ Lockean epistemology, by way of contrast, is committed to the unqualified universality of the knowing experience in virtue of its presupposition that bare presentation to passive consciousness, whether of idea or sense datum, constitutes an instance of cognition. "If the notion of perception as a case of adequate knowledge of its own object-matter be accepted, the knowledge relation is absolutely ubiquitous; it is an all-inclusive net."[44] Unable to draw any meaningful distinction between what appears in experience and what appears in the experience of knowing, epistemology tacitly affirms reason's right to colonize all experience, no matter how vigorously the latter resists assimilation to its reifications.

43. Dewey, EN, pp. 140–41.
44. Dewey, "Naive Realism vs. Presentative Realism," in EEL, p. 263.

This same argument can be made in a slightly different way. How is it that epistemology, whether of idealist or empiricist stripe, came to endorse the postulate of immediate knowledge, that is, of knowledge imprinted on consciousness without mediation by any form of embodied activity? From a quasi-genealogical perspective, this postulate expresses the fruits of epistemology's struggle to blend together the Pauline segregation of soul from body, classical metaphors representing knowing as a kind of perception, and the pre-Socratic conviction that the traits characteristic of objects known are of supreme value because they are the sole ultimate realities. The result, as we have seen, is a collapse of epistemic categories into ontological truths. This, in and of itself, is not new. Plato expressed this confusion when, in the *Theaetetus*, he claimed that "perception is always of something that *is*, and, as being knowledge, it is infallible" (152c); and Francis Bacon indicated this confusion's tenacity when, in his *New Organon*, he contended that "whatever deserves to exist deserves also to be known, for knowledge is the image of existence."[45] Because it is predicated upon an unambiguous mind-body split, however, modern epistemology cannot help but endorse a radically totalizing formulation of antiquity's conviction that embodied experience can transcend its native deficiencies only by submitting to and so assuming the forms definitive of cognition's refined objects. For example, from the premise that knowing should ponder only the "absolute . . . such as all which is considered as independent, causal, simple, universal, unitary, equal, similar, straight, or as having other qualities of this sort,"[46] Descartes moves without hesitation to the conclusion that the value of all lived experience turns upon its worthiness to be known: it must recapitulate the transparent coerciveness, the artificial simplicity, and the unequivocal order that characterizes disembodied knowledge whose first principles prove indubitable to all who are rational. He thereby completes the divestment of experience's capacity to constrain or criticize its disciplinary reconstruction by science.

In Chapter 7, I offer an account of the institutional structures through which the rationalizing dynamic of modern science, epistemologically construed, has made its way into the world of everday experience. For present purposes, the broad political implications of experience's subsumption beneath reason's categories are best indi-

---

45. Bacon, *The New Organon*, p. 109.
46. Descartes, "Rules for Direction of the Human Mind," p. 15.

cated by referring to the attributes characteristically ascribed to the God who stands as the ultimate guarantor of all knowledge. That God, suggests Newton in a typical formulation, "is eternal and infinite, omnipotent and omniscient; that is, his duration reaches from eternity to eternity; his presence from infinity to infinity; he governs all things, and knows all things that are or can be done."[47] When joined to Newton's contention that scientific inquiry is the vehicle through which humanity gains access to the signs of God's wisdom, it becomes apparent that epistemology furnishes quasi-secularized expression to Aquinas's conviction that "reason is to man what God is to the universe."[48] As such, epistemology perpetuates the traditional conviction that experience's pragmata must become clear and distinct objects of sight if they are to be assured of their own reality. Yet inasmuch as epistemology's individuated knowers now find themselves expelled from the cosmological structure that had securely anchored Aquinas's reason, each solitary self is now in effect thrust into the position once reserved to the Deity. Each such being, confronting an externalized world of independent objects, now knows that God's will is revealed through the exercise of a teleocratic reason whose perfection demands a domination of nature that is as thoroughgoing as humanity's subjection to its creator.

At first, this mortal god appears to pose no significant challenge to that worshipped by Aquinas. Thus Descartes is able to argue that if the term "substance" refers to "nothing other than a thing which exists in such a way that it needs no other thing in order to exist," then we may rightfully conclude, first, that the "only substance which needs absolutely no other thing" is God and, second, that "all others can exist only with the aid of God's participation."[49] In time, though, these two divinities cannot help but confront each other as rivals. As the possibility that God may at any moment suspend or alter nature's lawful regularities seems ever less imminent, the sense of His omnipotence grows dimmer. Correlatively, as humanity's collective capacity to reconstruct the material world grows ever greater, the created rather than the creator steps in to furnish whatever rationality is found in the world. Construing its autonomy in terms of the power of absolute self-determination, Descartes's cogito thus comes to define its freedom as

47. Newton, quoted in Matthews, *The Scientific Background to Modern Philosophy*, p. 150.

48. Aquinas, "On Princely Government," p. 67.

49. Descartes, "Principles of Philosophy," p. 239.

its success in mastering a world composed of aggregated objects that must remain intrinsically meaningless if that ego is to fancy itself the exclusive creator of all purpose. That ego's wholesale intolerance for the obscure, the vague, and the ambiguous sanctions the epistemic expropriation of all unrationalized practice on the grounds that the transparency of the rational self to itself, like God's apprehension of His own will, requires the construction of an enlightened order in which all being is characterized, first and foremost, by the quality of self-evidence.

Epistemology's science of nature, demanding that everything external to consciousness be deconstructed into discriminable bits of matter, drains its objects of all significance and so leaves them incomprehensible except as neutered targets of use-value. By the same token, epistemology's science of society dissolves the network of human relations into an aggregation of bodies who, deprived of the connections once sustained by God's will, now know one another only as objects of mutual exploitation. Hence whatever meaningfulness is possible within a "society" so composed can only be an expression of its efficient organization to produce maximal satisfaction of the brute desires advanced by utilitarianism as a surrogate for the ends of classical teleology.

Just how that fulfillment might be politically secured is suggested by the use to which Locke's empiricism is put by his Continental adherents. Qualifying his brief on behalf of the cognitive significance of ordinary sense perception, Locke insists that the "relations" established between the mind's simple ideas are the "workmanship of the understanding." This concession to Descartes is ignored, however, by Helvetius and Condorcet, who reduce these indispensable elements of scientific knowledge, like the epistemic atoms they link, to sensational form via a doctrine of extreme associationalism.[50] When that

50. For example, see Antoine-Nicholas de Condorcet, *Sketch for a Historical Picture of the Progress of the Human Mind*, trans. Jane Barraclough (London: Weidenfeld and Nicolson, 1955), pp. 132–33: "At last, Locke grasped the thread by which philosophy should be guided; he showed that an exact and precise analysis of ideas, which reduces them step by step to other ideas of more immediate origin or of simpler composition, is the only way to avoid being lost in that chaos of incomplete, incoherent and indeterminate notions which chance presents to us at hazard and we unthinkingly accept. By this same analysis he proved that all ideas are the result of the operations of our minds upon sensations we have received, or, to put it more exactly, that they are the combinations of these sensations presented to us simultaneously by the faculty of memory in such a way that our attention is arrested and our perception is thereby limited to no more than a part of such compound sensations."

view is wedded to Locke's conception of mind as a blank tablet whose accuracy is guaranteed by its passivity, it becomes exceptionally difficult to resist the conclusion that carefully regulated control of the mind's impressions and sensations, especially those relating to the production of pleasure and pain, can be employed to construct any sort of human character at will. A well-ordered polity, consequently, is one that systematically associates sensations of pleasure with socially useful conduct and sensations of pain with that which is harmful. It is not surprising, then, to find Holbach closing his *Du système de la nature* with a prayer to the material world; for that meaningless world, as constituted by the masterless ego, is now ascribed the same omnipotence over humanity that was once ascribed to its maker.

Epistemology's preoccupation with method, with what Descartes describes as those "certain and simple rules, such that, if a man observe them accurately, he shall never assume what is false as true, and will never spend his mental efforts to no purpose,"[51] is best understood in these political terms. As we have seen, classical and especially Aristotelian philosophy contended that although various forms of knowledge could be ranked hierarchically, all nonetheless betokened the realization of some level of Being. Hence to speak of appearance in contrast to reality was to speak of an imperfectly actualized form of Being rather than no Being at all. But "with the beginnings of modern thought, the region of the 'unreal,' the source of opinion and error, was located exclusively in the individual. The object was *all* real and *all* satisfactory, but the 'subject' could approach the object only through his own subjective states, his 'sensations' and 'ideas.' The Greek conception of two orders of existence was retained, but instead of the two orders characterizing the 'universe' itself, one *was* the universe, the other was the individual mind trying to know the universe."[52] Hence the Greek problem of accounting for the possibility of error was transformed into the peculiarly modern problem of accounting for the possibility of knowledge. For the possibility of mistake is implicit in the understanding of ideas as mental surrogates, as representations, whose nature is substantially different from the external objects they represent.

Embracing this formulation, Descartes and Locke agree that epistemic failure expresses defect in the knower rather than in the known.

51. Descartes, "A Reply by the Author," in *The Philosophical Works of Descartes*, vol. 2, p. 9.
52. Dewey, "The Experimental Theory of Knowledge," in *IDP*, p. 101.

They thereby replace the ancient hierarchy of cognitional forms with a unidimensional doctrine affirming that instances of knowing either fully grasp their object or grasp it not at all. Thinking that the mind's misapprehensions are not unlike the blurred or fragmentary images produced by poorly made carbon paper, Descartes and Locke set in motion the distinctively modern preoccupation with the rules of scientific method. Much like liberalism's constitutional procedures, those rules are justified by their ability to secure the intellectual self-purification of inconstant subjects and so guarantee their clear, distinct, and uniform perception of disqualified matter. If the mind is indeed like an imperfect telescope whose sights are trained on a world of distanced objects, then only thoroughgoing internalization of and hence self-surveillance by method's discipline can insure the self's emancipation from error. Only by submitting its cognitive lenses to grinding by method's abstract code can that self be saved from collapse into a frightening realm in which the distinction between subject and object no longer appears so real.

That fear offers a partial explanation for one of the defining features of so much modern thought, that is, its peculiar conjunction of a thoroughgoing distrust of faith and passion with a radical faith in reason and an all-absorbing passion for knowledge. Scientism, the idolatrous conviction that method-based knowledge furnishes the ontological ground as well as the exclusive organizing principle for all human conduct, is deeply implicated in a culture that cannot happily abide the frustration generated by subjects and objects that refuse to submit pliantly to the end-less telos of absolute domination. This distortion of science's initial emancipatory thrust has proven plausible only because, read as modernity's most powerful mythic agency, it has been required to answer questions previously posed by Catholic eschatology. When mixed with the pervasive desire to dispel Humean skepticism, fertile soil is prepared for those who know how to profit from the chronic search for lost bearings. "The philosophic theories which have set science on an altar in a temple remote from the arts of life, to be approached only with peculiar rites, are a part of the technique of retaining a secluded monopoly of belief and intellectual authority."[53]

Ironically, however, it is this same worship that, when defiled by recalcitrant beings, explains the present's infatuation with nihilism.

53. Dewey, EN, p. 382.

Such disillusionment, securing its most disturbing articulation in Max Weber's portrayal of charismatic politics, could never have become so pervasive had not modern science found imposed upon it the burdens once borne by theology. Demystification of the superstitious awe now afforded science, which grounds faith in the necessarily progressive character of history, is therefore a first step toward thinking about how thinking might deny the equation of reality with experience's ever more comprehensive subsumption beneath reason's imperatives.

V

"It is a commonplace that the chief divisions of modern philosophy, idealism in its different kinds, realisms of various brands, so-called common-sense dualism, agnosticism, relativism, phenomenalism, have grown up around the epistemological problem of the general relation of subject and object. Problems not openly epistemological, such as whether the relation of changes in consciousness to physical changes is one of interaction, parallelism, or automatism have the same origin. What becomes of philosophy, consisting largely as it does of different answers to these questions, in case the assumptions which generate the questions have no empirical standing? Is it not time that philosophers turned from the attempt to determine the comparative merits of various replies to the questions to a consideration of the claims of the questions?"[54]

To begin to criticize epistemology's refashioning of antiquity's teleocratic conception of reason, as well as the political dynamic it entails, it is necessary to remap the terrain indicated by the terms "nature," "experience," and "meaning." I cannot show all at once how thinking might develop an account of itself that closes rather than widens the gap between knowing and its concerns. The question of meaning I leave for Chapters 4 and 5; and much of what I say here about nature and experience is anticipatory and fragmentary. My aim at this point is simply to extend a bit farther than I did in Chapter 2 the moral implicit in my tale of reason's birth and maturation. That, perhaps ironically, is best accomplished by extracting the ingredient of truth in ancient metaphysics and then refashioning it in a way that casts doubt on the adequacy of the epistemological project.

54. Dewey, "The Need for a Recovery of Philosophy," in *ENF*, p. 43.

As we saw above, classical philosophy's utilization of visual metaphors to construe cognition, as well as its correlative disparagement of the more tactile senses, becomes hegemonic within epistemology. Galileo gives the sense of this development when he suggests that "the sense of touch, being more material than the other senses and being produced by the mass of the material itself, seems to correspond to the element of earth. . . . The sense of sight, most excellent and noble of all the senses, is like light itself. It stands to the others in the same measure of comparative excellence as the finite stands to the infinite, the gradual to the instantaneous, the divisible to the invisible, the darkness to the light."[55] Following Galileo's cue, Descartes and Locke read all cognitive experience as a kind of perceptual relationship between individuated but qualitatively empty objects and similarly individuated subjects who, of necessity, stand as exclusive creators of nature's ends. To quote Descartes: "In the matter of the cognition of facts two things alone have to be considered, ourselves who know and the objects themselves which are to be known."[56]

Yet the precise characterization of sight's sense undergoes an important revision as the modern theory of optics begins to develop. Whereas Plato and Aristotle thought of knowledge as active intercourse between the intellect and the epistemic object seen, Descartes and Locke conceive of the eye as a passive lens and vision as a kind of passive recording. As a result, the mind's eye is thrust out of the bodily realm, and the knowing agent severs its ties to the percipient organism. This essentially contemplative account of cognition fits neatly with the belief, also common to Locke and Descartes, that reality has a rational structure and that reason's concepts, when true, mirror that order in a context-independent way, that is, in a way that renders incidental the activity of grasping it as meaningful.

On this account, rationality can be assured of its own autonomy only insofar as its labor is governed by universal logical rules that owe nothing to experience's embodiment. Correlatively, the body's status as a law-abiding subject of scientific discourse turns upon its capacity to be represented as an interiorless object whose mechanical operations are construed as necessary causal responses to elementary sense impressions. Preservation of the gulf between cognition's conceptual

55. Galileo, quoted in Matthews, *The Scientific Background to Modern Philosophy*, pp. 58–59.
56. Descartes, "Reply to Objections II," in *The Philosophical Works of Descartes*, vol. 2, p. 35.

procedures and the body's perceptual receptions, an enterprise that finds its consummate expression in Kant, is therefore an essential condition of the possibility of scientific knowledge.

This amputation of body from mind entails a notion of experience that is foreign to the one suggested by the Greek term *empeiria*. This noun is etymologically rooted in a verb meaning "to attempt" or "to try" or "to make a trial of." That root is acknowledged when classical philosophy, generalizing from its observation of the intelligence displayed and embedded in *technai*'s skillful practice, characterizes ordinary nonphilosophical experience as the mutually transformational engagements and sufferings of embodied agents situated within shifting webs of qualitatively unique affairs. How, therefore, might one salvage some measure of the prephilosophical sense of experience and so rescue it from the hypostatizing ontologies of classical *theoria* and modern epistemology, each of which scorns it as a deficient form of knowing whose disabilities are finally overcome within reason's truth?

Let us begin by recollecting that the term *empeiria*, abstracted from its reference to any specific craft, refers to embodied skills whose habitual meanings accord conduct rule-of-thumb guidelines within diverse situations. This is the sense of Thucydides when, in his account of the Lacedaemonians' first naval defeat at the hands of the Athenians, he chides them for their failure "to take into account the long experience of the Athenians, as compared with their own brief practice" (2.85.2). Rooted in affirmation of relations connecting various concrete events occurring in time and space, the skills that *are* this learning are not merely perceptual, at least not in any thin sense of that term. Rather, they are historically engendered fruits whose capacity to elicit form from the materials given in experience turns upon their assimilation of motor, social, and linguistic dimensions within complexly structured media of action. As such, their grasp of their subject matters cannot be exhaustively articulated within reflective beliefs, expressible in propositional form. For such beliefs disclose only the explicitly articulable elements of modes of tactile understanding whose involvement within the world is, for the most part, tacit.

As ways of being that locate conduct within an intelligible world, the skills of *empeiria* furnish the vehicles through which agents fashion a world of experience from nature. But they are also, and at the same time, the vehicles through which the world fashions agents. Because the sensitive exercise of craft presupposes responsiveness and attunement to its materials, incorporation of their lessons informs its practitioners as much as its practitioners inform them. Hence, when genuinely skillful, techne's practice assumes the form not of unilateral manipulation, but of mutual transformation in which each party to this transaction participates in shaping the other.

Appreciation of this dialectical relationship hints at the misleading character of epistemology's strict demarcations between subject and object, mind and body, knowing and doing. These dualisms, abstracted from the rhythmic interplay of doing and undergoing in experience, reveal rationalism's inveterate conviction that experience must be forced into nonempirical confines if it is to rest assured of its true value. The ancient notion of empeiria, by way of contrast, suggests that the association between each of the entities artificially sundered by the imperatives of dualistic logic is much more immediate than epistemology can allow.

To get at the character of that association, we must first reject epistemology's denuded definition of experience in terms of the body's unmediated and stupid reception of discrete sense data. Instead, and following the clue offered by techne, we might say that "experience" is a "double-barrelled" term that "denotes both the field, the sun and clouds and rain, seeds, and harvest, and the man who labors, who plans, invents, uses, suffers, and enjoys. Innocent of the discrimination of the what experienced and the how, or mode, of experiencing," this term gestures at a form of being that is existentially prior to epistemology's various dualistic formulations inasmuch as it acknowledges "no division between act and material, subject and object, but contains them both in an unanalyzed totality. The primary and the persistent occurrence in the way of experience is a Res, an affair, a concern, a moving complex situation in which so-called primary, secondary and tertiary qualities are indissolubly blended or fused,—or from which, speaking more correctly, they have not yet been analyzed."[57]

Epistemology dissects the relational whole of such "primary" experience into the two separate causal structures identified by the terms "subject" and "object." Then, forgetting the derivative status of this abstraction, it offers its dissociation of reflectively constituted objects from their presence-in-experience as a truth given in the nature of things. Displacing the immediacy of qualitative existence with its ob-

---

57. Dewey, EN, p. 8; "Experience and Philosophic Method," in LW, vol. 1, p. 384; "Data and Meanings," in EEL, pp. 136–37n; "What Are States of Mind?" in MW, vol. 7, p. 37.

jectifying and subjectifying constructs, it can no longer re-member (as in "to put together again") that existential implication within primordial webs of contextualized experience precedes our capacity to render its pragmata intelligible through the fashioning and elaboration of sense-bearing meanings. Armed with the prepackaged goods labeled "subject" and "object," epistemology forgets that its terminology is but a circuitous way of denoting things that may be gestured at in words, but not thereby described or defined. Confusing its intellectually mediated objects for things contextualized by their participation in lived situations, epistemology mistakes the former's propositional modes of representation for the affairs so represented.

When we find ourselves in the midst of a qualitatively unique affair, our epistemological heritage encourages us to distinguish unambiguously between its things, on the one hand, and their qualities, on the other. Then, through use of the copula "is," we employ nouns to refer to the former qua objects whose truth is susceptible to scientific analysis, and adjectives to refer to the latter's properties, since these are adventitiously assigned to those objects by dislocated subjects. Assuming that the qualified character of ordinary experience testifies to its falsity, epistemology thus denies the reality of the irreducible and indescribable qualities that any thing must *have* in order to be, to participate in relations with other things, and finally to become a matter of formulated discourse. Convinced that quality's existence turns on its unmediated, noninferential, and indubitable appearance within the perceptual consciousness of individual knowers, epistemology's anthropocentric subjects cannot appreciate the existential facticity, the unconditioned "isness," of things just as they are. Were they to do so, they would soon come to question its equation of a mathematicized nature with genuine reality.

If epistemology's account of experience is suspect because it denies the ground out of which thinking emerges, then its unqualified characterization of nature must be questioned as well. Here, too, ancient usage furnishes a helpful starting point. Although overshadowed by an ontology that denied experience's qualitative dimensions full existential citizenship, Plato and Aristotle remained at least partly true to the import of *empeiria*. Both affirmed, via the hypostatized doctrine of Form, that the pragmata of experience are immediately and in their own right tragic, beautiful, humorous, barren, splendid, and more. Although twisting this insight to accommodate the imperatives of a misguided metaphysic, they nonetheless knew better than to endorse epistemology's representation of nature as so many chunks of homogeneous matter whose qualities are ascriptions generated within and by the human mind. "If experience actually presents esthetic and moral traits, then these traits may also be supposed to reach down into nature, and to testify to something that belongs to nature as truly as does the mechanical structure attributed to it in physical science. The traits possessed by the subject-matters of experience are as genuine as the characteristics of the sun and the electron. They are *found*, experienced, and are not to be shoved out of being by some trick of logic."[58]

When this ancient kernel is extricated from a teleocratic conception of reason, nature begins to appear as a relational scene that, under the pressure of time, gives rise to varying degrees of differentiated complexity. At its most primitive, as far as we now know, one finds the world of inanimate nature. Here the encounters between beings assume the form of "brute" connections in which the "accidental" conjunction of antecedent events is the external transitive condition of another's immediate and static qualities. But even at this most rudimentary level, where rock meets rock, the distribution of energies among nature's events, depending on their particular mode of conjunction, is capable of producing changes whose effects are something other than mere repetitions of what went before. "Even atoms and molecules show a selective bias in their indifferencies, affinities and repulsions when exposed to other events. With respect to some things they are hungry to the point of greediness; in the presence of others they are sluggish and cold. In a genuine although not psychic sense, natural beings exhibit preference and centeredness."[59] Hence, no matter how odd it may sound, it is not inappropriate to ascribe to inanimate existents "needs," if this term is taken to refer to concrete tensions sustained by patterned potencies pressing to discharge their energies and so resolve their dynamic possibilities within states of temporary equilibrium.

In moving from rocks to plants, we do not move to an essentially different order of being. If we stick to conventional usage by defining the "physical" as the inanimate, then the term "psychophysical" may be used to designate the class of animate organisms, where the prefix "psycho" denotes that physical activity has engendered capacities and potentialities absent from rocks. The difference between the animate

---

58. Dewey, *EN*, p. 2.
59. Dewey, *LW*, vol. 1, p. 162.

and the inanimate is not that the former is imbued with some special substance that is its essence; for there are no properties of a plant which are not products of the physicochemical energies that constitute rocks. Rather, that difference lies in the *way* in which physicochemical energies are interconnected, and hence in the forms of relationship of which each is susceptible and capable. In contrast to the relative indifference shown by nonliving beings toward the outcomes generated via their relations with other beings, the various constituent parts of a plant tend, when considered cumulatively, to sustain through time very specific forms of patterned activity. Making present use of consequences engendered by past activities, the plant adapts its subsequent changes to the future now bearing down on it. Inasmuch as those parts contribute to sustain the larger whole of which they are members, its "needs" may be said to express themselves as active "interests." "The root-tips of a plant interact with chemical properties of the soil in such ways as to serve organized life activity; and in such ways as to exact from the rest of the organism their own share of requisite nutrition. Thus with organization, bias becomes interest, and satisfaction a good or value and not a mere satiation of wants or repletion of deficiencies."[60] Life is thus causally dependent on events taking place on the merely physical plane of existence. But as these causes come to be organized in new and more intricate ways, they release new forms of causation that are only potentially present within the inanimate world.

This understanding of the continuity sustained among various forms of being indicates why atoms, interacting in increasingly intricate relations, give rise not merely to properties of mass and weight, but also to the equally real qualities we designate using terms of taste, color, feeling, beauty, and the like. In entering into new patterns of mutual implication, what in the realm of the inanimate was merely an abrupt and unique termination of interaction becomes a "quality."

In elucidating this complex term, it is important to sidestep the readings suggested by the classical account of Form as well as the epistemological account of nature's devitalized objects. To do so, we must first rekindle an appreciation of the temporality of all beings. The quality of temporality, as the practice of *technai* unreflectively grasped, is an immediate trait of every thing that is; and it is for this reason that

60. Dewey, *EN*, p. 256.

every existence is at the same time an event.[61] Nature, so construed, comprises events that are passing into other events such that the latter is a constitutive part of the former's existential character. As a conflux of organic and inorganic coincidents whose movements through time and space engender the mutual interpenetration of past, present, and future, nature is an affair of overlapping affairs. As such, its movement gives rise to and contains within itself endings or closings of temporal episodes that assume the form of pauses, resting place, and momentary consummations. Our everyday embodied experiences of immediate enjoyment and suffering thus presuppose and hint at the fact that nature's pregnant relationships sometimes issue forth in finalities and enclosures, each of which bears its own distinctive qualities.

When these issues enter into experience—that is, come to participate in the mode of being that is peculiarly human—their qualities in a sense are heard (although such hearing is never unambiguously clear). "In esthetic objects, that is in all immediately enjoyed and suffered things, in things directly possessed, they thus speak for themselves; Greek thinkers heard their voice."[62] Speaking more generally, those qualities are felt. This is not to say that feeling is an extraneous addition imposed by the subject on epistemology's neutered objects. Nor is it to say that feeling is the medium through which such objects cross from the realm of the purely physical to that of the purely psychical. Instead, the term "feeling" points to the newly actualized qualities events acquire when they pass into the more delicate and extensive relationships constitutive of experience. Before that time, those qualities can only be anticipated as possible realizations. But once actualized, the name of a particular "feeling" is appropriately employed to give communicable form to those irreducible differences that distinguish each affair from all others and so mark each off as *an* experience.

As parts of what constitutes a thing, experienced or felt qualities are qualities *of* natural events; for they are engendered by interactive relationships in which both extraorganic and organic agencies partake. This means that the relations in which something participates are

---

61. See ibid., p. 110: "Temporal quality is however not to be confused with temporal order. Quality is quality, direct, immediate and undefinable. Order is a matter of relation, of definition, dating, placing and describing. It is discovered in reflection, not directly had and denoted as is temporal quality."
62. Ibid., p. 87.

part of what makes it the qualified thing it is and not something else. To acknowledge that is, in turn, to suggest that our verbal copula "is" is the linguistic vehicle through which we "make a qualitative whole which is directly and nonreflectively experienced into an object of thought for the sake of its own development. The 'copula' stands for the fact that one term is predicated of the other, and is thus a sign of the development of the qualitative whole by means of their distinction. The logical force of the copula is always that of an active verb. It is merely a linguistic peculiarity, not a logical fact, that we say 'that is red' instead of 'that reddens,' either in the sense of growing, becoming, red, or in the sense of making something else red. Even linguistically our 'is' is a weakened form of an active verb signifying 'stays' or 'stands.'"[63]

The dilemmas apparently posed by the logic of predication therefore represent so much epistemological debris stemming from our supposition that its terms and their connections can be rendered meaningful apart from the relations of implication present within lived experience. They are the unfortunate fruit of our failure to recall that the more complex forms of experience that mark human life, including the linguistic, incorporate the relations characteristic of the simpler and so cannot be understood in isolation from them. Nature achieves more complete realization when its qualitative issues are taken up within human experience; and that is possible not because a "spiritual" element is thereby added to something otherwise lacking, but because experience constitutes a more complex revelation of nature's otherwise implicit potentialities.

To think of nature in this way is, by extension, to reject epistemology's recapitulation of the traditional conviction that to be and to be known are one and the same thing. Nature's emergents, drawn up and reshaped as experience's pragmata, are epistemically opaque in the sense that our immediate *having* of their qualities is never captured in, or equivalent to, our knowledge or discourse *about* them. Yet being and having things in ways other than the cognitive are the ontological prerequisites of the very possibility of knowing. "Without immediate qualities those relations with which science deals, would have no footing in existence and thought would have nothing beyond itself to chew upon or dig into. Without a basis in qualitative events, the

63. Dewey, "Qualitative Thought," in *ENF*, pp. 188–89.

characteristic subject-matter of knowledge would be algebraic ghosts, relations that do not relate."[64]

To grasp the point here, consider the difference between quenching one's thirst and inquiring into the molecular composition of water, between enjoying a conversation and researching the psychological makeup of its participants, between enjoying a painting and determining the compositional elements that account for its aesthetic power. As the first member of each of these pairings suggests, what I am now calling "primary" experience is immediate not in the sense that it stands outside all mediation, but rather in the sense that its character can only be inferred. Accordingly, as soon as such experience is rendered a discursive object, its defining characteristic disappears; for the more pragmata are simply "had" within experience, the more they are absorbed within the ongoing practices of acting agents, and so absent from the deliberate attention reflection entails. "Immediacy of existence is ineffable. But there is nothing mystical about such ineffability; it expresses the fact that of direct existence it is futile to say anything to one's self and impossible to say anything to another. Discourse can but intimate connections which if followed out may lead one to *have* an existence. Things in their immediacy are unknown and unknowable, not because they are remote or behind some impenetrable veil of sensation of ideas, but because knowledge has no concern with them."[65]

To acknowledge that the conduct of knowing is grounded in something more fundamental than itself is to render impossible the epistemological characterization of human beings as isolated subjects whose ideas bear meaning only to the extent that their perceptual representations, their ideas, accurately correspond to an independent realm of epistemic objects. This construction fails because it assumes that experience is composed of objects that are as clearly discriminated as are the objects of thinking. "We are accustomed to think of physical objects as having bounded edges; things like rocks, chairs, books, houses, trade, and science, with its efforts at precise measurement, have confirmed the belief. Then we unconsciously carry over this belief in the bounded character of all *objects* of experience (a belief founded ultimately in the practical exigencies of our dealings with

64. Dewey, *EN*, p. 86.
65. Ibid., pp. 85–86.

things) into our conception of experience itself. We suppose experience has the same definite limits as the things with which it is concerned."[66] But if experience involves a relationship of mutual inherence between actor and world, then the qualitative dimensions of experience belong neither to the experiencing self nor to the object experienced but rather are engendered through experience's situatedness in nature. Hence we need not, and should not, ask how much of our web of belief reflects the world in itself, and how much is our conceptual contribution; for that Kantian question presupposes the very dualism between subject and object that is rejected by this more inclusive notion of experience. Whatever meaning experience is capable of sustaining is generated *within* the medium established by the dialectical movement from interconnected existences to the disclosure of those relations within experience, and finally to the articulation of these involvements in discursive formations.

Consider also the implications of this departure from the epistemological formulation of experience for our thinking about thinking. The account advanced here can make use of Galileo's metaphor of nature as a text,[67] but it must shed the conviction that that text permits only a single correct interpretation. Absent this conviction, thinking might be analogically construed as a sort of reading that grasps the meanings nature intimates as possibilities when one of the more complex manifestations of its transactions, experience, reaches into its ambiguous depths. If nature is *what* is experienced, and if experience is *how* these things are brought into the world when mediated by human organisms, then thinking is a way of disclosing, making manifest, articulating the inferences immanent within experience. So construed, thinking "is not a distortion or perversion which confers upon *its* subject-matter traits which *do* not belong to it, but is an act which confers upon non-cognitive material traits which *did* not belong to it. It marks a change by which physical events exhibiting properties of mechanical energy, connected by relations of push and pull, hitting, rebounding,

---

66. Dewey, *AE*, p. 193.
67. See Galileo, quoted in R. G. Collingwood, *The Idea of Nature* (New York: Oxford University Press, 1960), p. 102: "Philosophy is written in that vast book which stands ever open before our eyes, I mean the universe; but it cannot be read until we have learnt the language and become familiar with the characters in which it is written. It is written in mathematical language, and the letters are triangles, circles and other geometrical figures, without which means it is humanly impossible to comprehend a single word."

splitting and consolidating, realize characters, meanings and relations of meanings *hitherto* not possessed by them."[68]

This, it should be stressed, does not mean that thinking is the medium within which the subject becomes self-consciously present to itself, or through which nature becomes transparent to mind. To engage in thinking is to participate in the activity through which some things, issues, and affairs become apparent within experience, while others recede. The term "appearance," consequently, does not refer, as it did in classical and medieval philosophy, to a realm of being infected with the defect of non-Being. Nor does it refer, as it does in modern epistemology, to the ontological gulf between things as they really are and things as they seem to be, where "seeming" designates what exists only in virtue of the subject's distortion of the single kind of Being that remains when the ancients' graded cosmos is denied its sense. Neither of these two understandings can acknowledge that things appear and disappear only because temporality, altering the relations among nature's interwoven affairs, presses experience past what would otherwise be contemplation's blank stare. The term "appearance," accordingly, denotes the fact that at any given moment in time some matters are showing and hence conspicuous, while others are latent and hence withdrawn. Its antonym is not reality but disappearance.

If the character of appearance in its primary sense is best suggested by a term like "conspicuousness," then thinking brings into play a second sense of this term, one better intimated by terms like "display" and "revelation." These latter terms, implying something more than the merely manifest character of the matter in question, call explicit attention to the connection sustained between an appearance and the encompassing temporally qualified whole within which it is located. To explicate the web of connections constituting that context is to transform an initial presentation into a re-presentation. So construed, the term "representation" refers not to an idea that reflects reality, but rather to the rendering intelligible of an apparent thing by locating it within a larger situation from which it elicits its sense. As a member, that thing is able to point to its status as part(icipant) within this more comprehensive web of circumstances only because thinking is able to

68. Dewey, *EN*, p. 381.

distinguish between it in its primary qualities, as these are had in experience, and it in its office as sign pointing beyond itself. Through thinking's intervention within the richly textured world of immediate experience, there arise representations that, like peaks emerging from the water in which glaciers are mostly submerged, assume the character of signs relating things that are immediately had by means not so immediately apparent.

Therefore, to call attention to error is to say that it is not at present possible to unproblematically refer a thing to a whole from which it might derive its intelligibility. When the issue of error arises, the question at stake is not which of several competing ideas corresponds accurately to a "real" object, but rather whether the present fit between a thing and its context, the inclusive but bounded relations it sustains to other things, succeeds in overcoming its partial character, its relative disappearance from the manifest world. The validity of employing one thing as a sign of an inferred other turns not on its connection to the knower, but rather on the specific relations it sustains to other things. As long as that issue remains unresolved, we can only speak of its "apparent" significance. When that question is closed, what was once only "apparently" so discloses and affirms its reality as a participant within some more extensive whole.

If this construction of the relationship between thinking and experience is adequate, then it follows that "as actual existence all 'appearances' stand on the same level; the real *esse* of things is neither their *percipi*, nor their *intelligi* alone; it is their *experiri*."[69] When Protagoras proclaimed "Man is the measure of all *things*," he intimated that when nature's affairs are taken up and shaped as the things of an experienced world, of necessity they assume one form as opposed to another. Accordingly, the things that constitute the circumstances in which we are presently situated, our pragmata, are what they are experienced as. "Existences *are* immediately given in experience; that is what experience primarily *is*. They are not given *to* experience but their giveness *is* experience."[70] To grant this is not to deny that as signs pointing toward a more inclusive whole some experienced things are better than others; one witness in a court of law may offer testimony that proves more satisfactory as evidence than that advanced by an-

69. Dewey, "Appearing and Appearance," in *PC*, p. 73; "Psychology as Philosophic Method," in *EW*, vol. 1, p. 151.

70. Dewey, *LTI*, p. 522.

other, even though their respective assertions are equally actual as empirical occurrences. Contra epistemology, however, this is to deny that reality is just what it would be to an all-competent all-knower were that knower to escape the limitations imposed by embodied subjectivity. For the world's pragmata can never be comprehensively, transparently, or finally known. As the relations sustained among nature's events are drawn up within the shifting parameters of contextualized experience, they make possible an indefinite plethora of meanings. Because what is really "in" experience extends much farther than what at any time is known, the same existential events are capable of an undelimitable wealth of meanings. Every thing resident in primary experience is charged with implicit potentialities that, until explicated through association with other things, limit the range of its meanings to those now had.

To acknowledge that one of the defining features of experience is its pluridimensional ambiguity is to grant that there exist a multiplicity of possible worlds, ways of fashioning the pragmata given by nature and in experience. This is not to suggest that experience plunges us into a Lockean miscellany of discrete sense impressions from which we can escape only through the arbitrary imposition of determinate concepts. For pragmata are pointed to in kinds. As our everyday use of adjectives implies, the issues of experience can be political, moral, economic, religious, esthetic, and more. In each case, the qualifying term calls attention to the characteristic way in which a contextualized affair presents itself qua experience. Each thing is what it is in virtue of the distinguishing traits and capacities, hues and tempos, called into being when organic and inorganic agencies relate to each other in this particular way as opposed to some other.

That the world now expresses the history of experience's differentiation into kinds poses no specifically epistemological dilemma for a radical empiricism of the sort advanced here. Unlike Locke's more timid rendition, this empiricism insists that all adjectivally qualified modes of experiencing represent ways in which some possibilities latent in nature have come to manifest realization. Hence it cannot privilege any one as exclusively ultimate or real. "If it is a horse that is to be described, or the equus that is to be defined, then must the horsetrader, or the jockey, or the timid family man who wants a 'safe driver,' or the zoologist or the paleontologist tell us what the horse is which is experienced. If these accounts turn out different in some respects, as well as congruous in others, there is no reason for assuming the content of one to be exclusively 'real,' and that of the others to be 'phenomenal'; for each account of what is experienced will manifest that it is the account *of* the horse-dealer, or *of* the zoologist, and hence will give the conditions requisite for understanding the differences as well as the agreements of the various accounts."[71]

Therefore, to advance the epistemological claim that modern science is peculiarly entitled to disclose or express the inner nature of things is to presuppose that reality is knowable apart from our experience of it. That, in turn, is to set in motion the quest for a method that will conclusively specify the determinate criteria that disqualify competing shapings of that which is.[72] If the argument presented here has merit, however, then our epistemic hold on the world cannot be anchored by either sense data, objects whose essence is to be perceived and in whose constitution thinking plays no part, or by "ideas," that is, "mental states" that represent consciousness's uncorrupted givens. To believe otherwise, whether tacitly or expressly, is to believe that we can gain access to a fixed external reality whose content, when compared with our ideas, can be employed to determine the latter's truth or falsity. And that, in turn, is to reaffirm the philosophic tradition's denigration of conventional belief as *doxa*, as the best that can be achieved by those who remain entrapped within the merely finite phenomenal world.

This last point can be put in a slightly different way. Let us assume that the history of human experience is a history of *technai's* gradual differentiation. On this assumption, modern science's emergence as a distinct mode of experience distinguishes but does not radically separate it from other modes, whether religious, political, or poetic. All of these ways of shaping experience, on the reading advanced here, "finally have the same *material*; that which is constituted by the interaction of the live creature with his surroundings. They differ in the media by which they convey and express this material, not in the material itself. Each one transforms some phase of the raw material of experience into new objects according to the purpose, each purpose demands a particular medium for its execution."[73]

Therefore, the various logical and technical instrumentalities of thinking we misleadingly gather together beneath the reifying rubric of "science" constitute but one of the many different ways of gathering

71. Dewey, "The Postulate of Immediate Empiricism," in *IDP*, p. 227.

72. See Michael Oakeshott in his *Experience and Its Modes* (Cambridge: Cambridge University Press, 1985), pp. 195–96, for a very nice statement of this point.

73. Dewey, *AE*, pp. 319–20.

and refashioning nature's offerings. As such, science can be grasped truly only when divested of its epistemological representation as a self-justifying agency whose unconditional stranglehold on truth renders its discourse autonomous from or superior to all others. For moral, political, and economic experiences, as well as the forms of thinking appropriate to each, reveal the traits of real things as truly as does the strictly scientific. Granted, like any other way of thinking things in relation to one another, science has recourse to its own peculiar form of abstraction from prereflective experience. But its abrogation of experience's qualitative dimensions, as when the physicist insists that the law of gravitation refers not to the behavior of common-sense objects but rather to the movement of homogeneous masses, does no more than reveal certain of the recurrent conditions under which individualities present themselves. To insist that the traits distinctive to this particular mode of thinking be universalized (for example, by insisting that the vocabulary of the physicist constitutes the only standard for estimating the "reality" of all other things) is to take the legitimate belief that the world can be grasped mathematically for certain purposes, and then to require that necessarily partial vocabulary to affirm its status as the exclusive principle of all cognition. But that is to move all too quickly from a recognition that the conduct of scientific inquiry intimates the suspect character of a philosophical tradition that categorically denies conduct's role in constituting knowledge to an insistence that the essence of knowing is identical in all experiential domains. To do that, in turn, is to ensure that thinking's conduct must either ignore, eliminate, or conquer the distinctive traits of individualized things appearing in contexts other than the scientific. In sum, the epistemological denial of epistemic pluralism reveals little about the meaning of science, but much about the pervasiveness of our desire to discover yet another guarantor of Being's unity.

VI

To note the rootedness of thinking within noncognitive experience to which it can secure only one-sided access is to be reminded that products of even the most refined forms of thought are secondary and derivative. The various arts of skilled mediation we call thinking can never be wholly independent of the nonpropositional dimensions of embodied experience. We can abstract from this experiential basis, and so in time it may come to appear that we are dealing with a priori structures of pure reason. But in fact these remote structures remain intelligible only because they have been elicited from the web of sense that *is* our being in and having of a world. Just as the meaning of language used in a particular situation is comprehensible only through reference to the larger context of ongoing practices within which it is embedded,[74] so too each occasion of thinking an affair secures its meaningfulness only through reference to that unknown experience from which its inferences originally emerged and to which its abstractions must ultimately return.

Thinking, to return to the close of Chapter 2, is a kind of poetic (in the sense of *poēisis*) experience that, at its best, participates in eliciting significantly shaped pragmata from nature's events. Although there are dangers in saying so, it is not altogether misleading to state that nature's telos is achieved and exhibited in (as opposed to apart from) thinking. For we live in a distinctively human way when the "brute" interpenetrations and termini of nature, fashioned into interwoven meanings, secure the quality of sensed significance. Thinking is correctly deemed "instrumental" only when its fruits are carried back and replanted within a mode of experience other than the reflective. Its end rests not in itself, but in its capacity to deepen and expand appreciation of the interconnections that fuse within the passing moments of lived immediacy. "Just what role do the objects attained in reflection play? Where do they come in? They *explain* the primary objects, they enable us to grasp them with *understanding*, instead of just having sense contact with them. But how? Well, they define or lay out a path by which return to experienced things is of such a sort that the meaning, the significant content, of what is experienced gains an enriched and expanded force because of the path by which it was reached."[75] How thinking might begin to mark out paths pointing toward a democratic rehabilitation of specifically political experience is the issue of the next three chapters.

74. In "Syllabus: Types of Philosophic Thought," in *MW*, vol. 13, Dewey uses the analogy of language to clarify his contextualist commitments: "All communication is through words and requires the supremacy of certain language standards; but the meaning of the words and of the linguistic standards can be adequately understood and tested only by resort to prior and subsequent (directly non-linguistic) situations. You can direct me to a certain place, and tell me what I will find there in language; but my going and finding, although so dependent upon language that it would not have occurred without it, is something other than language and necessary to define and test the meaning of the language used" (p. 355).
75. Dewey, *EN*, p. 5.

4 /
Liberalism and the Community of Facts

I

The presence of the past in the present means that any questioning of the quality of today's experience is at one and the same time an inquiry into that of yesterday. Such inquiry has been made an explicit object of reflective attention in the previous two chapters. Like the products of all thinking, the tale I have told cannot begin to exhaust the tangled webs of richly qualified experience about which it speaks. As a one-sided abstraction from what must be had before it can be known, its account of the emergence and history of teleocratic reason is of necessity unequal to the material from which my narrative has been wrought. Indeed, the very phrase "teleocratic reason" is merely a shorthand way of pointing to a thread of continuity that, to use an equally problematic reification, marks off what is conventionally called the "Western philosophical tradition." Whether that tale is adequate to its matter cannot be determined by laying it next to the "facts" in order to see whether it does or does not correspond; for any account of those facts must itself be crafted from the same materials as is my tale. Its adequacy can only be determined by exploring its capacity to elicit sense from the situation in which we presently find ourselves.

Although originally rooted in analogical extrapolation of metaphors suggested by craft's skilled conduct, teleocratic reason no longer acknowledges its prosaic ground. In fact, to sustain its claim to self-sufficient authority over the world of qualified experience, it cannot do so. Moreover, to the extent that teleocratic reason secures institutional embodiment and so succeeds in remaking the world in its own image, it slowly erodes the capacity to appreciate the partiality of its claim to universality. Hence at one and the same time it becomes ever more difficult and increasingly important to secure some critical distance from a conception of reason whose logic requires that the materials of cultural life be systematically subjected to its abstracted imperatives.

Teleocratic reason's capacity to fulfill its utopia of a completely rationalized world is frustrated by tensions present within its historically rooted self-understanding; it is in the space created by those tensions that criticism is possible. The characteristic forms presently assumed by that self-understanding, which are most readily apparent in conventional representations of modern science, draw their sense from an uneasy amalgam of classical and epistemological sources. As we have seen, the conduct of early modern science intimated the untenability of cosmotheological doctrines that, whether explicitly or implicitly, proclaimed that the world was somehow designed with the needs and aspirations of human reason in mind. Believing, however, that the method of science must furnish an alternative but equally powerful response to the questions that cosmotheological doctrine could no longer answer, seventeenth-century epistemology tried to assimilate its conduct to the presuppositional legacy supplied by that doctrine. This, as we saw, is apparent in epistemology's effort to furnish the practice of knowing with undeniable foundations, in its perpetuation of the ocular metaphors accounting for the construction of knowing as a kind of contemplative envisagement, in its failure to acknowledge the distinction between primary experience and thinking about the conditions on which such experience depends, and so on. So interpreted, the delegitimating promise of science was deflected and, in time, deployed in defense of inegalitarian institutional forms that might otherwise have come to appear increasingly suspect.

The political theory of liberalism offers an unusually fertile field for examination of the tensions present within the dense legacy we now call "reason." In Chapters 4, 5, and 6, which focus on the work of Émile Durkheim, Jürgen Habermas, and American policy science, I do not pretend to offer an exhaustive history of that tradition. Rather, I seek to show (a) how the presuppositions of teleocratic reason re-emerge in the thinking of liberals whom I would label "uneasy" in virtue of their common desire to counter liberal society's apparent thrust toward self-dissolution; and (b) to indicate in a preliminary way how the questions asked by Durkheim, Habermas, and American policy science might be reformulated and answered were we more completely to shed inherited assumptions about the relationship be-tween the claims of experience and those of reason. Since Durkheim, Habermas, and American policy science all employ pragmatism either as a source of inspiration or as a foil against which to develop their own views, I contest their readings at the same time that I offer an alternative; but that, it should be remembered, is incidental to my larger purpose.

II

Throughout its brief history, the theorists of liberalism have found it difficult to show why those who inhabit liberal orders should occasion-ally sacrifice their immediate welfare for the sake of a common good. This dilemma, although apparent to a greater or lesser extent in all schools of liberalism, is most pressing in that which presupposes a utilitarian psychology. Given the notion that each can know his or her own good only through private inspection of subjective preferences and their relative intensities, utilitarian liberalism has repeatedly fal-tered because its subjects cannot be regarded as *members* whose identi-ties are partly constituted by their birth into established communities entitled to their allegiance even in the absence of voluntary declara-tions of commitment.[1] This dilemma, however, is not confined to this particular branch of liberalism; it simply assumes a different cast, for example, in that which has recourse to the device of a social contract. Tangential bonds may be created when antecedently individuated agents contract with one another so as to better secure their egoistic aims; but these ties can never implicate their makers in enterprises whose claims exceed the sum of their separate wills. Thus the hollow-

---

1. On this point, see Michael Sandel, *Liberalism and the Limits of Justice* (New York: Cambridge University Press, 1982), passim.

ness of the liberal state's appeal to patriotism during times of war is merely the most extreme manifestation of a chronic dilemma within a doctrine that presumes the primacy of self-regarding desires.[2]

What is the relationship between this dilemma and the infatuation with scientific rationality that has marked so much liberal political theory? One familiar answer suggests that their affinity is a function of the analogy between science's method and liberalism's constitutionalism.[3] Participation within the scientific community and the liberal polity are formally identical in that neither presupposes the prior existence of universal consensus on points of substantive dogma. Both demand only that all agree to accept as authoritative whatever results are generated by the use of specified procedural mechanisms. The impersonal rules of constitutional politics regulate the competition between private interests and so produce legitimate policy, just as the impartial rules of scientific method adjudicate between competing hypotheses and so produce true knowledge. Liberalism and modern science thus conspire to create the conditions necessary for each other's existence. Liberalism induces the regularization of political conduct by eliciting habitual adherence to specified formal legal norms, while modern science uncovers lawlike generalizations that express the order thus fashioned.

This explanation is deficient because it accepts at face value the contention that liberalism neither requires nor solicits adherence to a shared vision of the social world. Granted, liberalism's affirmation of individual autonomy has rendered unavailable to it many more traditional sources of unity. The demands of consistency have left it unable to oppose the centripetal forces that its own conception of freedom encourages by advocating, for example, censorship, state-supported religion, or the suppression of political opposition. But acceptance of these strictures has proven compatible with the conviction that liberal-

2. To see this point, consider first John Locke, who in his *Two Treatises on Government* (New York: New American Library, 1960) claims that "neither the Serjeant, that could command a Souldier to march up to the mouth of a Cannon, or stand in a Breach, where he is almost sure to perish, can command that Souldier to give him one penny of his money; nor the General, that can condemn him to death for deserting his post, or for not obeying the most desperate orders, can yet with all his absolute Power of Life and Death, dispense of one Farthing of that Souldier's estate" (pp. 407–8). Then consider Rousseau's response in his *Emile* (New York: Dutton, 1911): "Self-interest, so they say, induces each of us to agree for the common good. But how is it that the good man consents to this to his own hurt? Does a man go to death from self-interest?" (p. 252).

3. For the most familiar example of this argument, see Sheldon Wolin, *Politics and Vision* (Boston: Little, Brown, 1960), pp. 388–93.

ism's subjectivist proclivities can be tempered if all can be induced to apprehend in common the facts disclosed by scientific analysis. That is, in its quest to discover a minimalist surrogate for the unifying power once exercised by classical and medieval conceptions of reason, liberalism has turned not so much to the authority of method per se, but rather to the determinate objects produced by science's procedures.

This turn to science's facts is intimated in those works that first disclose the specifically political bearing of the epistemological tradition initiated by Descartes and Locke. Although his authoritarian political commitments are clearly not those of a liberal, Thomas Hobbes nonetheless advances accounts of human nature, language, and society which inform the emerging discourse of liberalism for decades to come. In his *Elements of Law*, Hobbes explains that words are arbitrary creations that, as marks, remind an individual of past conceptions and, as signs, communicate these conceptions to others. Because of the diversity of bodily constitutions and the power of egoistic passions, however, the terms of ordinary language are necessarily of "inconstant signification."[4] It thus becomes unclear how persons can ever be certain of understanding one another. How can those who "take up maxims from their education, and from the authority of men, or of custom, and take the habitual discourse of the tongue for ratiocination" be assured that the names they employ to signify their particular ideas call to mind the same conceptions in others?[5] Accordingly, Hobbes concludes, the Sovereign can know that promulgated law is grasped clearly and distinctly by subjects only when its representational terms designate identical referents for those whose minds "are like clean paper, fit to receive whatsoever by public authority shall be imprinted in them."[6]

The third book of Locke's *Essay concerning Human Understanding* reworks certain of Hobbes's claims via a more refined articulation of the scientifically cleansed language that is to stand as "the great instrument, and common tye of society." Like Hobbes, Locke holds that speech renders perceptible the discrete ideas of distinct persons by

---

4. Thomas Hobbes, *Leviathan* (New York: Collier, 1962), p. 40.

5. Thomas Hobbes, *The Elements of Law Natural and Politic* (London: Frank Cass, 1969), p. 36. Cf. p. 25: The reformation of vulgar speech insures the "concomitance of a man's conception with the words that signify such conception in the act of ratiocination."

6. Hobbes, *Leviathan*, p. 249.

according them sensible form. Self-sufficient and complete meanings, originating in the private mind, are made public via words that, as "Signs of internal Conceptions," designate our apprehension of these antecedently existent objects. Because, however, the "confused Notions and Prejudices" we have "imbibed from Custom, Inadvertency, and common Conversation" invariably intermix with and so confound our efforts to speak sense to one another, the possibility of mutual intelligibility presupposes invention of an analytic method that secures a uniform correspondence between words and mental entities. Resolving the former into those "clear and distinct" ideas "out of which they are compounded," this method's application ensures that terms "become general by being made the signs of general ideas: and ideas become general by separating from them the circumstances of time and place, and any other ideas that may determine them to this or that particular existence." The abstract character of a language comprising such terms guarantees that discourse produces identical echoes in separated intellects and so generates meanings that are peculiarly common; for "*Men* who abstract their thoughts, and do well examine the Ideas of their own Minds, *cannot much differ in thinking.*" The communication of decontextualized words, in turn, establishes the possibility that specifically political conflict may be reasonably resolved. "*Justice* is a Word in every Man's Mouth, but most commonly with a very undetermined loose signification: Which will always be so, unless a Man has in his Mind a distinct comprehension of the component parts, that complex Idea consists of. . . . Till this be done, it must not be wondred, that they have a great deal of Obscurity and Confusion in their own Minds, and a great deal of wrangling in their Discourse with others." In sum, since "nobody" by nature possesses the "authority to establish the precise signification of words, nor determine to what Ideas any one shall annex them,"[7] the coherence of political practice demands a science whose excision of the ambiguous accretions that words acquire in concrete use protects liberalism from the consequences of its own inability to articulate the grounds of loyalty to the shared goods of an inclusive community.

Prior to the late nineteenth century,[8] it was not clear just how much

7. John Locke, *An Essay concerning Human Understanding,* ed. Peter Nidditch (Oxford: Clarendon Press, 1975), pp. 180–81, 402, 410–11, 479, 513.
8. For an eighteenth-century statement of liberalism's commitment to a scientifically purified language of politics, see Antoine-Nicolas de Condorcet, *Sketch for a Historical Picture of the Progress of the Human Mind,* trans. Jane Barraclough (London: Weidenfeld

weight had to be borne by this solution to liberalism's most fundamental dilemma. If only to a limited degree, the endurance of traditional foundations of commonality such as the extended family, the guild, the church, and the local community taught selves whose most elemental pursuits were ever more acquisitive to temper the pursuit of private advantage in the service of shared ends. Liberal practice, as the unintended recipient of the benefits wrought by this education in the virtues of dedication, loyalty, self-denial, and the like, went more or less unchallenged in its illusion that silence regarding the normative foundations of its own politics indicated the sufficiency of its formalistic proceduralism. But as the dislocating power of the free market enfeebled these parochial loci of customary bonds, as the secularizing impact of rapid industrial advance dissolved these familiar sources of received wisdom, it became increasingly unclear how one might disprove the truth of Hobbes's representation of the liberal state as a tenuous achievement whose relapse into the state of war is forestalled only by the ubiquity of fear.[9] As theoretical assertions regarding the utilitarian nature of all action and the contractual nature of all relationships became a more accurate description of liberal practice, it became imperative to ask once more whether its egos might hold in common anything other than the motive of self-aggrandizement.

The founding of modern social science in Europe at the turn of the twentieth century renews the attempt to forestall liberalism's slip into anarchic solipsism. That attempt takes shape as an effort to inject into its practice, via political education in the facts of science, a reason that will do the unifying work that cannot be done when cognition, following Hobbes, is defined as a mere instrument of unrationalized desire. Modern social science's creation reaffirms the hope that purification and stabilization of language subject to debasement in less refined contexts of discourse might substitute for the solidaristic bonds that liberal epistemology cannot otherwise sustain. Furnishing political

---

and Nicolson, 1955): "A universal language is that which expresses by signs either real objects themselves, or well-defined collections composed of simple and general ideas, which are found to be the same or may arise in a similar form in the minds of all men, or the general relations holding between these ideas, the operations of the human mind, or the operations peculiar to the individual sciences, or the procedures of the arts. So people who become acquainted with these signs, the ways to combine them and the rules for forming them will understand what is written in this language and will be able to read it as easily as their own language" (pp. 197–98).

9. For a parallel argument, see Fred Hirsch, *The Social Limits to Growth* (Cambridge: Harvard University Press, 1976).

expression to modernity's identification of objectivity with achievement of the standpoint assumed by an abstracted spectator who confronts an independent aggregation of precisely perceived objects, these sciences secure the certainty of the only public world liberalism can know.

III

This broad argument can be illustrated through a consideration of France's most noteworthy contributor to the liberal sciences of society. As he makes abundantly clear in his famous statement on the Dreyfus Affair,[10] Émile Durkheim's identification with liberal individualism, as well as the freedoms necessary to its accomplishment, is deep and abiding. Considered comprehensively, his various political writings are best understood, to quote Anthony Giddens, as so many efforts to think through the conditions of a "revitalized liberal republicanism which would fully realize the structural changes in society which had been promised but not achieved by the Revolution."[11] Yet this aspiration is qualified by Durkheim's gnawing fear that liberalism may prove unable to muster the resources necessary to keep its egoism in check. Accordingly, he seeks to furnish liberal society with a reason whose knowledge will secure the common ground upon which the play of individual desires and opinions can safely proceed. As I suggest below, however, because his account of that reason is so thoroughly shaped by the presuppositions of teleocratic rationalism, it cannot help but turn on and finally defeat the forms of individualism Durkheim is so eager to nurture.

Durkheim's understanding of liberalism's turn-of-the-century dilemma derives from his more global account of the decay of what he calls mechanical forms of solidarity. Within primitive social orders, Durkheim argues in the *Division of Labor in Society* (1895), the appetitive

---

10. Émile Durkheim, "Individualism and the Intellectuals," in *Émile Durkheim: On Morality and Society*, ed. Robert Bellah (Chicago: University of Chicago Press, 1973), pp. 43–57.
11. Anthony Giddens, "Durkheim's Political Sociology," *Sociological Review* 19 (1971), 513. I do not argue the point here, but it should be clear that I reject the representation of Durkheim as a reactionary who, appalled by the excesses of the Revolution, hoped to restore to France the sort of unity that allegedly characterized the medieval world. This caricature, made popular primarily by Robert Nisbet's *Émile Durkheim* (Englewood Cliffs, N.J.: Prentice-Hall, 1965), is at last fading from the interpretive scene.

ego is checked by the imperatives of small, isolated, and self-sufficient communities: "This particular structure enables society to hold the individual more tightly in its grip, making him more strongly attached to his domestic environment, and consequently to tradition."[12] Submerged in a social order whose essential features appear unalterable because given in the nature of things, the self regards itself first and foremost as a member whose identity is inseparable from the larger whole by which it is bound. Hence it has neither the opportunity nor the inclination to affirm its independence.

With expansion of the division of labor, however, such solidaristic consciousness becomes vaguer, and its power to navigate the individual toward collective ends grows more feeble. In the *Division of Labor*, Durkheim argues that the dissolution of mechanical solidarity and its homogeneous collective conconsciousness does not signify the imminent collapse of society into anarchy. With every increase in the complexity of the division of labor, there emerge new bonds of interdependence that, although often unacknowledged by those so joined, nonetheless display even greater resilience and unifying power than that peculiar to less differentiated societies. Hence Durkheim argues for the introduction of various institutional forms, most notably the occupational association, which will educate persons to a conscious apprehension of the intricate web of organic dependencies within which they are now enmeshed.

I do not mean to deny the adequacy of this familiar reading of Durkheim's *Division of Labor*. But I do argue that if one is to understand the specifically political dimension of the science Durkheim founds, one must attend to his account of the "abnormal forms" of organic solidarity. Throughout his life, Durkheim never quite rids himself of the nagging suspicion that these "abnormalities," manifest in the spread of anomie and the recurrence of class conflict, may signify the truth about modernity and hence the vanity of his appeal to organic solidarity. It is this anxiety, growing more pressing in his later years, that drives and informs the various shifts in his account of the logic of social science.

How does Durkheim explain the emergence of the abnormality that is the Hobbesian monad? As the individual ego is delivered from the womb of the traditional community, the pursuit of appetite, released

---

12. Émile Durkheim, *The Division of Labor in Society*, trans. W. D. Halls (New York: Free Press, 1984), p. 242.

from its former constraints, sets in motion a dynamic that, if left unchecked, culminates in what Durkheim calls the "malady of infinite aspiration."[13] Its symptoms are most dramatically disclosed by statistics demonstrating a linear relationship between the disintegration of cohesive communities and the frequency of suicide. But such self-destructiveness is merely a microcosmic expression of the larger crisis that afflicts any order that confuses the claims of individualism with those of self-interest, narrowly construed. There the supremacy of the utilitarian and the subordination of the moral conspire to create a society composed of self-aggrandizing individuals who, as slaves of petty desires that cannot be quenched, hope to live in a world of immediate gratification but find themselves doomed to perpetual frustration: "The more one has, the more one wants, since satisfactions received only stimulate instead of filling needs."[14] As these unbound creatures "tumble over one another like so many liquid molecules, encountering no central energy to retain, fix, and organize them,"[15] their order dissolves into a frenzied tangle of opposed opinions, each affirming the exclusive truth of its special fancy.

The disarray into which persons are thus thrust is sustained and aggravated by the meanings that constitute untutored common sense. This familiar way of "knowing" evolves out of regular intercourse among agents in their interaction with the affairs of ordinary experience. Bound together within the unsystematic miscellany that is unrefined speech, this body of uncriticized meaning is peculiarly "pragmatic," as Durkheim explains, because it expresses and organizes a given collectivity's appreciation of "what is useful or disadvantageous" about particular things and in what ways they "can render us service or disservice."[16] Yet because this body of meaning is so grounded in the shifting imperatives of daily practice, its terms are only as accurate as they need be to facilitate the performance of specific tasks: "For an idea to stimulate the reaction that the nature of a thing demands, it need not faithfully express that nature."[17] Still more problematic, precisely because common sense is so useful from the stand-

13. Émile Durkheim, *Moral Education*, trans. Everett Wilson and Herman Schnurer (New York: Free Press, 1961), p. 40.
14. Émile Durkheim, *Suicide*, trans. John Spaulding and George Simpson (New York: Free Press, 1951), pp. 247–48.
15. Ibid., p. 389.
16. Émile Durkheim, *The Rules of Sociological Method*, trans. W. D. Halls (New York: Free Press, 1982), p. 61.
17. Ibid., p. 61.

point of everyday life, its promptings cannot help but exert considerable power over its subjects. Woven into the very fabric of collective life and hence confused with the true data of experience, its authoritative meanings act as a "veil" that deludes us "even more effectively because we believe" it "to be more transparent"; its tissue of illusion, "interposed between the things and ourselves,"[18] comes to constitute the intelligible world for those who cannot penetrate its appearance of reality.

The common sense that is borne within and by the French language, Durkheim continues, is especially troublesome because the Cartesian structure of its grammar renders its speakers loathe to ascribe existence to anything that cannot be perceived clearly and distinctly.[19] The vernacular of contemporary France thus denies the truth of that unseen organic interdependence that now stays the wholesale decomposition of society into its atomic bits. Confirming liberalism's depiction of human order as "a huge constellation in which each star moves in its orbit without disturbing the motion of neighbouring stars," this "oversimplified rationalism" cannot help but intimate that the purpose of politics is merely to safeguard rights whose "function is not to link together the different parts of society, but on the contrary to detach them from one another, and mark out clearly the barriers separating them."[20] Even more perniciously, its endorsement of social contract theory's representation of human collectivity as "an artifact, a machine wholly constructed by the hands of men," invites the translation of liberalism's "limitless ambitions" into insatiable "revolutionary fancies."[21] As an idealism whose "ghost-like" meanings have become detached from their ground in reality, the deliverances of common sense incite "the mind, feeling completely unchecked," to imagine it possible to "construct—or rather reconstruct—the world through its own power and according to its wishes."[22]

18. Ibid., p. 60.
19. See Durkheim, *Moral Education*, p. 253: "Our language itself is not suited to translate the obscure superstructure of things that we may glimpse but do not understand. Precisely because our language is analytical it expresses well only those things that are analyzed—in other words, reduced to their elements. . . . The ideal thing for it would be to have one single word for each indivisible part of reality, and to express the totality formed by everything through a simple mechanical combination of these elementary notions."
20. Durkheim, *Division of Labor*, pp. 73, 75; *Moral Education*, p. 251.
21. Durkheim, *Rules*, p. 142; Émile Durkheim, *The Elementary Forms of the Religious Life*, trans. Joseph Swain (New York: Free Press, 1965), p. 30.
22. Durkheim, *Rules*, pp. 142, 60, 62.

How, Durkheim therefore asks, might these liberal agents be persuaded that contractarianism's myth of order's origins is merely a
"skilfull device" concealing the nonconventional source of "the snares
into which they have stumbled?" How might they, coming to "discern
more clearly the causes, of a different order of complexity, which
inspire the measures taken by the collectivity,"[23] realize the dangerous
foolishness of the Hobbesian account of liberty as the absence of
external impediments to motion? How, in sum, might they come to
understand that the coercive character of *faits sociaux* demands that
they renounce the limitless power they for so long have claimed as
their natural right?

As I noted above, a rehabilitated occupational association is the
central vehicle through which Durkheim hopes to overcome such
errors. The success of that institution ultimately turns upon its efficacy
as an agency of political education, that is, as an agency through which
such Hobbesian beings are made aware of truths of which they are
presently ignorant. Accordingly, Durkheim's political project is necessarily bound up with his understanding of the relationship between
scientific and unscientific apprehensions of *faits sociaux*.

Durkheim's initial formulation of that relationship appears in *The
Rules of Sociological Method*, first published in 1895. Appropriating
Francis Bacon's critique of the "Idols of the Market Place,"[24] Durkheim
urges his audience to acknowledge that "facts . . . are of necessity
unknowns for us, *things* of which we are ignorant, for the representations that we have been able to make of them in the course of our lives,
since they have been made without method and uncritically, lack any
scientific value and must be discarded." If they are to become the
objects of a science, "social phenomena must" therefore "be considered in themselves, detached from the conscious beings who form
their mental representations of them."[25] That accomplishment is made
possible by the rules of a scientific method whose systematic applica-

23. Ibid., pp. 37, 143.
24. See Francis Bacon, *The New Organon* (Indianapolis: Bobbs-Merrill, 1960), p. 56:
"But the *Idols of the Market Place* are the most troublesome of all—idols which have crept
into the understanding through the alliances of words and names. For men believe that
their reason governs words; but it is also true that words react on the understanding;
and this it is that has rendered philosophy and the sciences sophistical and inactive.
Now words, being commonly framed and applied according to the capacity of the
vulgar, follow those lines of division which are most obvious to the vulgar understanding."
25. Durkheim, *Rules*, pp. 36, 70.

tion to the world secures purified images that, like nondistorting mirrors, capture the fundamental features of social reality within explanatory constructs owing nothing to the mediation furnished by commonsensical understandings.

The capacity of science to meet the demands of this positivist ontology legitimates the political dimension of its project. Its cognition "immediately grounded firmly in reality," science is authorized to "direct the course of moral life."[26] Yet if it is true that the objectlike facts of society "present themselves to the sociologist in completely different terms than to the masses," then how is science to persuade the latter of its title "to play the part of legislator"?[27] How, that is, will Durkheim respond to the absence of that reservoir of shared intelligibility that might otherwise enable science to justify its regulation of collective existence to those whose commonsensical representations bear little if any "relationship to the intrinsic reality of the object to which they correspond"?[28]

At this early stage of his career, believing that common sense's "tyrannical . . . sway over the mind of the ordinary person" means that it will neither accede to correction by the facts nor even "tolerate its scientific examination," Durkheim cannot help but answer by conceiving of the relationship of knowledge to opinion as one of forced displacement. Hence what he calls "education" in the *Rules* can only take the form of a "continual effort" to cause its subject to submit to "penetrat[ion]" by "external" facts that "are endued with a compelling and coercive power by virtue of which, whether he wishes it or not, they impose . . . ways of seeing and acting which he himself would not have arrived at spontaneously."[29]

Accordingly, the pronouncements of the scientific community must appear to its extrascientific public as edicts whose revelation of an unperceived reality violates the web of commonsensical meaning that constitutes everyday life. Their rule cannot help but confront citizens reared on Enlightenment liberalism as a constellation of heteronomous hindrances whose constraint is illegitimate: "Far from being a

26. Ibid., p. 76; Émile Durkheim, "Replies to Objections," in *Sociology and Philosophy*, trans. D. F. Pocock (New York: Free Press, 1974), p. 65.
27. Durkheim, *Rules*, p. 160; "Replies to Objections," p. 73.
28. Émile Durkheim, "Note on the Definition of Socialism" [1893], in *Durkheim on Politics and the State*, ed. Anthony Giddens (Stanford: Stanford University Press, 1986), p. 115.
29. Durkheim, *Rules*, pp. 51–53, 73.

product of our will," the "moulds into which we are forced to cast our conduct . . . determine it from without."[30] Durkheim's central methodological injunction, which urges the scientific mind to surrender itself to nature's object, is thus transformed into a political mandate that commands submission of the liberal ego to rule by society's uncomprehended and unauthorized givens.

Although I do not in this context repeat the arguments needed to make this contention fully persuasive,[31] I think it possible to construe Durkheim's work after his publication of the *Rules* as so many attempts to temper the distinctly unliberal aspects of this response to liberalism's malaise. The cumulative impact of those attempts does not make its presence known until he elaborates the epistemological presuppositions implicit in his *Elementary Forms of the Religious Life* via a critique of American pragmatism.[32] In 1913, four years before his

30. Ibid., p. 70. Cf. p. 128: "The authority to which the individual bows when he acts, thinks or feels socially dominates him to such a degree because it is a product of forces which transcend him and for which he consequently cannot account. It is not from within himself that can come the external pressure which he undergoes; it is therefore not what is happening within himself which can explain it."

31. What follows is a highly abbreviated account of arguments that I present in more nuanced form in "Émile Durkheim and the Science of Corporatism," *Political Theory* 14 (1986), 638–59; and "Modernity's Myth of Facts: Émile Durkheim on Political Education," *Theory and Society* 17 (1988), 121–47. I believe that my thesis regarding the relationship between social science and liberalism at the end of the last century can also be defended through a consideration of Max Weber's work. In brief, the method of Weberian social science yields objective knowledge concerning the means necessary to accomplish projected political ends as well as the probable consequences of their achievement. This knowledge, although it cannot in and of itself resolve disputes of political value, may nonetheless furnish the ground for responsible debate within the legal framework of the liberal parliamentary state; and this it may do because, as Weber writes in "Objectivity in Social Science and Social Policy," in his *Methodology of the Social Sciences*, trans. Edward Shils and Henry Finch (New York: Free Press, 1949), "a systematically correct scientific proof . . . must be acknowledged as correct even by a Chinese" (p. 58). Only the reason of science, in short, can moderate conflicts between agents whose evaluative commitments, like those of Hobbesian selves, are by their very nature impervious to rational discourse.

32. That Durkheim is made uneasy by the political implications present in the *Rules'* conception of social facts is suggested by the "Preface" he adds to that work's second edition. There, in response to his critics, he (1) modifies his claim about the objectivity of social facts by arguing that their "thinglike" quality describes not their ontological status, but rather their methodological status as phenomena that are "not naturally penetrable by the understanding" (p. 36); (2) qualifies his insistence on the externality of social facts by asserting that, although incapable of being reduced to "purely psychological factors," they are nonetheless internal because they "express . . . the way in which the group thinks of itself in its relationships with the objects which affect it" (p. 40); and (3) downplays his emphasis on the coerciveness of social facts by declaring that the property of constraint, rather than delineating their essential attribute, merely describes one possible way to "pick out their location" (p. 43). Perhaps most important, he

death, Durkheim warns that pragmatism's insidious encroachment on the French intellect must be halted immediately. Introducing a course of lectures designed to counter the growing influence of Charles Peirce, William James, and John Dewey, Durkheim explains that this import's "attack on reason, which is truly militant and determined," threatens "to overthrow our whole national culture": "If we had to accept the form of irrationalism represented by pragmatism, the whole French mind would have to be radically altered." The stakes, though, are higher still. For pragmatism's principled justification of unprincipled expediency, predicated upon its denial of a truth that "express[es] what society is in itself, and not what it is subjectively to the person thinking about it," entails "a complete reversal of . . . the entire philosophical tradition, right from the very beginnings of philosophical speculation." Should the implications of this apostasy be popularized, Durkheim concludes, the forms of collective order definitive of the West may themselves be shaken: "Truth is the means by which a new order of things becomes possible, and that new order is nothing less than *civilization*."[33]

Why American pragmatists cannot resolve and indeed must aggravate the crisis of liberalism becomes apparent in considering the insufficiency of their account of "ideas." Inasmuch as pragmatism represents ideas as "human things that derive from temporal causes and give rise to temporal consequences," Durkheim grants that it shares the impulse animating his own reconstruction of social science. Pragmatists, however, misread the import of this historicist premise when they contend that "constructing truth and constructing reality are one and the same process." Representing general ideas as mere by-products generated through isolation and recombination of the characteristics shared by a given cluster of objects or experiences, pragmatism suggests that our most cherished ideational constructs are to be evaluated exclusively through reference to their capacity to facilitate intercourse with the affairs of everyday life; for "thought," on its account, "has as its aim not the reproduction of a datum, but the construction of a future reality." But this "logical utilitarianism," presupposing that "truth" is merely a "product of the gradual convergence of individual

tempers the antagonistic relationship between individuals and social facts by affirming that the authority the latter bears induces subjects not merely to submit, but to submit with an attitude of respect and even devotion.

33. Émile Durkheim, *Pragmatism and Sociology*, trans. J. C. Whitehouse (Cambridge: Cambridge University Press, 1983), pp. 1, 88, 92.

judgments," cannot grasp why it is that "men have always recognized in truth something that in certain respects imposes itself on us, something that is independent of the facts of sensitivity and individual impulse." Unable to explain the authority of the concepts it represents as indistinct "generic images," as shadowy images delineating nothing more than the "particular simplified and impoverished," pragmatists cannot resolve "the problem of knowing how several different minds can know the same world at once."[34]

Nor, therefore, can a science based on pragmatist premises offset the centrifugal forces called into being by a division of labor whose differentiation of occupational experience entails that each mind is ever more "oriented to a different point on the horizon, reflecting a different aspect of the world."[35] Because pragmatists believe that modern society is "made up of a plurality of small systems, each of which is endowed with an autonomous life," they must also hold that the conditions of social order are themselves "ceaselessly formed, deformed, and transformed."[36] But that in turn must lead pragmatists to conclude that society's ideas alter their identity as soon as those particulars take on a different shape. As such, pragmatism is peculiarly ill equipped to either explain or provide for the unification of individuals who, abstracted from traditional structures of local particularity, now share "nothing in common amongst themselves except . . . the constitutive attributes of the human person in general."[37]

Durkheim's encounter with pragmatism leads him to rethink the source of scientific knowledge's capacity to supplant traditional grounds of unity. Moderating his earlier insistence upon scientific method's capacity to penetrate to the essential facts of a coercive reality, he now emphasizes its peculiar ability to *abstract* from the commonsensical and thereby disclose epistemic objects that, because identical, can be shared by all. In other words, to bind together modernity's disconnected egos, Durkheim turns away from the externalized power of the *Rules'* *faits sociaux* and toward the interiorized power of what he now calls "concepts." In contrast to pragmatism's "generic

34. Ibid., pp. 54, 66–68, 73, 76, 85.
35. Durkheim, "Individualism and the Intellectuals," p. 51.
36. Durkheim, *Pragmatism*, p. 26. Cf. p. 36: "Pragmatism affirms the unity of the world, but it is a unity which is supple, flexible, polymorphous and consisting of a mass of phenomena which is undivided but everchanging, like a lake in which the water, blown about by the wind, looks different at every moment, as it separates and comes together again, moving and changing in a thousand different ways."
37. Durkheim, "Individualism and the Intellectuals," p. 51.

images," concepts are fixed inasmuch as "thinking in concepts means thinking of the variable, but subsuming it *under the form of* the immutable." Moreover, and even more important, they are "universal or at least capable of being universal amongst . . . all men who have the same language."[38] Their fixity and universality, in turn, express their status as elaborations of "a unique intelligence," which, because it "bear[s] the mark of no particular mind," has "its own nature distinct from that of the individual."[39] Inventing an anthropomorphized subject to ground Kant's contention that experience's objectivity presupposes the transcendental unity of consciousness, Durkheim argues that concepts "correspond to the way in which this very special being, society, considers the things of its own proper experience. . . . The collective consciousness is the highest form of the psychic life, since it is the consciousness of the consciousness. Being placed outside and above individual and local contingencies, it sees things only in their permanent and essential aspects, which it crystallizes into communicable ideas. At the same time that it sees from above, its sees farther; at every moment of time, it embraces all known reality."[40] Concepts, so construed, appear to retain the virtues but shed the vices of the *Rules'* *faits sociaux*. Because they are not the product of deliberate design, they are not to be remade by purposive agency. Yet at the same time their status as inherently meaningful entities enables them to bridge the gap between subject and object which had proven problematic in the *Rules'* account of political education. Making it possible to argue that the acquisition of "a more complete knowledge of things" is equivalent to incorporating the concepts through which the self comes to know itself as an autonomous agent, Durkheim concludes that submission to their dictates constitutes not "passive resignation but . . . enlightened allegiance."[41] Science thereby proves able to assume its rightful political office without violating the liberal will's right to see itself incorporated within the institutional and ideational structures that constrain it.

But does this move from the coercive fact to the universal concept do what it is designed to do? Does it in fact eliminate the authoritarian character of the *Rules'* account of political education? To answer that question, we must turn to Durkheim's essay "The Dualism of Human

---

38. Durkheim, *Pragmatism*, pp. 104, 140.
39. Durkheim, *Elementary Forms*, p. 482; *Moral Education*, p. 73.
40. Durkheim, *Elementary Forms*, pp. 483, 492.
41. Durkheim, *Moral Education*, pp. 115, 119.

Nature and Its Social Conditions," published in the same year as his polemic against pragmatism. There Durkheim advances a sociological reinterpretation of Descartes' dualism of mind and body. Finally making explicit the secularized version of Judeo-Christian theology that informs his reading of liberalism's sickness, Durkheim contends that human beings comprise two independent parts. The first, corresponding to the sacred, is constituted by the pure conceptual reality that society bequeaths to the individual; the second, corresponding to the profane, is constituted by the presocial body whose particularistic impulses, rooted in basic organismic drives, are defined by their passionate and egoistic orientation. The relationship between these two, he continues, cannot help but prove conflictual; for it is the latter that "breaks up and differentiates" the abstraction of the concept and so brings into being the "separate personalities" whose recalcitrance proves so problematic in a world destined to rule by the former: "It is the body that fulfills this function. As bodies are distinct from each other, and as they occupy different points of space and time, each of them forms a special centre about which the collective representations reflect and color themselves differently. The result is that even if all the consciousnesses in these bodies are directed towards the same world, to wit, the world of ideas and sentiments which brings about the moral unity of the group, they do not all see it from the same angle; each one expresses it in its own fashion."[42]

Serving as Durkheim's metaphor for those residual elements that determination by the concept can neither conquer nor absorb, it is the body that explains why society's self-consciousness must be "retouched, modified, *and consequently falsified*" in virtue of its internalization by individual selves.[43] No matter how willing, in other words, the subjects of a scientifically grounded political education, in appropriating society's concepts for purposes of everyday use, cannot help but "give words a particular meaning which they do not have" and so "pervert" its core curriculum.[44] Therefore, the ever receding goal of Durkheim's scientific project must be the inscription of hypostatized and homogeneous concepts upon souls whose recalcitrant bodies necessarily undermine their truth; for if indeed "the best part of us is only an emanation of the collectivity," the liberal self can "take on the shape

42. Durkheim, *Elementary Forms*, pp. 305–6.
43. Ibid., p. 484; emphasis added.
44. Durkheim, *Pragmatism*, p. 105; *Elementary Forms*, p. 484.

of the things it thinks about" only when it has become a tabula rasa awaiting imprint of a scientific content that it can "never manage to see in its entirety, or in its reality."[45] In sum, Durkheim cannot escape the conclusion that collective life must retain a coercive character if it is to overcome the decentralizing dynamic set in motion by persistence of the embodied self. Because the subjectivity that distinguishes each personality is opaque to the ministrations of reason, "to make it conform, we have to do some violence to it," although "we" shall "never completely succeed in triumphing over its resistance."[46]

If this abbreviated account of the opening and closing chapters in Durkheim's theoretical evolution is on the mark, then it is not at all clear that he has overcome modernity's crisis of disaggregation in a way that coheres with his liberal political commitments. That he is finally willing to sacrifice the latter for the sake of resolving the former becomes apparent when, in his final lectures on pragmatism, he explicitly returns to the question of political education. Since society's ruling concepts "undergo a process of elaboration" of which most are "not capable," how can "the collective consciousness . . . take possession of scientific truths and fashion them into a co-ordinated whole?"[47] No longer able to endorse the *Rules*' representation of education as penetration by externalized facts, yet unwilling to relinquish the privileged authority of science to dictate its content, Durkheim reluctantly concedes that "there is, and there always will be, room in social life for a form of truth which will perhaps be expressed in a secular way, but will nevertheless have a mythological and religious basis." Abandoning the Enlightenment's conviction that unrationalized common sense constitutes "one of the great obstacles which obstruct the development of sociology," Durkheim replaces the *Rules*' positivistic distinction between science and ideology with that between science and "mythology," each of which he now acknowledges as a legitimate form of knowledge. Scientific knowledge unites the members of its expert community in rational apprehension of "one object which is the same for all."[48] Mythological belief achieves the same end inasmuch as

45. Durkheim, *Moral Education*, p. 73; Émile Durkheim, *The Evolution of Educational Thought*, trans. Peter Collins (London: Routledge & Kegan Paul, 1977), p. 275; *Pragmatism*, p. 105.

46. Émile Durkheim, "The Dualism of Human Nature and Its Social Conditions," in *Émile Durkheim on Morality and Society*, p. 153.

47. Émile Durkheim, *Professional Ethics and Civic Morals*, trans. Cornelia Brookfield (Westport, Conn.: Greenwood, 1983), p. 92; *Pragmatism*, p. 89.

48. Durkheim, *Pragmatism*, pp. 88, 91.

it makes it possible for nonscientific consciousnesses, "otherwise . . . closed to each other," to establish a "real communion, that is to say, a fusion of all particular sentiments into one common sentiment"; but it does so by quite different means, for its content is "false with respect to things, but true with respect to the subjects who think them."[49] Comprising "simple, definite, and easily representable" symbols, a figurative rendering of the truth that *"constitute[s] a being who would not exist without it"* secures the acquiescence of those who cannot know it more immediately.[50]

Convinced that "the old gods are growing old or already dead, and others are not yet born," Durkheim responds to liberal society's absence of a shared ethical vocabulary and hence its "disintegrat[ion] into an inconclusive host of fragmented, petty creatures in conflict with one another" with a form of knowledge that fixes the sense of essential concepts and so quashes the peril of semantic ambiguity.[51] Vacillating meanings, on Durkheim's account, violate modern society's need for indubitable sources of "certainty," for convictions that ensure that there will be no hesitation "when the time comes . . . to transform" their imperatives "into action." To ward off such irresolution, Durkheim offers a functional creed that produces a "disposition to act *in conformity with a representation*" only because that representation, embraced "without . . . verification," is held to "conform to reality."[52] To put this less charitably, sensing the decay of the homogeneous stable cultural forms that once sustained the illusion of a fixed relationship between words and their objects, Durkheim fosters a neorealist understanding of science's constructs even as he comes to appreciate positivism's epistemological inadequacy.[53] Inculcating a

---

49. Ibid., p. 87; *Elementary Forms*, p. 262.
50. Durkheim, *Elementary Forms*, p. 251; *Pragmatism*, p. 82; emphasis in the original.
51. Durkheim, *Elementary Forms*, p. 475; "The Role of the State in Education," in *Durkheim on Politics and the State*, p. 177.
52. Durkheim, *Pragmatism*, pp. 86, 84, 99.
53. As I have already intimated, Durkheim's intellectual career, anticipating subsequent developments within the philosophy of science, displays a growing awareness of the incredibility of an arch-positivist account of the relationship between prereflective common sense, scientific knowledge, and cognition's objects. This is especially clear in *The Elementary Forms of the Religious Life*. There the epistemological autonomy of scientific rationality is considerably attenuated by Durkheim's demonstration of the derivation of all forms of thought, including modern science itself, from specific configurations of collective life. This argument, which posits the existence of a relationship of isomorphic dependence between the institutional forms and the logical categories of any given culture, implies that the enterprise of science is simply another object of analysis, which, like any other social fact, can be investigated with the tools of scientific method. But this, of course, renders exceptionally problematic the sense in which science is autonomous

cult whose universal endorsement creates the illusion of an order united not by the coercive necessities of hierarchically organized domination but by a common framework of value, Durkheim's politics of facticity restores a simulacrum of community to a world drained of its concrete conditions.

IV

By the close of his career, Durkheim effectively concedes that modernity cannot realize the Enlightenment's goal of assuring the freedom of liberal agents by securing their rational apprehension of and consent to the constraints by which they are governed. How exactly are we to make sense of this failure? Viewed from the perspective of its American foil, the impasse into which Durkheim is led exemplifies the difficulties liberalism encounters as a result of its attachment to epistemology's representation of cognition as the establishment of a relationship of correspondence between subjective consciousness and objective reality.

Liberalism and epistemology alike carry into the modern world the suspicion that Aquinas was right when he insisted that "many persons will never succeed in producing unity in the community if they differ among themselves. So a plurality of individuals will already require some bond of unity before they can even begin to rule in any way whatsoever. Just as the whole crew of a ship would never succeed in sailing it on any course unless they were in agreement among themselves."[54] Uncertain that what is given to our senses can locate a

---

from and hence authorized to pass critical judgment on common sense's adequacy. For science, if it is to sustain its claim to the possession of nonrelativistic criteria of truth, must explain how it has abstracted itself from and thereby come to stand outside the historical processes of which it is, and continues to be, the product; it must, in short, justify its claim to know the form of which it is the matter. To solve this dilemma, Durkheim suggests that truth is a function not of objectivity, as the *Rules* affirms, but rather of impersonality. The possibility of scientific knowledge, he argues, is predicated upon the existence of a community of inquirers whose joint commitment to the rules of scientific procedure enables its members to suppress the idiosyncratic effects otherwise produced by private perception and prejudice and so arrive at concepts that are true not because they perfectly mirror their objects, but rather because they are held in common. A true concept, then, is one whose excision of specific points of view ensures that it can be shared by all who engage in formally identical practices of rule-governed observation and reasoning.

54. Thomas Aquinas, "On Princely Government," in *Aquinas: Selected Political Writings*, trans. J. G. Dawson (Oxford: Basil Blackwell, 1978), p. 11.

principle of organization within its own history, epistemology's devotees show why modern beings must acknowledge the cognitive structures that make objective experience possible. Students of scientific liberalism, in turn, show why those same beings can halt their slide into so many private realities only by submitting to a world of objective facts. Together, epistemology and liberalism conspire to deter modernity's selves from appreciating the unsettling implications of their expulsion from the polis as well as the manor.

The precise character of this conspiracy is best read in light of Dewey's dictum that "it is easier consciously to ridicule Plato than to cease being his unconscious disciple."[55] Responding to the clash of incompatible claims elicited by competing Sophistic accounts of the nature of piety, justice, beauty, and the like, Socrates in Plato's *Cratylus* comes to suspect that "he who follows names in the search after things, and analyzes their meaning, is in great danger of being deceived" (436a). Certain that controversy signals the absence of reason, classical philosophers infer that disagreement is itself evidence of an underlying unity awaiting discovery. For persons cannot differ as long as they are talking about different things; and so the very possibility of intelligible disputation presupposes a community of intended reference on the part of separate minds. That, in turn, implies that language's aim is to disclose the common natures or kinds in which apparently diverse beings participate. Discourse can prove reasoned, in sum, only because it *means*, it intends, the object that is the ground of shared understanding.

Like Plato, Durkheim is persuaded that "the great trouble we have in understanding each other" stems from the fact that "we all use the same words without giving them the same meaning": "If left to themselves, individual consciousnesses are closed to each other; they can communicate only by means of signs which express their internal states."[56] The infinite regress of interpretation and reinterpretation that thus threatens to shred the fabric of liberal society can be halted only if its members come to hold in common objects that transcend their respective idiosyncrasies. "An observation," says Durkheim, "is more objective the more stable the object is to which it relates. This is because the condition for any objectivity is the existence of a constant, fixed vantage point to which the representation may be related and

---

55. Dewey, "Some Connexions of Science and Philosophy," in *LW*, vol. 17, p. 403.
56. Durkheim, *Elementary Forms*, pp. 484, 262.

which allows all that is variable, hence subjective, to be eliminated."[57] Durkheim departs from the classical formulation of this conviction, manifest in its idealization of the contemplative life, only insofar as he holds that the practice of modern science shows how such abstraction is achieved not through transcendence of this world, but rather through methodical regulation of inquiry within it. Purifying its constructions of the particularities that mark the commonsensical *doxa* of those still within the cave, science at last realizes the truth implicit in Plato's dream of an underlying whole in which all conflicting claims are finally adjudicated and all contradictions harmoniously resolved.

Agreement between persons, on this understanding, is an outcome necessarily generated by uniform apprehension of homogeneous epistemic objects; and it is for this reason that scientific truth, gifted with what Durkheim calls its "*de facto* necessitating power," is able to command collective belief.[58] Embracing a neo-Lockean account of mind as a receptacle whose capacity to discipline its otherwise unruly proclivities turns upon its correct use of the signs through which science's conclusions are externalized, Durkheim celebrates the politics of facticity because he is convinced that its monologic abstractions can be conveyed without distortion from their point of origin to so many discrete individuals. "Before this scheme of ideas," he remarks in a revealing phrase, "the individual is in the same situation as the *vous* of Plato before the world of Ideas."[59]

Durkheim's argument here, which articulates the premises common to most positivist accounts of science, only works if one presupposes some version of epistemology's representation of knowledge as a set of fully fashioned signals that, in coming to be known either by the voluntary application of mind or through the impression it makes on mind, elicits a fixed response. Why this claim is inadequate was implicit in the previous chapter's closing pages. To see its present import, consider Durkheim's representation of the object of knowledge as a "fact." In using the term *fait sociaux*, Durkheim is appropriating the sense of a distinctly seventeenth-century invention. Before that time, just as conventional English usage retained a sense of the etymological rootedness of "fact" in the Latin verb *facere*, the French noun *fait* preserved its connotational association with the same root via the verb

57. Durkheim, *Rules*, p. 82.
58. Durkheim, *Pragmatism*, p. 73.
59. Durkheim, *Elementary Forms*, p. 484.

faire. Thus, although occasionally employed within Scholastic writing to refer to an event or occasion, most commonly to speak of a "fact" was to speak of a deed or action, something that has been done. (In this way, "fact" and *fait* functioned semantically much like certain conventional uses of the term *pragma* in classical Greece.)

With the advent of epistemology, however, these nouns gradually came to designate a realm of discrete objects whose existence apart from the self's judgments about them is the condition of the inquiring mind's ability to determine the adequacy of the latter's correspondence with the former. The logic of this usage is clearly apparent when Bacon, in his *New Organon*, insists that "the human understanding is like a false mirror, which, receiving rays irregularly, distorts and discolors the nature of things by mingling its own nature with it."[60] Anticipating Durkheim's justification of method, Bacon continues: "There remains but one course for the recovery of a sound and healthy condition—namely, that the entire work of the understanding be commenced afresh, and the mind itself be from the very outset not left to take its own course, but guided at every step; and the business be done as if by machinery." For only when the natural proclivity of the mind to error is straightened by the discipline of such machinery, concludes Bacon, will it become possible to build "in the human understanding a true model of the world, such as it is in fact, not such as a man's own reason would have it to be; a thing which cannot be done without a very diligent dissection and anatomy of the world."[61]

Durkheim embraces and extends the general thrust of the Baconian posture when, in an effort to efface altogether the etymological connection between "fact" and "deed," he affirms that "les faits sociaux doivent être traités commme des choses,"[62] that social facts are to be thought of as "things." What, Durkheim then asks, "is a thing? The thing stands in opposition to the idea, just as what is known from the outside stands in opposition to what is known from the inside." This externalization of the object, he continues, is the condition of objective knowledge; for only when we "assimilate to the realities of the external world those of the social world" does it become possible for the student of society to "assume the state of mind of physicists, chemists and physiologists."[63]

60. Bacon, *New Organon*, p. 48.
61. Ibid., pp. 48, 34, 113.
62. Émile Durkheim, *Les regles de la méthode sociologique* (Paris: Alcan, 1927), p. x.
63. Durkheim, *Rules*, pp. 35–36.

As an heir of epistemology's misconceived dualism between mind and matter, Durkheim cannot help but think of facts as reified objects without intrinsic connection to the subject who comes to know them. This, in turn, undergirds his belief that the reality of such facts is most adequately disclosed when their existence is given expression within statements of statistical regularity: "Nothing is proved when, as happens so often, one is content to demonstrate by a greater or lesser number of examples that in isolated cases the facts have varied according to the hypothesis. From the sporadic and fragmentary correlations no general conclusion can be drawn. To illustrate an idea is not to prove it. What must be done is not to compare isolated variations, but series of variations, systematically constituted."[64] To sustain the plausibility of this latter claim, though, Durkheim must effectively "forget" that these statistical "objects," abstracted from situated circumstances of everyday life, are intellectual constructs fashioned by human thinking in an effort to make sense of experience that, in its qualitative immediacy, encounters "pragmata" but never "facts." Having effected this transposition, Durkheim then reimports these hypostatized entities within the realm of human association where, as the content of political education, they rule over the human affairs from which they have been dislocated.

Through this reversal, Durkheim secures the best of all possible worlds. By calling these intangible entities "facts," he indicates that they cannot be apprehended except through the lenses provided by scientific method. By simultaneously calling them "things," Durkheim assimilates to them the materiality that we associate with the matters of everyday experience; "like all other things in nature," *faits sociaux* are obdurate givens defined by their power to "resist the human will."[65] Transforming existence into essence and then subsuming existence beneath the hypostatized power of essence, Durkheim effectively quells his fear that rough hands might otherwise dare to grasp or refashion the truths that have been emancipated from the distorting subjectivity of the body politic.

Durkheim's "facts" begin to lose some of their coercive power, however, when the "things" of everyday experience are acknowledged to be pragmata rather than *choses*. To grasp the point here, consider the

64. Ibid., p. 155.
65. Émile Durkheim, *Montesquieu and Rousseau*, trans. Ralph Manheim (Ann Arbor: University of Michigan Press, 1965), pp. 3, 12.

etymology of the English term "thing." Rooted in Anglo-Saxon vernacular, the singular "ping" originally referred to a public assembly or
council in which matters of common concern were deliberated or
adjudicated. Abstracted from this institutional referent, the plural
bore the more general sense of "affairs" or "matters," that is, events or
incidents that might in time become the subject of resolution within
such a meeting. These resonances are still very much present when
Hobbes, in chapter 40 of his *Leviathan*, proves the authority of Moses
over all other prophets by noting that "when two of them prophesied
in the camp, it was thought a new and unlawful thing."[66] Such early
modern usage, not yet guilty of Durkheim's identification of things
with facts, also preserved the connotational association between, on
the one hand, the qualitative "things" with which one is presently
concerned and, on the other, deeds already completed as well as those
yet to be done. For example, when Mistress Quickly in Shakespeare's
Merry Wives of Windsor announces to Falstaff that "you shall hear how
things go" (4.5.126), she makes clear that those things are part of, and
derive their sense from, a moving situation whose resolution and
hence import are still very much unsettled. Finally, such usage also
registers the indeterminacy of that import by noting the relative formlessness of the some-thing toward which speech gestures. Thus does
Hamlet, unsure of the meaning of his amorphous nocturnal visitor, cry
out: "What, has this thing appear'd again to-night?" (1.1.21). In doing
so, he signals his emerging conviction that only more active engagement on his part will suffice to elicit from this ambiguous creature the
shape that is its sense.

The sense of "thingness" conveyed by these quotations has not yet
been lost altogether from contemporary speech. It is quite absent,
however, from Durkheim's representation of facts as disembodied
static objects whose self-sufficient meaning is best transmitted through
semantically determinate nouns; and it is just this abstraction from the
world of "things" that ensures the insignificance of those same facts.
For unless Durkheim does what he cannot, unless he rejects his Cartesian heritage by squarely acknowledging the ontological situatedness
of his "facts" within the moving and localized sociotemporal contexts
from which they have been excised, the political education he endorses
cannot prove other than nonsense.

Why is this so? Emerging out of qualitative circumstances whose

66. Hobbes, *Leviathan*, p. 346.

present import is unsettled, all thinking is "intentional" in the sense that its "objects" bear significance only in virtue of pointing beyond themselves. Their capacity to convey meaning presupposes their derivation from and reference to relations sustained between pragmata, as these are embedded within the temporally and spatially contextualized affairs of concrete human beings. As so many arte-facts, the sense of such objects stands or falls with the "truth" of the transactions they sustain between agents and an experienced world. Consequently, the symbols that express Durkheim's "facts," no matter how expertly fashioned, can neither displace nor supplant the experiential contexts that are the condition of their intelligibility.

Except for analytical purposes, the activity called thinking cannot be neatly segregated from what is thought, and so "facts" can designate no objective referents specifiable in strict isolation from our sensible engagement with them. The qualitative immediacy of that engagement is not a deceptive mask that, worn by social facts when dressed in common sense, is to be cast aside when the truth is known. We can never simply "take" social facts as they are, for they are never had *as* social facts. They are had only within the confines of so many immediately experienced contexts of everyday life; and inasmuch as each such context is distinguished from all others by its own peculiar qualities, no fact is ever simply reduplicated in moving from one to another. Political education's subject matter, therefore, cannot be conveyed to individual consciousnesses "as a pipe conducts water, and with even less transforming function than is exhibited when a wine-press 'expresses' the juice of grapes. Nothing enters experience bald and unaccompanied. Its very entrance is the beginning of a complex interaction; upon the nature of this interaction depends the character of the thing as finally experienced."[67] Hence, Durkheim's contention that individual appropriation "perverts" facts' essential meaning must be rejected, as must his construction of political education as the establishment of an unmediated correspondence between two independent relata. For that correspondence cannot help but dissolve into so many complex interrelationships between divergent knowers and contested knowns, each of which is mutually implicated in a world whose palpable reality always outruns the claims of knowledge.

Correlatively, a fact's capacity to bear meaning necessarily presupposes some being or beings for whom the symbol that conveys its

---

67. Dewey, *EN*, p. 169; *AE*, p. 162.

content is meaningful. The world's meanings are always meanings *of* particular persons located within specific situations, and so facts' sense entails their assumption of local habitations via vernacular ingestions that can neither proceed nor terminate in isolation from the interests, loyalties, and histories of those engaged. Aside from so many acts of importation that draw facts into a dialogue between meanings wrought from the experiences of the past and the possibilities projected by the present, they cannot be other than mere stimuli.

From this we may conclude that if the "education" Durkheim proposes is to be something other than the mere inculcation of senseless excitations, if these representations are to inform rather than further confuse habitual structures of meaning, then the abstractions called "facts" must enter into communities whose experience is already laden with some measure of embodied intelligibility. Experience is capable of generating and bearing an infinite load of intellectual content. But once that content's "facts" have been severed from *facta* and *facienda*, things done and things to do, that content cannot be grasped even in its own terms.[68] Its sense, in other words, requires the existence of a fund of meanings that cannot themselves be the fruit of rootless abstraction. Symbols are what they are by virtue of "what they suggest and represent, i.e., meanings. They stand for these meanings to any individual only when he has had *experience* of some situation to which these meanings are actually relevant. To attempt to give a meaning through a word alone without any dealings with a thing is to deprive the word of intelligible signification."[69] Yet Durkheim's own

---

68. Dewey, *DE*, p. 144. Cf. p. 233: "We are thus met by the danger of the tendency of technique and other purely representative forms to encroach upon the sphere of direct appreciations; in other words, the tendency to assume that pupils have a foundation of direct realization of situations sufficient for the superstructure of representative experience erected by formulated school studies. This is not simply a matter of quantity or bulk. Sufficient direct experience is even more a matter of quality; it must be of a sort to connect readily and fruitfully with the symbolic material of instruction. Before teaching can safely enter upon conveying facts and ideas through the media of signs, schooling must provide situations in which personal participation brings home the import of the material and the problems which it conveys."

69. Dewey, *HWT*, p. 236. In *SS*, Dewey makes an argument that, although intended to demonstrate the conditions necessary to fruitful education in public schools, may readily be read as a statement of the conditions of effective political education. These are "first that the pupil have a genuine situation of experience—that there be a continuous activity in which he is interested for its own sake; secondly, that a genuine problem develops within this situation as a stimulus to thought; third, that he possess the information and make the observations needed to deal with it; fourth, that suggested solutions occur to him which he shall be responsible for developing in an orderly way; fifth, that he have the opportunity and occasion to test his ideas by application, to make their meaning clear and to discover for himself their validity" (p. 192).

account of the disintegration of mechanical solidarity gives him little reason to think that there exists such a reservoir of meaning grounded in situated everyday practice. Hence the "knowledge" whose cause he advances cannot be other than "mythological" in the sense that it, as empty form without decipherable content, hovers uncannily above the irregular fleshy world from which it has been torn.

Unwilling to bend the facts so as to accommodate the sense-making needs of their knowers, Durkheim turns to reconstruction of the latter. That is, he concludes that uniform perception of *faits sociaux* presupposes the existence of knowers who are as devoid of local contextualization as the knowledge they behold in common. Social science, on Durkheim's telling, can generate a shared apprehension of "objective reality," which "must necessarily be the same for all men given its independence from the observing subject," only if each knowing agent proves "capable of raising himself above his own peculiar point of view and of living an impersonal life."[70] Believing that "the closer the collective consciousness is to particular things . . . the more unintelligible it is,"[71] Durkheim determines that science can fulfill its political mission only when its practice is situated within a community of knowers who, stripped of their capacity to generate subjective interference, are as radically disembodied as the untethered knowledge they confront. Just as method purges the latter of all qualitative irrelevancy, so too must methodical politics divest its objects of the differentiation that otherwise frustrates their joint participation in what he calls the "sphere of clear consciousness."[72]

Thus emptied and refilled, Durkheim's liberal subjects soon recognize that they are no longer capable of mustering or exercising the skills necessary to take part in the political matters that once appeared in the space generated and sustained by their intersecting activities. Learning that common sense mistakes the truth of things when it intimates that the roots of modernity's disease reside within the jurisdiction of present experience, those subjects must in time acquiesce in the modern state's expropriation of their collective political capacity. As Durkheim argues in his work on professional ethics, if the interdependent complexity that defines modernity is to be competently managed, the state must "become the instrument of the almost continuous reform that present-day conditions of collective existence demand."[73]

70. Durkheim, *Pragmatism*, p. 89; *Elementary Forms*, p. 494.
71. Durkheim, *Division of Labor*, p. 232.
72. Durkheim, *Professional Ethics*, p. 84.
73. Ibid., p. 90.

By implication, all bonds that obstruct the rational organization and reorganization of society's members must be loosened; the "ties which bind the individual to his family, to his native soul, to traditions which the past has given him," must be excised such that society becomes "all the more malleable."[74] If the distorting effect of such parochial bonds is analogous to, and in fact derived from, the individuation produced by the peculiar spatiotemporal location of liberalism's desiring bodies, then devitalization of mechanical solidarity's provincial residences must be pressed to its logical conclusion. These lagging "resistances of collective particularism," the incalculable "shadows" of the body social, hinder the ability of the state's "statistical services" to keep it "informed of everything important that goes on in the organism," and so mire the political organ in a web of custom from which it cannot escape. "We can almost say," writes Durkheim in his *Division of Labor*, "that a people is as much more advanced as territorial divisions are more superficial."[75]

With the ground of public meaning located in a sacred zone that a "people is forbidden to touch,"[76] the epistemological representation of consciousness assumes the character of a self-fulfilling prophecy. The key error of empiricist epistemology, its depiction of the mind as a passive receptor of isolated stimuli, becomes an ever more accurate account of everyday experience's subjection to a dizzying succession of degrounded factual particulars. Given its most revealing expression in the mass media's relentless invasion of private life, the integrity of ordinary intelligibility is overwhelmed by the anxiety common to those who, as solitary yet interchangeable components of a homogeneous audience, can no longer discriminate between the world's apparent chaos and the truth of its unyielding order. Simultaneously constructing and reinforcing the rigid boundaries between the insignificant events of everyday existence and the remote yet ultimately real domain where "news" takes place, the sensational spectacle of abstracted facticity can only confirm the irrelevance of sensibilities cultivated in more parochial arenas. Unable to remind their audience that human conduct gives ideas whatever fixity they presently display, modernity's facts create the conditions of their own fetishism. As such, they may in time secure something not unlike identity of vision;

---

74. Durkheim, *Division of Labor*, p. 400; *Professional Ethics*, p. 84.
75. Durkheim, *Division of Labor*, pp. 222, 187.
76. Durkheim, *Elementary Forms*, p. 244.

but when they do, it will be because the advance of rationalization's logic has finally and fully eradicated the textured capacity of tangibly grounded experience to hold at bay the "buzzing, blooming confusion" of undifferentiated sense stimuli.

V

Durkheim's resolution of the fundamental dilemma of late liberalism, turning upon its marriage to positivist social science, exacerbates the crisis it is intended to overcome. Believing that the facts of modernity render the collective empowerment of currently incompetent citizens an impossible and dangerous fantasy, Durkheim effectively reduces democracy's claims to the communication of knowledge between state and society regarding the unalterable structural imperatives embedded in an age of specialized functions. This ratification of the institutional confines that systematically generate a collective sense of impotence unites in an unhappy and self-defeating synthesis the ills of mechanical as well as organic solidarity. For democratization of the inability to exercise power in shaping the parameters of daily existence must spawn a renewed quest for bygone forms of wholeness, while the inevitable failure of that quest makes it necessary to try to manufacture order on the basis of factitious agreement. Yet unity fashioned from nothing more substantial than science's abstract imperatives cannot help but prove superficial, and so in time defeat its original purpose.

Although it may not be immediately apparent, Durkheim's failure bears within it some important implications for our assessment of the contemporary debate regarding the ground of commonality within late liberal political orders. That debate has now reached a stalemate in which each side offers little more than an inverted caricature of the other.[77] To the left, one finds those who endorse liberalism's refusal to embrace a teleological conception of community and so devote their energies to formulation of what John Rawls calls the "public system of rules" that is to resolve disagreements generated by the existence of "a plurality of opposing and even incommensurable conceptions of the

77. For commentaries on this debate, see Amy Gutmann, "Communitarian Critics of Liberalism," *Philosophy and Public Affairs* 14 (1985), 308–21; and John Wallach, "Liberals, Communitarians, and the Tasks of Political Theory," *Political Theory* 15 (1987), 581–611.

good."[78] Characteristically translating all political issues into questions of legal rights and obligations, thinkers of this stripe formulate liberalism's rules without reference to the expropriation of democratic political capacity and its resituation within antidemocratic institutional structures. Such thinking, for that reason, is ill suited to question a state-centered order whose legitimacy turns on the apparent neutrality of its abstracted proceduralism. Granted, Rawls has now tempered the formalism implicit in *A Theory of Justice*'s construction of the original position by acknowledging that justice's claims are grounded in "our public political culture" and the "shared fund of implicitly recognized basic ideas and principles" that are embedded in it.[79] But that, in and of itself, does not in any fundamental way alter his formulation of politics as, on the one hand, a matter of legally guaranteed rules and, on the other, a matter of competition between so many disconnected interest groups. It does not, in other words, transcend the familiar liberal assimilation of politics' qualitatively distinct affairs to those we conventionally call "economic."

To the right, one finds those who, convinced that liberalism's rule-bound politics can be nothing other than what Alasdair MacIntyre calls "civil war carried on by other means,"[80] seek to discover the shared ends that might unify the members of a postliberal body politic. Hoping to locate a surrogate for Aristotle's metaphysical biology in the solidaristic virtues cultivated by the determinate customs of small and homogeneous communities,[81] communitarians characteristically respond to liberal anomie by arguing that the task of modernity's politics is to discover a source of collective identity which will unproblematically harmonize all particular identities. Hankering after some secular proxy for God's capacity to assure a universal set of internally consistent identities, such political thinking all too quickly lapses into recommending reactionary programs whose success requires suppression of the heterogeneity that establishes the very possibility of politics.

The terms of debate thus posed, argument shuffles effortlessly be-

---

78. John Rawls, *A Theory of Justice* (Cambridge: Harvard University Press, 1971), p. 88; Rawls, "Justice as Fairness: Political Not Metaphysical," *Philosophy and Public Affairs* 14 (1985), 248.

79. See especially John Rawls, "Justice as Fairness: Political Not Metaphysical," p. 4.

80. Alasdair MacIntyre, *After Virtue* (Notre Dame: University of Notre Dame Press, 1981), p. 236.

81. Hence MacIntyre's appeal, in *After Virtue*'s conclusion, to create forms "of community within which civility and the intellectual and moral life can be sustained through the dark ages which are already upon us" (p. 263).

tween its familiar poles: Communitarians, pointing to the incontrovertible evidence that modern cultures are losing the resources of civility, demand that economistic liberals grant that mere rule-governed conduct cannot supplant the need for a politics of the common good. Finding communitarians unwilling to specify in any detail the unitarian good to which all must be committed if the twin evils of relativism and subjectivism are to be overcome, these liberals then respond by reaffirming the need to articulate those neutral rules that are to adjudicate between the claims of those whose peaceful coexistence presupposes no other shared ground.

In the remainder of this chapter, I suggest that we can break out of this debate's confines only when we acknowledge a truth neither of its present participants can afford to admit. To an ever greater extent, the real ground of order in late liberal societies is neither universal consensus on substantive doctrine nor the surrogate furnished by a fixed set of constitutional procedures. Rather, order is increasingly the product of joint subordination to the politics of facticity, the form of politics whose most articulate spokesman is Émile Durkheim. To ask how the problematic character of such politics might be overcome without becoming entangled in this sterile debate, I suggest that the deficiencies Durkheim identifies in American pragmatism are in fact virtues that enable it to offer a more democratic reading of the possibilities implicit in liberalism's decomposition. To make that claim plausible, I must begin by briefly retelling, from the perspective of the preceding two chapters, the tale of liberalism's malaise.

Durkheim is right to argue that that crisis is in large measure caused by decay of the past's parochial localities as well as emergence of forms of interdependence whose effects are presently felt but not known. "In static societies—those which the industrial revolution has doomed—acquiescence had a meaning, and so had the projection of fixed ideals. Things were so relatively settled that there was something to acquiesce in, and goals and ideals could be imagined that were as fixed in their way as existing conditions in theirs. The medieval legal system could define 'just' prices and wages, for the definition was a formulation of what was customary in the local community. It could prescribe a system of definite duties for all relations, for there was a hierarchical order, and occasions for the exercise of duty fell within an established and hence known order. Communities were local; they did not merge, ovelap and interact in all kinds of subtle and hidden ways."[82]

82. Dewey, "Individualism, Old and New," in *LW*, vol. 5, pp. 112–13.

Today the self-sufficient and homogeneous forms of association that spawned such ideals are for the most part no more. The invention of rapid modes of transportation, the growth of interconnected markets and mobile labor populations, the evolution of intricate networks of mass media, the emergence of major centers of urbanization, have all produced a vast complication of the ways in which persons find their lots impersonally cast together. As the loyalties that once held persons together and made them aware of their reciprocal obligations have weakened, their role has been assumed by expanding webs of regional, national, and even international interdependence. Collectively, these networks have conspired to dissolve the familiar bonds that once ordered the loci of immediate face-to-face relationships and rendered them intelligible to those whose identities were significantly bound up with their status as members. As these abstract and anonymous forces, felt but not known, have come to determine the basic parameters of everyday life, it has proven ever more difficult to locate the spatial and temporal dimensions of conduct within a coherent narrative of the agent's transformations. "No one knows how much of the frothy excitement of life, of mania for motion, of fretful discontent, of need for artificial stimulation, is the expression of frantic search for something to fill the void caused by the loosening of the bonds which hold persons together in immediate community of experience."[83]

To this point, my account of the sociohistorical origins of modernity's slip into senselessness is broadly congruent with that offered by Durkheim. Here, though, it diverges. Whereas Durkheim finds in modernity's dislocations a threat to reason's teleocratic rule, I locate a progressive depletion of ordinary citizens' capacity to find, grasp, and refashion political pragmata. As relations between citizens increasingly assume the character of momentary exchanges between fragmented beings situated in discontinuous contexts, the things that affect them collectively disappear. Experiencing no-things in common, those beings fall out of a world they might otherwise inhabit together.

Unable to muster a form of collective action that transcends that of interest group liberalism, the associated people Locke depicts as the origin of all legitimate political authority as well as the initiator of all rightful revolution are eclipsed. Caught up in the sweep of mysterious forces, the victims of modernity's dislocations retreat into various forms of apathetic privatism that, punctuated by periodic spasms of

83. Dewey, *PP*, p. 214.

ineffectual resentment, nationalistic fervor, and evasive criminality, aggravate their already acute inability to act with others who are similarly disenfranchised by the dynamic of rationalization. Disconnected and ever in motion, those whose sole bond consists in their loss of political capacity cannot slow the consolidation of a politicized economy that has neither place nor use for the uncombined and unintegrated. While the state that rules these disaggregated selves increasingly turns to the threat of punishment as compensation for the dissolution of older bonds, the hollowness of this ploy is revealed in the spread of craftier ways to outwit its sanctions.

If democracy's potential publics are to secure their status as vital currents in a larger fountain of political power, they must begin to remedy the asymmetry between the state's enormous power of collective action and its subjects' disabled capacity for reflection on the meaning of that power. Durkheim, in other words, is correct to insist that if modern agents are to find themselves coherently situated in a radically interdependent world, they require a form of knowing that in some way overcomes the limitations of that nurtured within the isolated communities of an imagined past. A vernacular inherited from an age that has passed away is no longer adequate to craft sense from a world where knowledge, haunted by the prospect of its own obsolescence, is efficiently manufactured and administered by the expert functionaries of a bureaucratized state.

The question of how to conceive of that knowing cannot be segregated from the question of how to characterize that to which it is related, that is, to common sense. To think about the latter, it is necessary to distinguish, as Durkheim does not, between common sense's ontological and its historical constitution. Although the first never exists except as the second, the former refers in formal terms to the know-how that, forged from direct use and immediate enjoyment of the concrete things and mundane affairs of everyday life, renders the lived world a medium of qualitatively significant things and persons rather than a senseless aggregation of discrete objects. Affixing a label to what went unnamed in the previous essay, "common sense" refers to the historically accumulated and socially conveyed modes of familiar acquaintance that emerge out of the recurrent involvements of embodied agents and, as such, explain the taken-for-granted character of all experience as long as it remains untroubled. Although not exhausted by its propositionally formulizable content, the understandings that constitute common sense secure partial expression within the grammar of a language whose orientation to the concrete *facienda*, things to be done or made, is "linguistically expressed by delimiting terms. The activities are pinned down to *this, that* and *the other*; they are further pinned down by specific references to date (*now, then, not yet*) and to place (*here, there, yonder*). These delimiting linguistic specificities reduce to their bare bones or, if one prefers, to their fighting weight, the chronological and geographical information necessary to establish the spatio-temporal location and connections of the commonsense activities involved."[84]

In its specifically historical sense, "common sense" refers to the general beliefs current in a given community, that is, the articulated shape assumed by common sense (ontologically construed) within a specific form of social life; and it is toward this, as opposed to common sense per se, that criticism is appropriately directed. As already noted, in late liberal political orders, common sense bears within itself sensibilities deriving from homogeneous, circumscribed, and largely self-sufficient collectivities; and in virtue of this implicit reference to structures of human relatedness which by and large no longer exist, it confuses rather than orients everyday practice. To cite just one example, whatever coherence was once possessed by a preliberal precept of conduct such as "Do unto others as you would have others do unto you" depended on the unspoken conviction that the nexus within which conduct takes place could be understood in terms of the deliberate intent of familiar persons and the accustomed regularities of proximate circumstances. Actors could safely assume the truth of this maxim as long as they knew with some measure of confidence which individuals were likely to be affected in what ways by a particular action as well as how they were likely to respond. But when an indefinite plethora of ramifying conditions intervene between conduct and its consequences, such a commonsense maxim is no longer sufficient to the defining structures of everyday life.

Moreover, as the deterioration of premodern forms of collective existence has eaten away at these customary sensibilities, liberalism's own structure of pretheoretical significances has compounded the political incompetence of those already confounded. Joining the individualistic thrust of Protestant theology to that derived from nascent capitalism, liberalism's doctrine of natural rights gives specifically political expression to epistemology's dualistic ontology. Thinking of the

84. Dewey, "Experience and Nature: A Re-introduction," in *LW*, vol. 1, p. 342.

self as a masterless monad whose autonomy demands that it sustain only external time and space relations with other sovereign egos, the common sense of liberalism leaves only self-interest in economic matters and the threat of retaliation in political affairs to hold human beings together. While selves, so construed, can know power as a commodity to be bought and sold in exchange for private advantage, they cannot know it as a good to be generated and exercised among those who share an identity as citizens.

How, then, to return to the question at hand, might citizens come to grasp the connections between their current political incapacity and the extended network of interdependence that, at present, assumes the form of a reified object rather than as a form of interrelatedness whose endurance through time presupposes their complicity as subjects? How might those who make up the audience of modernity's abstracted political spectacle recover a sense of the concrete reality of distinctively politika pragmata such that each comes to acknowledge that *pragma esti moi*, that these matters concern *me* because *we* are commonly implicated in their constitution?

With respect to the specific content of that sense, I can do no more than refer to the preceding chapters' historical narrative regarding metaphysical dispossession and reformation of the forms of knowledge that might yet sustain democratic political capacities. Nothing else can be specified apart from concrete investigations into existing modes of production, institutional structures, habits of conduct, and the like. It is, however, possible to say something, first, about the concrete conditions of the education through which a sense of translocal political pragmata might be diffused among those who do not now acknowledge the political qualities of their everyday engagements and, second, about the kind of commonality sustained among those associated by their participation in such sense.

As we have seen, Durkheim fails in his effort to halt liberal society's decomposition by requiring its "members" to draw the resources of self-identity from deracinated epistemic objects referring to an unfelt whole. His failure indicates why substitution of the epistemological relation of subject to object for that of person to person can never draw agents out of their solipsism and into a world that is experienced in common. Since there can be no significant connection of things and meanings prior to social discourse and intercourse—that is, prior to meanings' transformative implication within the concrete world *about* which thinking thinks—facts cannot take up residence among the things present in the world as long as they remain mere disconnected abstractions re-presented by individualized loci of consciousness. Persons cannot "perceive" what is abstract unless that perception can be rooted in what is already sensibly had as a result of active and embodied participation in the fashioning of a concrete world of lived experience. The domain of facticity, in sum, must remain without meaning unless it falls on a fertile ground whose capacity to assimilate what is nonimmediate presupposes that we are already in "touch" with the world.

Therefore, meanings pointing toward less immediate sources of everyday experience's qualitative dimensions can prove intelligible only when they enter associational forms possessing sufficient resilience to withstand the dynamics of a political economy otherwise bent on systematically effacing the parochial resources of coherence. If democratic citizens are to protect the fragile shoots of their collective sense from the numbing onslaught of disconnected "facts," they must first found and secure bounded sites that safeguard the conditions of debate, discussion, and persuasion. For, in the last analysis, the logic of a larger order of events can only be *had* when it passes through the medium of localized dialogue. The relationship between thinking and meaning, irreducibly informed by its passage through this medium, is a sort of intercourse via which the already familiar, enveloping what is more or less unfamiliar, engenders a reformation of each of its members. Accordingly, otherwise inert and artificial information can be brought to life and so become things shared within a community of partaking only when actualized within the public spaces that furnish political thinking with its indispensable and immediate atmosphere.

But to emphasize the "con" in "consciousness" is not to embrace the communitarians' effort to reconstitute at the translocal level the bonds appropriate to more immediate forms of sustained engagement. If it is true that in its deepest sense collective identity can only be engendered by face-to-face intercourse, then the term "community" is best confined to those forms of localized association, rooted in the ascriptive characteristics of gender, age, skin color, local custom, religion, and so on, that most intimately ground allegiance and elicit a sense of belonging. Yet if the members of such disparate communities are to acknowledge their overlapping and distinctively *political* concerns— for instance, their shared stake in reappropriating the expropriated powers presently resident within antidemocratic institutions and practices—then they must learn how to grasp the reality of what appears in the spaces created and sustained by the differences between them. They must learn to locate and repossess the domain of things that come into being only because the dissimilarities between them, relating and separating them at one and the same moment, establish the possibility of specifically political issues.

If such translocal things are to be "had" commonly, the meanings that bear their significance must possess not the property of clear and distinct visibility, but rather that of tangibility, the capacity to be refashioned by those engaged in making sense. Such meanings can e-ducate, draw persons out of their privatism, only if they are malleable artifacts that are capable of taking root in the structures of everyday intelligibility. Meaning, arising out of a dialectical tacking back and forth between what is settled and what is perplexing, emerges within and through the struggle to render determinate the significant content of presently problematic situations. Any symbol expressing the translocal determinants of primary experience can overcome its character as a mere indicator only as a consequence of its readaptation to meet the sense-making needs of those who are what they concretely are in virtue of the complex interrelationships in which they are specifically enmeshed. "Facts," one might say, can play a part in this readaptation only when they conduct themselves as so many travelers who, taken into others' homes, expand the spatial and temporal compass of their hosts' horizons. But that augmentation can bear sense only if those visitors grant their status as strangers whose welcome presupposes respect for the widely varied customs of the households into which they are received. To do otherwise, to think of facts as conquerors whose brute occupation of consciousness evicts the mind's previous "ideological" understandings, is to secure only thinking's homelessness.

"In its first estate, knowledge exists as the content of intelligent ability—power to do. This kind of subject-matter, or known material, is expressed in familiarity or acquaintance with things. Then this material gradually is surcharged and deepened through communicated knowledge."[85] With due respect to Durkheim, meaning is not well construed as a direct or immediate cause of particular actions. Human conduct involves answering the question posed by things in their meaning, whereas a response to a physical stimulus does not. Because such questioning always entails existential transformation of

---

85. Dewey, *DE*, p. 184.

the matter it considers, each "fact" is refashioned in the process of considering its significance for the circumstances at hand; and in that sense each fact actualizes itself as an event. Such events, as I suggest more thoroughly in Chapter 5, lose the ontological deficiency of all abstraction only when they become so thoroughly dissolved within a concrete web of conduct that they disappear within the medium they now reform. Consequently, one can say that one truly knows something remote from daily life only when its meaning, entering into an already complex network of interacting significations, is absorbed within the capacity to act intelligently in a world that makes sense.

Modernity's rule by despotic facts, imprisoning their subjects within the immediacy of a reified present, is checked when the targets of those facts refuse to grant them legitimacy until they have consented to participate as members within the projection of hitherto unrealized experiences. As the events of primary experience become known in their relation to events not directly felt, an extensive and enduring context becomes immediately implicated in present conduct. "It may be a mystery that there should be thinking but it is no mystery that if there is thinking it should contain in a 'present' phase affairs remote in space and in time. It is only a question of how far what is 'in' its actual experience is extricated and becomes focal."[86] Through forms of empowering action that move back and forth between the whole, as construed by its more or less proximate parts, and those parts, as informed by the situated whole within which they are embedded, a public capable of repudiating the politics of facticity becomes something other than an imagined fancy.

With this in place regarding political education's form, it is possible to turn to my second question: How are we to think about the commonality sustained among those who do not engage in regular face-to-face interaction but who nonetheless acknowledge that fate has cast their lot together in ways that are of mutual concern? If the creation of meaning is a contextually determined social process through which persons become significantly present to one another and thereby to themselves, in what sense can those otherwise absent take part in an experience that can be called common? In what way can the distant world of space-time relations become implicated in belief that is in some meaningful sense "shared"?

As preface to exploring this matter, let me emphasize once more that

86. Dewey, *EN*, pp. 279–80.

meaning is not the presupposition of reference, but rather the consequence of its adaptation to the exigencies of particular affairs. Consequently, just as the words constituting a given language establish the conditions of intelligibility but do not dictate what one is to say, so too the symbols that bear meaning furnish the materials with which one may *make* sense of the world but cannot determine identity of belief, much less of conduct.[87] A belief is not a determinate mental apparition, but rather a habit of inference, a customary way of drawing connections between some things and others. It follows that semantic ambiguity, like the quality of tangibility, is a condition of any symbol's capacity to bear meaning. For if symbols are to transform the reality of heterogeneity into overlapping patterns of political action among differentially situated persons, they must be vague, not precise. Their capacity to join together those otherwise disconnected turns on their ability to breed new meanings in contexts dissimilar to those in which they may have originated. Only then can they fulfill their mission as "messenger[s], liaison officer[s], making reciprocally intelligible voices speaking provincial tongues, and thereby enlarging as well as rectifying the meanings with which they are charged."[88]

Epistemology's account of language suggests that each word is meaningful in virtue of its unambiguous reference to determinate objects, whether external or internal to the self. That account says more about the growing power of written over oral communication at the time of its original formulation than it does about the actual conditions of intelligible meaning. "Where written literature and literacy abound, the intrinsic connection of language with community of action is then forgotten. Language is then supposed to be simply a means of expressing or communicating 'thoughts'—a means of conveying ideas or meanings that are complete in themselves apart from communal operational force."[89] By way of contrast, on the understanding sketched here, any given word expresses meaning only in virtue of its simultaneous divergence from and relatedness to others.

This simple conclusion carries important implications for how one conceives of the commonality that obtains between persons differently situated but jointly implicated in a translocal web of cause and consequence. Of necessity, that commonality will express and incorporate

87. On this point, I follow Anthony Cohen's argument in his *Symbolic Construction of Community* (Chichester: Ellis Horwood, 1985).
88. Dewey, *EN*, p. 410.
89. Dewey, *LTI*, p. 48.

the ambiguity present within the meanings that make it possible. For when disparately located persons appropriate symbols circulating in the fields wrought by their transactions, they participate in meanings whose content is grounded in nothing more certain than the practice of its open-ended application to matters at hand. "The sound h-a-t gains meaning in precisely the same way that the thing 'hat' gains it, by being used in a given way. The guarantee for the same manner of use is found in the fact that the thing and the manner of use are first employed in a *joint* activity."[90]

This does not imply that such meanings, because conventional, are "arbitrary" in the sense that they are inventions of willful subjectivity. "The meaning which a conventional symbol has is not itself conventional. For the meaning is established by agreements of different persons in existential activities having reference to existential consequences. The particular existential sound or mark that stands for 'dog' or 'justice' in different cultures is arbitrary in the sense that although it has *causes* there are no *reasons* for it. But *in so far* as it is a medium of communication, its meaning is common, because it is constituted by existential conditions."[91] The commonality of persons mutually implicated in activity via their shared use of such sounds is thus a fruit rather than a presupposition of the conduct through which collective identity is formed and reformed, both within and between groups. To the extent that such reformation gives rise to concerns shared by those not immediately implicated in one another's conduct, it can do so only because individuals who experience discontent in their daily circumstances respond in ways that carry such matters into a space of tangible public appearances. Formal articulation of those interests is therefore not the initial but rather the final moment in the dialectic engendered by the conduct of thinking.

The collaboration that obtains among such individuals is fully present within and sustained by their cumulative but not necessarily coordinated efforts to determine the import of presently underdetermined situations. The meanings shared by the members of any collectivity so constituted have no determinate existence apart from localized undertakings seeking to create and sustain the spaces necessary to such inclusive conduct. Correspondingly, the success of communication—that is, the making common of meaning—is given sufficient testimony

90. Dewey, *DE*, p. 15.
91. Dewey, *LTI*, p. 47.

by pointing to the confluence of actions whose mutuality resides in nothing more enduring than their cumulative consequences. The reality of such a collectivity is wholly manifest within a plurality of discontinuous, overlapping, and context-sensitive actions, each of which, in qualitatively unique fashion, questions that which is.

To fail to understand, to fail to make meaning common, is to fail to come into agreement in conduct. Dissensus among democratic citizens *is* their incapacity to muster the power necessary to call into being the confederated spheres of public action in which dialogue might serve as the condition of meaning's fullest sense. This means, of course, that there can be no antecedent guarantee that the coalitions necessary to challenge existing structures of antidemocratic power will in fact be mustered and sustained. To foreclose the possibility of failure by insisting on the achievement of common belief prior to action's inception is to close off the possibility of democratic politics as well. For the presupposition of such politics is not discovery of the foundations on which consensus can be securely built, but rather confidence that the dynamics of continual discussion, dissension, and experimentation are sufficient to anchor the play of differences. The "aim" of such politics is simply to preserve the media within which the interplay between identity and nonidentity can be expressed and contested without permitting either to abolish the other.

This way of thinking about commonality suggests that the coexistence of different points of view about a world existing in the space created by their ambiguous intersections is not an illusion to be overcome but an irreducible concomitant of any experience that hopes to make sense. Although the world furnishes common materials to those engaged in eliciting sense from experience, those materials cannot help but be appropriated in contradictory ways. The conflict engendered by such difference will appear incompatible with commonly oriented action only if one first presupposes the latter's impossibility in the absence of a uniform apprehension of reality's basic structure. Besides, there are important reasons for thinking that such conflict is to be cultivated, not lamented. For liberalism's citizens can grasp the contestable dimensions of the order they inhabit only by actively partaking of the controversies through which its meaningful shape is unmade and reworked.

If commonality comes into being not through the unadulterated transmission of decontextualized facts, but rather through the mutually transformative exchange of qualitatively distinct forms of symbol-laden experience, then participants in such exchanges must be as essentially ambiguous as the meanings they produce. "Through speech a person dramatically identifies himself with potential acts and deeds; he plays many roles, not in successive stages of life but in a contemporaneously enacted drama. Thus mind emerges."[92] In this sense, diversity of perspectives is present not simply in the interplay between localized collectivities, but within each decentered agency of conduct. Just as persons joined together within various forms of association can "know" the qualities distinctive to each only by distinguishing it from and relating it to that of others, so too the "self" constructs its identity out of acts of hypothetical reciprocity that bring into play what is not itself. To formulate experience "requires getting outside of it, seeing it as another would see it, considering what points of contact it has with the life of another so that it may be got into such form that he can appreciate its meaning. Except in dealing with commonplaces and catch phrases one has to assimilate, imaginatively, something of another's experience in order to tell him intelligently of one's own experience."[93] Hence the fashioning of a standpoint that includes the experience of others as well as one's own presupposes a mediation between tongues that does not collapse the integrity of each into a cosmopolitan language whose abstraction eliminates the need for subsequent acts of translation. "To cooperate by giving differences a chance to show themselves because of the belief that the expression of difference is not only a right of the other persons but is a means of enriching one's own life-experience, is inherent in the democratic way of life."[94]

When the notion of sameness of meaning is expressed through reference to links explicated in conduct rather than homogeneous apprehension of uniform ideas by discrete minds, it becomes apparent

92. Dewey, *EN*, p. 170.
93. Dewey, *DE*, pp. 5–6. Clifford Geertz's "The Way We Think Now: Toward an Ethnography of Modern Thought," found in his *Local Knowledge* (New York: Basic Books, 1983), quite nicely articulates the kind of skill to which I refer: "The problem of the integration of cultural life becomes one of making it possible for people inhabiting different worlds to have a genuine, and reciprocal, impact upon one another. If it is true that insofar as there is a general consciousness it consists of the interplay of a disorderly crowd of not wholly commensurable visions, then the vitality of that consciousness depends upon creating the conditions under which such interplay will occur. And, for that, the first step is surely to accept the depth of the differences; the second to understand what these differences are; and the third to construct some sort of vocabulary in which they can be publicly formulated" (p. 161).
94. Dewey, "Creative Democracy," in *The Philosophy of the Common Man: Essays in Honor of John Dewey*, ed. Sidney Ratner (New York: Putnam's, 1940), p. 227.

that there is no necessary contradiction between commitment to a larger public and loyalty to its constituent parts. Membership in the larger public occurs *through* the particularities by which it is mediated rather than in spite of them. Negatively, this enables us to evade the recurrent liberal temptation to slip from consideration of the conditions needed to facilitate democratic association to invention of the behavioral techniques needed to ensure that the same words conjure up the same ideas in all who see them. Positively, this enables us to affirm that a democratic *politikē technē*, incorporated within the tact of common sense and hence irreducible to a system of neutral procedures, is manifest in the discriminating ability to craft significant meaning out of the dialectic between local experience and less immediate content which gestures toward the structural constraints that now foreclose opportunities for its exercise. "The expert in thought" is not the master at manipulating determinate meaning, but rather the adept who exercises "skill in making experiments to introduce an old meaning into different situations and who has a sensitive ear for detecting resultant harmonies and discords."[95] To value that skill is to acknowledge that it is only our failure to apprehend the same world in the same way that makes politics possible. By extension, it is to entertain the hope that democratic citizens, deprived of the assurances furnished by secure epistemic objects, may prove able to fashion diverse forms of collective identity out of nothing more enduring than their shared capacity to elicit sense from experience in the presence of one another.

95. Dewey, *EN*, pp. 194–95.

5 /
Critical Theory and
the Politics of Talk

I

In the preceding chapter, I employed the work of Émile Durkheim to suggest, albeit in incomplete fashion, the outline of a larger argument regarding liberalism's fin-de-siècle crisis. Convinced that the extension of scientifically based technologies and scientifically grounded criteria of rationality was undermining the integrity of traditional stocks of shared belief as well as the more or less self-contained forms of local association in which such stocks had once been cultivated, many liberals on both sides of the Atlantic sought an antidote in modern social science. Because deployment of social scientific method appeared to overcome the deficiencies of common sense, it seemed to offer the stuff of a new political education. To the extent that ordinary liberal agents came to possess a shared apprehension of the social and political world's fundamental facts, they might overcome the forms of alienation that otherwise accompanied their thrust into modernity. Why that effort could not help but fail in virtue of its unwitting assimilation of dualistic epistemological presuppositions regarding the relationship between mind and its matter, I suggested in the second half of Chapter 4.

Over the last three decades of this century, epistemology's grip has relaxed considerably. That this is so is perhaps best indicated by the influence of those political thinkers who have insisted on the intimate relationship between political knowledge, the practice of dialogue, and democratic politics. No student of contemporary political theory can fail to acknowledge the cumulative impact produced by the works of Hannah Arendt, whose affirmation of public speech as the vehicle of self-disclosure undergirds her contention that "debate constitutes the very essence of political life";[1] of Hans-Georg Gadamer, whose vindication of hermeneutics against the pretensions of Cartesian methodism sustains his representation of political judgment as the fruit of dialogue between citizens; of Jürgen Habermas, whose elucidation of the conditions presupposed by all utterance oriented toward the achievement of shared understanding grounds his conception of politics as unconstrained communication; and of Richard Rorty, whose representation of "culture as a conversation" among divergent voices that can never be rendered commensurable through articulation of a single comprehensive vocabulary entails his political injunction to "keep pragmatic tolerance going as long as we can."[2] Thus Richard Bernstein obscures differences no more than required when he concludes his recent overview of Arendt, Gadamer, Habermas, and Rorty by arguing that the most urgent task confronting today's democrat is "to foster and nurture those forms of communal life in which dialogue, conversation, *phronēsis*, practical discourse, and judgment are concretely embodied in our everyday practices."[3]

Although by no means incontestable, I would argue that designation of collective talk as the paradigmatic exemplar of genuinely political action testifies to the power of the analysis offered by Max Horkheimer and Theodor Adorno in their *Dialectic of Enlightenment* (1944). An appreciation of that work is critical to any understanding of the way in which Marx's critique of capitalism was transformed at midcentury into critical theory's more encompassing attack on "instrumental rationality."[4] The scientific revolution of the seventeenth cen-

1. Hannah Arendt, "Truth and Politics," in her *Between Past and Future* (New York: Penguin, 1977), p. 241.
2. Richard Rorty, *Philosophy and the Mirror of Nature* (Princeton: Princeton University Press, 1978), pp. 319, 371.
3. Richard Bernstein, *Beyond Objectivism and Relativism: Science, Hermeneutics, and Praxis* (Philadelphia: University of Pennsylvania Press, 1983), p. 229.
4. In *Dialectic of Enlightenment* (New York: Continuum, 1986), Horkheimer and Adorno indicate why Marxism must now give way to the critique of instrumental

tury, through its ejection of teleological ends from the realm of nature, forced reason and value out of the cosmos and into the consciousness of the individual subject. The resulting dualism between humanity and nature, although the source of surplus production within the epistemological industry, was effectively bridged through the equation of theory with analytic decomposition and reconstruction of objects in accordance with mechanistic principles of cause and effect, and practice with application of this knowledge in technological fabrication. The problematic character of science, so construed, stems from its inability to determine the rationality of the ends to which these new resources of power are to be put, a point first intimated by Hobbes when he characterized thoughts as "spies" whose aim is to search out the most efficient means of securing unrationalized desires. Regarding everything outside the self as neutral instrumentality to be manipulated at will, this understanding reveals its specifically political dimension via its representation of human practice as a system of behavior to be modified without reference to the purposes of subjects whose status as objects is confirmed by the inaccessibility of consciousness to scientific empiricism. The inherent tendency of modern science to render inconceivable the critical scrutiny of ends reaches its acme when the efficient organization of means is transformed into an end in itself. That, in turn, is the key to making sense of a bureaucratic state whose purposes express, at best, merely the effort to maintain the order made possible by currently available technique and, at worst, the domination of subjective caprice masquerading as expertise.[5] In sum, say Horkheimer and Adorno, the self-propagating tyranny of technological means has generated a monistic ideology incapable of pressing beyond its own scientistic confines: "In the impartiality of

---

rationality: "But to recognize domination, even in thought itself, as unreconciled nature, would mean a slackening of the necessity to whose perpetuity socialism itself prematurely confirmed as a concession to reactionary common sense. By elevating necessity to the status of the basis for all time to come, and by idealistically degrading the spirit for ever to the very apex, socialism held on all too surely to the legacy of bourgeois philosophy. Hence the relation of necessity to the realm of freedom would remain merely quantitative and mechanical, and nature, posited as wholly alien—just as in the earliest mythology—would become totalitarian and absorb freedom together with socialism" (p. 41).

5. The first of these arguments is offered by Herbert Marcuse in "Industrialization and Capitalism in the Work of Max Weber," in his *Negations: Essays in Critical Theory* (Boston: Beacon Press, 1968). The second is offered by Alasdair MacIntyre in his *After Virtue* (Notre Dame: University of Notre Dame Press, 1981), pp. 79–108.

scientific language, that which is powerless has wholly lost any means of expression, and only the given finds its neutral sign."[6]

The critique of instrumental rationality is now one of the defining marks of left-leaning democratic political theory. With the exception of Rorty (whose domesticated pragmatism renders him immune to the angst of the early Frankfurt School), each member of Bernstein's gang of four embraces some version of the dialogical polity. Moreover, each does so on the grounds that the distinctively human can be protected only by drawing an unambiguous distinction between, on the one hand, that form of peculiarly political action whose interest in the preservation of intersubjective meaningfulness is secured through speech and, on the other, that form of antipolitical action whose interest in the maximization of efficient control is expressed in its reduction of politics to a science of public management.[7] Unmindful of Hegel's injunction to beware conceptual constructs that neatly partition experience into so many discrete realms, we have come to believe that our desire to master the utilitarian administration of domination is best served by sharply discriminating between qualitatively distinct forms of reason, some of which are sufficiently noble to participate in the political realm and some of which are not.

As the preceding chapter indicated, I do not challenge the contention that the overlapping forms of action bearing a family resemblance to what I have called "talk" (for example, "discourse," "communication," "dialogue," "conversation") are central to democratic politics. I do suggest, however, that claims of this sort conceal the pragmata about which we wish to say something and so unwittingly reinforce the antidemocratic forms of life that presently delegitimate and discourage that same activity. To indicate the bent of this critique, I cite Marx's famous dictum: "Philosophers have only *interpreted* the world in various ways; the point, however, is to *change* it." Excising the Hegelian baggage from this claim, we might ask just what the term "change" could possibly mean to one whose political education is limited to the texts of Arendt, Rorty, Gadamer, and Habermas? Will

6. Horkheimer and Adorno, *Dialectic of Enlightenment*, p. 23.
7. The remarks of this chapter are critical of the specific ways in which much contemporary political theory has formulated its response to the tyranny of instrumental rationality. As should be clear by now, however, I share the view that the hegemony of instrumental rationality has been accompanied by a profound loss of specifically political sensibilities. In the following chapter, I advance an argument regarding the shape that loss presently assumes in the United States.

that agent find that her sense of embodied agency, presupposed in any purposive effort to restructure the conditions that now shape the qualitative character of collective experience, has been deepened and intensified through this education? If the answer is no, as I suspect it is, then it may be inferred that much contemporary democratic theory does not elaborate a sufficiently complex or nuanced account of the conduct it means to inform. For that reason, we need to fashion ways of thinking about political conduct whose sensitivity to the interplay between the dialogic, the instrumental, and the aesthetic dimensions of reconstructive practice does less violence to the multifarious qualities of lived experience than that done by forms of conceptual reductionism whose chief attraction consists in their ability to gratify our will to believe in the intellectual tractability of the world.

II

The most significant contemporary effort to affirm the constitutive relationship between speech and democratic politics is found in the work of Jürgen Habermas. What makes Habermas especially noteworthy in this context is his acknowledged debt to Peirce and Dewey.[8] Yet as I suggest in the coming pages, it is precisely because that debt is not more thoroughgoing that Habermas fails to generate an adequate account of transformative political conduct.

Although given various formulations, Habermas's central preoccupation has remained essentially unchanged throughout the course of his career. Most recently, this concern has taken the form of a claim that modernity's "pathologies" are best understood not through reference to science's vitiation of the cosmological principles that sustained collective meaningfulness in the premodern world, but rather through

8. For the best indications of Habermas's debt to pragmatism, see his chapter on Charles S. Peirce in *Knowledge and Human Interests*, trans. Jeremy Shapiro (Boston: Beacon Press, 1971), pp. 91–112; his essays "Technical Progress and the Social Life-World" and "The Scientization of Politics and Public Opinion," in *Toward a Rational Society*, trans. Jeremy Shapiro (Boston: Beacon Press, 1970), pp. 50–61, 62–80; and his essay "Philosophy as Stand-in and Interpreter," in *After Philosophy: End or Transformation*, ed. Kenneth Baynes, James Bohman, and Thomas McCarthy (Cambridge: MIT Press, 1987), pp. 304–15. In his "Questions and Counterquestions," in *Habermas and Modernity*, ed. Richard Bernstein (Cambridge: MIT Press, 1985), note Habermas's claim that he has always identified his politics with the "radical democratic mentality which is present in the best American traditions and articulated in American pragmatism" (p. 198).

reference to the intrusion of its purposive rationality where it does not belong:

> The deformations that interested Marx, Durkheim, and Weber—each in his own way—ought not to be attributed either to the rationalization of the lifeworld as such or to increasing system complexity as such. Neither the secularization of worldviews nor the structural differentiation of society has unavoidable pathological side effects per se. It is not the differentiation and independent development of cultural value spheres that lead to the cultural impoverishment of everyday communicative practice, but an elitist splitting-off of expert cultures from contexts of communicative action in daily life. It is not the uncoupling of media-steered subsystems and of their organizational forms from the lifeworld that leads to the one-sided rationalization or reification of everyday communicative practice, but only the penetration of forms of economic and administrative rationality into areas of action that resist being converted over to the media of money and power because they are specialized in cultural transmission, social integration, and child rearing, and remain dependent on mutual understanding as a mechanism for coordinating action.[9]

The thrust of this argument is given more graphic expression in Habermas's assertion that the bureaucratic state and the capitalist economy have made "their way into the lifeworld from the outside—like colonial masters coming into a tribal society—and force[d] a process of assimilation upon it." This claim, in turn, depends for its force on Habermas's categorical distinction between social and system integration. The latter refers to those spheres that can be "integrated through the nonnormative steering of individual decisions not subjectively coordinated" without undermining the web of prereflective meanings that sustain the coherence of everyday practice. The former, by way of contrast, refers to those spheres of collective action that must be "integrated through consensus, whether normatively guaranteed or communicatively achieved," if that web is to be preserved from deformation. Since the political economy of late capitalism cannot acknowledge this distinction without calling into question the integrity of its administered order, it must ceaselessly vacillate between the market's "self-healing" powers and state interventionism in dealing with the legitimation crises provoked by this very vacillation. Yet no matter how vigorous its efforts, that order cannot overcome the "phe-

---

9. Jürgen Habermas, *The Theory of Communicative Action*, vol. 2, trans. Thomas McCarthy (Boston: Beacon Press, 1987), p. 330.

nomena of alienation and the unsettling of collective identity" that follow prolonged and systematic "disturbances in the symbolic reproduction of the lifeworld."[10]

Twenty years ago, Habermas made much the same argument, albeit in language that more clearly brought out its specifically democratic import. Discussing Marcuse's reading of Weber's concept of rationalization, Habermas argued that the "ideological nucleus" of "technocratic consciousness is *the elimination of the distinction between the practical and the technical*"; for this obfuscation makes our interest in "the maintenance of intersubjectivity of mutual understanding as well as . . . the creation of communication without domination . . . disappear behind the interest in the expansion of our power of technical control."[11] When the existence and maintenance of collective order is regarded as an end to be achieved through the manipulation of incentive structures rather than through the achievement of agreement among citizens who coordinate their action via the medium of language, the state cannot help but promote a systematic "depoliticization of the mass of the population":

> Old-style politics was forced, merely through its traditional form of legitimation, to define itself in relation to practical goals: the "good life" was interpreted in a context defined by interaction relations. . . . The substitute program prevailing today, in contrast, is aimed exclusively at the functioning of a manipulated system. It eliminates practical questions and therewith precludes discussion about the adoption of standards; the latter could emerge only from a democratic decision-making process. . . . To the extent that practical questions are eliminated, the public realm also loses its political function.[12]

Accordingly, very much like Horkheimer and Adorno, Marcuse errs when he locates the source of domination within technical rationality's

---

10. Habermas, *The Theory of Communicative Action*, vol. 2, pp. 150, 355, 386. Cf. p. 183: "The transfer of action coordination from language over to steering media means an uncoupling of interaction from lifeworld contexts. Media such as money and power attach to empirical ties; they encode a purposive-rational attitude toward calculable amounts of value and make it possible to exert generalized, strategic influence on the decisions of other participants while *bypassing* processes of consensus-oriented communication. Inasmuch as they do not merely simplify linguistic communication, but *replace* it with a symbolic generalization of rewards and punishments, the lifeworld contexts in which processes of reaching understanding are always embedded are devalued in favor of media-steered interaction; the lifeworld is no longer needed for the coordination of action."

11. Habermas, "Technology and Science as 'Ideology,' " in *Toward a Rational Society*, p. 113.

12. Ibid., pp. 103–4.

reduction of nature to an endlessly exploitable object and, on that basis, gestures at a science that embraces nature as a coequal subject. Rejecting critical theory's belief in "the original sin of scientific-technical progress," Habermas insists that our task is not to overturn but to contain the dynamic through which "the culturally defined self-understanding of a social life-world" is progressively "replaced by the self-reification of men under categories of purposive-rational action and adaptive behavior."[13]

This early statement of Habermas's argument, like its more recent formulation, relies for its intelligibility on postulation of a mutually irreducible distinction between instrumental and communicative action.[14] First introduced in his essay on Hegel's Jena *Philosophy of Mind* and elaborated (exaggerated?) in each of his subsequent works, this conceptual dichotomy distinguishes not between ontologically discrete kinds of being, but rather between different modes of constituting experience in accordance with fundamental interests of the human species.[15] Instrumental action arises out of the imperative to survive through reproduction of the conditions of material existence. Its character is most powerfully articulated within the empirical-analytic disci-

13. Ibid., pp. 89, 105–6. For Habermas's most explicit critique of Horkheimer and Adorno, see his "Entwinement of Myth and Enlightenment: Re-Reading the *Dialectic of Enlightenment*," *New German Critique*, no. 26 (1982), 13–30.

14. Although Habermas, in *Knowledge and Human Interests*, distinguishes between three basic cognitive interests, his later arguments, especially those advanced in *The Theory of Communicative Action*, make clear that his thought is fundamentally dualistic in character. His earlier insistence on the autonomy of an emancipatory interest has now been altered such that the human interest in liberation is taken to be a consequence of the increased rationalization of the sphere of communicative action.

15. This corresponds to Habermas's formulation in *Knowledge and Human Interests*, p. 196: "I term *interests* the basic orientations rooted in specific fundamental conditions of the possible reproduction and self-constitution of the human species, namely *work* and *interaction*." Cf. Jürgen Habermas, "A Postscript to *Knowledge and Human Interests*," *Philosophy of the Social Sciences* 3 (1973), 177: "The *universality* of cognitive interests implies that the constitution of object domains is determined by conditions governing the reproduction of the species, i.e., by the socio-cultural form of life *as such*." In his later work, this neo-Kantian transcendentalism is supplanted by what he calls "reconstructive analysis," whose more modest purpose is to explicate the presuppositions present within ordinary speech acts as well as the competencies that actors display in communicative action. For the evolution of Habermas's formulation of this distinction, see "Labor and Interaction: Remarks on Hegel's Jena *Philosophy of Mind*," in his *Theory and Practice*, trans. John Viertel (Boston: Beacon Press, 1974), pp. 142–69; "Technology and Science as 'Ideology,'" pp. 91–92; "Historical Materialism and the Development of Normative Structures," in his *Communication and the Evolution of Society*, trans. Thomas McCarthy (Boston: Beacon Press, 1979), pp. 117–20; and, finally, *The Theory of Communicative Action*, vol. 1, trans. Thomas McCarthy (Boston: Beacon Press, 1981), pp. 285–88. For the most thorough review of this distinction, as well as the criticisms it has spawned, see C. Fred Alford, *Science and the Revenge of Nature: Marcuse and Habermas* (Gainesville: University Presses of Florida, 1985), esp. pp. 139–77.

plines of natural science, whose rationality is rooted in their objectifying elaboration of nomologically formulated causal statements. When experimentally confirmed, those statements yield rules of monologic action that can be employed in the purposive exercise of technological power. Communicative action, in contrast, reflects the need of the species to sustain stable backgrounds of shared understanding. Its character is most fully disclosed by those hermeneutic sciences that secure access to the structures of symbolic meaning constitutive of specifically social reality. These sciences, unlike those aimed at the natural world, can secure their rational warrant only through reconstruction of the formal properties implicit within all utterances aimed at intersubjective consensus.

By thus differentiating between our efforts to dominate nature and the linguistically constituted context of shared meaning presupposed by such efforts, Habermas breaks Marx's concept of "practical-critical" activity into the discrete components of labor and social interaction. This enables him to evade the reduction of practice to "acting in the mode of producing."[16] Yet because he also identifies each as a form of action oriented toward cognition, he simultaneously salvages, without invoking essentialist premises, critical theory's case against the positivist identification of all knowledge with that peculiar to the natural sciences. Moreover, this a priori determination of the limits of autonomous knowledge-spheres proves directly applicable as social theory inasmuch as it enables Habermas to distinguish between those institutional spheres that promote an interest in technical control and those that enhance the integrity of the "life-world." Presupposing that "force exercised by one against others" is "the *only* alternative" when "interactions cannot be coordinated through achieved understanding," Habermas necessarily concludes that the possibility of political emancipation is now contingent on our ability to subordinate the forms of instrumental power "to decisions arrived at in unconstrained communication."[17]

16. Habermas, "The Classic Doctrine of Politics in Relation to Social Philosophy," in his *Theory and Practice*, p. 60.

17. Habermas, *The Theory of Communicative Action*, vol. 1, p. xxxvii; "A Reply to My Critics," in *Habermas: Critical Debates*, ed. John B. Thompson and David Held (Cambridge: MIT Press, 1982), p. 269. Cf. "Technology and Science as 'Ideology,' " pp. 118–19: "*Rationalization at the level of the institutional framework* can occur only in the medium of symbolic interaction itself, that is, through *removing restrictions on communication*. Public, unrestricted discussion, free from domination, of the suitability and desirability of action-orienting principles and norms in the light of the socio-cultural repercussions of developing subsystems of purposive-rational action—such communication at all levels

How, in light of the preceding chapters, are we to make sense of the core dualism informing Habermas's project? It is not implausible, I would argue, to read Habermas's resolution of the contemporary political problematic as a sophisticated reworking of early modern philosophy's struggle to protect the substance of traditional morality from the corrosive encroachment of rationalization. As I suggested through my reading of Descartes and Locke, the epistemological "adjustment which finally moderated, without completely exorcising, the earlier split between science and received institutional customs was a truce rather than anything remotely approaching integration. It consisted, in fact, of a device that was the exact opposite of integration. It operated on the basis of a hard and fast division of the interests, concerns, and purposes of human activity into two 'realms,' or, by a curious use of language, into two 'spheres'—not hemispheres. One was taken to be 'high' and hence to possess supreme jurisdiction over the other as inherently 'low.' That which is high was given the name 'spiritual,' ideal, and was identified with the moral. The other was the 'physical,' as determined by the procedures of the new science of nature. The new natural science was grudgingly given a license to operate on condition that it stay in its own compartment and mind its own business, as thus determined for it."[18]

Rooted in the distinction between technical and communicative interests, Habermas's basic conceptual equipment uneasily marries a content elicited from the ancient world to a form taken from the modern. The abstract opposition between purposive and communicative action, as Habermas acknowledges, has its roots in the distinction Aristotle draws between *technē* and *phronēsis*. That conceptual demarcation, we recall, serves in Aristotle's writings to explain the cognitional inferiority of those mechanical arts whose practice renders their adepts unable to specify the ends to which their products are to be put and hence, as a class, unfit to partake in public life.[19] But this classical

---

of political and repoliticized decision-making processes is the only medium in which anything like 'rationalization' is possible."

18. Dewey, *RP*, p. xxxi. On this point, see Dewey's essay "Peirce's Theory of Linguistic Signs, Thought, and Meaning," *Journal of Philosophy* 43 (1946): "It is, in my judgment, a too frequent practice to attempt to 'solve' problems by a distribution of subject-matters into different compartments—a procedure which also, in my judgment, evades the issues that are serious" (p. 86).

19. See Habermas, "The Classic Doctrine of Politics in Relation to Social Philosophy," p. 286n4, where he insists that the distinction between purposive-rational and communicative rationality was first brought to his attention through Arendt's affirmation of "the Aristotelian distinction between *technē* and *praxis*."

appropriation does not enter Habermas's thought in unaltered form. It is effectively recast in virtue of his conviction that modern science's demystification of the world demonstrates the untenability of Aristotelian cosmology and, by extension, its positing of a relationship of isomorphic interdependence between a complex hierarchy of self-realizing forms and a corresponding hierarchy of cognitional forms. Implicitly rejecting antiquity's contrast between perfect and defective Being, Habermas transforms the substance of his classical debt by assimilating it to epistemology's bifurcated categorization of all that exists as either end-positing mind or as end-less matter. Through this relocation, the Aristotelian *technē-phronēsis* distinction, which in its original statement presupposed their mutual rootedness and interrelatedness within an intrinsically meaningful nature, is represented as an unequivocal disjunction between two mutually exclusive interests and their corresponding epistēmēs.[20]

Habermas's struggle to protect the communicative interest by unambiguously partitioning it from the technical appears necessary only if one is convinced that we do in fact need to recapture the "values" that, on epistemology's account, Galileo expelled from nature. If that presupposition proves questionable, however, we may then ask whether Habermas's work offers a solution to the tyranny of instrumental rationality, or merely an expression of the alienation of human purpose from the cosmos within which it was once embedded. Granted, Habermas correctly identifies certain of the sociopolitical conditions that account for modernity's isolation of the intellectual from the material (for instance, its perpetuation, albeit in altered form, of antiquity's segregation of mental from manual labor). But these contingencies are simply accorded "quasi-transcendental" authorization when read back into the human condition as such. Not yet ready to part with the cosmological detritus that still informs so much contemporary thought about our present plight, Habermas's dualistic logic is ill equipped to offer distinctively democratic deliverance from the struggle to live in two unrelated worlds.[21]

20. See Dewey, "*Experience and Nature*: A Re-introduction," in *LW*, vol. 1, pp. 349–50: "The dualism of mind and matter may no longer overtly supply currently philosophical problems with their *raison d'être*. The assumptions underlying the cosmic dichotomy have, however, not been eliminated; on the contrary, they are the abiding source of issues which command today the attention of the very philosophers who pride themselves upon having replaced the philosophical 'thinking' of a bygone period with a mode of treatment as exact as the former discussions were sloppy."
21. See Dewey, unpublished ms. (53/13), where Marx's criticism of vulgar materialism is cited to this effect: "The distinction of the material and the non-material, while

The qualitative ethical content Galileo extracted from the world of human experience is refashioned and relocated within Habermas's ideal speech situation. The characterization of that situation is effectively dictated by Habermas's prior identification of purposive-rational activity with a narrowly instrumentalized and monologic conception of control ungrounded in intersubjective understanding and disconnected from any interest in collective emancipation.[22] The binary form of his logic then demands construction of that control's dialectically impoverished opponent, that is, the hypostatized counterfactual situation in which all arbitrary constraints on the flow of argumentation have been excised. Convinced that the achievement of human autonomy is conditional upon the self's ability to demarcate itself "in relation to the objectivity of a perceptible external nature,"[23] Habermas cannot help but represent the action appropriate to that situation as the intellectualized intercourse of neo-Kantian minds seeking immaterial union.

Granted, the formalism of Habermas's earlier characterizations of the ideal speech situation has now been tempered via the quasi-sociological analysis offered in the second volume of the *Theory of Communicative Action*. There, drawing heavily on Durkheim's tale of the transition from mechanical to organic solidarity, Habermas suggests that as the binding power once exercised by uncritically received tradition and religious revelation decays, the burden of normative regulation must shift to agreement achieved through rational communication:

---

necessary in study and inquiry, does not exist in culture as that which is studied, save as it itself is a characteristic of certain cultural beliefs. What is meant by this statement is that that which is called material and that which is called non-material cannot and do not *exist* apart from each other; the distinction made between them is one of inquiry and discourse, not a separation in what exists. Belief in their separation is itself a constituent of the non-material aspect of some cultures, and, like other elements of this culture, is maintained and carried only by elements of the material aspect."

22. For an excellent critique of Habermas and Arendt, which, from a Marxist perspective, argues against the equation of work with instrumental action, see Axel Honneth, "Work and Instrumental Action," *New German Critique* 26 (1982), 31–54.

23. Habermas, "Historical Materialism and the Development of Normative Structures," p. 100. Cf. pp. 105–6: "These fleeting allusions are meant only to render plausible the heuristic fruitfulness of the conjecture that there are homologies between the structures of the ego and of world-views. In both dimensions, development apparently leads to a growing decentration of intepretive systems and to an ever-clearer categorical demarcation of the subjectivity of internal nature from the objectivity of external nature, as well as from the normativity of social reality and the intersubjectivity of linguistic reality."

> The socially integrative and expressive functions that were at first fulfilled by ritual practice pass over to communicative action; the authority of the holy is gradually replaced by the authority of an achieved consensus. This means a freeing of communicative action from sacrally protected normative contexts. The disenchantment and disempowering of the domain of the sacred takes place by way of a linguistification of the ritually secured, basic normative agreement; going along with this is a release of the rationality potential in communicative action. The aura of rapture and terror that emanates from the sacred, the *spellbinding* power of the holy, is sublimated into the *binding/bonding* force of criticizable validity claims and at the same time turned into an everyday occurrence.[24]

In other words, as the domain of conduct ruled unproblematically by concrete custom diminishes, the "risk of dissensus" and hence the need for consensus, informed by "the ideal of an unlimited and undistorted communication community," grows more immediate. Unlike those more Romantically inclined, however, Habermas does not hold that this transformation in the fundament of community is to be lamented. As noted above, the freedom of modernity's selves requires that "the mask of a rationally impenetrable, basic, normative consensus" be stripped away so as to make room for a "rationalized lifeworld" in which "the authority of the better argument" is the exclusive foundation of "the unity of the collectivity."[25]

Consummation of the Enlightenment's promise thus requires a wholesale transcendence of the "sacred realm." That arena's articulation within various forms of ritual practice, promiscuously interweaving our interests in purposive activity and communication, expresses a primal version of the confusion between "relations of validity" and "relations of effectiveness." Reflecting the persistence of a mythical understanding of the world, this mixing of contraries fails to sever unequivocally action oriented to success from action oriented to mutual understanding, and so denies the structures of communicative action their right "to appear in an ever purer form."[26] In sum, Haber-

---

24. Habermas, *The Theory of Communicative Action*, vol. 2, p. 77. Cf. p. 107: "To the extent that communicative action takes on central societal functions, the medium of language gets burdened with tasks of producing substantial consensus. In other words, language no longer serves merely to *transmit* and actualize prelinguistically guaranteed agreements, but more and more to *bring about* rationally motivated agreements as well; it does so in moral-practical and in expressive domains of experience no less than in the specifically cognitive domain of dealing with an objectivated reality."

25. Ibid., vol. 2, pp. 82, 96, 145, 183.

26. Ibid., vol. 2, pp. 180, 193.

mas's appropriation of Durkheim simply reconfirms his earlier conviction that the intersubjective foundation of community must be rooted in "the discursive corroboration of truth claims, which occurs only under idealized conditions requiring that communication be *freed* of any compulsion to act."[27]

This dualistic formulation of the project of contemporary democratic theory engenders several problematic commitments, three of which I mention here. First, from Durkheim, Habermas learns that modernity can no longer rely on the power of religion, myth, or tradition to secure its unity. Hence it must now find an equally powerful substitute in universal agreement on the rules of a formalized reason. That quest, from my perspective, looks suspiciously like a refined version of liberalism's effort to counter the anomie of its subjects by ensuring the capacity of facticity to impose its truth on their disembodied minds. It takes no great ingenuity to see the parallel between, on the one hand, Habermas's contention that the task of reason qua technique is to dominate outer nature and, on the other, his contention that the task of reason qua communication is to master inner nature by employing its sublimated "spellbinding power" in the production of intersubjective consensus. Consequently, although he claims to welcome the diversity spawned by disintegration of mechanical solidarity's customary loci, Habermas's quasi foundationalism intimates his abiding fear that experience may prove unable to muster from within itself the resources needed to halt liberal society's fragmentation into so many atomic bits.

Second, while it may be true that "practical power" can be secured only "through the minds of enlightened citizens,"[28] it is not immediately clear how Habermas intends to join such enlightenment, once acquired, to significant transformative conduct. Habermas effectively subsumes beneath the category of purposive instrumentality all conduct not oriented toward mutual understanding. Then, like Arendt and Gadamer, he enjoins us to found anew the public spaces within which dialogue, conversation, speech, or communication might flourish. But how, we might ask, are we to think about the conduct that

27. Habermas, "A Postscript to *Knowledge and Human Interests*," p. 179. Note in this connection Habermas's admission that in his early years, overly "influenced by Dewey . . . I could not always resist the temptation to oppose the realist view of knowledge by stressing the instrumentalist idea of truth implicit in pragmatism" (p. 179).

28. Habermas, "Dogmatism, Reason, and Decision: On Theory and Praxis in Our Scientific Civilization," p. 255.

refashions the concrete media of lived experience and so makes such talk possible?[29] Through critical discourse, citizens may come to a partial understanding of the institutional and ideological barriers that presently reduce politics to technique. But this awareness, no matter how significant its implications for the self-reflective ego, is not identical to the forms of practical engagement through which structures of domination are reshaped.[30] Hence we need to know not how to purify the reason of autonomous subjects by abstracting from them their impulses to remake their world, but rather how to think about the ways in which agents might actualize the promptings of imagination in refashioning the political matters they locate in the spaces brought into being by their intersecting paths.

Third, and related, the difficulties stemming from Habermas's failure to articulate a suitable concept of transformative political conduct are compounded by his ambivalence toward institutions. In his early essays, Habermas complained of the gulf between our "growing power of technical control over the external conditions of nature on the one hand, and a more or less passive adaptation of the institutional framework to the expanded subsystems of purposive-rational action on the other"; in light of this complaint, he called for re-creation of "the institutionally secured forms of general and public communication

29. This, I take it, is part of what Anthony Giddens, in his *Studies in Social and Political Theory* (New York: Basic Books, 1977), is getting at when he states: "To differentiate labor and interaction, at least in the way Habermas does, treating the former as equivalent to strategic or instrumental action, seems to allow no conceptual mode of treating interaction as itself a productive enterprise" (p. 151). Habermas's response, which can be found in his "A Reply to My Critics," rejects the idea of a practice related "to the constitution of action complexes and to their reproduction" because such a notion, relying on "an anthropomorphistic concept of society," implies that "speaking and acting subjects 'produce' their social life-context in a way similiar to that in which they make products of instrumental action" (p. 268). Although Giddens might have made matters more difficult for Habermas had he not used the language of "production," it is nonetheless true that this reply confirms my contention that Habermas is unwilling to acknowledge any form of reconstructive practice that is not narrowly instrumentalist in orientation.

30. Habermas appears to perceive the need to carve out an alternative conception of action when, in his "A Postscript to *Knowledge and Human Interests*," he grants that he has not differentiated clearly "enough between instrumental action and experimental action" (p. 187n46). What he has in mind here is intimated when, in his "A Reply to My Critics," he writes: "Experimental action does not lie on the same level as the instrumental action of naive or scientised pratice. In its function of producing data, which is always gathered with a view to testing hypothetical validity-claims, experimental action is related to discourse from the start" (p. 275). Although this suggests that Habermas occasionally perceives the need to loosen the conceptual constraints imposed by his communicative-instrumental dualism, his unwillingness to do so in any politically relevant way is made clear by his representation of experimental action as a subordinate element within the logic of instrumental science.

that deal with the practical question of how men can live and want to live under the objective conditions of their ever-expanding power of control."[31] But here, too, his ability to indicate how we might engage in such re-creation is undermined by the reductionist thrust of his dualistic logic. As we have seen, Habermas effectively identifies purposive conduct as rule-governed action oriented to the achievement of instrumental control over a specified class of objects. Thinking within these confines, Habermas is impelled to equate the purposive conduct of institution making with the imposition of domination corresponding, at least in form, to that of our technological mastery of nature. That, in turn, leads him to suspect that the relationship between institutions and the achievement of social relations "bound only to communication free of domination" is antagonistic at best.[32] Echoing the liberal tradition he finds so problematic, he is thereby driven to represent emancipation as the counterfactual constitution of a purely procedural un-situation from which all impediments to the movement of unrestricted speech have been extirpated: "*Rationalization at the level of the institutional framework* can occur only in the medium of symbolic interaction itself, that is, through *removing restrictions on communication.* Public, unrestricted discussion, free from domination, of the suitability and desirability of action-orienting principles and norms in the light of the socio-cultural repercussions of developing subsystems of purposive-rational action—such communication at all levels of political and repoliticized decision-making processes is the only medium in which anything like 'rationalization' is possible."[33]

31. Habermas, "Technology and Science as 'Ideology,' " p. 115; "Technical Progress and the Social Life-World," p. 57. For Dewey's claim to the same effect, see *HNC*, p. 101: "We realize how little the progress of man has been the product of intelligent guidance, how largely it has been a by-product of accidental upheavals, even though by an apologetic interest in behalf of some privileged institution we later transmute chance into providence. We have depended upon the clash of war, the stress of revolution, the emergence of heroic individuals, the impact of migrations generated by war and famine, the incoming of barbarians, to change established institutions. Instead of constantly utilizing unused impulse to effect the reconstruction, we have waited till an accumulation of stresses suddenly breaks through the dikes of custom."
32. Habermas, *Knowledge and Human Interests*, p. 53.
33. Habermas, "Technology and Science as 'Ideology,' " pp. 118–19. Cf. Dewey, *HNC*, pp. 305–6: "Find a man who believes that all men need is freedom *from* oppressive legal and political measures, and you have found a man who, unless he is merely obstinately maintaining his own private privileges, carries at the back of his head some heritage of the metaphysical doctrine of free will, plus an optimistic confidence in natural harmony. . . . It is reasonably obvious that organization may become a hindrance to freedom; it does not take us far to say that the trouble lies not in organization but in over-organization. At the same time, it must be admitted that there is no effective or objective freedom without organization."

Hannah Arendt is surely correct to claim that "power comes into being only if and when men join themselves together for the purpose of action, and it will disappear when, for whatever reason, they disperse and desert one another"; and she is equally correct to insist that politics requires "a stable worldly structure to house" this "combined power of action."[34] But these claims simply reinforce my contention that theoretical work errs when it defines its task as clarification of the universal conditions necessary to rational consensus but fails to ask how our shared interest in political affairs might be actualized within institutional structures able to endure time. A commitment to the dialogical polity remains vacuous as a guide to the conduct its own possibility presupposes unless we recognize that our problem is always how to recraft existent institutional forms, not how to pass from one institutional setting to no setting at all.

Habermas dismisses such criticism by arguing that there is nothing of a theoretical nature to be said about questions of institution-creating and practice-reconstructing conduct because such "organizational" matters can only be resolved by those immediately embedded in specific contexts of action.[35] But this claim is tenable only if one first presupposes that the spectrum of choice is limited to either a form of theory that asserts the possibility of "a direct derivation" of action from its conclusions,[36] or alternatively a form that can only sustain an abstract and oblique relation to the practice it means to inform. To evade the authoritarian implications of the former, Habermas embraces the latter. Yet that makes it very difficult for him to acknowledge that organization of the quest for agreement through one institutional form as opposed to another is always a practical matter that presupposes specific "theoretical" commitments regarding the character of political membership, self-identity, reasoned choice, and so on.

Politics is indeed a matter of talking and arguing. But it is also a matter of struggling and fighting. To posit language and its distinctive logic as a sufficient model for understanding the nondiscursive forms

34. Hannah Arendt, *On Revolution* (New York: Penguin, 1977), p. 175.
35. See, for example, Habermas, quoted in Thomas McCarthy, *The Critical Theory of Jürgen Habermas* (Cambridge: MIT Press, 1981), p. 331: "If one calls democracies precisely those political orders that satisfy the procedural type of legitimation, then questions of democratization can be treated as what they are, i.e., as organizational questions. Which types of organization and which mechanism are better suited to produce procedurally legitimate decisions depends on the concrete social situation."
36. Habermas, "Some Difficulties in the Attempt to Link Theory and Practice," in *Theory and Practice*, p. 20.

of power incarnate in bureaucratic institutions, modes of production, disciplinary techniques, and the like is to respond to the vast accumulation of technical knowledge now employed in the service of domination with a theory of active reflection rather than a call for reflective action. Identifying human speech with practical reason, and practical reason with the resolution of collective misunderstanding, Habermas offers solace to those whose frustration at the diluted state of contemporary citizenship can be eased by equating democratic politics with the achievement of consensus via proceedings bearing a striking resemblance to those of an academic seminar.[37]

III

As epistemology's faith in the correspondence between the self's words and nature's objects has been shaken, its idealist alter ego has surfaced once again. Although appearing in many guises, the more familiar formulations of contemporary neoidealism presuppose in one way or another that discourse's propositions refer only to, and derive their full sense from, other propositions. In Habermas's case, the result is a coherence theory of truth that locates the criteria of verification wholly within the logic of speech. The problematic thrust implicit in such idealism is revealed much more pointedly when speech about political things is effectively equated with those things, as they are drawn up within and refashioned by language. To illustrate, I cite the example of Murray Edelman, who in his otherwise splendid *Constructing the Political Spectacle* makes the following assertion: "It is language about political events, not the events in any other sense, that people experience; even developments that are close by take their meaning from the language that depicts them. So political language *is* political reality; there is no other so far as the meaning of events to actors and spectators is concerned."[38] Here Edelman severs language from the

---

37. On this point, see William Connolly's comment in his review of Thomas McCarthy's *Critical Theory of Jürgen Habermas*, in *History and Theory* 18 (1979), 417: "The ideal speech situation, serving as the centerpiece of Habermas' theory, is more than an abstract theoretical construct. It symbolizes at once the ideal of enlightened politics and the threatened closure of public space for its realization. Unconstrained by any concrete political practice it provides a sanctuary of sorts for political reflection. In this space thought could run idle, even if politics ran out of control. We have here the idealized speech of stoics frozen out of effective participation in public life."

38. Murray Edelman, *Constructing the Political Spectacle* (Chicago: University of Chicago Press, 1988), p. 104.

forms of embodied experience in which it is embedded and, on that basis, identifies an ethereal intralinguistic world with the totality of political reality. At its most sublime, such academic conceit invites the construction of politics as a conversation whose sole end is its own agreeable perpetuation. The philosophical arms of Richard Rorty, in other words, wait to embrace those who, on strictly political grounds, might prefer to keep other company.

The critique of instrumental rationality, in giving birth to an equally one-sided caricature of the dialogic polity, has generated a vacuum in the space created by its binary formulation. "Philosophical dualism is but a formulated recognition of an impasse in life; an impotence in interaction, inability to make effective transition, limitation of power to regulate and thereby to understand."[39] Infatuated with distinctions whose form and content unwittingly reinforce the conditions to which they give expression, too much contemporary democratic theory conceives of political action as a war of words between hypostatized rivals who, at their most refined, identify the professional journal as the preferred field of combat.

What such theorizing does not need now is more rigorous typologies offering greater analytic precision as a surrogate for enhanced sensitivity to the ambiguities encountered in the course of concrete political activity. Rather, it needs imaginative projection of new forms of conduct whose capacity to empower by nurturing a sense of collective agency expands the potentialities of democratic experience. That, in turn, requires stepping outside the familiar terms of the hermeneuticist-instrumentalist debate. More precisely, we need to remap that terrain whose present exclusion from the political realm achieves consummate expression in Arendt's insistence that we unburden ourselves of a tradition that makes "it almost impossible to discuss" political matters "without using the category of means and ends and thinking in terms of instrumentality."[40]

Habermas, it is true, acknowledges the insufficiency of Arendt's dramaturgical conception of action, which, to escape all means-ends formulations of political action, stigmatizes as antipolitical violence any deliberate effort to refashion the world in the service of collective ends.[41] To do so, Habermas explicitly cites Dewey's critique of those

39. Dewey, EN, pp. 241–42.
40. Hannah Arendt, The Human Condition (Chicago: University of Chicago Press, 1958), p. 229.
41. In On Revolution's critique of James Harrington, Arendt argues that by equating action with fabrication, he introduces into politics "the means of violence which indeed

neo-Aristotelians who, certain that the ethical ends needed to guide use of our means are already known to us, overlook the glaring differences between the forms of culture out of which that knowledge originally emerged and the magnitude of the means presently available to us:[42] "Questions of life conduct demand a rational discussion that is not focused exclusively either on technical means or on the application of traditional behavioral norms. The reflection that is required extends beyond the production of technical knowledge and the hermeneutical clarification of traditions to the employment of technical means in historical situations whose objective conditions have to be interpreted anew each time in the framework of a self-understanding determined by tradition."[43] Hence, concludes Habermas, if political action is not to fall prey to a naive utopianism that neglects the reformulation of given ends in light of the means necessary to their satisfac-

---

are ordinary and necessary for all purposes of fabrication precisely because something is created not out of nothing, but out of given material which must be violated in order to yield itself to the formative processes out of which a thing, a fabricated object, will arise" (p. 200). The implication is clear: Any introduction of instrumental categories of action into the public realm signifies the degeneration of politics into terror.

42. See Dewey, *RP*, p. xxxvii. This criticism is readily leveled against Gadamer, who in his appropriation of the Aristotelian distinction between *technē* and *phronēsis* forgets that this way of carving up the world of human practice emerged out of a cultural matrix in which the ability of craft to alter the human and natural environments was radically circumscribed. Within this context, the conditions of collective life were not shaped in any fundamental way by technical instrumentalities; hence, as Chapter 4 suggested, the relations between its members could be satisfactorily regulated through recourse to the acquired virtues of practical wisdom and a nontheoretical stock of familiar maxims and proverbs. But as scientifically informed technology has radically altered the power of human action to produce consequences that extend, in space and time, far beyond its originating context, the characterization of our present mechanisms of control as *technai*—that is, as limited means with a determinate power of effecting specified proximate ends—has become untenable. Modern technology, whose most astonishing feature consists in its capacity to generate the resources needed to achieve ends that have not yet been conceived as desirable by those who must employ them, now creates the context within which political action must proceed. Failing to acknowledge that the instrumentalities of science no longer constitute an independent realm of tools that, like the implements of handicraft, may be employed or neglected at will, Gadamer fosters the illusion that it is still possible to isolate a purified realm of judgment within which human beings, unformed by what Foucault calls the "technologies of the self," debate the uses to which *technai*'s products are to be put.

43. Habermas, "Technical Progress and the Social Life-World," p. 53. Cf. p. 56, where, aside from a few terminological idiosyncrasies, Habermas makes a claim strikingly Deweyan in flavor: "The power of technical control over nature made possible by science is extended today directly to society. In the same measure, however, the problems of technical control solved by science are transformed into life problems. For the scientific control of natural and social processes—in a word, technology—does not release men from action. Just as before conflicts must be decided, interests realized, interpretations found. . . . Today, however, the practical problems are themselves in large measure determined by the system of our technical achievements."

tion, it must affirm a relationship of dialectical interdependence between the ends we deem worthy and the techniques now available for their realization.[44]

To explicate the practical significance of this claim, as we have seen, Habermas expresses the hope that the power of technical control can be "brought within the range of the consensus of acting and transacting citizens" by systematically cultivating reciprocal "communication between experts and the agencies of political decision."[45] Given his insistence, however, that we can disentangle the autonomous agent from its technological constructions only by radically dissociating our interest in linguistically mediated intersubjectivity from our interest in purposive-rational control, it is not clear how these antagonists can inform one another without compromising the life-world's integrity. Indeed, to ensure that world's purity, Habermas must ultimately characterize the relationship between communicative and instrumental rationality via a distinctively nondialectical notion of domination. For in the final analysis, either the life-world's conquest by technical rationality will in time be completed (in which case the prophecy of Horkheimer and Adorno will be proven correct) or, alternatively, technical rationality must be "subordinated"[46] to the life-world (in which case the mutual transformation of each by the other is suppressed in the interest of ensuring the victory of a subject whose autonomy is purchased at the price of substantive estrangement from the world in which it is situated).

To work between this Scylla and Charybdis, we must first question the effort to draw an unambiguous distinction between communica-

44. In "The Scientization of Politics and Public Opinion," Habermas cites Dewey when he argues that "there is obviously an interdependence between values that proceed from interest situations and techniques that can be utilized for the satisfaction of value-oriented needs. If so-called values in the long run lose their connection with the technically appropriate satisfaction of real needs, they become functionless and die out as ideologies. Inversely, new values can develop from new techniques in changed interest situations" (p. 66).

45. Habermas, "Technical Progress and the Social Life-World," p. 57; "The Scientization of Politics and Public Opinion," p. 68; cf. pp. 79–80: "The question is whether a productive body of knowledge is merely transmitted to men engaged in technical manipulation for purposes of control or is simultaneously appropriated as the linguistic possession of communicating individuals. A scientized society could constitute itself as a rational one only to the extent that science and technology are mediated with the conduct of life through the minds of its citizens."

46. Habermas, The Theory of Communicative Action, p. xxxvii. In this regard, see "The Dialectics of Rationalization: An Interview with Jürgen Habermas by Axel Honneth, Eberhard Knodler-Bunte and Arno Widmann," Telos 49 (1981), pp. 5–31, where Habermas makes reference to the "battle lines between life-world and system" (p. 19).

tive intercourse and conduct aimed at reshaping what is given in experience. The ground for such a questioning was prepared in my earlier discussion concerning the relationship between the what and the how of experience, but it bears recapitulating here. Contrary to classical teleology, nature is not a realm of fixed forms whose infection by intrinsically indeterminate stuff represents a regrettable degradation from its otherwise perfect state. Nor, contrary to epistemology, is it neutered matter whose lack of intrinsic form renders it infinitely malleable. Nor, contrary to Habermas's neo-Kantian version of the epistemological account, is "nature-in-itself" a transcendental presupposition to which we can secure only instrumental access.[47] None of these views adequately acknowledges that all existents are events inasmuch as they are qualified by temporal transition, and that all such occurrences are at one and the same time *con*currences. In virtue of its relationships with others without which it could neither be nor be conceived, each existent is shaped to individuated form by the concurrences in which it participates and which, together, account for its qualitatively unique and irreducible "itselfness." The promiscuous coincidence of these many events, moreover, is forever generating natural *termini* that are themselves as infinitely novel and irregularly varied as are the individual existents out of whose histories they proceed.

The event of experience is brought forth out of nature so characterized. "It is not experience which is experienced, but nature—stones, plants, animals, diseases, health, temperature, electricity, and so on. Things interacting in certain ways *are* experience; they are what is experienced. Linked in certain other ways with another natural object—the human organism—they are *how* things are experienced as well."[48] In being *of* nature, experience is caught up within and rooted in its qualitatively unique singularities. But those singularities are themselves the fruit of complex histories, and so experience's interception and incorporation of certain of the ends so generated bears within itself the capacity to become something more than a mere aggregation of isolated incidents. For it too possesses the character of a historical

47. For his disparaging characterization of another contemporary view of nature, see Habermas, "A Reply to My Critics," pp. 244–45: "The phenomena that are exemplary for a moral-practical, a 'fraternal' relation to nature are most unclear, if one does not want to have recourse here as well to mystically inspired philosophies of nature, or to taboos (e.g., vegetarian restrictions), to anthropomorphising treatment of house pets, and the like."

48. Dewey, *EN*, p. 4a.

emergent composed of events that are at one and the same time eventuations and initiations.

To see this is to see why it is a mistake to try to salvage some faint semblance of epistemology's conviction that our experience of the world's qualitative textures is a mere projection of subjectivity by arguing that such qualities are partly inherent in the object and partly derived from the human act of interpretation; that formulation, too, errs in its illicit importation of an antecedent subject-object distinction within experience that, in its immediacy, knows no such division. Rather, and as our language intimates when we say that a given landscape *is* beautiful or that a particular action *is* just, the qualitative fruits engendered by the transformation of a natural context into a lived environment—that is, a world—reveal as much about nature's events as it does about the beings who ingest and digest them. And it is for that reason that we may plausibly contend that "the main features of human life (culture, experience, history—or whatever name may be preferred) are indicative of outstanding features of nature itself—of centers and perspectives, contingencies and fulfillments, crises and intervals, histories, uniformities, and particularizations. The large features of human sufferings, enjoyments, trials, failures and successes together with the institutions of art, science, technology, politics, and religion which mark them, communicate genuine features of the world within which man lives."[49]

"Man begins as a part of physical and animal nature. In as far as he reacts to physical things on a strictly physical level, he is pulled and pushed about, overwhelmed, broken to pieces, lifted on the crest of the wave of things, like anything else. His contacts, his sufferings and doings, are matters of direct interaction only. He is in a 'state of nature.' "[50] In the animal, that state takes shape as singular patterns of response to distinct environmental disturbances. Its nature can be taken up within the more complex appearances of experience because the human animal, making use of the arts of memory and anticipation (the stuff of *empeiria*), is able to fashion multiple patterns of flexible response to its world and so, in time, lay hands on the matter of sense.

---

49. John Dewey, "Half-Hearted Naturalism," *Journal of Philosophy* 24 (1927), 59. Cf. p. 58: "Human affairs, associative and personal, are projections, continuations, and complications, of the nature which exists in the physical and pre-human world. There is no gulf, no two spheres of existence, no bifurcation."

50. Dewey, *EN*, p. 370.

The ground of meaning, as a potentiality implicit within the movement of nature's interweaving events, is established when experience encounters a thing as a *what*, that is, as this particular pragma in its qualitative immediacy. But what makes such a thing an identifiable event is the concretion effected by its articulation within the medium of language. This is not to say that the meanings of the things we encounter in daily life are invented by epistemology's disembodied and discrete minds. Instead, it is to affirm that when experience enters any given stretch of nature in a way that opens up the affairs of others, it can render these affairs meaningful only as they are additionally transformed through modes of linguistic appropriation that explore but neither create nor constitute the things of which we speak. "Without language, the qualities of organic action that are feelings are pains, pleasures, odors, colors, noises, tones, only potentially and proleptically. With language they are discriminated and identified."[51]

"When appetite is perceived in its meanings, in the consequences it induces, and these consequences are experimented with in reflective imagination, some being seen to be consistent with one another, and hence capable of coexistence of serially ordered achievement, others being incompatible, forbidding conjunction at one time, and getting in one another's way serially—when this estate is attained, we live on the human plane, responding to things in their meanings." It is via language's making manifest of some but never all the possible appearances intimated by experience's transactions that an otherwise truncated nature more completely real-izes its ontological potentialities. Language is "not a mere agency for economizing energy in the interaction of human beings. It is a release and amplification of energies that enter into it. When communication occurs, all natural events are re-adapted to meet the requirements of conversation, whether it be public discourse or that preliminary discourse called thinking. Events turn into things with a meaning."[52]

The transformative appropriation of things within language is a

51. Ibid., p. 258. Cf. p. 3a: Experience "tunnels in all directions and in so doing brings to the surface things at first hidden—as miners pile high on the surface of the earth treasures brought from below. . . . Experience as an existence is something that occurs only under highly specialized conditions, such as are found in a highly organized creature which in turn requires a specialized environment. There is no evidence that experience occurs everywhere and everywhen."
52. Ibid., pp. 166, 174, 370–71.

necessary condition of their capacity to bear meaning. Such meaning is always located within a context whose enduring structure is, in large measure, attributable to the concrete things crafted by human beings out of nature's historically qualified events. The constellation of such things includes the meaningful artifacts that constitute the "means" of everyday living. Hence those things are not objects that somehow span the otherwise empty space between mind's intentionality and nature's inert matter. Rather, they are immanent parts of that larger cultural medium in which human conduct, experienced things, and nature's whats are commonly situated. "A tool is a particular thing, but it is more than a particular thing, since it is a thing in which a connection, a sequential bond of nature is embodied. Man's bias towards himself easily leads him to think of a tool solely in relation to himself, to his hand and eyes, but its primary relationship is toward other external things, as the hammer to the nail, and the plow to the soil. A tool denotes a perception and acknowledgment of sequential bonds in nature."[53]

Additionally, the significant character of the various artifacts of ordinary experience testifies to their status as vehicles of collective import. Communication, as a natural function of existence, always implies at least two beings whose undertakings overlap in some way. The meaningfulness of the world's more enduring things, consequently, expresses the forms they assume when implicated in joint activity. Their significance is engendered not by association per se, but rather by their participation in recurrent situations of collective purpose and execution. Thus the "means" of everyday life can dig into qualitative experience and so complicate its immediacy only because they are already thoroughly embedded within linguistically saturated experience. "Spears, urns, baskets, snares may have originated accidentally in some consummatory consequence of natural events. But only repetition through concerted action accounts for their becoming institutionalized as tools, and this concert of action depends upon the use of memoranda and communication. At every point appliances and application, utensils and uses, are bound up with directions, suggestions and records made possible by speech."[54] Hence every artifact is itself

53. Ibid., pp. 122–23.
54. Ibid., pp. 168, 187. The capacity of artifacts to speak, Dewey argues, explains the origins of animism: "Animism, the attribution of desire and intent to inanimate things, is no mysterious projection of psychical traits; it is a misintepretation of a natural fact, namely, that significant things are things actually implicated in situations of shared or

an expressive vehicle of meaning. If "language in its widest sense—that is, including all means of communication such as, for example, monuments, rituals, and formalized arts—is the medium in which culture exists and through which it is transmitted," then a "tool or machine is not simply a simple or complex physical object having its own physical properties and effects, but is also a mode of language. For it *says* something to those who understand it."[55] Inasmuch as the distinctive human need is for appreciation of the meanings of things, appropriation of the artifacts we reductively designate as "means" is, in sum, the minister that conducts nature to this remarkable issue.

In grasping the relations of mutual implication sustained among nature's affairs, qualitative experience's linguistic metamorphosis does not transport human beings into an ontologically distinct supranatural realm. Converting existential connections into articulated relations of meaning, language surveys pragmata in ways that reveal new appearances in time; but it does not thereby remove them from the mundane. It is misguided, then, to partition lived conduct into autonomous realms by drawing a sharp separation between meanings that comment on the causal relationship of things and meanings that declare the terms of human association. To insist, as does Habermas, on a sharp ontological distinction between communicative encounters and efforts to reshape the lived contexts within which such communication takes place is to fail to see that words bear meaning only because they are immersed within forms of life which themselves cannot be dislocated from their embeddedness in nature's qualitative episodes. Language, in short, sits at the heart of the transactional relationships through which the means of daily life are used to initiate new possibilities in collective experience, and so contribute to more complicated and subtle fruitions of nature's otherwise partial end(ing)s. "Communication is uniquely instrumental and uniquely final. It is instrumental as liberating us from the otherwise overwhelming pressure of events and enabling us to live in a world of things that have meaning. It is final as a sharing in the objects and arts precious to a community, a

---

social purpose and execution. . . . 'Animism' is thus the consequence of a direct transfer of properties of a social situation to an immediate relationship of natural things to a person. Its legitimate and constant form is poetry, in which things and events are given voice and directly communicate with us" (pp. 180–81). For my understanding of Dewey on this point I am indebted to Anthony Cascardi, "The Genealogy of Pragmatism," *Philosophy and Literature* 10 (1986), 295–303.

55. Dewey, *LTI*, pp. 20, 46.

sharing whereby meanings are enhanced, deepened and solidified in the sense of communion. Here, as in so many other things, the great evil lies in separating instrumental and final functions."[56]

IV

Habermas's distinction between purposive and communicative action rides on the back of epistemology's alienation of experience from nature. As we saw in the previous section, that alienation is presupposed in his argument regarding the relationship between technical rationality and the objects it manipulates as well as in his argument regarding our collective need to resubordinate the realm of instrumentality to that of the life-world. Convinced that the claims of autonomy require that human subjects be located outside and above nature, Habermas imports into the core of his theoretical apparatus a notion of domination that effectively synthesizes Descartes' mind-body dualism with Zeus's representation of action as command from on high. An argument whose stated purpose is to reinvigorate the quality of democratic citizenship thereby discovers that it can achieve its end only by relocating the practice of univocal command in the relationship between citizens and the nature from which they have made their collective escape. The problematic character of this resolution is implicit in its conviction that experience can be carved up in strict conformity with the demands of a dualistic logic. Only that presupposition sustains Habermas's faith in the meaningfulness of an ideal speech situation from which all tainting considerations of power have been excised. If, however, we are uncertain whether such considerations, when relocated within experience, will remain neatly confined to their designated realm, perhaps we should ask whether it is possible to craft an understanding of conduct that, although purposive in some sense, nonetheless eludes the charges rightfully directed against instrumentalism, narrowly construed. My purpose in this section, in other words, is to sketch the outlines of a form of conduct which, because it respects the human situation's complex mediation of nature-in-experience, does not persist in the illusion that the qualitative dimensionalities of lived conduct can (or should) be subordinated to imperious dictates of "pure" reason.

56. Dewey, *EN*, pp. 204–5.

To start along that path, we can profitably begin by reworking the Aristotelian portrayal of deliberation as a form of conduct whose intelligence inheres in the establishment of an appropriate relationship between means and ends. Recall the ideological content of that portrayal. The familiar division of ends into the intrinsic and the instrumental is, as I suggested in Chapter 2, a metaphysical reification of antiquity's conviction that "there are classes of men who are necessary materials of society but not integral parts of it. Because Greek industry was so largely upon the plane of servile labor, all industrial activity was regarded by Greek thought as a *mere* means, an extraneous necessity. Hence satisfactions due it were conceived to be the ends or goals of purely animal nature in isolation. With respect to a truly human and rational life, they were not ends or goods at all, but merely 'means,' that is to say, external conditions that were antecedently enforced requisites of the life conducted and enjoyed by free men, especially by those devoted to the acme of freedom, pure thinking."[57] Not yet freed from antiquity's designation of the material as an enemy of the distinctively human, we remain captive to the characterization of means as mechanical conditions whose worth is derived exclusively from their strict subordination to ends that, because pure, are intrinsically valuable. So constrained, we find it all too easy to rationalize forms of collective practice, like that of industrial production in a capitalist economy, whose drudgery is endured for the sake of a higher good located at some unspecified point in an indefinite future.

To expose the problematic character of such justification, we must call into question Aristotle's contention, advanced in his *Politics*, that "when of two related things one is a means and the other an end, in their case there is nothing in common except for the one to act and the other to receive the action."[58] This claim, which Aristotle himself throws into doubt when he suggests that "each science produces its product well by focusing on what is intermediate,"[59] cannot recognize that the distinction between ends and means is temporal rather than ontological in character. "Means are means; they are intermediates, middle terms. To grasp this fact is to have done with the ordinary

57. Ibid., p. 369.
58. Aristotle, *Politics*, trans. Ernest Barker (London: Oxford University Press, 1958), 1328a29–31.
59. Aristotle, *Nichomachean Ethics*, trans. Terence Irwin (Indianapolis: Hackett, 1985), 1106b8–10.

dualism of means and ends. The 'end' is merely a series of acts viewed at a remote stage; and a means is merely the series viewed at an earlier one. The distinction of means and ends arises in surveying the *course* of a proposed *line* of action, a connected series in time. The 'end' is the last act thought of; the means are the acts to be performed prior to it in time."[60] Because the distinction between ends and means is a function of the temporal perspective from which action is surveyed, conduct cannot help but prove ill informed if it detaches each from the other on the ground that only one possesses unmediated value. If use of the term "intrinsic" is taken to mean that something is absolutely unrelated to all other things, then to acknowledge that any given end, once achieved, is a historical fruit produced by concatenation of its specific conditions is to deny this term the conditions of its intelligibility.

It follows that concern for the achievement of a particular end entails comparable solicitude for its means as well. To hold the contrary, given the status of means as relational states mediating between a present situation and one in the process of unfolding, is to reveal that one does not truly esteem the state of affairs that is engendered by their cumulative effect. In this sense, every means is an end, because each situation brought into being as means is also an outcome possessing its own qualitative uniqueness. Correlatively, every end is a means, because each "final" end stands at the close of one history and the beginning of another. The familiar claim, erroneously ascribed to Machiavelli, that "the end justifies the means" stands refuted, then, on the ground that each is simultaneously instrumentally and intrinsically valuable. To endorse that maxim "is equivalent to holding one of two views. One of the views is that only the specially selected 'end' held in view will actually be brought into existence by the means used, something miraculously intervening to prevent the means employed from having their other usual effects; the other (and more probable) view is that, as compared with the importance of the selected and uniquely prized end, other consequences may be completely ignored and brushed aside no matter how intrinsically obnoxious they are. This arbitrary selection of some one part of the attained consequences as *the* end and hence as the warrant of means used is the fruit of holding that *it*, as *the*

60. Dewey, *HNC*, p. 34. Cf. p. 36: "Means and ends are two names for the same reality. The terms denote not a division in reality but a distinction in judgment. . . . To think of the end signifies to extend and enlarge our view of the act to be performed. It means to look at the next act in perspective, not permitting it to occupy the entire field of vision."

end, is an end-in-itself and hence possessed of 'value' irrespective of all its existential relations."[61]

This understanding of the dialectic between means and ends is broadly congruent with that offered by Habermas in his account of the desirable relationship between democratic citizens and experts. It, like Habermas's formulation, implies that conduct is "grounded" in a concrete appreciation of the world's relational structure to the extent that it incorporates a self-correcting interplay between its future-oriented projection and present explorations of that project's conditions and consequences. But Habermas, as we have seen, encounters considerable difficulty in trying to show how purposive conduct might be informed by an account of the relational nexus into which it enters without undermining the categorical distinction between purposive and communicative action, and so inviting the degeneration of ethicopolitico questions into matters susceptible to technical resolution. Those difficulties begin to dissipate, however, when it is understood that purposive conduct and the relational thinking informing it are properly situated *within* (as opposed to *against*) the more comprehensive project through which human beings fashion common sense from the world into which they have been jointly thrust.[62]

To see how this is so, we need to take another step in undermining conventional formulations of the means-ends relationship. Our conventional way of thinking about that relationship represents an uneasy

---

61. Dewey, *TV*, p. 42. For a concrete application of this argument, see John Dewey, "Means and Ends: Their Interdependence, and Leon Trotsky's Essay on 'Their Morals and Ours,'" in *New International* 4 (1938), 232–33.

62. It is this view that explains Dewey's insistence that while the "aims, purposes, plans, and policies that direct intelligent human activity" may be "rationalized" when informed by "propositions about activities which are correlated as ends-means," this does not "enable us to tell directly, or upon bare inspection, the values of given particular ends" (*TV*, pp. 57–58). Dewey occasionally appears to be claiming more for his theory of valuation, as when he states that the "proposition in which any object adopted as an end-in-view is statable (or explicitly stated) is *warranted* in just the degree to which existing conditions have been surveyed and appraised in their capacity as means" (p. 25). Any reading of this claim, however, which mistakenly assumes that Dewey is offering a positivist science of morality—that is, a moral theory that claims the results of scientific investigation dictate correct conduct—ignores his distinction between the rules that inform intelligent evaluation and the discovery of "empirically ascertained and tested existential relations such as are usually termed those of cause and effect" (p. 21): "Propositions which lay down rules for procedures as being fit and good, as distinct from those that are inept and bad, are different in form from the scientific propositions upon which they rest. For they are rules for the use, in and by human activity, of scientific generalizations as means for accomplishing certain desired and intended ends" (pp. 22–23). For an example of such a misreading, see Morton White, *Social Thought in America* (Boston: Beacon Press, 1957), pp. 203–19.

amalgam of classical and modern sources. The former, as suggested above, contrasts the absoluteness of pure ends with the materiality of earthly means. With the advent of epistemology, however, that contrast was denied its cosmological foundation and then reinterpreted in the terms suggested by modern science's mechanistic universe. Hence the means-ends relationship was reformulated as one of external connection between discrete Galilean pushes and pulls; and that, in turn, implied that any given means is a cause but not a part of the end it effects.

Such an undialectical representation is not so much false as one-sided. To the extent that it affirms itself as an exhaustive truth, this characterization obscures the possibility of converting causal connections into relationships of meaning that express previously undetermined possibilities resident within nature. Failing to appreciate the transformation effected on "empirical" knowledge when it becomes embedded within the stocks of tacit know-how that agents draw upon in the constitution of meaningful activity, this familiar representation of means denies the potentialities disclosed by the incorporation of nature within significant experience.

If, however, we follow the clue offered by the ancient conception of *poēisis*, that form of conduct which brings nature's gifts to their meaningful consummation, means may become something other than the bare antecedent conditions required to produce distinguishable effects. That is, they may become constituents that, as immanent parts of more encompassing wholes, constitute the partial realization of the sense-bearing temporal closures to which they contribute. Keeping our ears open to the prephilosophical resonances intimated by Aristotle's phrase *ta pros ta tele* (usually translated as "what is towards the end"),[63] we are reminded of human conduct's capacity to accumulate deposits that, like so many layers of silt, become embedded within the significant soil of present experience. "A genuine instrumentality *for* is always an organ *of* an end."[64] Consequently, any conception of con-

63. See Aristotle, *Nichomachean Ethics* 1112b12–15. To the best of my knowledge, this aspect of Aristotle was first noted by L.H.G. Greenwood in the introductory essay to his *Aristotle: Nichomachean Ethics, Book VI* (Cambridge: Cambridge University Press, 1909), pp. 46–47. My understanding of this point has benefited from a reading of John Cooper's *Reason and Human Good in Aristotle* (Cambridge: Harvard University Press, 1975), esp. pp. 19–22.

64. Dewey, *EN*, p. 368. Cf. Dewey, *DE*, p. 101: "Any exhibition of energy has results. The wind blows about the sands of the desert; the position of the grains is changed. Here is a result, an effect, but not an end. For there is nothing in the outcome which

Critical Theory and Politics of Talk 189

duct that fails to pass beyond an abstract opposition between ends and means and on to a more comprehensive appreciation of the reciprocal transformation of parts and whole via the conduct through which its significance is disclosed in time must be deemed deficient. For means can contribute to the fulfillment of experience only to the extent that they, as constitutive mean-ings, participate in the fashioning of meaningfulness.

This assimilation of means qua transitive causes to means qua intrinsic constituents can be illustrated through the example of a medium, as it functions in specifically artistic experience. " 'Medium' signifies first of all an intermediary. The import of the word 'means' is the same. They are the middle, the intervening things through which something now remote is brought to pass. Yet not all means are media. There are two kinds of means. One kind is external to that which is accomplished; the other kind is taken up into the consequences produced and remains immanent in them. Physically, a brush and the movement of the hand in applying color to canvas are external to a painting. Not so artistically. Brush-strokes are an integral part of the esthetic effect of a painting when it is perceived. Paints and skill in manipulative arrangement are means of a picture as end, because the picture is *their* assemblage and organization."[65] Correlatively, as this illustration implies, an end worthy of the name—for instance, a painting by Rembrandt—is not simply an effect mechanically produced by the conjunctive aggregation of its senseless causes. Rather, as an integrated whole, it is that which expresses and informs the synthetic integration of its immanent media. Appropriately, the form of refashioning conduct suggested by this absorption of means within experience's media is best identified by the deliberately ambiguous term "art."

To more fully explicate the sense of this term, we need to see how this form of conduct is called into being through the confrontation between "habit" and a worldly "situation" whose qualitative unity has suffered disruption.[66] Experience's precognitive meaningfulness, as

---

completes or fulfills what went before it. There is mere spatial redistribution. One state of affairs is just as good as any other. Consequently there is no basis upon which to select an earlier state of affairs as a beginning, a later as an end, and to consider what intervenes as a process of transformation and realization."

65. Dewey, *AE*, pp. 197, 199; *EN*, p. 367.

66. For a recent attempt to develop a concept that does much the same work done by Dewey's notion of habit, see the discussion of "image schemata" in Mark Johnson, *The Body in the Mind* (Chicago: University of Chicago Press, 1987), esp. pp. 1–40.

indicated in the last two chapters, is not an effect of distinct facts, however clearly perceived. Rather, it is a consequence of accustomed patterns of culturally transmitted interpretive response, of habits that emerge out of the noncognitive intercourse between agents and the world to which they are heirs. "All of us have many habits of whose import we are quite unaware, since they were formed without our knowing what we were about. Consequently, they possess us, rather than we them."[67] In this sense, each human locus of experience is first and foremost a creature neither of reason nor of instinct, but of habit. For it is through the operation of habits that we come to in-habit a world that is home to our untroubled daily experience.

Habits, so construed, furnish resources in the form of taken-for-granted meanings serving not as external means of identification, but rather as atmospheric media whose entrance into the constitution of every situation provides the ill-defined yet meaningful field upon which specific phenomena are brought before focal consciousness. "That which is looked into, consciously scrutinized, has, like a picture, a foreground, middle distance, and a background—and as in some paintings the latter shades off into unlimited space. This contextual setting is vague, but it is no mere fringe. It has a solidity and stability not found in the focal material of thinking. The latter denotes the part of the road upon which the spotlight is thrown. The spatial context is the ground through which the road runs and for the sake of which the road exists."[68] Yet the metaphor of background and foreground, to the extent that it suggests two realms disconnected from each other, is not altogether apt. For the habits that constitute background thoroughly color and saturate foreground, that is, the pragmata that are of present concern. Hence if the term "consciousness" is taken to denote awareness of specific meanings, then its transient heres and nows secure their "subconscious" intelligibility only in virtue of their tacit rootedness in the noncognitive habits that give what is intentionally apprehended its current bearing.

The import of these claims for the epistemological self is clear. Should the Cartesian ego ever actually succeed in stripping away all of these active agencies of funded meaning, it will deprive itself of the only organs with which it can think. All knowing necessarily starts from some belief, some received habit of inference, which expresses

67. Dewey, DE, p. 29.
68. Dewey, "Context and Thought," in ENF, pp. 100–101.

the cumulative effect of so many prior occasions of thinking. Thinking, in this sense, is secreted in the interstices of those working habits that, when considered as an organic whole, go by the name "mind." Consequently, any form of Enlightenment rationalism which holds that the presence of habit signifies the absence of thinking must in the last analysis prove self-defeating.

Yet habits do more than furnish initial spatial location to the inference-making agent. If an activist spin is put on Continental phenomenology's concept of the life-world,[69] it becomes apparent that habits are the vehicles that effectively synthesize that which rationalism artificially sunders and then labels "mind" and "body." As so many incarnations of inarticulate anticipation and expectation, habits' structuring of associated activities involves the body by carrying it through time and space. "We may think of habits as means, waiting, like tools in a box, to be used by conscious resolve. But they are something more than that. They are active means, means that project themselves, energetic and dominating ways of acting."[70] Thus, in addition to furnishing a ground for the recognizability of conventional phenomena within everyday life, habits are dynamic potentialities that are vitally present even when not immediately engaged. As patterned dispositions to action whose incorporation of the past navigates each moment into the future and so insures that conduct's unfolding in time is something other than a meaningless juxtaposition of isolated reactions to discrete situations, habits' constellation constitutes our effective desires and furnishes us with our practical capacities. As such, the term "habit" does the work more often done by that of "will." But because it denotes the presence of open-textured and generalized *ways* of tending to the things of daily experience, it points not to the concretization of an otherwise abstract and empty faculty of choice, nor to the mechanical performance of routine acts, but rather to the skilled "application" of embodied "know-how."

As long as the locational powers of habit prove adequate to everyday experience, the situations it informs remain "conventional" in character. To say that the commuter is intellectually at home in his

---

69. See Victor Kestenbaum, *The Phenomenological Sense of John Dewey* (Atlantic Highlands, N.J.: Humanities Press, 1977), for an excellent phenomenological reading of Dewey. Because Kestenbaum is so eager to establish the congruence of pragmatism and phenomenology, however, he fails to recognize that Dewey regards habits not simply as accustomed meanings but also as meanings that carry an internal disposition to act in specified ways.

70. Dewey, *HNC*, p. 25.

automobile, the sculptor in her studio, the teacher in the classroom, is not to say that the habits that account for this situatedness "know" it in any strict sense; for habit is too thoroughly implicated in its medium to survey or analyze it. Nonetheless, and although it cannot be made the object of explicit discourse if it is to retain its taken-for-granted reality, each such situation "makes sense" insofar as familiar structures of embodied sensibility prove sufficient to elicit from what is given in experience a dynamic orientation to a coherent present. As long as that situation's events unfurl in anticipated fashion, there is settled belief.

The organic integrity of such passing moments is a function of the distinctive quality that defines each situation as *this* situation and not any other. "An experience has a unity that gives it its name, *that* meal, that storm, that rupture of friendship. The existence of this unity is constituted by a single *quality* that pervades the entire experience in spite of the variation of its constituent parts. This unity is neither emotional, practical, nor intellectual; for these terms name distinctions that reflection can make within it."[71] Neither an invention of the subject nor a property of the object, a situation's defining quality binds together the spatial and temporal constituents of each unduplicable and indivisible moment in a way that distinguishes it from the experience out of which it emerges and into which it passes. "The undefined pervasive quality of an experience is that which binds together all the defined elements, the objects of which we are focally aware, making them a whole. The best evidence that such is the case is our constant sense of things as belonging or not belonging, of relevancy, a sense which is immediate. It cannot be a product of reflecting even though it requires reflection to find out whether some particular consideration is pertinent to what we are doing or thinking. For unless the sense were immediate, we should have no guide to reflection. The sense of an extensive and underlying whole is the context of every experience and it is the essence of sanity."[72]

When habits' projective meanings prove inadequate to a given situation, when the familiar fund of habitual meanings previously woven

71. Dewey, *AE*, p. 37. Cf. p. 36: "Experience in this vital sense is defined by those situations and episodes that we spontaneously refer to as being 'real experiences'; those things of which we say in recalling them, 'that *was* an experience.' It may have been something of tremendous importance—a quarrel with one who was once an intimate, a catastrophe finally averted by a hair's breadth. Or it may have been something that in comparison was slight—and which perhaps because of its slightness illustrates all the better what is to be an experience."

72. Dewey, *AE*, p. 194.

into the world no longer suffice as means, then the immediacy of immediate experience suffers a rupture and becomes tensional.[73] This situation, like that out of which it grows, possesses *its* distinctive quality, which must be noncognitively had if it is to become an affair subject to thoughtful conduct's refashioning. But contra empiricist epistemology, what is given within such a situation is not a confrontation between uninterpreted sense data and a self who, to the extent that its contact with the world is defined by its reception of such data, must be as discontinuous as the discrete objects it knows; were that in fact an adequate account of experience, there could be no field upon which to articulate the meanings that define any particular encounter. Rather, when the qualitative character of a situation comes to be defined by its indeterminacy rather than its determinacy, its contingency rather than its matter-of-factness, particular things emerge within the space opened up by this fracture and so present themselves as questions, that is, as affairs asking for but lacking meaning. "A thing appears in the sense in which a bright object appears in a dark room, while other things remain obscure. We see islands floating as it were upon the sea; we call them islands because of their apparent lack of continuity with the medium that immediately surrounds them."[74] Only when the habit-laden world threatens to come apart, in short, does it become populated with matters of focal awareness.

Responding to such disintegration, the conduct of thinking takes

73. I adopt the term "tensional" from Dewey's "Introduction" to *EEL*, p. 11. Cf. Dewey, *EN*, p. 311: "Our deepest-seated habits are precisely those of which we have least awareness. When they operate in a situation to which they are not accustomed, in an unusual situation, a new adjustment is required. Hence there is shock, and an accompanying perception of dissolving and reforming meanings. Attention is most alert and stretched, when, because of unusual situations, there is great concern about the issue, together with suspense as to what it will be." In passing, it is worth noting the extent to which Habermas's characterization of both instrumental and communicative action reveals his appreciation of Dewey's understanding of thinking as a response to ruptures in ordinary experience. This is most clearly indicated in *Knowledge and Human Interests* where Habermas writes: "Both [communicative and instrumental action] are set off by disturbances of routinized intercourse whether with nature or with other persons. Both aim at the elimination of doubt and the re-establishment of unproblematic modes of behavior. The emergence of a problematic situation results from disappointed expectations. But in one case the criterion of disappointment is the failure of a feedback-controlled purposive-rational action, while in the other it is the disturbance of a consensus, that is, the non-agreement of reciprocal expectations between at least two acting subjects" (p. 175).

74. Dewey, *EN*, p. 137. In this regard, it is important to attend to Dewey's claim in *LTI*, pp. 105–6: "It is the *situation* that has these traits. *We* are doubtful because the situation is inherently doubtful. . . . Consequently, situations that are disturbed and troubled, confused or obscure, cannot be straightened out, cleared up and put in order, by manipulation of our personal states of mind."

shape as the exercise of artifice in delving beyond a situation's present appearances so as to locate its particular history within some more inclusive state of affairs. In referring to thinking's appropriation of experience's partly figured and partly disfigured appearances, we may elect to refer to them as cognition's "objects." But if we do, we should not forget that such a designation serves only to mark off specified dimensions or phases of a complex and dynamic whole by abstracting them from the larger contextualized situation within which they find their home. "By 'object' is meant some element in the complex whole [of a situation] that is defined in abstraction from the whole of which it is a distinction. The selective determination and relation of objects in thought is controlled by reference to a situation, so that failure to acknowledge the situation leaves, in the end, the logical force of objects and their relations inexplicable." Nor should we forget that this moving situation is always implicit within these "objects" insofar as the latter, qua differential meanings, draw their bearings from and shade off into that indeterminate penumbra constituted by the world from they have been abstracted. Nor, finally, should we forget that the aim of such selective determination is set by that same situation in the sense that its purpose is to reconnect activities that are now dislocated. "The situation controls the terms of thought; for they are *its* distinctions, and applicability to it is the ultimate test of their validity."[75]

Deliberation, elicited from the dialectic between unreflective habit and the habit of reflecting, is one moment within the more comprehensive form of conduct that is "art." In deliberating, agents imaginatively project conduct into the potential implications of so many imminent futures by refining the ambiguity of an indeterminate situation into an anticipation of its possible reconstitution as embodied "sense." "Deliberation is a dramatic rehearsal (in imagination) of various competing possible lines of action. Although overt exhibition is checked by the pressure of contrary propulsive tendencies, this very inhibition gives habit a chance at manifestation in thought. Deliberation means precisely that activity is disintegrated, and that its various elements hold one another up. Activity does not cease in order to give way to reflection; activity is turned from execution into intra-organic channels, resulting in dramatic rehearsal."[76] These projections are inescapably informed by our acquired premonitions regarding what to

75. Dewey, "Qualitative Thought," in *PC*, pp. 97–98.
76. Dewey, *HNC*, pp. 190–91.

select and emphasize as well as what to slur over or ignore amid the multiplicity of inchoate meanings currently suggesting themselves. As such, deliberation takes its point of departure not from non-sense, but rather from insufficient sense; and it culminates not in Archimedean vision of a determinate terminus, but rather in conduct's emergence on a path whose sense can be fully ascertained only by following it into the situations toward which it points. Just as we can come to "know" a highway only by finding out what we experience as we travel on it, so too we can know the sense of proposed meanings only by practically explicating their import within situations now in the making.

The term " 'sense' covers a wide range of contents: the sensory, the sensational, the sensitive, the sensible, and the sentimental, along with the sensuous. But sense, as meaning so directly embodied in experience as to be its own illuminated meaning, is the only signification that expresses the function of sense organs when they are carried to full realization."[77] Signification, "making sense," designates conduct that reforms a situation by disclosing previously "unseen" relations whose referential connections, pointing beyond themselves, become immanent as interwoven meanings when reabsorbed within a reconfigured context of situated activity. The achievement of such sense, although an organic "product" of the "means" drawn up within it, is not to be confused with the artful action that explicates its implications. For the "sense of a thing is an immediate and immanent meaning; it is meaning which is itself felt or directly had. When we are baffled by perplexing conditions, and finally hit upon a clew, and everything falls into place, the whole suddenly, as we say, 'makes sense.' In such a situation, the clew has signification in virtue of being an indication, a guide to interpretation. But the meaning of the *whole* situation as apprehended is sense."[78]

Although formally identical to the sense that nondiscursively qualifies the world of everyday routine, the sense engendered by art differs inasmuch as it is animated by a comprehensive awareness of itself as the realized issue of a dramatically unfolding situation whose various phases are now grasped *as* parts of a larger but demarcated whole.

---

77. Dewey, *AE*, p. 22. Reiner Schurmann, in *Heidegger on Being and Acting: From Principles to Anarchy*, trans. Christine-Marie Gros (Bloomington: Indiana University Press, 1987), notes that "the English 'sense' and the French *sens*—'sense' of a river, or of traffic—stems, not from Latin [*sensus*], but from an Indo-European verb [*sinno*] that means to travel, to follow a path" (p. 13).

78. Dewey, *EN*, p. 261.

"The qualities of situations in which organisms and surrounding conditions interact, when discriminated, make sense. Sense is distinct from feeling, for it has a recognized reference; it is the qualitative characteristic of something, not just a submerged unidentified quality or tone."[79] More precisely, when brute existential events acquire significance via an active fusion of old meanings and new situations in which each is dialectically transfigured by the other, there results a unification of body-mind in concentrated sensitivity to the world's opportunities and possibilities. "Experience in the degree in which it *is* experience is heightened vitality."[80] Here knowing, passing beyond Habermasian talk, finds its fruition within embodied engrossment in the situated luminosity of a moment that, although fulfilled in the present, is hardly a condition of stasis. Its mobile resolution of the tensions present within experience discloses a path whose implications, if followed into the future, helps experience sustain its always precarious escape from the ephemera of insignificance.

This characterization of the relationship between habit, thinking qua artful conduct, and sense largely recapitulates the assimilation of seeing and partaking suggested by Homer's use of the verb *noein* (which is retained in the literal meaning of perception, "to take in," as well as in our use of the term "mis-take"). To sense the full significance of a present situation is not to analytically reduce it to the conjunction of its simplest timeless elements. "Perception is not an instantaneous act of carving out a field through suppressing its real influences and permitting its virtual ones to show, but is a process of determining the indeterminate."[81] Even when more overtly apparent elements of motor activity are submerged, perception (as opposed to bare recognition) is still a matter of locating a situation in its widest set of vital interconnections by "means" of the exploratory attendings that achieve insight, that sort of inference-making vision whose apprehension of the not yet seen sustains a posture of alert expectancy toward what is yet to come.

---

79. Ibid., pp. 260–61.
80. Dewey, *AE*, p. 19. Cf. p. 19: "There is much in the life of the savage that is sodden. But when the savage is most alive, he is most observant of the world about him and most taut with energy. As he watches what stirs about him, he, too, is stirred. His observation is both action in preparation and foresight of the future. He is as active through his whole being when he looks and listens as when he stalks his quarry or stealthily retreats from a foe. His senses are sentinels of immediate thought and outposts of action, and not, as they so often are with us, mere pathways along which material is gathered to be stored away for a delayed and remote possibility."
81. Dewey, "Perception and Organic Action," in *PC*, p. 214.

The crafting of such consummatory sense, such "cultivated na-ivete," is rightly deemed "poetic." As a form of experience whose ineffability may become something about which one speaks but cannot itself be reproduced in language, its embodied meaning is captured within what might be called "intuition." But intuition's immediacy is not to be equated with spontaneous—that is, unformed—reaction to the superficial aspects of what is disclosed by conduct. "The scope and content of the relations measure the significant content of an experi-ence. Meaning may be determined in terms of consequences hastily snatched at and torn loose from their connections. Or, we may be aware of meanings that unite wide and enduring scope with richness of distinctions. It is not bare enjoyment but enjoyment as *consummation* of previous processes and responses that constitutes appreciation. These previous states and operations involve reflective observation that partakes of the nature of analysis and synthesis, of discrimination and integration of relations. Appreciation, if genuine, is toward a subject-matter that is *representative*. It is not representative of some-thing outside the appreciated object. The object in question is repre-sentative of that which has led up to it as fulfillment or consummatory close."[82] Thus, in the sense used here, the term "intuition" expresses the qualitatively meaningful sense of an experiential whole that binds together its various developmental phases in a way such that they are immediately appreciated as the interwoven meanings of *that* experi-ence. When those meanings qua the means of thinking are thoroughly integrated within their media of expression and so engender experi-ences whose depth and texture raise them out of the ordinary, the immediacy of that sense neither precludes nor excludes the mediation that has called it into being. Indeed, it is only in virtue of that mediation that a once tensional experience can become genuinely sufficient rather than deficient.

Experience's capacity to be drawn into celebration of those moments in which the future is the quickening of a present laden with the past turns upon its capacity to fold the mediate into the immediate. In that sense, the quality of such moments is indicated by their achievement of "form." So construed, the problem of defining form is not the Platonic problem of identifying the metaphysical essence that roots something in the order of the cosmos. Nor is it a matter of peeling off the abstractable skeleton that accounts for the order sustained by a

---

82. Dewey, AE, p. 44; *EN*, p. 371; *LTI*, p. 175.

singular experience. Nor is it a question of locating those causes that explain an experience's assumption of its particular character. Each of these accounts, construing the term "form" as a noun rather than as a verb, fails to appreciate its reference to the mutual engagement sustained among an experience's constituent parts, that is, to the means by which it is carried forward to a finished whole. Form's relational existence, as the sympathetic interweaving of the powers that carry an experience to its integral fulfillment, is what is implicated in its moving events such that they, in passing from the tensional to the consummatory, grow together as an organic whole. As such, form joins the beginning to the ending of an experience by locating both within the context of a narrative that marks off this concrete existential eventuation as a distinguishable *res*, an affair. That affair's depth of significance, in turn, is measured by its capacity to yield a pregnancy of meaning that before was not so much hidden as unrealized in nature.

This account of form, it should be clear, pays homage to the truth of the experiences that classical philosophy misconstrued as contemplative knowledge of self-determining and transcendent ends. Testifying to the rhythm of loss and recovery that characterizes the experience of any being whose existence is marked by episodes of resistance, ambiguity, and dislocation, these cathartic moments are to be celebrated because of the possibilities they offer for the amplification of present powers and meanings. "Art is the living and concrete proof that man is capable of restoring consciously, and thus, on the plane of meaning, the union of sense, need, impulse and action characteristic of the live creature."[83] Human experience finds its promise stated when the suspenseful ambiguity of a dislocating situation is not so much eliminated as refined into a projective sense of its possible meaningfulness; and that promise is redeemed but never finalized when this particular history, situated within a life understood as an affair of many histories, each with its own plot and individual quality, is brought to a lucid close that is "had" rather than known.

Artful action, sharing classical philosophy's conviction that experience is susceptible of different degrees of being but shedding the ontology the ancients believed necessary to sustain this conviction,

83. Dewey, *AE*, p. 25. This, of course, is not to deny that ends may be "mere closures" rather than fulfillments. See Dewey, *EN*, p. 269: " 'Ends' are not necessarily fulfillments or consummations. They may be mere closures, abrupt cessations, as a railway line may by force of external conditions come to an end, although the end does not fulfill antecedent activities."

takes issue with the peculiarly modern presupposition that the world is equally real at each moment in time. Being's most complete revelation of its potentialities occurs when ego and nature overcome their ascribed status as independent systems of causality and join forces to initiate an experience in which the two are so fully integrated that each fuses with the other in vital appreciation of the "truth" of their intercourse. Most purely exemplified by the sense of concentrated intelligibility we occasionally achieve in the presence of great art, such moments implicate depths of the active agent's relational connections that remain either merely potential or only superficially sensed in the unproblematic flow of everyday conduct. "We are, as it were, introduced into a world beyond this world which is nevertheless the deeper reality of the world in which we live in our ordinary experiences."[84] Wholly invested in a qualitatively unique experience that releases new existential potentialities while unveiling its own significant possibilities, the drama of lived experience testifies to its capacity to give birth to new ways of being in the world.

V

The foregoing explication of conduct's art suggests that my initial genealogy of Habermas's political theory was insufficiently radical; it failed to get at the root of his lacunae. That root can be isolated, ironically, by showing how Habermas shares a crucial presupposition with utilitarianism (and, by implication, with the caricatured version of pragmatism as America's utilitarianism). The theory of utility, although praiseworthy inasmuch as it assesses social and political practice through reference to the satisfaction of concrete human needs and wants, mistakenly envisions the acting self as a formless repository of discrete appetites and aversions to which it merely reacts. In other words, it treats desires in the same way that epistemology treats sense data: as isolated and externally related to one another as well as to the world. As such, it forgets that what is ultimately at stake in deliberation is the sort of being one is now becoming.[85] Substituting

84. Dewey, AE, p. 195.
85. See Dewey, HNC, pp. 216–17: "Deliberation is not an attempt to do away with this opposition of quality by reducing it to one of amount. It is an attempt to *uncover* the conflict in its full scope and bearing. What we want to find out is what difference each impulse and habit imports, to reveal qualitative incompatibilities by detecting the dif-

the technical question of how to manufacture something already taken to be a desired end for the practical question of what is to be done, utilitarianism confines the notion of instrumentality to the discharge of efficient action. It thereby limits intelligence to a mechanical determination of means and their application in the production of an aggregation of acts, each of which abandons its predecessors in time and so fails to enter into the constitution of a significant end.

Conflating the distinction between accounting in a capitalist economy and ethical deliberation, utilitarianism testifies to but cannot remedy the fragmentation of modern life into a patchwork of semi-autonomous compartments, each of which affects the others only externally and accidentally. Reducing all qualitative distinctions to those of quantity, the disconnected self learns that no real or significant conflict among its various interests is possible, and hence that the tragic cannot prove a vital dimension of human experience. Never pressed beyond accumulation and on to the integration of diverse experiences, that ego cannot help but uncritically embrace the ends given by current convention; and so it cannot pierce utilitarianism's rationalization of a life denied the resources of sense.

Utilitarianism's failure to transcend the tradition it claims to leave behind is a function of its retention of the classical belief that the rationality of action presupposes its direction by a determinate final end. Giving a hedonistic twist to Aristotle's contention that there is "an end of the things that we do, which we desire for itself, desiring all other things on its account,"[86] this doctrine inverts the classical tradition by identifying the maximization of pleasure as the abstract goal of all purposive action. But, demonstrating that inversion is not equivalent to transcendence, utilitarianism then conceptualizes conduct as a kind of coerced necessity, that is, as a matter of effecting the inherently valueless conditions necessary for the manufacture of an intrinsically valuable end.

Habermas shares the utilitarian's repudiation of classical philosophy's insistence that fixed ends are given to reason through its priv-

---

ferent courses to which they commit us, the different dispositions they form and foster, the different situations into which they plunge us. . . . Deliberation as to whether to be a merchant or a school teacher, a physician or a politician is not a choice of quantities. It is just what it appears to be, a choice of careers which are incompatible with one another, within each of which definite inclusions and rejections are involved. With the difference in career belongs a difference in the constitution of the self."

86. Aristotle, *Nichomachean Ethics* 1094a18–19.

ileged access to a teleologically structured nature. But unfortunately, and also like the utilitarian, he fails to undercut the traditional conviction that the rationality of action's ends entails their formulation prior to and independent of that action itself. He thereby unwittingly retains the pivotal assumption that sustains all instrumentalized conceptions of practice. Neither the utilitarian nor Habermas, in sum, trusts that ordinary experience is capable of developing from within itself the "means" of its own significance.

In an early essay, Habermas criticizes Dewey because he "did not take into account the difference between the control of technical recommendations by means of their results and the practical confirmation of techniques in the hermeneutically clarified context of concrete situations."[87] As we have seen, on Habermas's reading, it is this misstep that makes clear the need to secure the conceptual and institutional isolation of communication aimed at securing agreement from action aimed at transforming a situation; the "process of enlightenment," if it is to retain its integrity, must be construed in a way that makes no reference to the "organization of action."[88] To safeguard the former from the taint of fabrication, Habermas insists that the achievement of consensus precede effectuation of "the *plans* that participants draw up on the basis of their interpretations of the situation, in order to realize their ends."[89] This follows necessarily, he insists, from the difference between two distinct kinds of "risk" embedded in the human condition: "the risk of not coming to some understanding, that is, of disagreement or misunderstanding, and the risk of a plan of action miscarrying, that is, of failure."[90] Hence when "efforts to come to some agreement within the framework of shared situation definitions fails, the attainment of consensus, *which is normally a condition of pursuing goals*, can itself become an end"; for "*averting the former risk is a necessary condition of managing the latter*."[91]

By the same token, in order to safeguard the rationality of consensus from the taint of positivist verificationism, Habermas argues that the truthfulness of consensus, considered as a ground for possible action, must not turn upon anything apart from its intersubjective formulation (or, more precisely, its intersubjective formulation when that

87. Habermas, "The Scientization of Politics and Public Opinion," p. 66.
88. Habermas, "Some Difficulties in the Attempt to Link Theory and Praxis," p. 33.
89. Habermas, *The Theory of Communicative Action*, vol. 2, p. 127.
90. Ibid.
91. Ibid., vol. 2, pp. 126–27. Emphasis added.

satisfies the conditions stipulated by the ideal speech situation). Distinguishing between the *"objectivity* of experience," which means that "everybody can count on the success or failure of certain actions," and the *"truth* of a proposition," which means that "everybody can be persuaded by reasons to recognize the truth claim of the statement as being justified," Habermas argues that the latter "is not corroborated by processes happening in the world but by a consensus achieved through argumentative reasoning."[92] Unwilling to entertain the hypothesis that the ground of every warranted judgment resides in the transformative consequences of sense-making conduct, Habermas represents "coming to an understanding" as that talk through which "participants in communication reach an agreement concerning the validity of an utterance; agreement is the intersubjective recognition of the validity claim the speaker raises for it."[93]

Consequently, Habermas can entertain as potentially rational only action that, via language, "has the goal of ascertaining which elements of the situation can count as identically perceived and interpreted components of the external world"; *or* action that, via technical manipulation, "realizes defined goals under given conditions,"[94] that is, secures the production of an antecedently conceived object or state of affairs. On my account, of course, it is precisely this dualism that proves Habermas has yet to relieve himself of the conception of rational action fashioned out of classical philosophy's (mis)appropriation of the intelligence incarnate in ancient *technē's* skills and products.[95] Recall the conclusion of Chapter 2: classical philosophy's abstraction from the ground of primary experience is effected by its reification of metaphorical understandings elicited from the realm of craft. The notion of action that results is teleocratic in the sense that it

92. Habermas, "A Postscript to *Knowledge and Human Interests*," pp. 169–70.

93. Habermas, *The Theory of Communicative Action*, vol. 2, p. 120. Cf. "What Is Universal Pragmatics?" in *Communication and the Evolution of Society*, p. 3: "The goal of coming to an understanding is to bring about an agreement that terminates in the intersubjective mutuality of reciprocal understanding, shared knowledge, mutual trust, and accord with one another. Agreement is based on recognition of the corresponding validity claims of comprehensibility, truth, truthfulness, and rightness."

94. Jürgen Habermas, "Aspects of the Rationality of Action," in *Rationality Today*, ed. T. F. Geraets (Ottawa: University of Ottawa Press, 1979), pp. 196, 199; "Technology and Science as 'Ideology,'" pp. 91–92.

95. Cf. Dewey, *HNC*, p. 224: "When men believed that fixed ends existed for all normal changes in nature, the conception of similar ends for men was but a special case of a general belief. Such a view, consistent and systematic, was foisted by Aristotle upon western culture and endured for two thousand years. When the notion was expelled from natural science by the intellectual revolution of the seventeenth century, logically it should also have disappeared from the theory of human action."

universalizes as a property of all action the error it makes regarding a single domain of conduct. Contending that "the *eidos* must stand in view beforehand, and this appearance selected in advance is the end, that of which *technē* has know-how,"[96] Aristotle assumes that craft's achievement of form is a function of its subordination to antecedently formulated unambiguous ends. This hypostatization of *technē*'s metaphorical content is, in turn, the ground of Aristotle's more general conclusion, first, that all action, whether theoretical or practical, is end or goal oriented; and, second, that action's rationality is determined by its achievement of that end. All becoming, understood as the motion through which form is made durably visible, is thus explained through reference to its determinate termination in an end that, already given to reason, has greater value than the activity that realizes it (just as, Aristotle states, a completed building is understood as the finally worthwhile "end" of the builder's craft): "Everything that comes to be moves toward an end, that is, a telos; in fact, that for the sake of which a thing is, is its end, and becoming is for the sake of its telos."[97] Accordingly, even when Aristotle insists that there is a distinction between forms of action which are incomplete because they aim at a product beyond the activity of the maker and those, like philosophy and politics, which do not aim at any extrinsic end, he nonetheless construes the latter as action oriented to and ruled by (immanent) ends; for "every craft and every investigation, and likewise every action and decision, seems to aim at some good."[98]

"The teleological structure," states Habermas, "is fundamental to *all* concepts of action."[99] On that basis, he counters the hegemony of instrumentalism with a telos-centered conception of discursive action whose logic "grounds" its practice in anterior agreement on the process by which validity claims are justified as well as the substantive conclusions generated by its application.[100] In making this claim, Habermas recapitulates the essential misstep of the Western philo-

96. Aristotle, quoted in Schurmann, *Heidegger on Being*, p. 102.

97. See Aristotle, *Metaphysics*, trans. Richard Hope (Ann Arbor: University of Michigan Press, 1960): "Then, too, actuality is prior to power in being. One reason is that what comes later in genesis is prior in form and being: the man is prior to the son, as a human being is prior to the seed; for the one already has form, and the other does not. Also, everything that is produced proceeds according to its principle, for its wherefor is its principle, and at the same time its coming into being is directed by the end; hence the actuality is the end, and it is thanks to it that a power is possessed" (1050a–e).

98. Aristotle, *Nichomachean Ethics* 1094a.

99. Habermas, *The Theory of Communicative Action*, vol. 1, p. 101.

100. On this point, see Brian Fay's informative discussion of Habermas in his *Critical Social Science* (Ithaca: Cornell University Press, 1987), pp. 184–90.

sophical tradition. By ascribing full ontological status to its reflectively derived distinction between subject and object, and then characterizing agency in the terms thus engendered, he cannot help but think of action as the goal-oriented imposition of antecedent ends upon recalcitrant matter. Although correctly sensing that the energies necessary to generate new cultural forms have evaporated as a result of the progressive "rationalization" of experience, he nevertheless imposes upon the "ideal of an unlimited and undistorted communication community" the burden of re-creating the bonds that more traditional sources can no longer sustain.[101] Additionally, to ensure that that community's judgments are strictly disciplined by the imperatives of truth rather than custom or opinion, he subjects their formulation to universal principles abstracted from the wishes and hopes of those subject to them. As such, Habermas's critical theory is best read as a symptom of rather than an antidote to the crisis of Western rationalism.[102]

I have suggested, by way of contrast, that the subversion of instrumental rationality can be better effected by taking the term "means" to refer to the conduct (along with its linguistically saturated instrumentalities) through which experience left unresolved by prereflective meanings is reformed in a way that restores situated intelligibility. On this account, all knowing is practical in the sense that exploration of the implications disclosed through the refashioning of experience is the condition of sense, whether individual or collective. Why this account does not engender another teleocratic conception of conduct is suggested, albeit with some misdirection, by Dewey's use of the term "end-in-view."[103] On the face of it, the first third of this term

101. Habermas, *The Theory of Communicative Action*, vol. 2, p. 96.
102. The inability to conceptualize *technē* as a form of art that is not bound to the achievement of determinate and antecedently formulated ends, as well as the conviction that human life should be construed as teleological in the sense that it is goal-oriented, appears common to virtually all proponents of the dialogic polity. See, for example, Hans-Georg Gadamer's *Truth and Method* (New York: Crossroad, 1975): "Here we see a fundamental modification of the conceptual relation between means and end, which distinguishes moral from technical knowledge. It is not only that moral knowledge has no merely particular end, but is concerned with right living in general, whereas all technical knowledge is particular and serves particular ends. . . . The end towards which our life as a whole tends and the elaboration of it into the moral principles of action, as described by Aristotle in his *Ethics*, cannot be the object of a knowledge that can be taught" (pp. 286–87).
103. See, for example, Dewey, *HNC*, p. 250: "The end-in-view of desire is that object which were it present would link into an organized whole activities which are now partial and competing. It is no more like the actual end of desire, or the resulting state attained, than the coupling of cars which have been separated is like an ongoing single train. Yet the train cannot go on without the coupling."

appears to imply a commitment to goals or plans whose antecedent formulation as determinate objects dictates the conduct that applies it; its remaining two-thirds appear to imply the existence of what the epistemological tradition calls "ideas," self-contained figments existing in the "minds" of discrete knowers. Neither of these implications, though, is congruent with the meaning evoked here.

Since artful conduct seeks to reconstitute the meaningfulness of qualitative experience following its dislocation, its "aims" emerge from the womb of ongoing situations. Although susceptible to information by the larger network of cause and consequence within which it is enmeshed, that conduct issues from within the conflicts determinative of a concrete context rather than in isolation from them. The conduct of thinking is in this sense always *in media res* and so perpetually unfinished. Accordingly, conduct cannot be informed by determinate goals articulated prior to the engagement that brings them into being. Let us reject the Platonic characterization of action (the imposition of cognized shape upon formless matter) as well as its Christian counterpart (the unpremediated but purposive expression of a radically unconstrained will). Once we do so, we are in a position to grant that intelligent conduct, as a *search* for the meaning of a present situation, takes shape as the *refashioning* of experience in accordance with an "aim" that is itself in constant reenactment at each stage of its actualization. "The 'end' is the figured pattern at the center of the field through which runs the axis of conduct."[104] Here, as before, the example of "fine" art is suggestive. "A statement that an artist does not care how his work eventuates would not literally be true. But it is true that he cares about the end-result as a completion of what goes before and not because of its conformity or lack of conformity with a ready-made antecedent scheme. He is willing to leave the outcome to the adequacy of the means from which it issues and which it sums up. Like the scientific inquirer, he permits the subject-matter of his perception in connection with the problems it presents to determine the issue, in-

---

104. Ibid, p. 262. On the Platonic conception of action, see Dewey, *AE*, p. 138: "A rigid pre-determination of an end-product whether by artist or beholder leads to the turning out of a mechanical or academic product. The processes by which the final object and perception are reached are not, in such cases, means that move forward in the construction of a consummatory experience. The latter is rather of the nature of a stencil, even though the copy from which the stencil is made exists in mind and not as a physical thing." On the Christian conception, see Dewey, *AE*, p. 65: "Even the Almighty took seven days to create the heaven and the earth, and if the record were complete, we should also learn that it was only at the end of that period that he was aware of just what He set out to do."

stead of insisting upon its agreement with a conclusion decided upon in advance."[105]

Contrary to Habermas's situationless account of speech's universal theoretical presuppositions, the notion of "ends" advanced here entails their formulation as limits of specifiable histories within a present construed not as a complex of barriers to be removed, but as the ground out of which action cannot help but evolve. Artful conduct seeks not to transform the whole qua whole, but rather to respond adeptly to indeterminate situations by effecting a spiraling series of partial resolutions. As such, it is guided not by prior design, but rather by its continually developing sense of the meanings intimated within and by its own tendencies. Because conduct's momentary pauses contribute to consummation of the situation in which they find themselves, it is only in working out the means to some vaguely specified end that conduct discovers what it is about. The intentionality of such conduct is fully instantiated within the more or less continuous flow of deliberative agency passing through the medium of space/time.

Artful conduct aims to invest an indeterminate sense of emergent significance with substantive content by taking actions that qualify as sufficient constituents of a larger whole whose meaning can only be appreciated within its impermanent terminations. For this reason, its "ends-in-view" must have as their "purpose" the contribution they make to what I have called consummatory experience. What this connotes with respect to our conventional notion of goal-oriented activity can be intimated by reflecting on the origin and purpose of games. "Men shoot and throw. At first this is done as an 'instinctive' or natural reaction to some situation. The result when it is observed gives a new meaning to the activity. Henceforth men in throwing and shooting think of it in terms of its outcome; they act intelligently or have an end. Liking the activity in its acquired meaning, they not only 'take aim' when they throw instead of throwing at random, but they find or make targets at which to aim. This is the origin and nature of 'goals' of action. They are ways of defining and deepening the meaning of activity. Having an end or aim is thus a characteristic of *present* activity."[106] A "goal" of action, so construed, is what traditional theory

105. Dewey, *AE*, p. 138–39.
106. Dewey, *HNC*, pp. 225–26. Cf. p. 265: "Over and over again, one point has recurred for criticism;—the subordination of activity to a result outside itself. Whether that goal be thought of as pleasure, as virtue, as perfection, as final enjoyment or salvation, is secondary to the fact that the moralists who have asserted fixed ends have

calls a means. For instead of lying beyond activity as an end not yet attained, it stands as a redirecting pivot within conduct whose "purpose" is to enhance the sense of formed experience. Correlatively, present experience, which traditional theory regards as an unavoidable means to intrinsically valuable ends, is in fact the "aim" of conduct.

If the intercourse sustained between artful conduct and the more or less plastic qualities of emerging experience is to retain its dialogic quality, it must acknowledge that its rationality does not turn on success in mastering a world of independent objects. Rather, its intelligence is measured by its responsiveness to the meanings intimated by those intersecting events that have now crystallized within an insufficient situation. To subordinate conduct to ends formed outside the sediment generated by the dialectic of doing and suffering is to deny its rootedness in habits' projection into an as yet unknown future. Furthermore, it is to deny conduct its dexterity since its skill is gauged by its sensitivity to the internal relation between action within a partly disordered medium and receptivity to that medium's replies. Most important, by attempting to vanquish rather than transform a situation, it is to render impossible the achievement of knowledge. Such anthropocentric authoritarianism forgets that thinking can attain its end only when the ends of conduct are wrought from within the subtle interplay between things done and things undergone. If knowing is one way we ingest experience, then the transactional involvement that constitutes thinking can be brought to *its* integral fulfillment only when our effort to assimilate the world's pragmata to the simplifying abstractions of any given cognitive schema first concedes their existential capacity to overflow its terms. "Experience is limited by all causes which interfere with perception of the relations between undergoing and doing. There may be interference because of excess on the side of doing or of excess on the side of receptivity. Unbalance on either side blurs the perception of relations and leaves the experience partial and distorted, with scant or false meaning."[107] In sum, the human and nonhuman partners in knowing must acknowledge their co-related status as members in the organic project of enculturing nature with meaning.

---

in all their differences from one another agreed in the basic idea that present activity is but a means. We have insisted that happiness, reasonableness, virtue, perfection, are on the contrary parts of the present significance of present action."

107. Dewey, *AE*, p. 44.

By blurring the distinction between learning the meaning of a situation and acting to transform it, this conception of conduct takes exception to Habermas's cognitivist conviction that oppression is a consequence of the internalization of propositional objects from which we may be liberated through self-reflective discourse. By extension, it also suggests the problematic nature of his contention that the first step toward emancipation occurs when human beings, "through communication . . . form themselves into a collective subject of the whole, *that is capable of action*."[108] Critical intelligence is the fruit not of acknowledging the universal presuppositions of formal discourse, but of refashioning forms of life in response to unsatisfied needs and felt confusions. Consequently, the present's constraints cannot be understood independently of, or prior to, conduct that is "experimental" in the sense that its "ends" are neither had nor known apart from so many efforts to uncover the meanings implicit within experience.

We may grant that such conduct is guided by "ideas," but only if we recognize that this term designates nothing other than that phase of habituated meanings that is presently enduring transitive transformation. It follows that the potentialities of the present cannot be *known* till *after* they have been called into being. "In an experience of thinking, premises emerge only as a conclusion becomes manifest. The experience, like that of watching a storm reach its height and gradually subside, is one of continuous movement of subject-matters. Like the ocean in the storm, there are a series of waves; suggestions reaching out and being broken in a clash, or being carried onwards by a cöoperative wave. If a conclusion is reached, it is that of a movement of anticipation and cumulation, one that finally comes to completion."[109]

Hence "emancipation" is possible only through the embodied agent's adoption of what might best be called new "postures" toward the world. "*If* we could form a correct idea without a correct habit, then possibly we could carry it out irrespective of habit. But a wish gets definite form only in connection with an idea, and an idea gets shape and consistency only when it has a habit back of it. Only when a man can already perform an act of standing straight does he know what it is like to have a right posture and only then can he summon the idea required for proper execution. The act must come before the thought, and a habit before an ability to evoke the thought at will."[110] The

108. Habermas, "Dogmatism, Reason, and Decision," p. 255.
109. Dewey, *AE*, p. 38.
110. Dewey, *HNC*, p. 30. Cf. p. 29: "Now in fact a man who *can* stand properly does

possibility of liberation, in other words, is inseparable from immediate engagement of the intelligent body-mind. "In the hyphenated phrase body-mind, 'body' designates the continued and conserved, the registered and cumulative operation of factors continuous with the rest of nature, inanimate as well as animate; while 'mind' designates the characters and consequences which are differential, indicative of features which emerge when 'body' is engaged in a wider, more complex and interdependent situation."[111] Separable only for analytic purposes, the body-mind can move past the confines of the present only by mobilizing various forms of improvisational doing whose versatility in overcoming experienced disjunctions derives from the play of imagination, that is, the aspect of underdetermined events that are moving toward eventualities that are now mere possibilities.

Inasmuch as such conduct disintegrates old situations and forms new ones within a medium that is beyond the latter but not yet in the former, it might well be called "subjective." "When an old essence or meaning is in process of dissolution and a new one has not taken shape even as a hypothetical scheme, the intervening existence is too fluid and formless for publication, even to one's self. Its very existence is ceaseless transformation. Limits from which and to which are objective, generic, stateable; not so that which occurs between these limits."[112] The charge of subjectivism seems all the more apt when we recall that, just as talk about love is not the same thing as being in love, the experiences generated by such doing must remain incommunicable in an important sense. "All statement is of means; we cannot *state* consummations but only means to or conditions of them."[113] Yet such action is not for that reason arbitrary, as Habermas would no doubt contend. If what we call selves are themselves events located not

---

so, and only a man who can, does. In the former case, fiats of will are unnecessary, and in the latter useless. A man who does not stand properly forms a habit of standing improperly, a positive, forceful habit. The common implication that his mistake is merely negative, that he is simply failing to do the right thing, and that the failure can be made good by an order of will is absurd. One might as well suppose that the man who is a slave of whiskey-drinking is merely one who fails to drink water. Conditions have been formed for producing a bad result, and the bad result, will occur as long as those conditions exist. . . . Only the man who can maintain a correct posture has the stuff out of which to form that idea of standing erect which can be the starting point of a right act." By way of contrast, Habermas's cognitivist understanding of ideology makes clear his unacknowledged retention of a dualistic conception of the relationship between mind and body.

111. Dewey, *EN*, p. 285.
112. Ibid, p. 221.
113. Dewey, "Syllabus: Types of Philosophic Thought," in *MW*, vol. 13, p. 385.

beside but within experience, then the distinction between knowing subjects and a world of objects is functional rather than ontological. Correlatively, the truth or falsity of that which is known resides within rather than without the relationships that give any situation its qualitative uniqueness. That is, the adequacy of conduct's transformative disclosure of the habit-laden world is determined not by the antecedent achievement of an abstracted consensus, but rather by its "success" in restoring sense to the body-mind. "Thought or inference becomes knowledge in the complete sense of the word only when the indicative or signifying is borne out, verified in something directly present or immediately *experienced*—not immediately known."[114] As correspondence theories rightly suggest, the question of truth *is* a question concerning the agreement between meaning and the world. But this property is ascribed to a meaning only insofar as it acknowledges the brute reality of nature's existents and so proves able to elicit *their* qualitative significance, as these participate, qua things, in the constitution of experience.

This view entails the contemporaneous validity of incongruent but nonetheless "true" ways of shaping the world's pragmata. With due respect to Habermas, this account of truth implies that there can be no *theory* whose stipulation of abstract procedures to which ethical or political choice must conform in order to prove rational shows how disagreement might be eradicated from the human condition. To rethink the "sense" in Habermas's "consensus" is to learn that collective significance exists not as universal assent to specified propositional content, but rather as knowledge that "absorbs the intellectual into immediate qualities that are experienced through senses that belong to the vital body."[115]

Thus if and when agents attain a consensus on the meaning of "fairness," this achievement does not signify the unification of otherwise discrete minds regarding an unambiguous concept of justice which, formed under conditions ensuring that only the force of the better argument will prevail, is known to be true prior to its employment in resolving particular cases. Rather, this achievement is fully actualized when interrelated agents practice together the habits that

114. Dewey, "Realism without Monism or Dualism," in *MW*, vol. 13, p. 52.

115. Dewey, *AE*, p. 216. As is perhaps clear, this account of the fulfillment of knowing in sense renders untenable Richard Rorty's claim that, for a pragmatist, what is true is what "our peers will, *ceteris paribus*, let us get away with saying" (*Philosophy and the Mirror of Nature*, p. 176). On this point, I see no significant difference between Habermas and Rorty, except insofar as the former wishes to justify the imposition of constraints upon what our peers should allow us to say.

enable them to take the sense of—that is, to secure a significant grasp of—those situations calling for their deliberative exercise.

Just as there are no rules that can dictate in advance the conduct best suited to elicit significant form from experience, so too there are no determinate standards that can relieve judgment of its contingency. "No rules can be laid for the performance of so delicate an act as determination of the significant parts of a whole, and of their respective places and weights in the whole."[116] Because judgments regarding conduct's meaningfulness are instances of ex post facto appreciation rather than antecedent cognition, "theory" can do no more than cultivate, on the one hand, the art of discrimination, appreciation of the particulars of a situation as parts that may or may not contribute to an eventual sense-bearing whole; and on the other hand, the art of synthetic unification, appreciation of the way in which that more comprehensive whole may enter into and inform those parts without denying the particularity that is the condition of their contribution to the cause of vital sense. Granted, this repudiation of theory's hubris deprives actors of the security offered by rationally warranted judgments to which all must eventually give their assent. In exchange, it holds forth the promise of that fullness of meaning that now and then grips those whose contextualized initiatives remain fully exposed to and appreciative of the ambiguities and uncertainties of concrete conduct.

VI

At the outset of this chapter, I suggested that Hannah Arendt, Jürgen Habermas, Hans-George Gadamer, and Richard Rorty have been primarily responsible for encouraging the vision of the dialogic polity. The inclusion of Rorty's name suggests that to call oneself a pragmatist is not in and of itself sufficient to secure protection against the pitfalls I noted via my exploration of Habermas. What chiefly distinguishes Rorty's account from these others is its failure to derive significant critical leverage from this vision and so to muster an effective challenge to the tyranny of instrumental rationality. As a way of bringing this segment of my larger argument to a close, let me briefly indicate why and how this is so.

As a pragmatist, Rorty cannot advance the sort of metaphysical

116. Dewey, *AE*, p. 310.

premises often invoked by his more Continentally minded brethren to substantiate the distinction between forms of action appropriate to the human and nonhuman realms, that is, between communication and control. This he makes most adequately clear in his critique of Charles Taylor's oft-cited "Interpretation and the Sciences of Man."[117] In a nutshell, Taylor argues, first, that the essence of being human is to possess the capacity for self-description; second, that any social science that eliminates reference to intersubjective meaning in order to represent society as a mechanistic field of homogeneous bits of mute matter in motion misconceives its subject matter; and, third, that only a science of humanity that defines its task as the interpretation of action rather than the explanation of behavior is true to its object. The larger implication is clear: When politics is construed as an object to be regulated in accordance with nomological knowledge rather than as an affair sustained among coequal speaking subjects, it cannot help but violate that which makes persons distinctively human.

Taylor's surreptitious appeal to a notion of human nature is the focal point of Rorty's critique. The attribution of an essence to humanity, Rorty argues, simply perpetuates now discredited understandings that, seduced by originally Platonic metaphors, identify knowing as a form of seeing and hence knowledge with correspondence to reality. This mistake, which accounts for the view that the aim of the natural sciences is to furnish a representation of the world as it is apart from the meanings accorded it by human subjects, is simply transposed to a new arena when it is claimed that an underlying ontological distinction between different kinds of beings (for instance, people and rocks) mandates the establishment of a corresponding methodological distinction between categorically different forms of reason or action. As Rorty states, "To be told that only a certain vocabulary is *suited* to human beings or human societies, that only *that* vocabulary permits us to 'understand' them, is the seventeeth century myth of Nature's Own Vocabulary all over again."[118]

When this error is exposed, when it becomes apparent that Taylor is mistaken in thinking that our heterogeneous linguistic practices reveal ontological features of the world, his quasi-theological affirmation of humanity's special dignity collapses. This in turn is the premise of

---

117. Charles Taylor, "Interpretation and the Sciences of Man," *Review of Metaphysics* 25 (1971), 3–51.

118. Richard Rorty, *Consequences of Pragmatism* (Minneapolis: University of Minnesota Press, 1982), p. 198. For an additional statement of this criticism, see Richard Rorty, "Reply to Dreyfus and Taylor," *Review of Metaphysics* 34 (1980), 39–46.

Rorty's contention that the human condition is defined by the existence of so many mutually irreducible discourses whose sole criterion of value is their respective ability to contribute to successful achievement of whatever ends are specified by the language game currently being played:

> "Explanation" is merely the sort of understanding one looks for when one wants to predict and control. It does not contrast with something else called "understanding," as the abstract contrasts with the concrete, or the artificial with the natural or the "repressive" with the "liberating." To say that something is better "understood" in one vocabulary than another is always an ellipsis for the claim that a description in the preferred vocabulary is more useful for a certain purpose. If the purpose is prediction, then one will want one sort of vocabulary. If it is evaluating, one may or may not want a different sort of vocabulary.[119]

To grant this, Rorty continues, is not to give up the ability to criticize, say, an attempt to analyze the practice of moral deliberation in stimulus-response terms, or to reduce the practice of politics to administered manipulation. Rather, it is to say, first, that such complaint must be advanced on either moral or political rather than ontological grounds and, second, that the authority of the norms upon which such criticism relies can be justified only through reference to the social practices out of which they have evolved, not through illicit importation of untenable essentialist postulates.[120]

In this way, Rorty rejects the ontological assumptions underpinning the positivist insistence that all experience may be reduced to materialist terms *as well as* the hermeneuticist insistence that human spirituality

---

119. Rorty, *Consequences of Pragmatism*, p. 197.

120. Parenthetically, it should be noted that Rorty's criticism of Taylor entails a criticism of Gadamer as well. Although his appropriation of *Truth and Method*'s understanding of hermeneutics is more or less uncritical, Rorty should find Gadamer suspect when the latter, in his "The Problem of Historical Consciousness," in *Interpretive Social Science*, ed. Paul Rabinow and William Sullivan (Berkeley: University of California Press, 1979), p. 114, challenges the Cartesian formulation of modern science by asking rhetorically whether its method "does not, in the human species, lead to a misapprehension of the natural mode of being specific to this domain?" To imply, as Gadamer does here, that the ontological significance of hermeneutics stems from its special revelation of what it is to be a being whose essential mode of being consists in interpretation is to offer yet another form of metaphysical idealism whose purpose is to secure the authority of the sciences of humanity over the sciences of nature. For much the same reason, Rorty should find Gadamer suspect when, in his *Reason in the Age of Science* (Cambridge: MIT Press, 1981), p. 137, he insists that "the claim to universality on the part of hermeneutics consists of integrating all the sciences, of perceiving the opportunities for knowledge on the part of every scientific method wherever they may be applicable to given objects, and of deploying them in all their possibilities."

constitutes the essence of being human. He thereby overcomes the temptation to which Habermas falls prey: to reestablish a secularized version of the ontological dualism between the sacred and the profane. Exhorting us to finally overcome our felt need to ground various cultural practices in some more fundamental reality, Rorty offers an unbounded field of possible discourses, no one of which can be excluded on a priori grounds from the domain of the perculiarly human. Only when we have thus matured will we endorse his representation of culture as a conversation among divergent voices that can never be rendered commensurable through articulation of a single and more comprehensive vocabulary. Correlatively, only when we no longer engage in the hypostatization of some privileged set of descriptions will we lose the justificatory basis for constraining those who depart from a truth we wish to believe is given rather than made. Only then, in sum, will we come to grant that our most pressing political injunction is to foster the virtue of tolerance among, as Rorty puts it, "persons whose paths through life have fallen together, united by civility rather than by a common goal, much less by a common ground."[121]

Hence, although Rorty denies the hermeneutic enterprise any special grounding, he does so only in order to more effectively establish the legitimacy of a dialogical conception of rational action, one that regards knowing as "more like getting acquainted with a person than following a demonstration"; a Socratic conception of "practical wisdom," one that equates prudence with the "willingness to talk, to listen to other people, to weigh the consequences of our actions upon other people";[122] and a conversational conception of politics, one which envisions ruling and being ruled in turn as the interpretive exchange of diverse perspectives through the vehicle of end-less discourse. Considered in this way, it is difficult to understand why *Philosophy and the Mirror of Nature* has generated the controversy it has; for under the guise of a radical critique of contemporary philosophy, Rorty defends an account of politics whose metaphorical dependence on the conduct of ordinary talk simply confirms the defining prejudices of much contemporary democratic theory.

Note, moreover, that Rorty's celebration of linguistic pluralism entails no effort to recast our accustomed understanding of instrumental rationality. Granted, he denies such rationality its hubris by representing it as merely one among the many ways we meet the world. But that

---

121. Rorty, *Philosophy and the Mirror of Nature*, p. 377.
122. Ibid, p. 319; Rorty, *Consequences of Pragmatism*, p. 172.

in and on itself offers no challenge to our familiar sense of the forms of conduct through which we refashion experienced things. "Forgetting" the epistemological metaphysic substantively implicated in most contemporary technology and the institutional vehicles through which its power is organized and deployed, Rorty provides additional ammunition for those already eager to endorse Max Horkheimer's representation of pragmatism as the Americanized expression of an ethic that commends the manipulative domination of independent objects by subjects not radically enmeshed in the world they master.[123]

By way of contrast, this chapter has suggested that because the agent is neither a self-propelled source of autonomous designs nor a psychic mechanism capriciously responding to a welter of external impulses, the relationship between actor, conduct, and things conducted cannot be understood in simple causal terms. In place of reductive understandings whose embrace of atomistic presuppositions requires that any given whole be comprehended from the standpoint of its discrete elements and their mechanical aggregation, the argument advanced here presents the "situation" as a more or less integrated totality that cannot, without distortion, be dissolved into its separate moments. For the experiencing-experienced transaction is a single structure in which what are reflectively distinguished as subject and object are in fact dialectically interrelated constituents of the larger web of relationships constituting a lived situation. Because each, as cause, acts on the other and, in so doing, affects the other's causality, which it in turn must undergo, expression of the self through the medium of the world entails that both acquire a form neither previously displayed. "Things and events belonging to the world, physical and social, are transformed through the human context they enter, while the live creature is changed and developed through its intercourse with things previously external to it."[124] Blending the terminology of classical metaphysics into this claim, we might say that in artful conduct's recrystallization of the field of meaningful habit, neither form nor matter is logically prior or primary. Each is shaped to existence as the other makes its appearance within the world.

For much the same reason, the argument of this chapter suggests why pragmatism ought not to be represented as a doctrine equating value with specification of the technical imperatives necessary to pro-

---

123. See Max Horkheimer, *The Eclipse of Reason* (New York: Seabury Press, 1974), especially pp. 48–57.
124. Dewey, *AE*, p. 264.

duce predicted consequences. This caricature, which Rorty does little to challenge, fails to acknowledge that "arts that are merely useful are not arts but routines, and arts that are merely final are not arts but passive amusements and distractions"; and so it forgets that "the realm of immediate qualities contains everything of worth and significance. The object of foresight of consequences is not to predict the future. It is to ascertain the meaning of present activities and to secure, so far as possible, a present activity with a unified meaning."[125] When this is appreciated, it becomes clear that anything construed as a means is but a candidate whose worthiness to participate within a reformed context of conduct turns upon its suitability to enter, as an organic instrumentality, into the habits that sustain the world's intelligibility and the active agent's potentialities. For conduct qua art seeks not successful mastery, but rather the fecund constitution of a community of meaning in which all parts, transformed through their reciprocal exchange, relate to one another in a way such that no one violates the others' contribution to the experience of sense.

When the "means" that is knowing is situated within a more comprehensive grasp of experience's consummatory possibilities, science's isolation from everyday life's chief affair—that is, concern with its own significance—becomes open to question. If the collective noun "science" refers to specific but complex forms of analytic enterprise that state the relations between things by reducing them to conceptual form, then its telos is fulfilled only when it, as one phase within the structure of a more extensive situation, is merged with experience's noncognitive phases in the constitution of a qualitatively significant moment in time. To reject the notion of "pure" science on the grounds that it is abstract, that it lacks something that warrants recovery, is not thereby to advance a defense of technical rationality. Instead, it is to urge a fundamental rethinking of what we take science to be. For if the application of science means its involvement in rather than its mastery over experience, then its conduct must be deemed ontologically deficient until it participates in engendering histories and revealing potentialities previously hidden in nature. In a strong sense, therefore, science whose moment of abstraction fails to intensify the sensed intelligibility of experienced affairs cannot claim to be knowledge, for it does not evince the correspondence with reality that is the mark of all knowledge worthy of the name.

125. Dewey, *EN*, pp. 361, 114; *HNC*, pp. 205–6.

6 /
The State of
Political Science

Although their writings differ significantly in form and content, Émile Durkheim and Jürgen Habermas share the fear that modernity is falling into a condition of irrationalism. In response, each seeks to articulate a conception of reason whose truths, whether achieved through deployment of scientific method or discourse within the ideal speech situation, are sufficiently determinate and authoritative to secure consensus among those whose forms of living no longer guarantee a unitarian vision of the world. Yet each can succeed in this endeavor only by illicitly smuggling into his account of rationality much of the conceptual baggage that first emerged out of the classical city-state and was later refashioned as a result of the epistemological effort to situate the practice of early modern science within these inherited confines. In consequence, both prematurely cancel the question of how we might craft significance from the materials now given to us in experience. Neither squarely faces the unsettling dimensions of our current collective fate.

Turning away from Germany and France, in this chapter I explore a characteristically American effort to forestall the present's slide into a future denied the assurances of the past. The argument of this chapter is intended to complement that of its two immediate predecessors. In Chapter 4, I claimed that the fruits of thinking can bear sense only when rooted in tangible forms of noncognitive experience. That, in turn, led to the proposal that we abandon the quest to find some translocal conceptual surrogate for the unity once guaranteed by what Durkheim calls "mechanical solidarity." In Chapter 5, I explicated the sense of the term "sense" through an indication of conduct's capacity to elicit form from the media of experience and so engender those consummatory moments in which significance is most vitally embodied. That, in turn, led to the conclusion that the instrumentalities of science violate the terms of their existence when their entry into the constitution of ordinary experience undermines its struggle to sustain and enrich some sense of what it is about. Here I show the import of these arguments for the practice of what is conventionally but inappropriately called "political science."

II

More often than not, American social scientists committed to what has come to be known as "policy science" locate the origins of this enterprise in the years immediately following the close of World War II and identify as its inaugural statement Harold Lasswell's influential essay "The Policy Orientation."[1] This genealogy, while not entirely false, is quite one-sided unless it is also noted that the soil necessary to Lasswell's founding deed was prepared long before. Political science's constitution as a professional academic discipline in the first decades of this century was justified, in large measure, through reference to its potential role in rationalizing the formulation and implementation of public policy.[2] Hence, in 1925, when Charles Merriam asked rhetorically, "Have we not reached the time when it is necessary . . . to apply the categories of science to the vastly important forces of political and social control?"[3] he repeated a theme already articulated by A. L.

1. For a typical claim to this effect, see Ronald Brunner, *Public Policy Analysis: An Introduction* (Englewood Cliffs, N.J.: Prentice-Hall, 1982), p. 125.
2. On this point, see Albert Somit and Joseph Tanenhaus, *The Development of American Political Science* (Boston: Beacon Press, 1967), passim.
3. Charles Merriam, *New Aspects of Politics*, 3d ed. (Chicago: University of Chicago Press, 1970), p. 55.

Lowell, F. J. Goodnow, W. B. Munro, A. B. Hart, Woodrow Wilson, and many others. In this way, policy science is accurately regarded as the most conventional branch of the larger discipline within which it grows ever more prominent.

To point out policy science's deeper roots is to call to mind its relationship to pragmatism. Lasswell makes it a point to cite the continuity of his work with that of "John Dewey and other American philosophers of pragmatism";[4] David Braybrooke and Charles Lindblom, in *Strategy of Decision*, suggest that their account of policy science's incremental rationality merely "corroborates Dewey's theses with complementary but independent results";[5] Aaron Wildavsky, in his *Speaking Truth to Power*, insists that "policy analysis has its foundations for learning in pragmatism";[6] and Heinz Eulau, offering Dewey's *Logic* as the best available guide to the problematic situations that regularly confront political decision makers, urges that this science self-consciously honor its forebears by renaming itself "policy pragmatics."[7]

What are we to make of policy science's claim to the legacy of pragmatism? To answer this question, I argue, first, that references to pragmatism by policy scientists are best read as attempts to legitimate its status as a vital source of the modern state's reason;[8] second, that insofar as policy science succeeds in its rationalizing ambitions, it proves complicitous in obscuring the contours of distinctively political

4. Harold Lasswell, "The Policy Orientation," in *The Policy Sciences*, ed. Daniel Lerner and H. D. Lasswell (Stanford: Stanford University Press, 1951), p. 12.

5. David Braybrooke and Charles Lindblom, *A Strategy of Decision* (New York: Free Press, 1970), pp. 18–19. The quotation continues: "Yet can the results be independent, when Dewey has done so much to affect the climate of the social sciences, at least in America? So many of us who have grown up in that climate have come to hold similar views, after reflecting seriously on the difficulties of evaluation and on observable evaluative practices, that we can make at most only incremental claims to saying something new." This quotation would appear to confirm Richard Rorty's claim, advanced in his *Consequences of Pragmatism* (Minneapolis: University of Minnesota Press, 1982), that "Dewey made the American learned world safe for the social sciences" (p. 63).

6. Aaron Wildavsky, *Speaking Truth to Power* (Boston: Little, Brown, 1979), p. 393.

7. Heinz Eulau, "Skill Revolution and the Consultative Commonwealth," *American Political Science Review* 67 (1973), 173; "The Interventionist Synthesis," *American Journal of Political Science* 21 (1977), 422.

8. For a useful but uncritical account indicating how the discipline of political science appropriated Dewey in order to articulate and legitimate its own professional ambitions, see David Ricci, *The Tragedy of Political Science* (New Haven: Yale University Press, 1984), pp. 101–14. For a work that acknowledges but does not elaborate on the conflict between pragmatism and policy science, see Benjamin Barber, *Strong Democracy* (Berkeley: University of California Press, 1984), esp. pp. 52–53.

experience; third, that a critique of this enterprise from the perspective suggested by the preceding chapters intimates the possibility of a political science that digs beneath the sediment of administered expertise and so assists in recovering our sense of the tangibility of political things; and, fourth, that the democratic character of such a science is best revealed by considering its implications for what it means to speak truth to power.

In his *Psychopathology of Politics*, published in 1930, Harold Lasswell contended that the purpose of politics, which he defined as the "process by which the irrational bases of society are brought out into the open," is less to "solve conflicts than to prevent them; less to serve as a safety value for social protest than to apply social energy to the abolition of recurrent sources of strain in society."[9] In 1939, sensing that the walls holding the irrational at bay were rapidly crumbling, he called upon a dedicated core of social scientists to save democratic citizens from manipulation by less discriminating elites: "It is indisputable that the world could be united if enough people were impressed by this (or by any other) elite. The hope of the professors of social science, if not of the world, lies in the competitive strength of an elite based on vocabulary, footnotes, questionnaires, and conditioned responses, against an elite based on vocabulary, poison gas, property, and family prestige."[10] Joined together, this conception of the purpose of politics and the promise of expertise furnish the unstated premises of his explication and defense, in 1951, of a policy science whose aim is to "reduc[e] the level of strain and maladaptation in society" by diagnosing society's ills and then prescribing "comprehensive programs" of therapeutic treatment.[11]

It takes no great ingenuity to discover in Lasswell's work, from start to finish, a thinly veiled apology for a form of rule that, following Comte, might well be called "sociocracy."[12] Employing a revealing

9. Harold Lasswell, *The Psychopathology of Politics* (New York: Viking Press, 1960), pp. 184, 197.

10. Harold Lasswell, *World Politics and Personal Insecurity* (New York: McGraw-Hill, 1939), p. 20.

11. Lasswell, *The Psychopathology of Politics*, p. 197.

12. This tendency within Lasswell's thought is given most forthright expression in his *World Politics and Personal Insecurity*: "The pre-requisite of a stable order in the world is a universal body of symbols and practices sustaining an elite which propagates itself by peaceful methods and wields a monopoly of coercion which it is rarely necessary to apply to the uttermost. This means that the consensus on which order is based is necessarily non-rational; the world myth must be taken for granted by most of the population. The capacity of the generality of mankind to disembarrass themselves of the

metaphor, Lasswell describes the institution of policy science as a "maternity hospital for the delivery of . . . historically viable policy proposal[s]."[13] Implying that politics has an end whose rational determination guides its practice in much the same way that the goal of successful delivery informs the obstetrician's craft, this representation presupposes science's mastery of the criteria of civic well-being, and so its ability to combat the discrepancies between society's real needs and its conventional but "pathological" practices. This, in turn, justifies Lasswell's implicit assumption that the state, as the vehicle through which such knowledge is wedded to power, must be granted considerable autonomy from the subjects it is to cure. For in the absence of generalized competence in the relevant forms of expertise, it is no more possible for a democratic citizenry to participate in assessing and refashioning forms of collective practice than it is for laypersons to take part in decisions regarding how or whether an obstetrician should perform a cesarean section.

The patently antidemocratic implications of this argument might have been tempered had Lasswell embraced Aristotle's dictum to the effect that the wearer of a shoe knows best where it pinches, and on that basis argued that ordinary citizens are entitled to express their sense of pressing collective ills by selecting those who are to remedy them. But even so qualified, the body politic's disclosure of its symptoms, via the mechanism of elections, gives it no special title to identify either the causes of its current distress or the treatments appropriate to it. Hence the public's role in the processes whereby policy science confirms its diagnosis and prescription can extend, at best, only to ex post facto determination of whether state-initiated programs have in fact restored its collective feet to good standing. Appreciating this, Lasswell insists that the practitioners of what he calls the "sciences of democracy" must "gradually win respect in society among puzzled people who feel their responsibilities and who respect objective findings."[14] Verification of its hypothetical excursions presupposes a citi-

---

dominant legends of their early years is negligible, and if we pose the problem of unifying the world we must seek for the processes by which a non-rational consensus can be most expeditiously achieved" (p. 237).

13. Lasswell, "The Policy Orientation," p. 12. Cf. p. 10: "It is, I think, safe to forecast that the policy-science approach will bring about a series of 'special' sciences within the general field of the social sciences, much as the desire to cure has developed a science of medicine which is distinct from, though connected with, the general science of biology."

14. Lasswell, "The Policy Orientation," p. 10; The Psychopathology of Politics, p. 202. In the absence of such respect, warns David Bobrow, in his "Beyond Politics and Markets,"

zenry whose members accept the authority and defer to the imperatives of its interventions. The creation of a positivist culture, as Durkheim understood, is a condition of the very possibility of social scientific knowledge.

Given these implications, it is perhaps fortunate that policy science, for the most part, has not followed the path Lasswell recommended. While the Lasswellian formulation continues to elicit at least token endorsement, policy science's most prestigious expressions have drawn inspiration as well as method not from the craft of medicine, but rather from the discipline of microeconomics.[15] Embracing the positivist presupposition that all evaluative statements are noncognitive in nature, this science has in fact largely confined itself to developing techniques for securing ends that cannot themselves be defended on rational grounds.[16] Premised upon the utilitarian view that social welfare consists of the aggregated desires of discrete individuals, these techniques suggest that the purpose of the state is not to restore society to a condition of health, but rather to determine those policies best calculated to secure maximal satisfaction of expressed wants. In doing so, policy science escapes the transparently authoritarian bent of its Lasswellian formulation; but in rendering itself a mere instrument of aggregate desire, it also loses the critical edge Lasswell hoped to locate at its core.

So construed, the work of Aaron Wildavsky reveals the character of policy science more adequately than does that of its putative founder. In *Speaking Truth to Power*, Wildavsky opposes all forms of policy analysis that aid the state in its efforts to achieve preconceived goals via the formulation and implementation of rationalistic designs man-

---

American Journal of Political Science 21 (1977), pp. 415–19, the policy scientist must take precautionary steps to guard against "adaptive actions by those adversely affected to foil the policy options which emerge by blocking their choice or their impact"; only such measures can "protect the continuing validity of the conclusions and hinder unwarranted use of them" (p. 418).

15. For a good example of policy science that takes its cues from microeconomics, see Edith Stokey and Richard Zeckhauser, *Primer for Policy Analysis* (New York: Norton, 1978). It should be noted that Lasswell invited this displacement of the medical analogy when, in "The Policy Orientation," he offered economics as the enterprise that, because it most thoroughly adopted "the methods of physical science" (p. 5), had proven most useful to the national government in the years between the world wars.

16. Lasswell also prepares the ground for policy science's repudiation of his belief in the rationality of the goals for which power is exercised when, in "The Policy Orientation," he writes: "It is not necessary for the scientist to sacrifice objectivity in the execution of a project. The place for nonobjectivity is in deciding what ultimate goals are to be implemented. Once this choice is made, the scholar proceeds with maximum objectivity and uses all available methods" (p. 11).

dating the coercive regulation of behavior. In place of such "central direction by one mind that decides everything once and for all," he recommends that policy science devise planning techniques that, as tools, may be wielded by agents who wish to "figure things out for themselves." The autonomy of democracy's citizens is both preserved and exercised, that is, through their engagement in market-rational calculations regarding the likely advantages and disadvantages of either pursuing or declining various strategies of action structured but not required by the state. For example, Wildavsky argues that if the quality of public education is to improve, its consumers must find it possible to assert their preferences more efficiently than is presently the case. To this end, he urges not federal imposition of uniform curricular standards, but rather development of a voucher plan that makes it possible for parents to evaluate the schools their children now attend and then, should their dissatisfaction prove sufficient, move them elsewhere. Such a plan, Wildavsky insists, will achieve social coordination without coercion. Moreover, by inviting citizens to "act as analysts" and so become a "part of public policies," it will simultaneously foster "capacity for moral development on public purposes." As each comes to know "what other people prefer and are willing to give up" in fulfilling self-regarding aims, action becomes ever more informed by an "awareness" of its "consequences for others." The generation of "common understandings," therefore, is the unintended by-product of the state's manipulation of its invisible hand.[17]

I do not mean to minimize the differences between Lasswell's and Wildavsky's conception of the method and purpose of policy science. I do suggest, however, that this distinction fades considerably when it is understood that they both express and contribute to the historical dynamic through which matters political, especially in liberal regimes, have been constituted as specialized objects of disciplinary professionalization and expert administration. Here I cannot trace political science's contribution to the objectification of political pragmata with the care it deserves.[18] Suffice it to note that during the first several decades of its formal existence—during the closing decades of the nineteenth

17. Wildavsky, *Speaking Truth to Power*, pp. 8, 13, 19, 114, 255, 260, 270. In much the same vein, Wildavsky supports abolition of the U.S. Post Office's monopoly over the delivery of first-class mail so that consumers will find it necessary to choose among various private firms; and he urges the development of energy policies that foster both decreased consumption and increased production by, for example, raising the domestic price of gasoline.

18. For a work that largely does what I shall not do here, see Raymond Seidelman's *Disenchanted Realists* (Albany: State University of New York Press, 1985).

century and the opening years of the twentieth—the self-definition of American political science did not unequivocally privilege its scientific as opposed to its political purpose. This ambiguity is suggested by the fact that its most notable practitioners identified their cause with that of the Progressive movement, and especially with its campaign to initiate governmental reorganizations aimed at weakening the power of city bosses, party machines, and exploitative captains of industry. Its neo-Enlightenment hope, best exemplified by the work of Charles Beard and Woodrow Wilson, was that broad dissemination of the results generated by social scientific inquiries might animate coalitions of predominantly middle-class citizens to mobilize around issues of common concern. Acting through vehicles ranging from the referendum to civil service reform, these civic-minded movements hoped to free the channels of government from the forces presently corrupting their neutrality.

Political scientists' faith in the possibility of rousing broad-based reformist energies through an education in the facts of a muckraking science began to wane as early as World War I, and it has continued to do so throughout this century. This occurred initially in reaction to the late liberal state's evolution, which, responding to the cultural decomposition effected by a capitalist economy, found itself called upon to exercise supervisory control over ever wider areas of collective practice. Correctly sensing that the capacity for significant action was undergoing rapid centralization, practitioners of the emerging discipline of political science recognized that their original desire to speak truth to the power of a liberal citizenry now threatened to secure the discipline's own obsolescence. Thus, as the instrumentalities of party politics were displaced by those of a bureaucratized civil service, that discipline turned away from those citizens and toward the state in an effort to "rationalize" the operation of its regulatory imperatives. Growing ever less troubled by the indistinct memory of its Progressive past and ever more envious of the honor and place accorded to the rival discipline of economics, its practitioners increasingly measured the discipline's success by its ability to market the managerial skills cultivated within newly established schools of public administration.

To legitimate its self-representation as a vital source of the specialized knowledge necessary to the state's policy-making ventures, political science affirmed its reason as the sine qua non of democracy's capacity to endure in a highly complex and interdependent world. Hence Lasswell in 1941: "Without science, democracy is blind and

weak. With science, democracy will not be blind and may be strong."[19]
So construed, political science has become an eager accomplice contributing to the rationalizing processes through which broad matters
of public concern, expropriated from democratic citizens in the name
of democracy, have been redefined as depoliticized objects of expert
superintendence and so withdrawn from the public sphere. Employing the claims of objectivity to buttress the state's insistence that
formulation of comprehensive policy requires considerable administrative autonomy from the pressures of party politics and public
opinion, professionalized political science has evolved into one of the
more effective vehicles through which the claims of popular sovereignty have been eroded without engendering significant opposition.
For the discursive strategies of social science, displacing an earlier
discourse that spoke the language of equal rights, liberties, and
powers, repose questions regarding the accountability of representa-
tives as questions regarding the efficacy of various forms of asym-
metrical intervention. As citizens come to find natural the positions
prescribed for them as objects of so many state-initiated policies,
subtle mechanisms of disciplinary control, like the cost-benefit ploys
recommended by Wildavsky, penetrate deeper and deeper into the
body politic's constitutive organs. There, once assimilated, they obvi-
ate the need for grosser displays of sovereign power.

III

At the beginning of this chapter, I indicated that the enterprise of
policy science, in both therapeutic interventionist and microeconomic
instrumentalist form, claims pragmatist parents. It is disappointing
but not surprising, therefore, to find that the sins of its alleged off-
spring have been visited upon pragmatism itself. On the one hand,
following Lasswell's cue, pragmatism has been found to ratify the
state's efforts to reeducate a democratic citizenry when its members
resist reforms aimed at replacing the irrationalities of popular politics
with the ministrations of an expert civil service. Thus Christopher
Lasch argues that the intellectual veneer furnished by pragmatism is
but one of the many sources of the managerial state's hubristic convic-

19. Harold Lasswell, *Democracy through Public Opinion* (Menasha, Wis.: Banta, 1941),
p. 12.

tion that it possesses the knowledge necessary to concoct remedies for society's current diseases: "The new psychology, the child-study movement, the new education, the idea of scientific management, the philosophy of pragmatism, the science of evolution, all confirmed the experience of a century of unimpeded material and social progress, that the turmoil and conflict which had so long troubled the course of history could at last be eliminated by means of a scientific system of control. . . . Accordingly, they [Dewey and his followers] proposed to reform society not through the agencies of organized coercion . . . but by means of social engineering on the part of disinterested experts."[20] This interpretation has since found echoes in the work of John Diggins, Jeffrey Lustig, and Bruce Kuklick, to name but a few;[21] and without exception all endorse the conclusion, summarized by Arthur Murphy, that pragmatism's celebration of comprehensive social planning, informed by a psychotherapeutic conception of politics, is thoroughly implicated in producing and legitimating the "engineered complacency in which we live today."[22]

On the other hand, theorists following Wildavsky's cue, have found in pragmatism a paradigmatic expression of America's Benthamite bent. Because it offers no "clearer criterion for practice than a common and popular notion of scientific method," insists Bernard Crick, pragmatism can never successfully maintain that one "specific situation is rationally preferable to another."[23] From this premise, Louis Hartz

20. Christopher Lasch, *The New Radicalism in America* (New York: Knopf, 1965), pp. 161–62. Defenses of what Lasch calls social engineering politics are to be found in James Shotwell, *Intelligence and Politics* (New York: Century, 1921); and Edward Ross, *Social Control and the Foundations of Sociology* (Boston: Beacon Press, 1959).

21. R. Jeffrey Lustig, *Corporate Liberalism* (Berkeley: University of California Press, 1982). See p. 140: Dewey "appealed to people to 'internalize' the existing 'corporateness.' He ended *Individualism, Old and New*, with this announcement: 'By accepting the corporate and industrial world in which we live, and by thus fulfilling the precondition for interaction with it, we . . . create ourselves as we create an unknown future.' The definition of healthy individualism that emerged from such ideas was that of 'adjusted' individualism—the individual adjusted to external functions. That was the real thrust of Dewey's formalistic emphasis on 'integration.' " In his *Churchmen and Philosophers: From Jonathan Edwards to John Dewey* (New Haven: Yale University Press, 1985), historian Bruce Kuklick argues that Dewey believed that "power in the modern world rightly belonged to the intellectuals; and that power could be exercised dispassionately, impartially, and objectively only if they had control" (p. 260). Finally, in *The Lost Soul of American Politics* (New York: Basic Books, 1984), John Diggins writes: "The idea of 'liberty' . . . underwent a significant change of meaning in Dewey's philosophy. It no longer suggested political independence but social control" (p. 161).

22. Arthur Murphy, *Reason and the Common Good* (Englewood Cliffs, N.J.: Prentice-Hall, 1963), p. 260.

23. Bernard Crick, *The American Science of Politics* (Berkeley: University of California Press, 1959), pp. 89–90.

deduces the appropriate conclusion: Like cost-benefit analysis, pragmatism cannot help but prove an acquiescent servant of whatever ends are presently valued by its employers; and so, in its native land, it cannot do other than reinforce the uncritical core of American liberalism. This argument was given its earliest statement by Randolph Bourne, who in the early years of World War I sought to explain the embarrassing eagerness with which those who called themselves pragmatists embraced American involvement in that conflict. In his famous essay "Twilight of Idols," Bourne argued that the mobilization of pragmatist intellectuals for a military engagement whose aims had never been democratically defined revealed their philosophy's natural tendency to collapse into nihilistic celebration of *raison d'état*:

> The war has revealed a younger intelligentsia, trained up in the pragmatic dispensation, immensely ready for the executive ordering of events. . . . His [Dewey's] disciples have learned all too literally the instrumental attitude toward life, and, being immensely intelligent and energetic, they are making themselves efficient instruments of the war technique, accepting with little question the ends as announced from above. That those ends are largely negative does not concern them, because they have never learned not to subordinate idea to technique. . . . They have, in short, no clear philosophy of life except that of intelligent service, the admirable adaptation of means to ends. . . . They have absorbed the secret of scientific method as applied to political administration.[24]

On the domestic front, George Santayana continues in much the same vein, pragmatism furnishes an intellectualized glorification of the commitment to "redoubl[e] your effort when you have forgotten your aim."[25] More perniciously, argues C. Wright Mills, pragmatism's abolition of the salutary distance between knowledge and power obscures underlying structural conflicts over the distribution of political and economic resources and thereby sustains the hegemony of capitalist individualism.[26]

As should be apparent, all parties to the debate about pragmatism's

24. Randolph Bourne, *The Radical Will* (New York: Urizen Books, 1977), pp. 342–43.
25. George Santayana, quoted in Murphy, *Reason and the Common Good*, p. 259. It should be noted that Lasswell himself opens up the possibility that policy science will do nothing more than uncritically confirm the values of American liberalism. Compensating for his failure to offer any account of the criteria of social health in "The Policy Orientation," he asserts that the "dominant American tradition" (p. 10) will supply the apparently uncontestable ends necessary to orient the practice of this science.
26. C. Wright Mills, *Pragmatism and Sociology* (New York: Oxford University Press, 1966), pp. 400–413.

politics share the conviction that America's most celebrated contribution to philosophic discourse authorizes the union of knowledge, qua
technical expertise, and power, as that resource is institutionalized
within the modern state. Their disagreement concerns the most apt
characterization of this alliance, not its existence per se. The suspect
character of this presuppositional core can be suggested, however, by
invoking a passage in which Dewey satirizes arguments on behalf of
"rule by those intellectually qualified, by expert intellectuals":

> This revival of the Platonic notion that philosophers should be kings is
> the more taking because the idea of experts is substituted for that of
> philosophers, since philosophy has become something of a joke, while
> the image of the specialist, the expert in operation, is rendered familiar
> and congenial by the rise of the physical sciences and by the conduct of
> industry. A cynic might indeed say that the notion is a pipe-dream, a
> revery entertained by the intellectual class in compensation for an impo-
> tence consequent upon the divorce of theory and practice, upon the
> remoteness of specialized science from the affairs of life: the gulf being
> bridged not by the intellectuals but by inventors and engineers hired by
> captains of industry.[27]

Those who advance this neo-Comtist position, Dewey goes on to say,
are committed to a kind of pseudoknowledge, which, under present
circumstances, cannot help but assume the character of "a mystery in
the hands of initiates, who have become adepts in virtue of following
ritualistic ceremonies from which the profane herd is excluded."[28] Its
relationship to collective life, as long as it remains an arcane commodity, can take shape only as externalized intervention that further
erodes the fragile remnants of America's democratic culture.

While these quotations are sufficient to cast doubt on any unvar-
nished technocratic reading of pragmatism, they do not make clear the
thoroughgoing incompatibility between it and policy science, whether
clad in Lasswellian or Wildavskian garb. That, though, is Dewey's
import when he insists that a "class of experts is inevitably so removed
from common interests as to become a class with private interests and
private knowledge, which in social matters is not knowledge at all."[29]
To glean the meaning of this curious claim, it is useful to begin with a

27. Dewey, *PP*, p. 205. For Dewey's ironic presentation of the sorts of arguments most
commonly used to justify deference to the claims of expertise in contemporary politics,
see pp. 123–25.
28. Ibid., p. 164.
29. Ibid., p. 207.

brief critique of positivist social science, because the subfield of policy science is merely the most forthright expression of the transposition of positivism into political science.

For the sake of argument, I define "positivism" as that theory of scientific explanation that (1) advances a nomological conception of knowledge, one that identifies the end of inquiry with the construction of causal explanations relating the occurrence of specific events through reference to universal laws that predict an invariant relationship between certain antecedent conditions and their necessary consequences; (2) claims that a presupposition of such knowledge is generation of a neutral language whose content stands in some isomorphic relationship to the antecedently existent objects it describes; and (3) affirms the ideal of value-free knowledge. Leaving the first of these claims for last, let me indicate why positivism's (and hence policy science's) commitment to the second and third are untenable.

The quest for a neutral observation language can be satisfied only if it proves possible to maintain a strict distinction between fact and theory. Yet as the preceding chapters suggest, "facts" have no existence apart from the inarticulate preunderstandings contained within our meaning-construing habits. "Objects of knowledge are not given to us defined, classified, and labeled. We bring to the simplest observation a complex apparatus of habits, of accepted meanings and techniques. Otherwise observation is the blankest of stares, and the natural object is a tale told by an idiot."[30] Because our experience is always *of* that which habit appropriates from the indefinite matrix of concrete possibilities implicit in nature's doings, the ideal of knowledge purged of all "distortion" introduced by the self's subjectivity is unintelligible.

Equally indefensible is any notion of objectivity that holds that truth is determined by an unmediated appeal to the naked sense certainty of uncompromised facts-in-themselves. Experience, whether of the natural or the social worlds, is not some uncooked material to which scientific methods can be directly applied. "If the idea, the theory, is tentative, if it is pliable and must be bent to fit the facts, it should not be forgotten that the 'facts' are not rigid, but are elastic to the touch of theory. In other words, the distinction between the idea and the facts

---

30. Dewey, *EN*, p. 219. This quotation is sufficient to show the error of Bernard Crick's contention, made in his *American Science of Politics*, that the "prior importance of theory to observation scarcely occurred to them [pragmatists]. To the pragmatist a prior commitment would seem like a prejudice; the task of the social philosopher was to let the facts bring themselves to order" (pp. 92–93).

is not between a mere mental state, on one side, and a hard and rigid body on the other. Both idea and 'facts' are flexible, and verification is the process of mutual adjustment, of organic interaction."[31]

The Cartesian conception of scientific method as a system of prophylactic procedures whose employment enables an observer to overcome the ontological gap between the mind qua subjective knower and the object qua matter is further compromised insofar as facts become constituted as cognitive entities only within situations deemed problematic and only by means of transformative conduct seeking to determine their cumulative import for an as yet unreal future. Apprehensiveness is a vital moment of all significant apprehension because the observation of concrete "facts" always emerges out of a sense of dislocation as well as some preliminary sense of that situation's possible import for subsequent experience. As transitive abstractions discriminated from a context of moving events, facts are thus objects by which we come to know rather than things known. Their final office is to overcome their deficient status as signs in becoming meaningful part(icipant)s within the experience of enlarged sense. Hence if they are not to be left as artificial ossifications within a science devoted to what is ontologically deficient, facts must be relocated within the qualitatively experienced whole from which their meaning is finally derived.

When positivism denies that relocation, it makes apparent its inability to acknowledge adequately the temporality of the human condition. It forgets, that is, that our quests for knowledge are inseparable from but not identical to our questions about an event's potential significances within the multiple contexts in which it plays a part. "Because we are afraid of speculative ideas, we do, and do over and over again, an immense amount of dead, specialized work in the region of 'facts.' We forget that such facts are only data; that is, are only fragmentary, uncompleted meanings, and unless they are rounded out into complete ideas—a work which can only be done by a free imagination of intellectual possibilities—they are as helpless as are all maimed things and as repellent as are needlessly thwarted ones."[32] Unable to grant this truth without undermining its self-understanding, positivist inquiry cannot help but culminate in truncated pursuit of a miscellaneous heap of insignificant objects.

31. Dewey, "The Logic of Verification," in EW, vol. 3, p. 87.
32. Dewey, "Philosophy and Civilization," in PC, p. 11.

To relocate inquiry within the qualitative situational wholes in which it may play a part is to see that positivism's insistence upon a categorical distinction between empirical description and normative prescription must also be reconfigured. That difference, in the last analysis, is merely a dessicated reincarnation of the Kantian attempt to safeguard a sphere of free moral choice by rigidly segregating it from the encroachments of a mechanistic science. From the perspective suggested here, however, to claim that a fact is value-neutral means not that an observer has achieved a standpoint outside all situational contexts, but rather that this particular fact has no apparent bearing on the emergent meanings of this specific situation. Thinking is first and foremost concerned with *facienda*, things done and yet to be done. As a means by which the past is navigated into the future, all thinking bears the qualitative impress of interest in the directionality of the affairs in which it is embedded. Consequently, the quality of care is implicated whenever its conduct is significantly present. To hold otherwise is to justify intellect's withdrawal from the affairs of human culture, and so to invite its degeneration into methodism, the practice of polishing analytic techniques whose chief raison d'être is to aid in the development of more sophisticated formal techniques.

To contest the sufficiency of positivist science's claim to cognitive status is, by extension, to attack the specifically political bearing of its pseudoknowledge. Introduced into the public realm, positivism's facts add to the weight of an order whose basic institutional arrangements appear increasingly rigid and impermeable. For when such historyless reifications are effectively equated with the partly ordered and partly disordered sociotemporal events of lived experience, they cannot help but abridge the conduct of thinking. "If the social situation out of which these facts emerges is itself confused and chaotic, the facts themselves will be confused, and we shall add only intellectual confusion to practical disorder."[33] Much the same effect is achieved, moreover, when such epistemological realism takes shape as a claim to know the body of interrelated nomological regularities that rules the particulars subsumed beneath them. Defining its end in a way such that it can become a mode of professional discourse of and for itself, that science first abstracts its conclusions from the recurrent patterns of institutionalized conduct without which they have no being, and it then ascribes to these hypostatized entities the dignity and power

33. Dewey, "Social Science and Social Control," *New Republic* 67 (1931), 276–77.

once ascribed by myth to Zeus's *archē*. Not surprisingly, such an "ab-
negation of human intelligence save as a bare reporter of things as they
are and as a power of conforming to them consecrate[s] the existent
state of affairs, whatever its distribution of advantages and disadvantages. That such a doctrine should work out, no matter how personally benevolent its holders, in the direction of *Beati possidentes*, is
inevitable."[34]

At first glance, it might appear that Lasswell acknowledges the truth
of this critique of positivism. After all, he opposes the neo-Kantian
conviction that knowledge gives birth to itself and is capable of afford-
ing its own justification. Correlatively, he holds that reason can discharge its duties only by refashioning the present state of things rather
than merely knowing it. These superficial resemblances, though, fail
to tell the whole story. Lasswell's account of verification, functioning
as the vehicle through which he legitimates the antipolitics of a social
engineering state, incorporates significant teleocratic presuppositions
and, as such, must be rejected.

Lasswellian policy science derives its title to navigate the ship of
state from its tacit commitment to a hierarchy of forms of judgment.
That is the necessary presupposition of his claims regarding the superiority of expert, as opposed to lay, assessments of everyday practice's
truth-value. Because the "individual is a poor judge of his own interest," Lasswell argues, "the time has come to abandon the assumption
that the problem of politics is the problem of promoting discussion
among all the interests concerned in a given problem." Rational politics, he continues, requires the forging of more "intimate techniques of
communication among research workers, policy advisers, and the
makers of final decisions"; for "our problem is to be ruled by the truth
about the conditions of harmonious human relations, and the discovery of the truth is an object of specialized research."[35]

It is not difficult to locate in these quotations the dense legacy of our
collective conceptual inheritance. In the opening book of his *Meta-*

34. Dewey, "Nature and Reason in Law," in *PC*, pp. 168, 172.
35. Lasswell, *The Psychopathology of Politics*, pp. 3–4, 194, 196–97. Cf. p. 194: "The
individual who chooses a political policy as a symbol of his wants is usually trying to
relieve his own disorders by irrelevant palliatives. An examination of the total state of
the person will frequently show that his theory of his own interests is far removed from
the course of procedure which will give him a happy and well-adjusted life. Human
behavior toward remote social objects, familiarity with which is beyond the personal
experience of but a few, is especially likely to be symptomatic rather than a healthy and
reflective adjustment."

physics, Aristotle contends that "we take experts in an art to be wiser than men of mere experience; because wisdom presumably comes only with knowledge, and we believe that the experts can analyze and explain, whereas others cannot."[36] To this classical affirmation of *epistēmē*'s peculiar capacity to grasp the "true" nature of lived experience, Lasswell joins epistemology's conviction that the "real" world is populated by positivism's self-sufficient facts. The net result is his unformulated belief in the ontological priority of individuated subjects whose unambiguous dissociation from an antecedent realm of similarly individuated objects is the condition of knowledge's objectivity, and hence of technique's authority to rule the merely conventional. In sum, when Lasswell accords superior reality to policy science's scarce judgmental goods and then demands that society's appearances be made over in their image, he makes manifest the authoritarian thrust implicit in any notion of expert competence that immunizes itself from politics by denying that its abstracted discourse emerges from and always refers to its ground in more comprehensive forms of noncognitive experience.

To reverse this reversal and so ensure reason's piety toward the experience that sustains it, a science of politics must become self-consciously what it already is in fact. That is, it must become a distinct but derivative part(icipant) within the more encompassing activities through which collective affairs are refashioned in significance-creating ways. This is not to erase the difference between the kinds of judgments appropriate to ordinary modes of practice and those appropriate to more specialized practices of inquiry. It is, however, to insist that there are no essences behind those appearances to which science has privileged access. And relatedly, it is to insist that the worth of political science's conduct is contingent upon its capacity to serve as an "organ" (as opposed to an autonomous industry) contributing to proliferation of the consummatory meanings resident as so many potentialities within experience-in-nature. The pertinent question regarding the conjunction of science and politics within political science is, therefore, not how the conclusions of the former are to be applied to the latter. Rather, it is how this particular mode of conduct is to be related to the other modes of encultured experience from which it is derived and to which it must return.

36. Aristotle, *Metaphysics*, trans. Richard Hope (Ann Arbor: University of Michigan Press, 1960), 980a27–30.

What shape such conduct might take can be intimated by expanding the discussion of truth in Chapter 5. In this context, my more particular aim is to rethink our accustomed understanding of verification, that is, the activities through which human beings take part in fashioning truths from the affairs of everyday experience. Because truth is ultimately grounded in knowing's contribution to the struggle through which experience's implicit meaningfulness is nurtured and sustained, it is not in the last analysis an epistemic notion. To use the term "truth" is not to refer to a logical property of propositions—for instance, their internal consistency with one another. Nor is it to claim a statement's correspondence with reality. Rather, it is to testify to the truthfulness of a qualitatively distinct situation refashioned by the activity through which it is known. "The question of truth is not as to whether Being or Non-Being, Reality or mere appearance, is experienced, but as to the *worth* of a certain concretely experienced thing."[37] To profess a situation's truthfulness is to make a statement regarding the appearance of a distinctive quality permeating the concrete affairs of a specific situation. It is, more precisely, to affirm the adequacy of sensed significance, as that significance is embodied within the meaning-disclosing habits of live creatures, and so to provisionally trust its capacity to inform subsequent conduct. The term "truth" thus indicates an experienced relation resident among the pragmata of meaningful experience, and it has no tangible significance outside such relation.

While truthful moments are temporally circumscribed, they are not disconnected from the present's emergence out of the past and into the future. Given its appropriation of antiquity's ocular metaphors, epistemology cannot help but compress the durational processes of thinking into a distinct moment of instantaneous apprehension which it then calls knowledge. If, however, the gerundial form is taken to indicate the truth about knowledge—that is, if we take seriously William James's insistence that "truth *happens* to an idea"—then the event that is knowing is well characterized as a "directed transformation of an indeterminate situation into one that is so determinate within its constituent distinctions and relations as to convert the elements of the original situation into a unified whole."[38] From this point of view, it follows that "verification and truth are two names for the

---

37. Dewey, "The Postulate of Immediate Empiricism," in *IDP*, p. 235.
38. Dewey, *LTI*, pp. 104–5 (emphasis deleted from entire quotation).

same thing. We call it 'verification' when we regard it as process; when the development of the idea is strung out and exposed to view in all that makes it true. We call it 'truth' when we take it as product, as process telescoped and condensed."[39]

If thinking's fruits can only be assessed relative to the specific contexts out of which they are teased, then expertise's successful candidacy for the title of truth can be confirmed only when, relocated within the determinate forms of experience from which it was derived, it cultivates the coherent vitality of the sense present within and presented by the associated activities that constitute its particular subject matter. "Individuals in every branch of human endeavor" must come to act as "experimentalists engaged in testing the findings of the theorist"; such collective confirmation "is the sole final guaranty for the sanity of the theorist."[40] This, it should be noted, is not to say that confirmation of these fruits is private in the sense that it is confined to the incorrigible experience of so many singular subjects. Contra Descartes, who insists that the ultimate test of certainty is found in the individual consciousness, a claim to knowledge, as a claim to a particular sort of meaning, always makes reference to a wider association of knowers. To know is to partake in the mutual exchange of symbols whose full reality is contained in the consummatory conduct through which such meanings are explicated. Hence social scientific knowledge is possible only when its hypothetical claims become subject to transformation in accordance with the sense-making habits and capacities of those whose relatedness sustains that association.

Our prereflective situatedness in noncognitive experience is a con-

39. Dewey, "The Intellectualist Criterion of Truth," in *IDP*, p. 139.

40. Dewey, "The Logic of Judgments of Practice," in *EEL*, p. 442. The longer quotation immediately preceding this claim reads as follows: "But lest the man of science, the man of dominantly reflective habits, be puffed up with his own conceits, he must bear in mind that practical application—that is, experiment—is a condition of his own calling, that it is indispensable to the institution of knowledge or truth. Consequently, in order that he keep his own balance, it is needed that his findings be everywhere applied. The more their application is confined within his own special calling, the less meaning do the conceptions possess, and the more exposed they are to error. The widest possible range of application is the means of the deepest verification. As long as the specialist hugs his own results they are vague in meaning and unsafe in content." In a sense, Dewey's conclusion here is not wholly unlike that drawn by Aristotle in the eleventh chapter of book 3 in the *Politics*, trans. Ernest Barker (London: Oxford University Press, 1958). At 1282a, Aristotle answers Plato's arguments on behalf of philosopher-kings by arguing that while "each individual may indeed be a worse judge than the experts . . . when they meet together," they are "either better than experts or at any rate no worse." Dewey's claim is much stronger, though, inasmuch as he argues that truthfulness is realized not in correct judgments, but rather in the constitution of peculiarly democratic practice.

dition of our ability to think about and know its concerns. Its pragmata, moreover, have no existence prior to, or apart from, the persons
who take part in shaping and reshaping them. Their specific qualitative dimensions are engendered by the relations sustained among
those whose crisscrossing and conflicting paths call into being a field
that would have no existence in their absence. Consequently, if experience's issues are to be appreciated truly, they must be known in a way
that acknowledges the contextualized tissue of contingent relations
that gives rise to their appearance as worldly things and so establishes
the possibility of talking about them. To subject such matters to rule by
the agencies and categories of expertise, as predicated upon epistemology's monologic conception of knowing, is to deny their reality as
intersubjective concerns woven from a world made by no *one* in particular.

The truth or falsity of any meaning lies *within* rather than without
the relationships that define a problematic situation. It follows that
any science that joins "knowledge" to the power of an interventionist
state dedicated to "rational" planning of a society unable to appreciate
its own needs precludes the possiblity of its own confirmation.
Lasswell, as we have seen, *pre*supposes the congruity of policy science's expert assessment with the (unarticulated) reason of those immediately implicated in insufficiently significant forms of experience
when he holds that the abstracted cognition affirmed by expertise can
be applied indiscriminately, that is, moved about from situation to
situation without paying heed to the qualitative peculiarities that define each. As such, the science he recommends cannot help but mistake the hypothetical for the actual.

For much the same reason, any science that equates the achievement of public sense with its efficacy in manufacturing specified results short-circuits the distinctively collective dimension of truth making. Thus when Wildavsky identifies verification with the success
of economic incentives in producing behavior congruent with that
deemed desirable by policy makers, he contributes to experience's
falsification. His prescription for educational reform, for example,
does not aim to render articulate, comprehensible, and collective the
discontent experienced by parents who share an inclusive interest in
remedying the quality of instruction received by their children; and so,
although disdaining the politics of direct command, his science does
nothing to overcome the manipulative character of a state that characterizes "planning" as the reorganization of market cues so as to "rein-

force or modify" the behavior of target populations.[41] By preserving the appearance of autonomous choice and so enhancing the likelihood that policy will encounter but limited resistance, that science's "reason" proves an all the more insidious weapon within the arsenal of state power.[42]

In the case of Lasswell and Wildavsky alike, the pseudorationalism of state planning, taking as warranted knowledge what is at best a possible vehicle of experience's enhanced truthfulness, produces only meaninglessness. To use the language of the previous chapter, each fails to acknowledge that experience's capacity to bear meaning becomes most adequately embodied only when each part of the larger whole that is sense dynamically calls forth the distinctive qualities of all others. For when order is imposed from without, form remains external to that whole and so cannot be present in the constitution of each of its members. Or to put this point in more overtly political terms, Wildavsky and Lasswell deny citizens their full participation in the dialectic of doing and suffering which reconstitutes a refashioned situation, and so deny that situation its most sufficient intelligibility. Rendering political things intangible, expertise's abstracted rule loosens our collective grip on the significant flesh of the political world and thereby encourages our fall into the epistemological equivalent of solitary confinement. The upshot is so much nonsense.

IV

If we give up our inveterate conviction that predominantly middle-class intellectuals are specially entitled to speak truth to power in virtue of their ability to generate unbiased assessments of social events, what then will science do? Alternatively, what might be the character of a science that did not recapitulate the intellectualist fallacy under the guise of a claim to expert knowledge, and so did not falsify experience in the name of truth? "Theory having learned what it cannot do, is made responsible for the better performance of what needs to be

41. Wildavsky, *Speaking Truth to Power*, pp. 395–96.
42. For a general critique of the educative consequences that attend reliance on market rationality in the implementation of public policy, see William Connolly, *Appearance and Reality in Politics* (New York: Cambridge University Press, 1981), pp. 90–119. For a review of Wildavsky that makes some similar points, see Marc Landy, "Policy Analysis as a Vocation," *World Politics* 33 (1981), 468–84.

done: study of the conditions out of which come the obstacles and the resources of adequate life."[43] A science *of* politics acknowledges its derivative status when it offers its claims in the form of provisional interpretations that, when presented to those who share an interest in experience's significant reconstitution, account for the sources of their current senselessness and intimate ways to (a)mend that condition.[44] Such offerings, which cannot be verified in any strict positivistic sense, canalize aspiration by weaving together apparently unrelated affairs in a way that challenges the forms of description now dominant. Suggesting the dependence of noncognitive situations immediately experienced as problematic on a nexus of relations hitherto uncharted, these narratives locate the power of collective action by indicating how agents came to be thus situated, as parts related in particular ways, within so many sense-deficient contexts. For to grasp the meaning of a thing or event is to behold the relations it sustains with other things and events, and thus to render the former significant. Exposing the forms of relatedness among matters presently apportioned between and subjected to the epistemic imperatives of so many bodies of isolated expertise, such a science might help to bring into the world of appearance things that, at present, remain unseen.

Like its positivist rivals, such a science may incorporate "lawlike" statements of empirical regularities. But unlike positivism, it will not confuse their abstracted exposition with science's "end." If the aim of thinking is to invest concrete affairs with a fuller sense of their own significances, then the full reality of knowledge, as an eventual event, is carried in the present instance. The form of such a science, accordingly, must remain true to its situation within a world whose distinc-

43. Dewey, "Intelligence and Morals," in *IDP*, p. 68.
44. For a provocative effort to articulate a conception of social science that does not employ pragmatism as its foundation but is largely congruent with that developed here, see Brian Fay's *Social Theory and Political Practice* (London: Allen & Unwin, 1975) and *Critical Social Science* (Ithaca: Cornell University Press, 1987). My reading of pragmatism owes a great deal to Fay's work, although he, I suspect, would not embrace my claim that Dewey's philosophy is largely compatible with the conception of social science he delineates. For other efforts to spell out the possible significance of a reinterpretation of the pragmatic tradition for political science, see Charles Anderson, "Political Theory and Political Science: The Rediscovery and Reinterpretation of the Pragmatic Tradition" in *What Should Political Theory Be Now?* ed. John Nelson (Albany: State University of New York Press, 1983); and Alfonso Damico, "Analysis and Advocacy: Pragmatism and the Study of Politics," *Polity* 7 (1974), 193–208. Finally, for an essay that moves in much the same direction, albeit on the basis of an appropriation of Karl Popper rather than Dewey, see James Farr, "Situational Analysis: Explanation in Political Science," *Journal of Politics* 474 (1985), 1085–1107.

tive qualities can make their presence felt only because the regular and the uniform are so thoroughly interwoven with the contingent and the unpredictable. "If natural existence is qualitatively individualized or genuinely plural, as well as repetitious, and if things have both temporal quality and recurrence or uniformity, then the more realistic knowledge is, the more fully it will reflect and exemplify these traits."[45]

The circumstantial generalizations of such a science, we must recall, are neither necessary nor essential to the being of the connections they express. Although the relations in which individuals participate may be abstracted as cognitive objects within the context of situations calling for reflection, the being of those relations does not derive from the knowing that discloses them. "In art, as in nature and life, relations are modes of interaction. They are pushes and pulls; they are contractions and expansions; they determine lightness and weight, rising and falling, harmony and discord. The relations of friendship, of husband and wife, of parent and child, of citizen and nation, like those of body to body in gravitation and chemical action, may be symbolized by terms or conceptions and then be stated in propositions. But they *exist* as actions and reactions in which things are modified."[46] As discursive formulations of the immanent recurrences sustained among discriminated phases of spatiotemporal transactions, the "laws" of political science designate not truths to which persons must accommodate themselves, but rather conditional means by which connections are instituted and continuity introduced where hitherto there had been only fragmentation. The ultimate existential reference of such means, therefore, is to the truth that is either cultivated or violated within the immediate experience sustained by the relations to which those means refer.

On the understanding advanced here, the conduct of political science must pass beyond the aggregation of positivism's brute "facts" in order to explicate the meanings that, qua habits, inform any given medium of conventional conduct. But unlike any hermeneuticist science that regards such explication as the end of inquiry,[47] such inquiry's representations cannot assume the adequacy of that medium as presently constituted. For meanings, like facts, are truly appreciated only when their facticity is overcome in anticipating the eventua-

---

45. Dewey, *EN*, p. 160.
46. Dewey, *AE*, p. 134.
47. For a defense of such a hermeneutic endeavor, see Charles Taylor, "Interpretation and the Sciences of Man," *Review of Metaphysics* 25 (1971), 3–51.

tions toward which they are capable of moving. "All things that we experience have *some* meaning, but that meaning is always so partially embodied in things that we cannot rest in them. They point beyond themselves; they indicate meanings which they do not fulfil. All thinking grows out of this discrepancy between existence and the meaning which it partially embodies and partially refuses, which it suggests but declines to express. Perception of things as they are is but a stage in the process of making them different. They have already begun to be different in being known, for by that fact they enter into a different context, a context of foresight and judgment of better and worse."[48] Stating the possible significances of immediate qualities that are now ambivalent in their import, science necessarily questions the authority of things as they are presently given.

If it is to motion beyond experience's present insufficiencies, science must have recourse to a kind of abstraction. Drawing out the common elements embedded within seemingly unrelated situations experienced by seemingly unrelated agents is a vital moment in the emancipation of significance from beneath the accumulated weight of layer upon layer of objectified expertise. Such abstraction, however, must conserve the possibility of its reintegration within the habitual skill of conductors shifting dialectically between the exigencies of local detail and the parameters of translocal structure such that each makes reference to the other and both point beyond themselves. Persons already "know" far more than they can say about the social reality within which they are habitually embedded. If science is to respect that prosaic "knowledge" even as it explores the present's deficiencies, its temporary abrogation of the qualitative dimensions of immediate experience must grant the priority of conventional opinion over the truth of theory.

More specifically, science must fashion its claims in rhetorically appropriate ways, that is, in ways that grow out of and relate intelligibly to the vernacular soil in which they offer themselves as candidates for sowing. Too often we forget that truth in its original sense was neither a logical nor an epistemological term. Its most naive use was in reference to a virtue called into being by recurrent intercourse among those who had found cause to worry about each other's sincerity. As intimated by Greek antiquity's use of the verb *aletheuein* in praise of those who engage in right dealings with one another, "telling the

48. Dewey, "The Intellectualist Criterion of Truth," in *IDP*, p. 117; *HNC*, p. 298.

truth, telling a thing the way it is, means designating things in terms that observe the conventions of proper social intercourse. Truth telling has always been a matter of adaptation to a social audience."[49] Consequently, if it is to be reflexively appropriated within ordinary experience, the language of political science must meet the criteria of adequacy implicit within such experience. To hold otherwise is to arrogate to science a responsibility that can only be met by those who in time either will or will not breathe life into its otherwise deficient abstractions.

Just how such inquiry is to show respect for its ground can be clarified by specifying the character of its instrumentality. That science's constructions, inviting its audiences to have for themselves the sort of immediately experienced situation "intended" by these discourses, are not unlike tools. Unlike Lasswell's state-concocted cures and Wildavsky's state-orchestrated manipulations, however, these instrumentalities are more like maps than hammers. The aim of any such map is to facilitate the interpretation of a locally present situation through reference to that which is now apparently absent, that is, the larger wholes to which it, as part, makes tacit reference. Like any other map, just how much distance it covers depends on the scope of its scale. It may take in only those relations that enter most tangibly into the medium of present experience; or it may abstract from their relative detail in order to explore that experience's more comprehensive background. Which map is appropriate at any given moment can never be answered apart from the particularities of a given situation and its troubles. For one purpose, a maximum of concreteness is just what is needed; for another, such detail means that any sense of the more enduring limits on conduct is blurred at best. In either case, though, it is important to emphasize that such a map's charting of collective space and time can be neither confirmed nor falsified by, for example, a photograph taken at the spot where agents are presently lost. To identify science with the production of such duplicative images is to ensure that actors remain disoriented in a senseless present. Only by deliberately distorting the world as it is positivistically constituted can we come to perceive that the way in which experience is currently fashioned by so many forms of teleocratic expertise is not given in the nature of things.

To appreciate such coherent deformations of the world's facticity,

---

49. Dewey, "The Problem of Truth," in *MW*, vol. 6, p. 15.

even apart from practical explication of its existentially emergent possibilities, is to come to inhabit a transfigured world. To grasp the
medium of collective experience as so many interpenetrating but more
or less alterable situations is to find the facts of domination and suffering invested with new qualitative significance. "Discovery of America
involved insertion of newly touched land in a map of the globe. This
insertion, moreover, was not merely additive, but transformative of a
prior picture of the world as to its surfaces and their arrangements. It
may be replied that it was not the world which was changed but only
the map. To which there is the obvious retort that after all the map is
part of the world, not something outside it. It was not simply states of
consciousness or ideas inside the heads of men that were altered when
America was actually discovered; the modification was one in the
public meaning of the world in which men publicly act."[50]

Yet in the last analysis, to acquire an awareness of others who share
the same lot, the empowering possibilities engendered by such awareness, and the tactics that might prove serviceable in overcoming obstacles to those possibilities is not in and of itself to move from lost
to found. Science's interpretations secure partial confirmation when,
transformed in the process of their appropriation, they shape sufferings passively borne into anticipations of alterable conditions. Their
truth becomes more completely manifest as they demonstrate their
capacity to overcome the privatism common to those who believe that
the plight of each, as particularized in accordance with expertise's
antecedent classifications, is unrelated to that of others. They achieve
full epistemic status, however, only when their participation in bringing intelligibility to a moving course of events is actualized within and
by a collectivity whose power to act is exercised in ways that elicit
sense from its mutual situation.

Accordingly, science must incorporate within its offerings counsel
regarding possible forms of associated activity among those mutually
implicated in the experience toward which its accounts gesture.
"Truth is a character which belongs to a meaning so far as tested
through action that carries it to a successful completion."[51] Such "completion" might be termed a kind of agreement, but only on condition
that we remember that the term "agreement" points toward the collective expression of congruous embodied habits rather than universal

---

50. Dewey, *EN*, pp. 156–57.
51. Dewey, "The Intellectualist Criterion of Truth," in *IDP*, p. 139.

intellectual endorsement of specified propositional content (as in Habermas). The know-how embedded in such characteristic ways of dealing with similar situations cannot be fully explicated in discursive form. Hence science's "maps" can fully overcome their abstraction only in guiding conduct through space and time by means of habits reconstituted en route. Their "utility" is a function of their *aretē*, that is, their capacity to perform this service; and their correspondence to reality is like that between an answer and the question it is intended to address.

It follows that the truthfulness of science's inventions can become apparent only *after* they have been found helpful to those searching for new ways through the thickets of experience. By implication, should a practitioner of the science sketched here advance an interpretation that fails to render the predicaments of everyday experience less opaque, then its partiality in this respect must be taken as a measure of its falsity. What aspires to the title of knowledge is "refuted not by denial that one finds things to be thus and so, but by giving directions for a course of experience that results in finding its opposite to be the case. To convince of error as well as to lead to truth is to assist another to see and find something which he hitherto has failed to find and recognize. All of the wit and subtlety of reflection and of dialectic find scope in the elaboration and conveying of directions that intelligibly point out a course to be followed."[52] To endorse a senseless account of some situation is to find that conduct in accordance with its intimations further entangles those caught within a web of cause and consequence not of their own making. "To represent things as they are is to represent them in ways that tend to maintain a common understanding; to misrepresent them is to injure—whether wilfully or no—the conditions of common understanding."[53]

V

How might such a science assist in recapturing the expropriated skills, resources, and knowledges that presently assume the form of teleocratic expertise? How might it assist in revitalizing our sense of the tangibility of ordinary experience? To answer these questions in a way

---

52. Dewey, "Experience and Philosophic Method," in *LW*, vol. 1, p. 391.
53. Dewey, "The Problem of Truth," in *MW*, vol. 6, p. 16.

that pulls together several of the arguments of the preceding chapters, let me suggest the sort of inquiry that might be undertaken were such a science to take as its object the conduct of work within a late capitalist economy. (What makes this conduct an appropriate topic for analysis by a specifically *political* science is indicated in the next chapter.)

If science is to demonstrate its piety toward vernacular meanings, its offerings must acknowledge temporality as a defining quality of all intelligible experience and so assume narrative form. "To explain is to employ one thing to elucidate, clear, shed light upon, put in better order, because in a wider context, another thing. It is thus subordinate to more adequate discourse, which, applied to space-time affairs, assumes the style of narration and description. Speaking in terms of captions familiar in rhetoric, exposition and argument are always subordinate to a descriptive narration, and exist for the sake of making the latter clearer, more coherent and more significant."[54] Therefore, an interpretation aimed at exploring that complex of institutionally structured relations we designate as a capitalist economy in light of its contribution to the production of experience's insignificance might well take as its premise the tale of reason's history, as related in Chapters 2 and 3.

It requires no elaborate explication to show that a capitalist economy takes the ancient division of classes into those who had to labor for a living and those who were relieved from this necessity, and then shapes this disjunction into a form adapted to the present industrial regime. Nor does it take extensive argumentation to show that the roots of our segregation between fine and useful art, as reinforced by the separation of liberal education from professional and vocational education, extend back to antiquity. "To these two modes of occupation, with their distinction of servile and free activities (or 'arts') correspond two types of education: the base or mechanical and the liberal or intellectual. Some persons are trained by suitable practical exercises for capacity in *doing* things, for ability to use the mechanical tools involved in turning out physical commodities and rendering personal service. This training is a mere matter of habituation and technical skill; it operates through repetition and assiduity in application, not through awakening and nurturing thought. Liberal education aims to train intelligence for its proper office: to know. The less this knowledge

54. Dewey, *EN*, p. 284.

has to do with practical affairs, with making or producing, the more adequately it engages intelligence."[55]

It also takes little ingenuity to show that the justification of capitalist property relations is intimately bound up with the presuppositional core of Enlightenment epistemology. For the most part, such epistemology secularizes but does not abandon the Christian conviction that "nature" is thoroughly good because it comes from the creative hand of God, and that evil is a form of corruption introduced into the world by the "artificial" choices of God's specifically human creatures. When interwoven with epistemology's subjectivism, the effort to rescue the purity of the natural finds expression in the liberal conviction that free self-determination by discrete Galilean atoms requires the elimination of all barriers to the unobstructed play of wants in industry and commerce, the unrestricted enjoyment of labor's fruits, and the limitation of government to essential police functions. The persistence of this cluster of understandings is essential to continued legitimacy of the forms of economic exploitation characteristic of an order in which the value produced by wage labor exceeds its compensation rate, and this difference is appropriated by those who privately own or control the means of productive activity.

Matters grow more complex, though, when these inheritances participate in shaping the meaning of an economic order bearing little resemblance to that of either Aristotle or Adam Smith. In early modernity, and in spite of its various political revolutions, the preindustrial demarcation between labor and reason remained largely intact. Work, for the most part, continued to be practiced in accordance with the traditional patterns of skill that, cumulatively, the ancients called *technai*, while theory retained its independence by preserving its purity free of the mutable and the apparent. The division between intellectual and embodied labor, however, took on a decidedly different cast during the late nineteenth century. To an ever greater degree, "capital" became not a reward for the practice of self-denying virtues, but rather a legally protected institution managed and controlled by bureaucrat-

---

55. Dewey, *DE*, p. 253. Cf. p. 318: "Those who are in a position to make their wishes good, will demand a liberal, a cultural occupation, and one which fits for directive power the youth in whom they are directly interested. To split the system, and give to others, less fortunately situated, an education conceived mainly as specific trade preparation, is to treat the schools as an agency for transferring the older division of labor and leisure, culture and service, mind and body, directed and directive class, into a society nominally democratic."

ized corporations whose accountability to workers and citizens became more and more attenuated; and at the same time, theory abandoned its status as distanced critic of the actual and embraced its new
role as capital's most productive tool of technological innovation.

The conjunction of these twin developments has stimulated a mutually reinforcing dynamic between, on the one hand, the drive to
generate ever more sophisticated technical knowledge and, on the
other, the desire to incorporate that knowledge within ever more
powerful instrumentalities of mass production. Industry's *technē* is
now technological, and so it can no longer be handed down in the
form of so many rule-of-thumb procedures and through the medium
of apprenticeship. The disempowering consequences of this dynamic,
illustrated by the deskilling of artisanal practice and the proliferation
of discrete categories of vocational expertise, have been exacerbated as
the organization of the workplace has itself become subject to comprehensive planning. As the productive process has been subdivided
into multiple partial operations whose efficient execution demands the
imposition of ever more minute controls, the temporal and spatial
structures of earlier work experience have rapidly decomposed. "Under the old régime all workers in a craft were approximately equals
in their knowledge and outlook. Personal knowledge and ingenuity
were developed within at least a narrow range, because work was
done with tools under the direct command of the worker. Now the
operator has to adjust himself to his machine, instead of his tool to his
own purposes."[56] Together, the agents inserted at strategic locations
within the confines of such instrumentalities "inevitably sink to the
rôle of appendages to the machines they operate. The remainder of
their lives is spent in enslavement to keeping the machinery going at
an increasingly rapid rate."[57]

Threatened by disintegration of the nuclear family, the Protestant
work ethic, the self-contained community, and other familiar resources of meaning, the sense-denying anticulture of late capitalism
seeks to guarantee reproduction of its existence by entwining its fate
ever more tightly with that of the bureaucratic state. As the achievement of national military and economic security becomes increasingly
dependent on the subsidized invention of new forms of technological

56. Ibid., p. 314.
57. Ibid.; Dewey, *HNC*, p. 272.

prowess, the production of knowledge is systematically defined as the state's special prerogative. Hence out of the patterned but unplanned accumulation of individualized responses to various concrete needs— for instance, to carve out new investment opportunities for capital, to ensure continued docility on the part of those bearing outmoded labor skills, to maintain a citizenry's diffuse loyalties to the existing order, to ensure imposition of the most severe burdens on those least able to resist—there emerges a politicized economy whose dependence on the monopolistic reproduction of certain forms of "knowledge" and the radical dispossession of other forms mocks in practice the theory-practice disjunction it perpetuates in mythology.

So constrained, work in the modern world has been deprived of whatever experiential unity it once possessed. That this expropriation has occurred without engendering more resistance than it has is, as I have already noted, a testament to the continued power of classical categories of thinking. To appreciate that power more fully, recall the invidious distinction Aristotle draws between activity (*praxis*) and production (*technē*). Activity is a species of actualization (*energeia*), and production is a species of change (*kinēsis*). Actualization, Aristotle tells us, is an end in itself inasmuch as activity's aim is realized throughout the time it takes place. Change, by way of contrast, is an intrinsically valueless means inasmuch as its aim is not realized until it is brought to a determinate close in the creation of a tangible good. Employing this distinction, Aristotle concludes that only forms of activity done entirely for their own sake rather than for the sake of something else can count as immanent parts of a life worth living. He thereby strips productive activity of any claim to stand and be judged as an integral part of a flourishing life.

The durability of this classical baggage contributes to our acceptance of work's organization exclusively in terms of technical and efficiency oriented imperatives. Strictly segregated from all other modes of activity in which persons participate, consideration of its larger "ethical" import is forgotten. Work, to use Arendt's categories, becomes "mere" labor, because it cannot raise those engaged in it above the level of the animal and into a significance-bearing world. "To animals to whom acts have no meaning, the change in the environment required to satisfy needs has no significance on its own account; such change is a mere incident of ego-centric satisfactions. This physically external relationship of antecedents and consequents is perpetuated; it continues to hold true of human industry wherever labor and its materials and products are externally enforced necessities for securing a living."[58]

So degraded, the pressure to create articles of use is severed from that urge for consummatory experience that, undenied by more "primitive" peoples, is given expression through work's information by ceremonial, ritual, and other "gratuitous" accompaniments. "Men make a game of their fishing and hunting, and turn to the periodic and disciplinary labor of agriculture only when inferiors, women and slaves, cannot be had to do the work. Useful labor is, whenever possible, subordinated to art that yields immediate enjoyment."[59] When radically stripped of such accompaniments, modernity's denuded labor is at the same time deprived of all possible meaning. For the insertion of scientific knowledge within the technological apparati of modern production transcends the capacity of the embodied agent to locate her activity within an immediately grasped whole. As such, such production deprives the things and affairs of ordinary experience of the "reality" they once appeared to bear. "Production apart from fulfillment becomes purely a matter of quantity; for distinction, quality, is a matter of present meaning. Esthetic elements being excluded, the mechanical [that is, the ontologically deficient] reign."[60]

To relate this genealogical tale is in and of itself to render the current organization of work suspect. To show how institutionalized self-understandings express a hodgepodge of elements derived from several past worlds is effectively to inquire about their present capacity to make sense. But that is insufficient to fulfill the imperatives of the science sketched in the previous section. The world of work is never experienced as an unreflexive recapitulation or simple effect of the transformations discursively elaborated here. The character of the workaday world is always contextualized in the lives of concrete agents who experience these global changes as so many mundane impositions. Accordingly, the implications of this genealogical account must now be teased out in a way that indicates how the experience of work might be reformed by those who, although occupied in discrete vocational spheres, nonetheless share an interest in making this particular mode of conduct an immanent part of the larger struggle to live a life of unfolding vital significance. More specifically, the argument of

58. Dewey, *EN*, pp. 368–69.
59. Ibid., pp. 78–79.
60. Dewey, *HNC*, p. 272.

the preceding chapter intimates at least two avenues of protest against the systematic production of insignificance within this dismembered medium of human practice, each of which derives from the conception of conduct that follows from a refashioned understanding of the means-ends relationship.

The character of the first route can be suggested by asking the following: If "art" describes the form of conduct in which means and ends contribute dialectically to the generation of significance, then how might the practice of work in a late capitalist economy be internally organized in light of this ideal? To answer this question, I will show how an exploration of "play" might contribute to the possibility of artful work. The modern world presupposes an unambiguous distinction between the experiential realms of work and play. The authority of that disjunction, in turn, is vitally bound up with the capacity of the reifying rhetoric of "growth" and "progress" to justify the stultifying character of most conventional workplace experience.

Habermas, it will be recalled, implicitly embraces this distinction when he defines work as "purposive-rational action" that "realizes defined goals under given conditions."[61] In doing so, he transforms a legitimate objection against the quality of much of our daily life into a "theoretical" account of an ahistorical species interest. That is, he "naturalizes" those contingent circumstances that explain why play so often takes the form of spasms of escape from the thralldom of enforced work. "The idea that work, productive activity, signifies action carried on for merely extraneous ends, and the idea that happiness signifies surrender of mind to the thrills and excitations of the body are one and the same idea. The first notion marks the separation of activity from meaning, and the second marks the separation of receptivity from meaning. Both separations are inevitable as far as experience fails to be art:—when the regular, repetitious, and the novel, contingent in nature fail to sustain and inform each other in a productive activity possessed of immanent and directly enjoyed meaning. Our classificatory use of the conception of some arts as merely instrumental so as to dispose of a large part of human activity is no solving definition; it rather conveys an immense and urgent problem."[62] To sanction work's

---

61. Jürgen Habermas, "Technology and Science as 'Ideology,'" in *Toward a Rational Society*, trans. Jeremy Shapiro (Boston: Beacon Press, 1970), p. 92.

62. Dewey, *EN*, pp. 361–63. Cf. p. 361: "For arts that are merely useful are not arts but routines; and arts that are merely final are not arts but passive amusements and distractions, different from other indulgent dissipations only in dependence upon a certain acquired refinement or 'cultivation.'"

anaesthetic character because of its contribution to an essential species interest is, however unwittingly, to frustrate our desire to ask about the relationship between its conditions and those of sense making. "We bring into view simply their efficacy in bringing into existence certain commodities; we do not ask for their effect upon the quality of human life and experience. What they also *make* by way of narrowed, embittered, and crippled life, of congested, hurried, confused and extravagant life, is left in oblivion."[63]

But are play and work as antithetically opposed as Habermas's dualistic logic suggests? In play, Aristotle's heirs often claim, activity is its own end; as a kind of actualization, it does not aim at that end as an ulterior result. This is surely correct. But the import of this claim is mistaken if, on the basis of an artificial separation between process and product, we conclude that play is momentary, having no elements of anticipation and foresight. Like much subdivided work, if an activity is its own end in the sense that the action of the isolated moment is radically self-contained, then it is purely physical; it can have no meaning. Even play, therefore, is guided by a "purpose" that gives significance to the events it informs; and since artful conduct is that form of activity in which means, qua media, are progressively drawn up within a consummatory end, then play is a sort of means-ends activity. Correlatively, if conducted artfully, work can to a greater or lesser degree assume the character of play.

This is not to deny the difference between work and play, but rather to reconstrue it. The distinction between play and work is largely one of duration, of time span between the deployment of means and the achievement of ends. In the former, where the end of activity is a continuation of present activity, it is not necessary to look far ahead in time and space, and so it is possible to alter any given course of action easily and frequently. In the latter, where some definite external outcome is wanted, more remote results of a specific character must be anticipated and employed to navigate the efforts necessary to their accomplishment. Work does indeed bear within it an interest in meaning's adequate embodiment in a determinate object. But that does not warrant the positing of a dualistic distinction that effectively denies its receptivity to play. For work, through its orientation to enduring

---

63. Dewey, *EN*, p. 362: "We identify utility with the external relationship that some events and acts bear to other things that are their products, and thus leave out the only thing that is essential to the ideal of utility, inherent place and bearing in experience."

consummations, can lend play its structure and plot; and play can repay its debt by investing work with responsiveness to what is given to experience in the present.

Work sustains its continuity with play to the degree that the means necessary to the achievement of a complex issue are recognized as vital organs of a qualitatively complete end. Or to put this in more classical terms, work assumes the character of *poēisis* insofar as an emergent whole is present in each of the intermediate parts of a production unfolding in time, and each of those parts is at one and the same time deemed instrumentally and finally valuable. "To a person building a house, the end-in-view is not just a remote and final goal to be hit upon after a sufficiently great number of coerced motions have been duly performed. The end-in-view is a plan which is *contemporaneously* operative in selecting and arranging materials. The latter, brick, stone, wood and mortar, are means only as the end-in-view is actually incarnate in them, in forming them. Literally, they *are* the end in its present stage of realization. The end-in-view is present at each stage of the process; it is present as the *meaning* of the materials used and acts done; without its informing presence, the latter are in no sense 'means;' they are merely extrinsic causal conditions."[64]

By contrast, work takes shape as constrained labor when, ruled by utilitarian logic, the achievement of goals *within* activity is supplanted by the pursuit of goals *by means of* activity, that is, when the conduct of work is merely a means to the acquisition of some reward or the avoidance of some penalty. It becomes anaesthetizing violence when, ruled by the logic of capitalism, a maldistribution of power enables some to foist upon others prefabricated tasks dissociated from the needs of sense-making conduct. "Given ready-made, they must be imposed by some authority external to intelligence, leaving to the latter nothing but a mechanical choice of means."[65]

To question the segregation of work from play is not to argue that the coherence of work requires abolition of the division of labor and a return to some preindustrial idyll. It is, however, to suggest that an appreciation of the possibilities of artful conduct, understood as a means *of* consummatory experience, might furnish fruitful direction to critical questioning aimed at refashioning work's situation within a democratic culture. "The labor and employment problem cannot be

64. Ibid., pp. 373–74.
65. Dewey, *DE*, p. 204.

solved by mere changes in wage, hours of work and sanitary conditions. No permanent solution is possible save in a radical social alteration, which effects the degree and kind of participation the worker has in the production and social disposition of the wares he produces. Only such a change will seriously modify the content of experience into which creation of objects made for use enters. And this modification of the nature of experience is the finally determining element in the esthetic quality of the experience of things produced."[66]

More precisely, to criticize the current constitution of work in light of its meaning-bearing capacities is to pose questions like the following: Is that work characterized by sufficient innovation to stimulate challenges to accustomed meanings and hence contribute to an enlarged sense of competence? Does it furnish opportunities for sufficient interchange of tasks and so overcome what is otherwise labor's entrapment within the immediacy of a present whose integral connections in space and time are neither felt nor known? Does organization of the workplace provide for sufficient empowerment such that those whose habits are formed within it appreciate the possibility of engaging in its "playful" reconfiguration? Are the contributions of fellow workers simply aggregated in the production of a given commodity, as is the case on a standard assembly line? Or are they integrated in a way such that the conduct of each is what it is only in virtue of its relationship to the conduct of those others with whom an understanding of this more comprehensive project is shared? Do those engaged in production have sufficient appreciation of the eventual disposition of their goods to determine their fitness to enter, as constituting media, into more comprehensive forms of experience?

This last question suggests a second and more global critique of current economic arrangements which, because it anticipates the argument of the following chapter, I shall only mention here. Whereas the first line of criticism focuses inward on the conduct of work, the second looks outward to its situation within the constitution of a democratic culture. The present's power to constrict the future's immanent possibilities rests at least in part on our institutionalized recapitulation of epistemology's conviction that reality is an aggregation of atomic, fixed, and independent entities whose connections to one another are relations of external causal conjunction rather than mutual implication within an organic whole. Following this cue, the anatomy of the cultural body is effectively dissected into so many discontinuous

66. Ibid., p. 343.

provinces, each of which is managed by a separate agency and regulated in accordance with its own peculiar brand of expert knowledge. So reified, these partitionings discourage experimentation with more inclusive wholes that, by reconfiguring the boundaries currently demarcating the insulated realms of experience, might give rise to a fuller sense of the web of association tying each to the others.

To question these familiar segregations, we might begin by seeking to recapture a sense of the inclusive web of activities Locke calls "civil society" but which, in order to break its narrowly economistic connotations, is better designated by the term "culture." "It is a prime philosophical consideration that 'culture' designates, in their reciprocal interconnections, that immense diversity of human affairs, interests, concerns, values which compartmentalists pigeonhole under 'religion,' 'morals,' 'aesthetics,' 'politics,' 'economics' etc."[67] To consider "the economy" as an entity unto itself, as does most classical liberal theory, is to hide the relations it sustains with other spheres of associated activity and so, strictly speaking, to fail to grasp what it is. To recontextualize this sphere by returning it to the qualitative medium from which it emerges is, by way of contrast, to deny it the autonomy that now sustains its abstraction from a democratic culture and so to understand it truly. "The subject-matter of full-fledged 'scientific' economics has been identified with aspects of life economists designate as *material*. The consequence of this identification or definition is to separate and isolate the economic from the moral and political. It is a fact that modern means of production and distribution of commodities are the consequences of technologies made possible by physical (or material) science. But it is also a fact that the sphere of economic activity— the economic enterprise in all its vast and intricate complications—is inextricably enmeshed in social life, that it serves human needs, personal and institutional, and is to be judged by how well or ill it serves them."[68]

67. Dewey, "Experience and Nature: A Re-introduction," in *LW*, vol. 1, p. 363.
68. Ibid., vol. 1, p. 358. Cf. Dewey, *QC*, p. 283: "When economists were told that their subject-matter was merely material, they naturally thought they could be 'scientific' only by excluding all reference to distinctively human values. Material wants, efforts to satisfy them, even the scientifically regulated technologies highly developed in industrial activity, are then taken to form a complete and closed field. If any reference to social ends and values is introduced it is by way of an external addition, mainly hortatory. That economic life largely determines the conditions under which mankind has access to concrete values may be recognized or it may not be. In either case, the notion that it is the means to be utilized in order to secure significant values as the common and shared possession of mankind is alien and inoperative."

To think of productive arrangements as a subordinate but integral part of this larger cultural whole is to throw into doubt liberal society's identification of material well-being as its chief source of self-definition and collective power. More generally, it is to ask whether the current ordering of economic life does or does not contribute to the creation of a democratic culture that "is so free in itself that it conceives and begets political freedom as its accompaniment and consequence."[69] It is at just this point, when inquiry turns to the relationship between character and culture, that this second avenue of criticism merges with the first. To interrogate the conduct of work is to demand that the economy justify its present form. "Just what response does *this* social arrangement, political or economic, evoke, and what effect does it have upon the disposition of those who engage in it? Does it release capacity? If so, how widely? Among a few, with a corresponding depression in others, or in an extensive and equitable way? Is the capacity which is set free also directed in some coherent way, so that it becomes a power, or its manifestation spasmodic and capricious? Are senses rendered more delicately sensitive and appreciative, or are they blunted and dulled by this and that form of social organization? Are minds trained so that the hands are more deft and cunning? Is curiosity awakened or blunted? What is its quality?"[70]

VI

"If the ruling and the oppressed elements in a population, if those who wish to maintain the status quo and those concerned to make changes, had, when they became articulate, the same philosophy, one might well be skeptical of its intellectual integrity."[71] The knowledge-power configuration represented by the unholy alliance of policy science and the late liberal state is stabilized by a culture that unreflectively endorses the epistemological construction of knowledge as a property of individual minds produced via isolated contacts with unambiguous objects. When knowledge is taken to be a private possession consisting of ideas mastered by so many discrete selves, it is difficult to evade the conclusion that participation in regulating distinctively political

69. Dewey, *FC*, p. 6.
70. Dewey, *RP*, p. 197.
71. Dewey, "Philosophy and Civilization," in *PC*, p. 9.

affairs is best limited to those certified as competent in the determinate bodies of technical expertise deemed necessary to efficient ordering of modernity's complex interdependence. That conclusion, by effectively disqualifying all, invites common acquiescence in a condition of powerlessness. When agents share nothing save a sense of private incapacity, their discontent remains inarticulate, uncrystallized, incoherent.

It is a mistake to suppose that political science, however construed, can serve as the vehicle through which democratic politics is rescued from what now threatens it. Indeed, in an important sense, political science's salvation is conditional on a revival of politics itself. Only through reformation of the latter can peculiarly collective affairs reconstitute a public world and so furnish political science with its true subject matter. Still, properly chastened, that science is not without work to do in the present. While the content of its explorations cannot be specified in advance, its larger purpose is to challenge the antidemocratic inferences born of the marriage of epistemology and expertise. To do so, it must identify loci of vulnerability within existing knowledge-power configurations and so assist presently unfocused pluralities of potential power in their struggles to recollect those features of everyday life—for instance, the objectified embodiments of the dualisms between labor and leisure, practical and intellectual activity, humanity and nature, individual and society—which fracture the possibilities for consummatory experience. Because knowledge is a collective achievement whose vitality turns upon its continued animation by those who undergo it, that science must find suspect any institutionalized formation that thwarts the impulse to take part in the conduct of knowing. Its research must be informed by a call to unsettle those settled domains of administered practice which presently account for the disappearance of experience's more prosaic pragmata. Only by repoliticizing those realms of managerial competence whose authority turns upon the apparent autonomy of their epistemic endeavors can the integrity of everyday affairs be collectively repossessed.

Fulfillment of this charge entails deconstruction of those positivist social sciences that have proven complicitous in subsuming ordinary competencies beneath the rule of expertise's teleocratic injunctions. When political science gives up its pretense of privileged access to an otherwise hidden domain of objects, it effectively acknowledges that its distinctive mode of conduct issues from, belongs to, and acts within

the form of experience it explores. Cutting sharply against its constitution as a self-enclosed profession, that science thereby recovers the
salutary ambiguity preserved by Aristotle in his use of the term *politikē*
to designate the interpenetration of acting and knowing in distinctively political conduct.[72] That conduct, in turn, is the medium through
which political science realizes its status as a refined but not discrete
form of thinking whose conditional purpose, always in media res, is to
contribute to the explicative endeavors through which the multiple
significances of experienced things are drawn into the world of appearances.

So construed, political science might take part in redeeming the
promise whose unfolding was aborted when intelligence and its fruits
were first dispossessed and then reconstituted as reason. That redemption entails grasping the present as an opportunity made possible only because presuppositions central to the Western rationalist
tradition are today so questionable. Only when the classical equation
of knowledge with contemplation of antecedent being, and the epistemological construction of the subject-object relationship, begin to lose
their grip on our collective imagination does it become possible to see
that knowing is a form of conduct whose exercise transforms what is
known. Only when nature qua *physis* is grasped as a medium of
immanent potentialities can "knowing" be acknowledged as mutually
transformative responsiveness to experience's dialectic of doing and
suffering. Only when conduct qua *poēsis* assumes the character of that
tendance through which these possibilities issue forth within the
world can power assume the form of collective cultivation of those
parts of a larger cultural whole that show their capacity to elicit significance from the textured things of "had" experience.

To take "truth" not as intellectualized representation of an external
object, but as collective affirmation of experience's fuller realization of
its incipient meaningfulness is to refuse to equate the world that
knowing knows with a reality that is fully present in the present. It is
to perceive that potentiality, what may yet be called into being, is
a category of existence whose actuality is a condition of knowing's
viability. Expansion of experience's significance-bearing capacity can
occur only if particular centers of agency have powers or capacities

72. I draw this point from Mary Nichols, *Socrates and the Political Community* (Albany:
State University of New York Press, 1987). Nichols writes: "The word [*politikē*] is an
adjectival form that Aristotle uses as a noun. Its gender allows it to agree either with
science or knowledge (*epistēmē*) or action (*praxis*)" (p. 222n).

that are latent in the sense that they are not fully actualized in the present moment. Consequently, any political science that hopes to contribute something other than nonsense to the culture in which it is embedded must spurn those forms of antipolitical order that effectively deny potentialities' necessary concomitants—for example, the acknowledgment of time, the provisionality of all that is now taken to be true, and the unanticipated transformations that are inseparable from the existence of individuals. "Genuine time, if it exists as anything else except the measure of motions in space, is all one with the existence of individuals as individuals, with the creative, with the occurrence of unpredictable novelties. Dictatorships and totalitarian states are ways of denying the reality of time and the creativeness of the individual. Freedom of thought and of expression are not mere rights to be claimed. They have their roots deep in the existence of individuals as developing careers in time. Their denial and abrogation is an abdication of individuality and a virtual rejection of time as opportunity."[73]

Among many other connotations, the term "democracy" implies "the ideal of a continuous reconstruction or reorganizing of experience, of such a nature as to increase its recognized meaning or social content, and as to increase the capacity of individuals to act as directive guardians of this reorganization."[74] Hence the connection between this science and the cause of democratic experience is not, contra Lasswell and Wildavsky, a contingent matter turning upon the subjective "values" of its practitioners. Given that every form of knowing entails a particular way of ordering the associated capacities of those who live by it, this science affirms an essential connection between the possibility of knowledge, the exercise of power, and the forms of democratic experience. Its contribution to disclosure of experience's possibilities among those partaking of the most comprehensive category of collective life—citizenship—is the measure of its enabling truth. Therefore, its devotion to getting at the truth of things is inseparable from its commitment to *demos-kratia*, that is, power that is broadly distributed among and exercised by ordinary persons. Political science's otherwise unverified speculations become knowledge in its most complete sense only when, absorbed throughout collective life, they become the means (read: media) of significant public experi-

---

73. Dewey, "Time and Individuality," in *ENF*, pp. 241–42.
74. Dewey, *DE*, p. 322.

ence. "Genuine theoretic knowledge penetrates reality more deeply, not because it is opposed to practice, but because a practice that is genuinely free, social, and intelligent touches things at a deeper level than a practice that is capricious, egoistically centered, sectarian, and bound down to routine."[75] Because egalitarian appropriation of the resources of collective conduct is a necessary condition of experience that remains receptive to the potentialities tendered by nature, we may legitimately conclude that democratic politics (rather than science) is the means by which truth is most adequately revealed.

75. Dewey, "Perception and Organic Action," in *PC*, pp. 205–6.

7 /
The Constitution of Democratic Political Experience

I

Each of the preceding chapters has tacitly asked the same question: What qualities might experience, whether political or otherwise, exhibit were we to abandon our inveterate conviction that its capacity to bear and deliver meaning derives from its subordination to the imperatives of teleocratic reason? To disclose the origins, history, and characteristic manifestations of this conviction, I have examined reason's initial emergence in the ancient city-state; the reformation of that reason within certain typical forms of Enlightenment epistemology; and the appearance of this rationalizing project, in various guises, in the work of Durkheim, Habermas, and the exponents of American policy science. Each of these discussions, gesturing beyond itself, has suggested the sense-denying import of any attempt to establish reason's self-sufficient autonomy by repudiating the noncognitive ground out of which thinking arises; and that in turn has intimated several ways of relocating thinking within the conduct through which experience's capacity to bear qualitative significances is deepened and enhanced.

In this chapter, my aim is not to deduce the implications of the preceding arguments and thereby construct a comprehensive *theory* of politics. To harbor such an ambition is to miss the point of what it means to call ordinary experience to a recollection of its potentiality for meaning. My aim instead is to consider once more the question with which this work commenced: If the most powerful structures of modernity mandate modes of behavior consistent with established notions of reason, and if that requirement systematically undermines experience's meaningfulness, then how might we begin to fashion that dynamic's reversal? A "practical" response is offered in the postscript that follows this chapter. Here my purpose is simply to work toward a formulation of this issue which is more adequate than that offered in Chapter 1.

To do so, I begin by indicating how the history Weber describes using the term "rationalization" complements the history of what I have called "teleocratic reason." More specifically, making use of the tale of reason's history developed in Chapters 2 and 3, I show why Max Weber was essentially correct to contend that Western rationalism most adequately reveals its specifically political import within the complex of practices that constitute the bureaucratic state. From there I contend that we can escape the manufactured state of bureaucratic nihilism only by acknowledging that the ontological conditions of meaningful experience are correlative with those necessary to sustain democratic politics. That, finally, leads to the conclusion that the possibility of meaning's recovery from rationalism's antipolitics turns on our capacity to fashion a culture whose "reason of state" is fully articulated by and within the vital relations that make up its constitutional form.

II

The argument of the preceding chapters entails no particular quarrel with Max Weber's prophecy that Western rationalism discloses its full and final meaning within a cell whose bars are made of finely tempered steel. The bitter irony of Weber's reading of modernity resides in its intimation that the rationalizing mind, having enfeebled the metaphysical and theological rivals that once limited its pretensions to universality, has now turned on and conquered its disillusioned creator. The iron cage is indeed an apt symbol for an age whose infatuation with science's fruits cannot quite dispel its gnawing fear that

modernity's will to know, intruding on and shaping to its own imperatives every domain of practice, has produced forms of organizational
and technological power which can be neither mastered nor dismissed.

Modernity, on this account, signifies not the antithesis of classical
metaphysics, but rather the repressive fulfillment of its identification
of true Being with the mind qua ruler, as well as its correlative representation of the most perfect world with what has been comprehensively re-created in accordance with reason's monomaniacal injunctions. The difference between the ancient and modern worlds consists
in the latter's discovery that forms of practice which in the former were
considered impervious to theoretical guidance are in fact susceptible
to technical control in accordance with the objectifications of scientific
discourse. The traditional understanding of culture as a fragile complex of works produced through reference to models furnished by an
independent nature is thus displaced by the idea of civilization as a
systematic construct whose wholesale fabrication renders irrelevant
the distinction between artifice and its pregiven material. As the dualism of theory and practice collapses within the realized ideal of a
totalistically ordered system, the intellect is confounded by the obdurate embodiments of its own superfluous achievement. The senseless
order so produced can no longer hear, let alone appreciate, the irony in
Hegel's insistence that "reason governs and has governed the world."[1]
Denied the capacity for significant reconstruction that was preserved
in a less mindful age, the intellect is left with nothing more demanding
than descriptive social science.

"The marks and signs of this 'impersonalization' of the human soul
are quantification of life, with its attendant disregard of quality; its
mechanization and the almost universal habit of esteeming technique
as an end, not as a means, so that organic and intellectual life is also
'rationalized'; and, finally, standardization. Differences and distinctions are ignored and overridden; agreement, similarity, is the ideal.
There is not only absence of social discrimination but of intellectual;
critical thinking is conspicuous by its absence. Our pronounced trait is
mass suggestability. These are then the marks of the Americanization
that is conquering the world."[2]

1. G.W.F. Hegel, *Reason in History*, trans. Robert Hartman (Indianapolis: Bobbs-
Merrill, 1953), p. 16.
2. Dewey, "Individualism, Old and New," in *LW*, vol. 5, p. 52.

To this degree, I share Weber's vision. The burden of this chapter, however, is to show the contingent character of the impasse into which his thinking is necessarily led. In the last analysis, Weber argues, the peculiarly modern self is faced with a dichotomous choice: Either it must spurn that which is by espousing some version of the credo that contends, "My kingdom is not of this world"; or it must affirm the essential structure of the world as it presently stands, and then struggle dutifully to meet its requirements. This conclusion, whose apparently opposed halves effectively reduce to resignation in the face of what Weber calls the present's "polar night of icy darkness and hardness,"[3] can be read as an expression of his wedding of a teleocratic model of rational action to neo-Kantian epistemology. The fruit of that conjunction is illustrated by the general typology of social action he offers in Economy and Society. That schema suggests that meaningful action consists of so many purposive acts, each of which is subjectively aimed at the production of an antecedently determined end. More exactly, to prove meaningful, action must be self-consciously oriented either to maximization of the capacity for efficient control (zweckrationalität) or to the realization of determinate absolute ends (wertrationalität).[4]

Weber's account of Western history (and so of the choice we are now condemned to make) is implicit in this typology. That history is best understood as a dynamic through which zweckrationalität, most completely exemplifed by the practice of modern science, has progressively emptied wertrationalität of all public content. Holding that "the cosmos of natural causality and the postulated cosmos of ethical, compensatory causality stand in irreconcilable opposition,"[5] Weber asserts that rationalization of the world spells its disenchantment. Disenchantment, in turn, means that human life is ever more completely denied the resources necessary to engender a feel for its own significance:

3. Max Weber, From Max Weber, ed. Hans Gerth and C. W. Mills (New York: Oxford University Press, 1958), p. 128.
4. See Max Weber, Economy and Society, vol. 1, ed. Guenther Roth and Claus Wittich (Berkeley: University of California Press, 1978), pp. 24–26. Weber initially suggests two additional types of social action, those labeled "affectual" and "traditional." He then, however, more or less denies their status as categories of meaningful action on the grounds that the former is "often a matter of almost automatic reaction to habitual stimuli," and the latter "consist[s] in an uncontrolled reaction to some exceptional stimulus" (p. 25).
5. Weber, in From Max Weber, p. 355.

Abraham, or some peasant of the past, died "old and satiated with life" because he stood in the organic cycle of life; because his life, in terms of its meaning and on the eve of his days, had given to him what life had to offer; because for him there remained no puzzles he might wish to solve; and therefore he could have had "enough" of life. Whereas civilized man, placed in the midst of the continuous enrichment of culture by ideas, knowledge, and problems, may become "tired of life" but not "satiated with life." He catches only the most minute part of what the life of the spirit brings forth ever anew, and what he seizes is always something provisional and not definitive, and therefore death for him is a meaningless occurrence. And because death is meaningless, civilized life as such is meaningless; by its very "progressiveness" it gives death the imprint of meaninglessness.[6]

Draining ancient cosmology and medieval theology of the teleological ends once located within the world's very structure, modern science destroys the resources that might otherwise permit it to believe that reason's cause is still bound up with either the "grace of seers and prophets dispensing sacred values and revelations" or "the contemplation of sages and philosophers about the meaning of the universe."[7] As the vehicle through which Hume's logical distinction between fact and value becomes the practical alienation of humanity (qua creator of all meaning) from nature (qua a constellation of meaningless objects mechanically joined to one another), reason learns all too well that it can no longer certify that, quoting Weber, the world it probes "has any 'meaning,' or that it makes sense to live in such a world."[8]

Although unable to engender anything to replace that which it devours, modern science nonetheless "come[s] forward with the claim of representing the only possible form of a reasoned view of the world."[9] Consequently, Weber is persuaded that the sphere of judgment must in time be reduced to a potentially limitless number of nonrational preferences: "The fate of an epoch which has eaten of the tree of knowledge is that it must know that we cannot learn the *meaning* of the world from the results of its analysis, be it ever so perfect; it must rather be in a position to create this meaning itself. It must recognize that general views of life and the universe can never be the products of increasing empirical knowledge, and that the highest

6. Ibid., p. 140.
7. Ibid., p. 152.
8. Ibid., p. 144.
9. Ibid., p. 355.

ideals, which move us most forcefully, are always formed only in the struggle with other ideals which are just as sacred to others as ours are to us."[10] As human beings find themselves unable to ground or constrain the power acquired through the various objective manifestations of their own instrumental rationality, the generation of significance becomes the privatized prerogative of autonomous centers of manipulative agency who can become assured of the truth of their most cherished convictions only by imposing them on otherwise senseless things. Yet because most of those centers cannot summon the willpower necessary to such imposition, an ever larger number seek escape from this "senseless hustle in the service of worthless, moreover self-contradictory, and mutually antagonistic ends" through universal subordination to the arbitrary resolution of a charismatic ruler.[11]

From among the many manifestations of rationalization, Weber elects to focus on the modern state. Through his account of this institutional form's genesis, Weber sheds considerable light on the concrete strategies through which teleocratic rationality has made its presence palpably present in the world of everyday experience. The complex struggle to coordinate power's resources within the centralized state could succeed as it has only because of the mutually reinforcing effects produced by what Weber labels "expropriation." To clarify the meaning of this complex term, Weber takes issue with Marx's contention that separation of workers from the instrumentalities of industrial production is sufficient to account for modernity's most characteristic forms of power. In fact, he argues, appropriation of workers' tools and skills is but a single instance of a more pervasive dynamic through which agents in all spheres of conduct have been gradually dispossessed of the means of significant action.

Such divestment, on Weber's account, is an inescapable concomitant of any order committed to integration of the powers engendered by the division of labor among so many specialized capacities. To ensure that such powers coherently served the cause of national power, the early modern state aggressively asserted its right to monopolize the management of all matters of public import:

> The "separation" of the worker from the material means of production, destruction, administration, academic research, and finance in general

10. Max Weber, " 'Objectivity' in Social Science," in *The Methodology of the Social Sciences*, ed. Edward Shils and Henry Finch (New York: Free Press, 1949), p. 57.
11. Weber, in *From Max Weber*, p. 357.

is the common basis of the modern state, in its political, cultural and military sphere. . . . The whole process is a complete parallel to the development of the capitalist enterprise through gradual expropriation of the independent producers. In the end, the modern state controls the total means of political organization, which actually come together under a single head. No single official personally owns the money he pays out, or the buildings, stores, tools, and war machines he controls. In the contemporary "state"—and this is essential for the concept of state—the "separation" of the administrative staff, of the administrative officials, and of the workers from the material means of administrative organization is completed.[12]

The triumph of such expropriation presupposed the exercise of domination through the medium of permanent hierarchical organizations staffed by professionally trained and salaried civil servants acting in accordance with prescribed and impersonal rules. Especially via the establishment of uniform revenue-collection systems and the provisioning of public armies, the early modern state gave ever sharper bureaucratic teeth to its claim to control the resources of all effective action. That claim secured its initial theoretical formulation in the account of sovereignty suggested by Marsilius' *Defender of the Peace*; and it received its most stark expression, three centuries later, in Hobbes's *Leviathan*. So construed, the early modern state came to define its being in terms of its exclusive authority to make laws regulating the conduct of all political affairs within a given jurisdiction as well as to punish those who dared contest such regulation.

On the whole, early liberal discourse endorsed this representation of the state as an independent institutional complex affirming its standing as the sole object of political allegiance. Accordingly, it showed little nostalgia for the parish, the village, the councils, and the estates—that is, all those "irrational" and "outmoded" features of the social landscape, which had once served as institutional buffers for the

---

12. Max Weber, *Economy and Society*, vol. 2, p. 1394; *From Max Weber*, p. 82. Cf. *Economy and Society*, vol. 2, p. 1394: "Sociologically speaking, the modern state is an 'enterprise' just like a factory: This exactly is its historical peculiarity. Here as there the authority relations have the same roots. The relative independence of the artisan, the producer under the putting-out system, the free seigneurial peasant, the travelling associate in a *commenda* relationship, the knight and vassal rested on their ownership of the tools, supplies, finances and weapons with which they fulfilled their economic, political and military functions and maintained themselves. In contrast, the hierarchical dependence of the wage worker, the administrative and technical employee, the assistant in the academic institute *as well as* that of the civil servant and the soldier is due to the fact that in their case the means indispensable for the enterprise and for making a living are in the hands of the entrepreneur or the political ruler."

defense of seigneurial and ecclesiastical rights, customs, and immu-
nities. In their stead, and reflecting the cultural fragmentation generated by the slow detachment of capitalist market operations from
feudalism's undifferentiated manorial economies, liberalism offered
its principles of abstract individualism. Holding that the primary realities of the political world are autonomous egos bent first and foremost
upon the pursuit of private happiness, and convinced that the relations among such egos leave their characters essentially unchanged,
that discourse defined each individual in terms of his or her possession of the noncontextualized rights and liberties that all, by nature,
share. So identified, each liberal self came to confront the growing
power of the bureaucratic state without allies and without any determinate sense of membership other than that furnished by allegiance to
a nation whose unity was at first symbolized and later constituted by
that same state.

As Michel Foucault has reminded us, however, the history of the
bureaucratic state is more complex than this reading suggests. As
premodern domains of collective action were slowly dispossessed of
the material and intellectual resources necessary to insure the integrity
of their own practice, rationalizing techniques bent on fostering forms
of behavior consistent with the requirements of bureaucratized order
made increasingly effective inroads into these same spheres. More
specifically, since at least the middle of the nineteenth century, if not
before, the liberal state has found it necessary to stabilize the order
over which it rules by seeking more comprehensive coordination between the accumulation of scientific knowledge, the translation of
such knowledge into technological instrumentalities, the stimulation
of economic production, and the manufacture of supportive secularized myths. (Think, for example, of contemporary efforts to link the
cause of "reindustrialization" to renewal of the Protestant ethic, even
though the existence of Luther's God can no longer be guaranteed.)

Not surprisingly, as more and more domains of collective experience
have been subordinated to the calculations of instrumental rationality,
liberalism's representation of society as an independent and self-regu-
lating arena of private relationships has proven less and less persuasive. Familiar categories that unambiguously distinguish the political
from the economic now merely occlude the character of a highly
politicized economy. Moreover, inasmuch as conventional liberal
thinking continues to define the state as the sovereign locus of politically significant power, it effectively turns attention away from the

disciplinary techniques that have come to penetrate ever deeper into the ostensibly nonpolitical fabric of everyday life. As Foucault points out:

> Historically, the process by which the bourgeoisie became in the course of the eighteenth century the politically dominant class was masked by the establishment of an explicit, coded and formally egalitarian juridical framework, made possible by the organization of a parliamentary, representative regime. But the development and generalization of disciplinary mechanisms constituted the other, dark side of these processes. The general juridical form that guaranteed a system of rights that were egalitarian in principle was supported by these tiny, everyday, physical mechanisms, by all those systems of micro-power that are essentially non-egalitarian and asymmetrical that we call the disciplines. And although, in a formal way, the representative regime makes it possible, directly or indirectly, with or without relays, for the will of all to form the fundamental authority of sovereignty, the disciplines provide, at the base, a guarantee of the submission of forces and bodies.[13]

In other words, while liberalism's juridical order is premised on the myth of popular control over the state, the constitution of collective order is in fact determined by the body politic's absorption of non-juridical strategies of normalization; and the legitimacy of those strategies in turn is premised on collective acknowledgment of the authority of so many expert discourses to manage discrete realms of social life.

The dynamic of expropriation thus finds its complement in the march of professionalization, the processes through which specialists, appropriately trained and certified, come to displace and replace pre-modern bearers of authority within ever more spheres of regularized conduct. It follows, accordingly, that Weber's generalized application of Marx's thesis regarding divestment of the worker from control over the means of production can be broadened still farther. Such expropriation, externalized within bureaucratic organizational forms and internalized within normalized selves, receives its most ambitious expression when cast as a project of epistemic objectification. Through the manufacture of science's objects, a multiplicity of practices of knowing are abstracted from their original bearers, systematized within various forms of expertise, and finally, as vehicles of control and supervision, turned against the subjects they now constitute. In sum, liberalism's

13. Michel Foucault, *Discipline and Punish*, trans. Alan Sheridan (New York: Vintage Books, 1979), pp. 221–22.

citizens are effectively deprived of their political capacities through their reification as so many targets of rationalization's interwoven macro and microscopic projects.[14]

Contra Weber, therefore, the power-depriving thrust produced by expropriation in all of its many forms cannot be understood as a simple transfer of action's instrumentalities from a plurality of localized sites to a monolithic juridical state claiming a monopoly over *"the legitimate use of physical force within a given territory."*[15] To endorse this famous Weberian characterization is to think of the power generated by this dynamic as a homogeneous possession or commodity whose scope may be precisely demarcated and whose location may be clearly specified. Again, I quote Foucault:

> It would be wrong to believe that the disciplinary functions were confiscated and absorbed once and for all by a state apparatus. "Discipline" may be identified neither with an institution nor with an apparatus; it is a type of power, a modality for its exercise, comprising a whole set of instruments, techniques, procedures, levels of applications, targets; it is a "physics" or an "anatomy" of power, a technology. And it may be taken over either by "specialized" institutions (the penitentiaries or "houses of correction" of the nineteenth century), or by institutions that use it as an essential instrument for a particular end (schools, hospitals), or by pre-existing authorities that find in it a means of reinforcing or reorganizing their internal mechanisms of power, . . . or by apparatuses that have made discipline their principle of internal functioning (the disciplinarization of the administrative apparatus from the Napoleonic period), or finally by state apparatuses whose major, if not exclusive, function is to assure that discipline reigns over society as a whole (the police).[16]

14. On this point, see Michel Foucault, "Two Lectures," in *Power/Knowledge*, ed. Colin Gordon (New York: Pantheon, 1980), p. 105: "Why has the theory of sovereignty persisted in this fashion as an ideology and an organising principle of these major legal codes? For two reasons, I believe. On the one hand, it has been, in the eighteenth and again in the nineteenth century, a permanent instrument of criticism of the monarchy and of all the obstacles that can thwart the development of disciplinary society. But at the same time, the theory of sovereignty, and the organisation of a legal code centred upon it, have allowed a system of right to be superimposed upon the mechanisms of discipline in such a way as to conceal its actual procedures, the element of domination inherent in its techniques, and to guarantee to everyone, by virtue of the sovereignty of the State, the exercise of his proper sovereign rights. The juridical systems—and this applies both to their codification and to their theorisation—have enabled sovereignty to be democratised through the constitution of a public right articulated upon collective sovereignty, while at the same time this democratisation of sovereignty was fundamentally determined by and grounded in mechanisms of disciplinary coercion."

15. Weber, in *From Max Weber*, p. 78.

16. Foucault, *Discipline and Punish*, pp. 215–16. Cf. p. 213: "But, although the police as an institution were certainly organized in the form of a state apparatus, and although

Taken in by liberalism's equation of power with sovereignty, Weber's legalistic formulation overlooks the many ways in which expropriated means of action have returned to and spread through a multiplicity of coalescing but distinguishable realms of formally nonpolitical practice. He thereby fails to appreciate adequately those nongovernmental domains of institutionalized activity which furnish the cohesion that liberalism falsely ascribes to its formal constitution of public right.

If the production, distribution, and legitimation of power in late liberal orders can be adequately grasped only by assimilating Foucault and Weber in the manner sketched above, then utmost caution is advised in making reference to "the state." "The concept of the state, like most concepts which are introduced by 'The,' is both too rigid and too tied up with controversies to be of ready use. It is a concept which can be approached by a flank movement more easily than by a frontal attack. The moment we utter the words 'The State' a score of intellectual ghosts rise to obscure our vision."[17] In an important sense, liberalism's "state" is a mythical abstraction. It possesses neither the unity nor the individuality intimated by this term. Additionally, inasmuch as this term connotes a complex of public institutions demonstrably distinct from its private counterparts, it hides from view the forces that have eroded liberalism's public-private distinction by diffusing power among a multiplicity of overlapping sites.[18] Rationalization—that is, all the patterned effects engendered by narrowly instrumentalized ways of giving shape to collective affairs—appears in more or less concentrated form at different sites within the body politic. At one of its more dense loci, we find the complex configuration conventionally

this was certainly linked directly to the centre of political sovereignty, the type of power that it exercises, the mechanisms it operates and the elements to which it applies them are specific. It is an apparatus that must be coextensive with the entire social body and not only by the extreme limits it embraces, but by the minuteness of the details it is concerned with."

17. Dewey, *PP*, p. 8. Cf. Foucault, "Two Lectures," p. 99: "The important thing is not to attempt some kind of deduction of power starting from its centre and aimed at the discovery of the extent to which it permeates into the base, of the degree to which it reproduces itself down to and including the most molecular elements of society. One must rather conduct an *ascending* analysis of power, starting, that is, from its infinitesimal mechanisms, which each have their own history, their own trajectory, their own techniques and tactics, and then see how these mechanisms of power have been—and continue to be—invested, colonised, utilised, involuted, transformed, displaced, extended, etc., by ever more general mechanisms and by forms of global domination."

18. Perhaps the best account of this process is still that offered by Grant McConnell in his *Private Power and American Democracy* (New York: Vintage, 1966). Theodore Lowi, *The End of Liberalism* (New York: Norton, 1969), offers a helpful but not nearly so insightful extension of McConnell's argument.

referred to as the "bureaucratic state." Where those effects are not yet
so compacted, we find forms of practice whose conformity to the ideal
implicit in rationalization is less total because of "impurities" produced
by noninstrumentalist ways of relating persons to the things and
affairs that make up their shared world. Therefore, although I use the
term "state" to refer to the specific institutional configuration that
preoccupies Weber, it is important to recall that that configuration is
simply one expression of the much more comprehensive constellation
of processes suggested by the term "rationalization."

The working out of the complex dialectic between the concentration, proliferation, and dispersion of powers which is characteristic of
rationalization generally, and the bureaucratic way of politics more
particularly, presupposes a particular ontology, an understanding of
what is real and what is not, as well as an understanding of the sorts of
relations into which the things that are real can and cannot enter. That
ontology, read through the lenses furnished by the preceding chapters, is best understood as an expression of the movement through
which the mind of the Enlightenment, born of an unhappy synthesis
of classical philosophy's teleocratic conception of action and epistemology's subjectivist conception of the sovereign self, sheds its derivative status and becomes a hypostatized reality increasingly detached
from its ground in primary experience. As an unusually well-formed
expression of the dynamic through which the surplus powers of associated human beings are expropriated and then wielded in the consolidation of established ways of relating persons and things, the bureaucratic state embodies the Enlightenment's attempt to reconcile ancient
and modern conceptions of reason.

Just why that state cannot succeed in finally legitimating its own
authority can be suggested by redrafting Weber's ideal typical characterization of the bureaucratic state. As with all ideal types, my aim
here is not to offer an account that is descriptive of any currently
existing state, but rather to construct the broad outlines of a model that
highlights the logic of the specifically bureaucratic way of giving form
to the materials found in cultural experience. Although empirically
false, this account is nonetheless "true" in the sense that its deliberately one-sided statement indicates the totalistic but sense-denying
dream that informs rationalization's politics and gives meaning to the
dystopia toward which it necessarily drives.

The legitimacy of the late liberal state, to the extent that bureaucratic
rationality comes to define its character, must prove suspect. That

state inherits the ancient conception of action, as that conception was reshaped in accordance with the demands of medieval theology. When Aquinas relocated Aristotelian ontology within the comprehensive context furnished by Catholic eschatology, he recapitulated the classical view that "to govern is to guide what is governed to its appointed end."[19] To this teleocratic inheritance, however, he made a significant alteration. The classical formulation, in its Aristotelian version, suggested that the ends of politics are immanent within its practice. But Aquinas's faith in the ultimacy of an end standing apart from and above nature mandated that political rule assume a quasi-utilitarian cast: "Now when something is ordered to an end which lies outside itself, as a ship is to harbor, it is the ruler's duty not only to preserve its integrity, but also to see that it reaches its appointed destination. If there were anything with no end beyond itself, then the ruler's sole task would be to preserve it unharmed in all its perfection. But . . . there is no such example to be found in creation, apart from God who is the end of all things."[20] Aquinas concludes: "Government is of a higher order according to the importance of the ends it serves," because the "final aim of social life" is "not merely to live in virtue, but rather through virtuous life to attain to the enjoyment of God."[21] Accordingly, and because its this-worldly good is subordinate to humanity's supranatural end, the conduct of politics assumes the status of a means whose practice is necessary but not equal to the achievement of our ultimate telos.

The liberal state inherits this instrumentalist notion of politics, but cannot have recourse to the cosmology that determined and legitimated the ends toward which it was once directed. As such, it exists in a state of perpetual tension. Predicated upon the neo-Kantian fact-value distinction, the modern administrative state cannot justify either its own practice or the ends toward which it is directed. Mimicking science's contention that conformity to method is the sole guarantor of its knowledge, the liberal state defines itself as a neutral arbiter upholding the rules that regulate competition between so many private interests; that is, it substitutes formal correctness of legal enactment for satisfaction of concrete needs as the measure of its worth. But this, in and of itself, is insufficient to overcome its legitimacy deficit. For to

19. Thomas Aquinas, "On Princely Government," in *Aquinas: Selected Political Writings*, trans. J. G. Dawson (Oxford: Basil Blackwell, 1978), p. 73.
20. Ibid., p. 73.
21. Ibid., p. 75.

define its constitutional instrumentalities as universally available end-
less techniques is to acknowledge that the state's administrative institutions can and will be placed at the disposal of any unrationalized
desire with sufficient strength to grasp and put them to private advantage.

How, therefore, is the bureaucratized liberal state to defend its
status as a peculiarly public institution worthy of the power it wields?
In the absence of more traditional forms of legitimation, only the
consent of the governed can answer this question. To delegitimate
feudalism's Church-based justification of decentered power, the early
modern state offered popular sovereignty as a new ground for political
authority. That sovereignty was institutionalized initially through the
creation of parliamentary bodies and later through expansion of the
electorate. But once the war against feudalism is won, these innovations come to appear as arbitrary sources of opinionated interference
with administrative rationality, and so their capacity to innovate must
be depreciated. As an objectified expression of the belief that experience's truth turns on its rationalistic reconstruction, the bureaucratic
state must conclude that the rightness of its rule can be assured only if
it remains untouched and unmodified by that on which it acts.[22] In
short, the state requires the legitimation furnished by society's consent; but as a formal embodiment of intrumentalism's characterization
of all action as the maximally efficient production of antecedently
formulated ends, it cannot abide any politically significant manifestation of that authorization.

The late liberal state can conclusively escape the conflict between
what Weber calls its substantive rationality (its status as an agency of
popular will) and its formal rationality (its commitment to bureaucratic
modes of analysis and procedure) only through the construction of
subjects who find it increasingly senseless to ask about that state's
grounding. Weber describes such engineered production of mass loyalty using the phrase "passive democratization":

> The *demos* itself, in the sense of an inarticulate mass, never "governs"
> larger associations; rather, it is governed, and its existence only changes

22. On this point, see Weber, in *From Max Weber*, pp. 200–201: "In all circumstances,
the designation of officials by means of an election among the governed modifies the
strictness of hierarchical subordination. . . . Therefore popular elections of the administrative chief and also of his subordinate officials usually endanger the expert qualification of the official as well as the precise functioning of the bureaucratic mechanism."

the way in which the executive leaders are selected and the measure of influence which the *demos*, or better, which social circles from its midst are able to exert upon the content and the direction of administrative activities by supplementing what is called "public opinion." "Democratization," in the sense intended here, does not necessarily mean an increasingly active share of the governed in the authority of the social structure. . . . The most decisive thing here—indeed it is rather exclusively so—is the *leveling of the governed* in opposition to the ruling and bureaucratically articulated group, which in its turn may occupy a quite autocratic position, both in fact and in form.[23]

So construed, "passive democratization" is best understood as one expression of that larger dynamic through which the objectifications of teleocratic reason evacuate experience's capacity to engender a sense of its own significance. For when all come to equate what exists with what can be known in virtue of its correspondence to administrative classification schemes, then intelligibility is denied to those who might otherwise dispute the contention that the state is the exclusive vehicle through which experience is to be reductively remade by the hypostatized objects of management science.

Revealing the durability of the classical representation of form as the source of the intelligible element in the things of this world, rationalization's politics cannot help but treat the matter it meets as the inherently chaotic and irrational stuff upon which its designs are to be impressed. Joining this appropriation to epistemology's suspicion that experience's relations are products of the mind's constitution, the logic of state-defined order presupposes that its discrete subjects cannot give rise to any independent association, and so are incapable of articulating their own organs of joint action. Convinced that only penetration of its directives into every sphere of human experience thwarts their decomposition into centrifugal disarray, this way of organizing human and material energies secures the conditions necessary to the state's autonomy by gradually vitiating its charges' capacity to unlearn their need for constant supervision and discipline. Expropriating whatever resources might be deployed to counter its abstraction from nonrationalized spheres of practice, the state ceaselessly manufactures the evidence necessary to validate its own claim to self-evident inevitability.[24]

23. Ibid., pp. 225–26.
24. On this point, see ibid., pp. 228–29: "Once it is fully established, bureaucracy is among those social structures which are the hardest to destroy. Bureaucracy is *the* means

"The importance of organization has increased so much in the last hundred years that the word is now quite commonly used as a synonym for association and society. Since at the very best organization is but the mechanism through which association operates, the identification is evidence of the extent in which a servant has become a master; in which means have usurped the place of the end for which they are called into existence."[25] The late liberal state, unable to check its desire to monopolize all resources of significant action, unwittingly aspires to displace and ultimately replace its cultural ground. Coming to equate the fulfillment of collective purposes with accumulation and concentration of the power that secures its right to rule the merely apparent, this superimposed shell of ossified reason can neither generate nor sustain an organic connection between itself and its disaggregated wards. Assuming that state and society, like mind and matter, are radically distinct, the former comes to believe that its power is the sustaining cause of the latter's being. Recall that Cartesian epistemology, ascribing ontological status to the subject-object dualism generated by its own misguided reflection, cannot sense the interwoven textures of prereflective experience, and so cannot escape a manipulative conception of action. By the same token, the disengaged state cannot confront the subjects of its rule as anything other than so many externalized objects to be instrumentally mastered or, better still, absorbed within itself. Comparable to a scaffolding whose structure cannot enter into the movements it struggles to contain, that state subsumes all forms of heterogeneous cultural experience beneath the dictates of comprehensive planning.

Calling into being a plane of politicosocial space whose absence of significant differentiation suits the deficiencies of its own reason, the logic of rationalization commits the state to incorporation of all that is doubtful within the fixed grasp of the theoretically certain. Descartes, we should remember, represented scientific method as a kind of con-

---

of carrying 'community action' over into rationally ordered 'societal action.' . . . The ruled, for their part, cannot dispense with or replace the bureaucratic apparatus of authority once it exists. For this bureaucracy rests upon expert training, a functional specialization of works, and an attitude set for habitual and virtuoso-like mastery of single yet methodically integrated functions. If the official stops working, or if his work is forcefully interrupted, chaos results, and it is difficult to improvise replacements from among the governed who are fit to master such chaos. This holds for public administration as well as for private economic organizations of private capitalism. The idea of eliminating these organizations becomes more and more utopian."

25. Dewey, FC, p. 166.

ceptual bulldozer whose task is to level the disorderly jumble of inherited wisdom and so make possible the reconstruction of knowledge on a foundation owing nothing to the past: "Buildings planned and carried out by one architect alone are usually more beautiful and better proportioned than those which many have tried to put in order and improve, making use of old walls which were built with other ends in view. In the same way, those ancient towns which, originally mere villages, have become in the process of time great towns, are usually very badly constructed in comparison with those which are regularly laid out on a plain by a surveyor who is free to follow his own ideas."[26]

Analogously, thinking of time as a mechanical order of successive moments rather than as the soil from which significant emergents may grow, the bureaucratic state recapitulates the philosophic tradition's fallacy of unlimited universalization. Just as the latter asserts that the end of thinking is to draw all existents into a single, all-inclusive, and timeless whole, so too the former identifies its cause with efficient imposition of transparent grids upon society's time-consuming sense particulars. The theoretical violence perpetrated by Enlightenment science is thus reiterated by a state convinced that endless conversion of experience's qualitative diversity into the manufactured material of managed meaning is the condition of its truth.

Bureaucratic classificational categories are created by systematically abstracting the features of things deemed useful to production of the state's antecedently defined ends. Each such category tacitly represents the differentiating characteristics of persons and things as less real than the standardized groupings through which they are known by insertion. Recurrent application of such classifications to the field of collective action in time elicits a routinized world in which administration's quest for the uniform, the stable, and the substitutable slowly eviscerates the capacity of agents to sense the reality of what is variable and heterogeneous.[27] Convinced that managerial science's abrogations of experience's particularities are authorized to displace its con-

26. René Descartes, "Discourse on Method," in *The Philosophical Works of Descartes*, vol. 1, ed. Elizabeth Haldane and G. R. T. Ross (Cambridge: Cambridge University Press), pp. 87–88.

27. On this point, see Weber, in *From Max Weber*, p. 198: "The reduction of modern office management to rules is deeply embedded in its very nature. The theory of modern public administration, for instance, assumes that the authority to order certain matters by decree—which has been legally granted to public authorities—does not entitle the bureau to regulate the matter by commands given for each case, but only to regulate the matter abstractly."

crete tangles, those agents come to endorse the state's conversion of statistical regularities into the desiderata to which those relations must conform. Reimposition of that "knowledge" is then justified through reference to society's need to constitute itself as a clear and distinct object presented for unambiguous "re-presentation" by the state's centralized organ of sight.

Aristotle, we learned earlier, insists that only form's presence in things renders them knowable. Epistemology, following suit, contends that subjection of nature's affairs to immutable law is the condition of their being. As the inheritor of this legacy, the logic of the bureaucratic state holds that only subsumption beneath the abstracted idealizations through which its particulars, when sensed, are immediately recognized and exhaustively known assures them of their existence. Hence those particulars that submit without regard for their contextually delimited idiosyncrasies are regarded as formally equivalent cases of some more general law, whereas those that resist are either dismissed as anomalous or condemned as unreal.

In pressing toward full realization of its covert aspiration, the bureaucratized state reconfigures the liberal distinction between public and private in ways that considerably attenuate the demand for tangible manifestations of consent.[28] No longer corresponding to the functional and conditional differentiation of state from civil society, that distinction comes to refer to the unbridgeable gulf between, on the one hand, institutions whose objective obduracy makes them appear given in the nature of things and, on the other, the ethereal subjective space into which the routinized self retreats so as to preserve the illusion of autonomy. Moving disconnectedly between so many compartmentalized spheres of existence, that self finds its beliefs stripped of their internal relatedness as well as their connections to a world of experience concretely shared with others. Shaped to a form that is appropriately accessed through public opinion polls and their aggregating techniques, it learns that the communication of politically

28. See ibid., p. 239: "Only with the bureaucratization of the state and of law in general can one see a definite possibility of separating sharply and conceptually an 'objective' legal order from the 'subjective rights' of the individual which it guarantees; of separating 'public' law from 'private' law. Public law regulates the interrelationships of public authorities and their relationships with the 'subjects'; private law regulates the relationships of the governed individuals among themselves. This conceptual separation presupposes the conceptual separation of the 'state,' as an abstract bearer of sovereign prerogatives and the creator of 'legal norms,' from all personal 'authorizations' of individuals."

significant information can only proceed in a vertical direction, because lateral exchanges are merely the trading of opinions. As "ideas" about political things become fantasies to be enacted in a world of free-floating signifiers, that ego ever more completely equates the meaning of the term "democracy" with the corollary of such polls, that is, with the electoral mechanisms through which individual and group interests are rendered homogeneous and then impersonally combined. "Analytic abstraction, having perchance already deprived men of all their qualities due to their social relations, now proceeds further to reduce them into merely numerical individuals, into ballot-projecting units."[29] Yet in accepting the translation of such interests into commensurable terms as a condition of their entry into the public realm, those interests are denied their qualitative rootedness in the tangible concerns of concrete life. The overweening abstraction of the public realm, overcome only through the pseudopolitics of civil society's hierarchically organized economic institutions, is thereby mirrored by the particularistic concreteness of all that is relegated to the mutually impoverished private domain.

Encased in institutional forms that reinforce conventional oppositions between the sane and the insane, the mind and the body, the autonomous and the heteronomous, the natural and the artificial, the bureaucratized ego has no doubt that its freedom turns on experience's wholesale subjection to reason's unifying dictates. It retains in eviscerated form the cosmological conviction that humanity was created for happiness, whether by nature or by God, on condition that all submit their will to the dictates of reason. That ego, in other words, clings to the faith that the world's scientific administration can finally establish a tension-free congruence between its native impulses and the forms of identity made available by Enlightenment culture. As such, it must suppress its suspicion that articulation of any particular form of collective association enables certain modes of being and disables others. And it must suppress its suspicion that the fashioning of any determinate notion of rational selfhood necessarily invokes some notion of the not rational, and so frustrates the desire to create a world in which all oppositions have been finally overcome.

United in common endorsement of a state whose pretensions give secularized expression to the view that God is perfect mind and humanity is created in the image of the maker, ruler and ruled bow before

29. Dewey, "The Ethics of Democracy," in *EW*, vol. 1, p. 233.

this creature of thinking's conduct. Its effects are daily felt even though "it" can no longer be seen. As such, that state becomes a fetish whose power, although everywhere and so nowhere, is experienced as that of an externalized agency hovering eerily above the ruled. Thrusting on it the burden of modernity's quest for certainty, that unseen agency is ascribed the capacities of the epistemological self whose autonomy turns on its ability to secure total propositional objectification of and absolute mastery over the world's contents. Yet precisely because it defines itself as an omnipotent agent whose need to abolish insecurity justifies its unfettered right to marshal the psychophysical energies necessary to its ambitions, it cannot openly admit its incapacity to anticipate and subjugate the unforeseen consequences generated by its own interventions. In a desperate effort to secure some magical safeguard against the world's uncertainty and so occlude its own ineptitude, the state turns to ritualistic affirmation of the ubiquity of cause and effect, the necessity of progress, and the inherent rationality of the universe. Unable to legitimate its own ends, yet committed to the goal of perfect mastery, that state redefines all political matters as technical problems whose solutions can be had if only all have abiding faith in the natural correspondence between the world it creates and the reason that knows it.

Surrounded by insurance schemes that distribute more equitably but never overcome their apprehension of the future, the ruled for their part seek increasingly effective protection from the disorder they fear will surely overwhelm should they be thrown together without benefit of prior design. Knowing that the qualitative dimensions of lived experience must now find refuge within the "values" entertained by solo egos, they eagerly embrace the state's perpetuation of the enfeebling dualities that protect us from experience's contingency. The institutionalization of those bifurcations, rendering life a malleable resource awaiting analytic reduction and conceptual reification, secures experience's distance from what might otherwise be its intensities, ambiguities, and vagaries. Asking for little more than assured provision of social welfare services and benefits, the state's subjects thus become suitable objects for management psychology, market analysis, and other forms of practical power fashioned from the practice of positivist social sciences. As the habits of sense crafted out of activity in common with others decompose, those whose conduct grounds the state's power (but no longer share the forms of experience that might enable them to recall that this is so) endorse its banality in return for the guarantees customarily given to customers and clients.[30] Jointly conspiring to withdraw from its distinctive affairs, ruler and ruled sustain an antipolitics whose truth consists in a falsehood that turns the state into an end-in-itself to which all owe their essential existence.

Parodying Newton's representation of nature as a divinely devised machine, adherents of the late liberal state dream of the day when it will at last constitute all experience as a self-enclosed and perfectly stable substance. But that ambition, were it to succeed without limit, would effectively transform the world into a timeless and senseless brute entity, and the domain of experience would, in a way, disappear. "A world that was all necessity would not be a world of necessity; it would just be."[31] For unless the field of accustomed meanings is sufficiently tensed or dislocated to call forth discernible figures from the world constituted by preobjectified habit, no-things can appear. "Unless there were something problematic, undecided, still going-on and as yet unfinished and indeterminate in nature, there could be no such events as perceptions."[32] Hence the drive to subject all experience to the imperatives of bureaucratized routine intimates the moment when the flickering light of thinking may finally be extinguished.

III

Weber's construction of the problem of meaning leaves him without the critical leverage necessary to contend with reason's slow suicide. That explains why he must heap scorn on those who seek escape from the unyielding structures of calculable administration.[33] But belief in the inexorability of that end only follows because Weber has already confined the scope of thinking to neutered analysis of the world's facticity, and hence to a science that cannot do other than express and reinforce reason's march to self-annihilation.

30. See Weber, in *From Max Weber*, pp. 212–13: "Increasing bureaucratization is a function of the increasing possession of goods used for consumption, and of an increasingly sophisticated technique of fashioning external life—a technique which corresponds to the opportunities provided by such wealth. This reacts upon the standard of living and makes for an increasing subjective indispensability of organized, collective, inter-local, and thus bureaucratic, provision for the most varied wants, which previously were either unknown, or were satisfied locally or by a private economy."
31. Dewey, *EN*, p. 64.
32. Ibid., p. 349.
33. See especially Weber, *Economy and Society*, vol. 1, p. 224.

If, however, we question the traditional conviction that reason constitutes the exclusive vehicle through which existence achieves value,
we open up the possibility of asking how the mode of experience we
call knowing is now *had*. That, in turn, makes it possible to suggest
that the present's institutionalized embodiments of reason are suspect
insofar as they eviscerate the conditions of qualitative significance. In
other words, the bureaucratic state analyzed by Weber is subject to the
same criticism that is appropriately directed against any knowledge
that is abstract in the sense that it is ontologically deficient. Just as
knowledge that is all-inclusive ceases to have meaning because it has
lost all context, so too the imperialistic pretensions implicit in that
state's attempt to capture all experience within the confines of its
teleocratic logic renders it an expression of modernity's senselessness.

If this is so, then the irrationality Weber locates at the heart of
rationalization is a contingent matter that relies for its perpetuation on
the systematic production, distribution, and consumption of meaninglessness. Its undoing requires not nostalgic resurrection of the
past's objectivism (its God), nor subordination to charismatic embodiments of the present's subjectivism (its many gods), but rather artful
refashioning of the cultural conditions that nourish experience's potential to become pregnant with a sense of its wider involvements in
space and time. " 'Social reform' is conceived in a Philistine spirit if it is
taken to mean anything less than precisely the liberation and expansion of the meanings of which experience is capable."[34]

In the last analysis, experience's potential for meaning turns on the
collective cultivation of a nature that is neither perfectly formed nor
perfectly formless, neither pure flux nor pure structure, neither unchanging substance nor random accident. "Nature is characterized by
a constant mixture of the precarious and the stable. This mixture gives
poignancy to existence. If existence were either completely necessary
or completely contingent, there would be neither comedy nor tragedy
in life, nor need of the will to live. The significance of morals and
politics, of the arts both technical and fine, of religion and of science
itself as inquiry and discovery, all have their source and meaning in the
union in Nature of the settled and the unsettled, the stable and the
hazardous. Apart from this union, there are no such things as 'ends,'
either as consummations or as those ends-in-view we call purposes.
There is only a block universe, either something ended and admitting

34. Dewey, *EN*, p. 411.

of no change, or else a predestined march of events. There is no such thing as fulfillment where there is no risk of failure, and no defeat where there is no promise of possible achievement."[35]

As unwittingly intimated by the philosophical tradition's distinctions between subject and object, freedom and necessity, particular and universal, nature is inherently ambiguous. For it comprises an infinitely varied conflux of events whose intersecting histories yield the recurrent as well as the discontinuous, the firm as well as the inconstant. That ambiguity, in turn, is an indispensable condition of meaning. "Unless nature had regular habits, persistent ways, so compacted that they time, measure and give rhythm and recurrence to transitive flux, meanings, recognizable characters, could not be. But also without an interplay of these patient, slow-moving, not easily stirred systems of action with swift-moving, unstable, unsubstantial events, nature would be a routine unmarked by ideas."[36] Weber holds that the susceptibility of meaningful moments to the erosions of time as well as their failure to cohere as parts within a cosmologically sanctioned whole entails the nihilism of death and so of life as well. In fact, however, it is only because nature proffers meanings, and then teases its creatures with the prospect of their incompletion or withdrawal, that it can take part in the birth of significant experience.

A human being capable of cultivating the potentialities implicit in such experience is a creature who acknowledges without desiring to overcome the ambiguity of its situation within a nature that is indeterminate but not shapeless. "An individual existence has a double status and import. There is the individual that belongs in a continuous system of connected events which reinforce its activities and which form a world in which it is at home, consistently at one with its preferences, satisfying its requirements. Then there is the individual that finds a gap between its distinctive bias and the operations of the things through which alone its need can be satisfied; it is broken off, discrete, because at odds with its surroundings. It either surrenders,

---

35. Dewey, QC, pp. 243–44. Cf. Dewey, EN, pp. 64–65: "The common failure to note the fact that a world of complete being would be a world in which necessity is meaningless is due to a rapid shift from one universe of discourse to another. First we postulate a whole of Being; then we shift to a part; now since a 'part' is logically dependent as such in its existence and its properties, it is necessitated by other parts. But we have unwittingly introduced contingency in the very fact of marking off something as just a part. Its being what it is, is not necessitated by the whole or by other parts: its being what it is, is just a name for the whole being what it is."
36. Dewey, EN, p. 351.

conforms, and for the sake of peace becomes a parasitical subordinate, indulges in egotistical solitude; or its activities set out to remake conditions in accord with desire." When most fully prepared to summon the consummatory possibilities latent in experience, the incompletion of the human being thus replicates that of a nature "whose events have their own distinctive indifferencies [sic], resistances, arbitrary closures and intolerances, and also their peculiar openness, warm responsiveness, greedy seekings and transforming unions. Existentially speaking, a human individual is distinctive opacity of bias and preference conjoined with plasticity and permeability of needs and likings. One trait tends to isolation, discreteness; the other trait to connection, continuity. This ambivalent character is rooted in nature."[37]

As a partly constant and partly inconstant locus of conduct moving suspensefully through life's interwoven incidents, the individuated human creature is not a unified substantial being who *has* so many overlapping histories. Whatever continuity each self exhibits over time cannot be an expression of some underlying essence, for there is no prefabricated singular self lurking behind the complex of unstable habits and impulses that have now come to more or less amicable terms with one another. Rather, that continuity is a function of the constellation into which that being's working habits are currently resolved. "Were it not for the continued operation of all habits in every act, no such thing as character would exist. There would be simply a bundle, an untied bundle at that, of isolated acts. Character is the interpenetration of habits."[38] As a complex historical emergent that cannot be isolated, except for analytical purposes, from the situations within which "it" finds itself, the individual is its life activity rather than something that acts.

Like the nature from which it emerges, each human life deals with so many unique situations about which complete assurance is never possible. Cumulatively, such experiences can only engender meaning in the process of becoming. Meaning, complete and undefiled, is a prerogative of the gods, not of human beings for whom it sometimes happens to appear in time. Shaping and being shaped by the scriptless stories of the others with which it is interwoven, each life is the adverbial site upon which so many histories overlap. That intersection, in turn, is the transactional ground of those punctuating mo-

37. Ibid., pp. 242, 245.
38. Dewey, *HNC*, p. 38.

ments that, if demarcated *and* integrated within the general stream of lived experience, are taken up into the funded mean(ing)s that convey the past's presence into the future. "Each resting place in experience is an undergoing in which is absorbed and taken home the consequences of prior doing, and unless the doing is that of utter caprice or sheer routine, each doing carries in itself meaning that has been extracted and conserved."[39]

While the meanings of such a life can build upon one another, there is no significance to life per se. For meaning, as William James insists, grows up within finite experiences that "lean on each other, but the whole of them, if such a whole there be, leans on nothing. . . . All 'homes' are in finite experience; finite experience as such is homeless. . . . Nothing outside of the flux secures the issue of it. It can hope for salvation only from its own intrinsic promises and potencies."[40] In sum, as an emergent like any other, each agent's life is an adventure whose meaning cannot be fully known until after it is no longer capable of producing surprises. "No one discovers a new world without forsaking an old one; and no one discovers a new world who exacts [a] guarantee in advance for what it shall be, or who puts the act of discovery under bonds with respect to what the new world shall do to him when it comes into vision."[41]

As we have seen, the insecurity engendered by the human creature's immersion in such ontological ambiguity has spawned many efforts to transcend this condition by securing some pledge that Being is good, or that the world can be made so if only human beings muster sufficient power to transform its things in accordance with determinate ideals of rational perfection, or that its affairs are of such little moment that it is not worth the trouble to overcome their insignificance. "Oppositions of mind and body, soul and matter, spirit and flesh all have their origin, fundamentally, in fear of what life may bring

---

39. Dewey, *AE*, p. 56. Cf. Dewey, "Time and Individuality," in *ENF*, p. 230: "It is impossible for a biographer in writing, say the story of the first thirty years of the life of Lincoln, not to bear in mind his later career. Lincoln as an individual is a history; any particular event cut off from that history ceases to be a part of his life as an individual. As Lincoln is a particular development in time, so is every other human individual. Individuality is the uniqueness of the history, of the career, not something given once for all at the beginning which then proceeds to unroll as a ball of yarn may be unwound. Lincoln made history. But it is just as true that he made himself as an individual in the history he made."

40. William James, quoted in Michael Weinstein, *The Wilderness and the City* (Amherst: University of Massachusetts Press, 1982), p. 112.

41. Dewey, *EN*, p. 246.

forth. They are marks of contraction and withdrawal."[42] All such evasions entail a refusal to acknowledge the anxiety that is qualitatively present within contingent, partial, and discontinuous situations where there can be neither unquestionable justification for the rightness of a cause nor indubitable guarantee for the happiness of its issue. Forcing the multifariousness of lived experience to conform to reason's imperatives and equating success in doing so with the truth of existence, such impositions violate reality. When such violence is objectified within powerful institutional forms, it cannot help but squeeze from the interrelated situations that constitute a human life the prerequisites of meaning; and that, in turn, must spawn intense pressure to locate, in either spasms of meaningless savagery or in otherwordly reconciliations, "symbolic" substitutes for the fleshier meanings available to those who still know that qualitative experience always exceeds knowledge's capacity to encapsulate, exhaust, or tame its vital possibilities.

Teleocratic rationalism cannot acknowledge the appearance of gaps and discontinuities in nature without forsaking the presuppositions of its own intelligibility. Hence it cannot grant that mutability gives meaning to immutability, that novelty is possible only because of recurrence, that defect is the condition of grace, that without vice there could be no virtue. "If disharmony were not in both man and nature, if it were only between them, man would be the ruthless overlord of nature, or its querulous oppressed subject. The anomaly apparent in the occurrence of consciousness is evidence of an anomalous phase in nature itself."[43] Convinced of the need to safeguard meaning from time's corrosive effects, such rationalism cannot see that experience is able to deliver its promise of significance only because nature's events are what they qualitatively are in virtue of the "from which" and the "to which" they are related in time. Oriented backward, experience can make sense of its emergents only because their disclosure points to meanings, borne within sedimented habits, which are more intimately present than the term "memory" can suggest. Oriented forward, experience can make sense of its eventualities only because those same informing habits propel it into a world that must be had before it is known. "Apart from language, from imputed and inferred meaning, we continually engage in an immense multitude of immediate organic selections, rejections, welcomings, expulsions, appropriations, with-

42. Dewey, *AE*, p. 22.
43. Dewey, *EN*, pp. 421, 349.

drawals, shrinkings, expansions, elations and dejections, attacks, wardings off, of the most minute, vibratingly delicate nature. Formulated discourse is mainly but a selected statement of what we wish to retain among all these incipient starts, following ups and breakings off."[44]

Insofar as temporally qualified situations *fail* to engender significant discord within the "subconscious" resources of mind, individual loci of conduct begin to "lose consciousness" of themselves within an abyss of effortless, unfocused, and inertial response. "It is this double relationship of continuation, promotion, carrying forward, and of arrest, deviation, need of supplementation, which defines that focalization of meanings which is consciousness, awareness, perception. Every case of consciousness is dramatic; drama is an enhancement of the conditions of consciousness."[45] Only through their capacity to resist do experienced pragmata affirm their status as somethings rather than nothings. Correlatively, only when thinking is challenged by that which it meets in experience is "mind" impelled to modify its formed content by departing from the drift of the present. "Impulsion forever boosted on its forward way would run its course thoughtless, and dead to emotion. For it would not have to give an account of itself in terms of the things it encounters, and hence they would not become significant objects. The only way it can become aware of its nature and its goal is by obstacles surmounted and means employed; means which are only means from the very beginning are too much one with an impulsion, on a way smoothed and oiled in advance, to permit of consciousness of them. Resistance and check bring about the conversion of direct forward action into re-flection; what is turned back upon is the relation of hindering conditions to what the self possesses as working capital in virtue of prior experiences."[46] Incarnate in the activities of reidentifying, collecting, separating, grasping, pointing, discriminating, criticizing, and so on, thinking is called into play only when the world threatens to come apart. "The point of maximum apparency is the point of greatest stress and undetermined potentiality; the point of maximum of restless shift, is also the point of greatest brightness; it is vivid, but not clear; imminent, urgently expressive of the impending, but not defined."[47]

44. Ibid., pp. 299–300.
45. Ibid., p. 306.
46. Dewey, *AE*, pp. 59–60.
47. Dewey, *EN*, p. 349.

The sense of collective powerlessness that stabilizes the present is crucially dependent on an anaesthetization of ordinary experience which obviates the call to think. Deaf to experience's potential for qualitative textures and depths, actors accept its currently dessicated form as normal, and so forget how to know themselves as agencies of transformative conduct. "Only occasionally in the lives of many are the senses fraught with the sentiment that comes from deep realization of intrinsic meanings. We undergo sensations as mechanical stimuli or as irritated stimulations, without having a sense of the reality that is in them and behind them: in much of our experience our different senses do not unite to tell a common and enlarged story. We see without feeling; we hear, but only a second-hand report, second hand because not reënforced by vision. We touch, but the contact remains tangential because it does not fuse with qualities of sense that go below the surface. We use the senses to arouse passion but not to fulfill the interest of insight."[48] Most particularly, in a culture where all things become signs of their possible use-value, the sense of sight degenerates into an agency of arrested recognition. In such bureaucratized seeing, an isolated detail is taken as a cue (as opposed to a clue) which permits summary assignment of an object to the larger class from which it derives its entire meaning. Rarely does sight yield sufficiently to its seens such that it proves able to per-ceive—that is, to take in and appropriate—their qualities as members contributing to the organic constitution of a complete act of consummatory appreciation. Rarely do agents achieve the alert and active commerce with the world that is paradigmatically exemplified by the hunter whose intelligently animated body displays its synthesis of animal vigor and human thinking.

Shrinking of the body's affective senses strangles experience's vitality by obliterating the resources of memory. Alternately conforming to and rebelling against an order unable to check its surplus production of atrophied being, everyday conduct vacillates between rigid abstinence and aimless indulgence. "In much of our experience we are not concerned with the connection of one incident with what went before

---

48. Dewey, *AE*, p. 21. For an insightful analysis of the way this sensed powerlessness stimulates action qua violent self-assertion, see Joseph Kupfer, *Experience as Art* (Albany: State University of New York Press, 1983). Also, for a splendid essay on the bureaucratization of the senses, see Walker Percy, "The Loss of the Creature," in his *Message in the Bottle* (New York: Farrar, Straus and Giroux, 1987). The following remarks owe much to these suggestive works.

and what comes after. There is no interest that controls attentive rejection or selection of what shall be organized into the developing experience. Things happen, but they are neither definitely included nor decisively excluded; we drift. We yield according to external pressure, or evade and compromise. There are beginnings and cessations, but no genuine initiations and concludings. One thing replaces another, but does not absorb it and carry it on. There is experience, but so slack and discursive that it is not *an* experience."[49] Such "behavior" cannot engender the sort of differentiation necessary to any sense of experienced significance. For in the absence of a sufficient gap between received habits and that which appears now, conduct remains dormant. Flattening the qualitative distinctions between its different moments, the present's sense certainty lowers the tension between conduct and its medium, and so induces thinking to accept premature termination of its exploratory possibilities.

Human beings, bereft of any expansive feel for experience's temporal stretch and hence of any feel for the relational implications embedded in that stretch, lose all but a radically impoverished sense of their own qualitative individuality as well. "Genuine time, if it exists as anything else except the measure of motions in space, is all one with the existence of individuals as individuals, with the creative, with the occurrence of unpredictable novelties."[50] When individual participants in meaning's generation, aping the bureaucratized order within which they are encased, demand antecedent assurance that their conduct will produce gratification or security, actualization of nature's implicit powers is aborted. Time ceases to be present as an immanent reality in such routinized being, as its creatures adapt all too readily to the confines of the iron cage.

IV

"Mind," Dewey argued in his *Psychology* (1887) "has not remained a passive spectator of the universe, but has produced and is producing certain results. These results are objective, can be studied as all objective historical facts may be, and are permanent. . . . Such objective manifestations of mind are, in the realm of intelligence, phenomena

49. Dewey, *AE*, p. 40.
50. Dewey, "Time and Individuality," in *ENF*, p. 241.

like language and science; in that of will, social, and political institutions; in that of feeling, art; in that of the whole self, religion."[51] Weber, in his essay "Parliament and Government in a Reconstructed Germany," published three decades later, also turned to the relationship between mind and its creations: "An inanimate machine is mind objectified. Only this provides it with the power to force men into its service and to dominate their everyday working life as completely as is actually the case in the factory. Objectified intelligence is also that animated machine, the bureaucratic organization, with its specialization of trained skills, its division of jurisdiction, its rules and hierarchical relations of authority. Together with the inanimate machine it is busy fabricating the shell of bondage which men will perhaps be forced to inhabit some day, as powerless as the fellahs of ancient Egypt."[52]

Together, these two passages indicate why revitalization of experience's potential for significance entails pitting thinking's conduct against the objectifications of "mind." Any conception of mind is made tangible through institutionalization of the distinctions—for instance, between health and disease, education and indoctrination, sanity and insanity, cleanliness and uncleanliness—it employs in working its way through the thickets of experience. To the degree that individual selves come to be what they are in virtue of their assimilation and endorsement of such objectified distinctions, they can be said to express that mind. It follows, therefore, that "the mind that appears *in* individuals is not as such individual mind. The former is in itself a system of belief, recognitions, and ignorances, of acceptances and rejections, of expectancies and appraisals of meanings which have been instituted under the influence of custom and tradition."[53] The latter, by way of contrast, emerges only on those rare occasions when individuals in their individuality, that is, as embodiments of unique histories, import new twists and turns into reproduction of culture's habitual ways of being.

To construe the appearance of individual mind in this fashion is to render problematic what epistemology takes for granted. Reflecting its Christian heritage, Cartesian/Lockean epistemology starts with an ensouled self, and then endows or identifies that self with its formal capacity to know. On the basis of this assumption, it concludes that any particular mind is in principle capable of entertaining whatever

51. Dewey, *Psychology*, in *EW*, vol. 2, p. 15.
52. Weber, *Economy and Society*, vol. 2, p. 1402.
53. Dewey, *EN*, p. 219.

beliefs it chooses. As such, it cannot begin to appreciate the difficulty of lightening, however incompletely, the cumulative load of institutionalized mind. On the divergent account suggested here, the fact that individual minds do on occasion prove able to contest the condensation of accustomed ways of being into settled truths is precisely what requires explanation. Moreover, this account implies that the refashioning of belief cannot be construed as an exclusively intellectual matter. Because such settled truths are incarnate in the habits through which individuals, relating to one another and to the world of things, regenerate mind's objectifications, the possibility of belief's recrafting cannot be segregated from a recrafting of the relations that sustain it through time.

If mind becomes individual by a process of functional differentiation from a more comprehensive whole that hitherto was only potentially differentiated, then its revival can be construed as a matter of animating its verbal and adjectival senses. In its original verbal sense, as we saw in Chapter 2, the term "mind" referred to certain qualitatively unique modes of doing and suffering. "Consider its inclusiveness. It signifies memory. We are reminded of this and that. Mind also signifies attention. We not only keep things in mind, but we bring mind to bear on our problems and perplexities. Mind also signifies purpose; we have a mind to do this and that. Nor is mind in these operations something purely intellectual. The mother minds her baby; she cares for it with affection. Mind is care in the sense of solicitude, anxiety, as well as of active looking after things that need to be tended; we mind our step, our course of action, emotionally as well as thoughtfully. From giving heed to acts and objects, mind comes also to signify, to obey—as children are told to mind their parents. In short 'to mind' denotes an activity that is intellectual, to *note* something; affectional, as caring and liking, and volitional, practical, acting in a purposive way." In its adjectival (or, better, adverbial) formulations, as we saw in Chapter 5, "mind" designates the indispensable conditions of everyday experience's intelligibility, that body of habitual meanings by means of which events appear within the realm of significance. As such, it "forms the background upon which every new contact with surroundings is projected; yet 'background' is too passive a word, unless we remember that it is active and that, in the projection of the new upon it, there is assimilation and reconstruction of both background and of what is taken in and digested."[54]

54. Dewey, AE, pp. 263–64.

It is these two senses of mind that must be recalled if we are to appreciate how thinking might come to question rationalism's teleocratic usurpations. The only "solution" to the problem posed by a reason whose authority requires continued concealment of its existential origins is to reveal its hubris. To counter the grip of the too familiar structures of everyday interaction, we need to discover what is withdrawn from the realm of potentiality by sedimentary ways of eliciting experiential form from an intrinsically ambiguous nature. We need, that is, to repose the question of the present's sufficiency of meaning; and to the extent that that sense proves insufficient, we must counterpose thinking to the consolidations of reason.

Routinized selves can begin to acknowledge that cultivation of the aleatory, the precarious, and the adventitious dimensions of nature is a condition of meaning's rebirth only when the present becomes a matter of discontent. Animation of sense-making conduct must commence, in other words, by awakening desire. "Desire is the forward urge of living creatures. When the push and drive of life meets no obstacle, there is nothing which we call desire. There is just life-activity. But obstructions present themselves, and activity is dispersed and divided. Desire is the outcome. It is activity surging forward to break through what dams it up."[55] To enliven a feeling, no matter how ill formed, of the violations done by a world whose defining institutional forms systematically frustrate the need to fashion sense from the materials of concrete experience is to open the way for a possible release of embodied intentionality.

When desire stimulated by a sense of incompletion begins to pass into action, it does so initially as an amorphous drive which, as impulse, must remain unnamed inasmuch as neither its source nor its end are yet known. "Impulses are the pivots upon which the reorganization of activities turn, they are agencies of deviation, for giving new directions to old habits and changing their quality."[56] But to vitalize an impulse to make *suf*ficient what is presently *de*ficient is not in and of itself to give action's opening wedge a sense of its imminent directionality. Hence significance-seeking agency must transform its lack into some preliminary sense of its potential means of fulfillment. Such projections, grounded in a search for what is at present indescribable, can only be fashioned by imagination. Imagination, the

55. Dewey, *HNC*, p. 249.
56. Ibid., p. 93.

responsive application of meanings borne by habit to the novel elements present within an immediate situation, is the vehicle through
which thinking metaphorically extrapolates the past into the future.
"There is always a gap between the here and now of direct interaction
and the past interactions whose funded result constitutes the meanings with which we grasp and understand what is now occurring.
Because of this gap, all conscious perception involves a risk; it is a
venture into the unknown, for as it assimilates the present to the past
it also brings about some reconstruction of that past."[57]

Grasping the unknown as a possible participant in a sense-making
whole that is not yet, imagination may shape its summonings into
dramatically enhanced distillations of the more precious things found
in experience's most pregnant moments. Although pointing beyond
the present, such ideals are nonetheless firmly rooted in the tangible
stuff of everyday experience. Grounded in what might be called nature's "idealizability," these "ends" express the tendency of things that
now exist carried to their fullest imaginable limit. An end-in-view, as
we saw in Chapter 5, is a directional pivot that gives focus to present
conduct. "About this central figuration extends infinitely a supporting
background in a vague whole, undefined and undiscriminated. At
most intelligence but throws a spotlight on that little part of the whole
which marks out the axis of movement. Even if the light is flickering
and the illuminated portion stands forth only dimly from the shadowy
background, it suffices if we are shown the way to move. To the rest of
the consequences, collateral and remote, corresponds a background of
feeling, of diffused emotion. This forms the stuff of the ideal."[58] Accordingly, the credibility of our ideals requires no external guarantor.
Their relationship to what is, reciprocally constitutive but always in
tension, affirms their reality by calling for their continued articulation
and rearticulation through the medium of artful conduct.

The ideal is made actual in its navigation of perception, from among
the welter of possibilities offered by any immediately experienced

57. Dewey, *AE*, p. 272.
58. Dewey, *HNC*, p. 262. Cf. Dewey, *CF*, p. 49: "What I have been objecting to . . . is
not the idea that ideals are linked with existence and that they themselves exist, through
human embodiment as forces, but the idea that their authority and value depend upon
some prior complete embodiment—as if the efforts of human beings in behalf of justice,
or knowledge or beauty, depended for their effectiveness and validity upon assurance
that there already existed in some supernal region a place where criminals are humanely
treated, where there is no serfdom or slavery, where all facts and truths are already
discovered and possessed, and all beauty is eternally displayed in actualized form."

situation, to those that bear most pertinently on that ideal's present import. That meaning is itself constituted by the conduct through which impulsion's initial emotion begins to assume more definite form via practical exploration of the paths it opens up. The "aim" of such exploration is to call into being a transformed constellation of habits whose worth is measured not by its conformity to some speculative abstraction, but rather by its capacity to foster enhanced receptivity to the world's sense-engendering possibilities. "Now an animal given to forming habits, is one with an increasing number of needs, and of new relationships with the world about it. Each habit demands appropriate conditions for its exercise and when habits are numerous and complex, as with the human organism, to find these conditions involves search and experimentation; the organism is compelled to make variations, and exposed to error and disappointment. By a seeming paradox, increased power of forming habits means increased susceptibility, sensitiveness, responsiveness. Thus even if we think of habits as so many grooves, the power to acquire many and varied grooves denotes high sensitivity, explosiveness."[59]

The authority of an ideal, so construed, is neither a function of its detachment from what is, nor of its status as an eternal property of the antecedently real. It is to be justified by its works, by its capacity to challenge the present's appearance of immobility and so open up a space for conduct. In this sense, any ideal's practical engagement is, of necessity, critical. Criticism is the imaginative assumption of a new posture toward what previously appeared within the world. The critical elaboration of an ideal's meaning, therefore, entails crafting and recrafting its intimations into unfolding complexes of conduct within the context of situations that are never closed, complete, discrete, or wholly consistent. Pointing toward what must be either reformed or excised because it does not at present contribute to the unfolding sense of a dynamic consummatory whole, "ideal/critical" conduct begins to retether the abstract but all too mundane creatures of Weber's mind to the ground of ordinary experience.

V

The roots of the contemporary political dilemma reach down to the most basic ways we now experience, and hence to the forms of life that

59. Dewey, *EN*, p. 281.

accord those ways their pragmatic explication. The enunciation of a democratic ideal can come about only as a result of conduct's reformulation of what is, and so is capable of truthful articulation. How the world's matters might appear in virtue of such reshaping can be intimated by an exercise of the sort undertaken in this chapter; but that exercise, it should be recalled, is a relatively insignificant part of the art toward which it gestures. It is not to be confused with realization of the ideal whose meaning it can only anticipate.

If new spirit is to be infused within a decaying body politic, conduct must prove able to sense the tangible affairs whose distinctive qualities are designated by the adjective *political*. The possibility of such grasping will appear utopian as long as our relations with the matters of daily life receive their principal articulation through the categories of bureaucratic rationality. Institutionalized via a state committed to systematic regulation of the things it abstracts from the sites of their original emergence, that reason is defined by its desire to overcome experience's potential to reveal and sustain the political qualities of everyday affairs. Hence to the extent that we now equate politics with the state's management of its expropriated things, the rediscovery of such quality must appear an "antipolitical" task.

Recrafting of sense-bearing experience through rehabilitation of the forms of democratic association is not a matter for which the state can assume responsibility. Such recovery requires that diversely associated agents, coming to know how the experience of dispossession manifests itself in one another's lives, engage in so many distinct but overlapping struggles to relocate the powers resident within the web of relations engendered by their ongoing transactions. To suggest the content of an ideal that might intimate the possibility of such artful reappropriations, I propose a critical recovery of the ancient notion of constitution (*politeia*).[60] In this section, I offer a preliminary account of the sense of this term; and in the next I indicate certain of the conditions that must be met if a constitution is to participate, qua medium of artful conduct, in disclosing and sustaining distinctively political pragmata.

Let us take the term "culture" to refer to the vast complex of things that emerge out of nature and in experience. As I noted above, every particular culture presupposes a distinctive ontology—that is, a non-

---

60. For Aristotle's broader use of the term *politeia*, see *The Politics*, trans. Ernest Barker (Oxford: Oxford University Press, 1958), 1292a34. For an example of his more narrow usage, see *The Politics* 1289a15.

cognitive sense of what can appear within experience and what cannot, as well as how the things that appear in experience can and
cannot relate to one another. Such sense expresses a culture's constitutional form, the shape assumed by its established ways of experiencing in virtue of the relations they characteristically sustain to one
another. "Experience always carries with it and within it certain systematized arrangements, certain classifications (using the term without intellectualistic prejudice), coexistent and serial. Social institutions, established political customs, effect and perpetuate modes of
reaction and of perception that compel a certain grouping of objects,
elements, and values. A national constitution brings about a definite
arrangement of the factors of human action which holds even physical
things together in certain determinate orders."[61] The term "constitution," in sum, refers not to a specified plan of governmental institutions, but rather to a "way of life" sustained among agents whose
interweaving conduct sometimes elicits specifically political significances.

The bureaucratic state, considered in constitutional terms, expresses a particular way of giving form to the matter that is culture.
When this way is married to liberalism's nominalistic ontology, the
objects of that state's management are taken to be so many discrete
individuals cohabiting within a society that is itself taken to consist of a
simple aggregation of such beings. Working from within the confines
of epistemology's subject-object dualism and the mechanistic conception of causality that attends it, this ontology opens up two basic ways
of thinking about the relation between constitutional form and the
selves so related. At one extreme, it suggests that each individual is an
entity whose essential character requires no explanation because that
individual's identity is antecedent to the form it creates. This view is
given classical expression in the conviction, common to most forms of
social contract theory, that persons stand apart from all forms of relatedness until they fashion a compact to regulate the terms of their
intercourse. At the other extreme, this ontology suggests that each
individual is a subject whose character is radically determined by the
constitutional form that confronts it as a source of externalized power.
This view is given paradigmatic expression in the conviction, common
to most forms of policy science, that the plasticity of human being is
the sine qua non of positivism's capacity to verify its predictive claims.
In either case, the possibility of significant institutional transforma-

---

61. Dewey, "Experience and Objective Idealism," in *IDP*, pp. 208–9.

tion, the participation of individuals in refashioning their shared constitutional form, is effectively denied. The former, intimating that change is simply a matter of exerting the manipulative will, invites resignation on the part of those who soon discover that constitutional form possesses none of the elasticity this model suggests. The latter, counterposing the puny efforts of impotent selves to the inert embodiments of routinized habit, deters transformative conduct before it ever thinks to act.

The previous chapters, by way of contrast, have suggested the inadequacy of any account of the relationship between experience and conduct predicated upon belief in an antecedent disjunction of subject from object. The things encountered in experience are not objects but pragmata embedded in the affairs of contextualized social situations; and the beings whose lives are entangled in such affairs are not subjects but fountains of agency whose conduct can be distinguished analytically but never existentially from the things of their experience and the relations that account for those things' qualitative dimensionality. Hence while constitutional form cannot be understood as a simple effect produced by the impress of will's voluntaristic designs on indifferent matter, nor can it be understood as an abstraction whose independent causal power operates over and above that will.

To grasp the more subtle sense in which constitutional form is appropriately construed as an expression of human conduct, we must recall experience's rootedness in those prereflective habits that emerge out of the mutually informing dialectic of doing and suffering. Such habits are the "means" of our being in the world insofar as they locate us within the situations through which we daily pass. As ways of engaging what appears in experience, habits can take on varying degrees of solidity. Through terms like "practice," "custom," "institution," we articulate our sense that established ways of doing exist along a continuum stretching from the more flexible to the more standardized (as in Durkheim's social facts). Because habitual ways of relating persons to persons and persons to things sometimes come to exercise considerable power over those they relate, conduct always takes place in a public medium whose more durable structural dimensions, elicited from complex interactions sustained among diverse agencies acting in time, are not the products of autonomous individual creation. The range of conduct available to agents acting in a particular complex of circumstances is, in other words, always circumscribed to a greater or lesser degree.

If habit is the link that establishes continuity between the sense-making conduct of individuals and society's more enduring institutional forms, then liberalism's dualistic construction of their relationship must be rejected in favor of an account that more fully acknowledges the reciprocity between individual conduct and constitutional transformation. To make this point, I suggest that constitutional form's peculiarly human realities are not epistemology's subjects, but rather "individuals-in-relations."[62] The hyphenation of this phrase is intended to indicate that neither of its defining elements can exist apart from the other. Contra liberalism, the relations in which individuals participate are neither external nor contingent to their being. Human beings are what they are in virtue of the characteristic modes of being in which they take part; and modes of being, as distinctive ways of crafting significance from the things offered in experience, are never creations of singular authors. They emerge and are sustained in time only through conduct that implicates others whose presence, whether explicit or implicit, is indispensable to their present sense. All distinctively human conduct is in this sense "ethical," for its character as meaningful indicates its acknowledgment of the reality of others with whom one relates in varying degrees of complexity.

These relations, however, do not exhaust the being of those they relate. As we have seen, liberalism abstracts the qualities peculiar to individuals by defining persons as undifferentiated bearers of homogeneous natural rights. This definition, in turn, is an essential prop of its Enlightenment utopia, that condition in which perfect harmony between self and the order it occupies has been finally achieved. But as the first half of the phrase individuals-in-relations suggests, the particularity of each individual is co-constitutive of his or her being, and so cannot be dismissed as the merely "accidental." To abstract the qualities that constitute that particularity is to deny the brute and irreducible uniqueness, the "itselfness," of each distinctive being. That quality, although an expression of the relations in which that individual participates, is not reducible to them. For relations have their being in the temporally qualified fields that emerge out of the joint activity of individuals, and so cannot be exhaustively located within the specific individuals whose qualitative uniqueness makes manifest their mode of confluence upon a particular site. Hence, the existence of individ-

62. I appropriate this hyphenated expression from Carol Gould's *Rethinking Democracy* (New York: Cambridge University Press, 1988). I am considerably indebted to the explication of political ontology she develops especially in chapter 2 of that work.

uals is a precondition of relations' being; as relations *of* those individuals, they cannot exist apart from those they relate.

To intellectually peel off all the habitual ways of relating persons to persons and persons to things from the concrete affairs in which they are mutually imbricated is, as suggested above, to develop an account of a culture's constitution. To see how those ways interact with one another in recurrent patterns of varying degrees of stability and instability is to articulate a constitution's morphology, that is, its anatomical "structure." That structure, because comprising a constellation of relations, is not immediately accessible to thinking. Nor is it wholly plastic to human touch. For "its" movement through time occasions effects that are real although neither intended nor immediately apparent to those caught up within it. Yet constitutional structure is not for that reason a substantial reality existing apart from the relations it comprises. For it is always "structure *of* something. A house has a structure; in comparison with the disintegration and collapse which would occur without its presence, this structure is fixed. Yet it is not something external to which the changes involved in building and using the house have to submit."[63] Structure's existential occurrence, accordingly, can no more be discovered apart from some realized constitution than can form be existentially isolated from its embodiment in matter.

Because a culture's constitution is at one and the same time the medium within which present conduct is situated and an expression of the accumulated sediment left behind by so many collective doings and sufferings, its structure is always subject to rearticulation. Because it *is* the patterned concurrence of events happening within boundaries specified with more or less fixity, structure is forever available for renegotiation via the partly associated and partly dissociated conduct of those who are what they qualitatively are in virtue of their participation in its relations. Hence its articulation of a determinate field of experience is never as static as teleocratic reason commands or as the bureaucratic way of politics demands.

As we saw above, the constitution toward which the bureaucratic state tends is distinguished, at least in part, by its denial of the truth of structure's temporal qualification. Regarding structure as a product to be manufactured through the reduction of all associated movement to the literal repetition of atomistic units of behavior, that state subjects

63. Dewey, *EN*, p. 72.

social existence to the categories of determinate spatiality by establish-ing its imperatives as a rigid framework to which all change must accommodate itself. Yet this hypostatized self-representation cannot persist when it is acknowledged that constitutional structure *is* "cer-tain basic relationships among the activities of the citizens of the country; it is a property or phase of these processes, so connected with them as to influence their rate and direction of change. It is no cause or source of events or processes; no absolute monarch; no principle of explanation; no substance behind or underlying changes—save in the sense of substance in which a man well fortified with this world's goods, and hence able to maintain himself through vicissitudes of surroundings, is a man of substance. The name designates a character in operation, not an entity."[64] Even the bureaucratic state, in other words, is in the last analysis only an unusually brittle cluster of indi-viduals-in-relation. Measuring its success by its capacity to get individ-uals to stand to one another in the concrete but objectified relations defined by the sciences of public administration, that state can secure complete release from the reality of gross experience only by taking leave of this world.

To think of constitutional structure in these terms is to refashion our sense of those enduring forms of relatedness we call "institutions." Neither classical nor modern liberal thought, in virtue of each's hypo-statizing bent, is able to forgo thinking of institutions as mere instru-ments whose value derives from the intrinsic worth of the anteced-ently apprehended purposes they make possible. The latter, best exemplified by Bentham's subjection of all institutions to the calcula-tions of the felicific calculus, regards constitutional instruments as deliberately constructed external means enabling antecedently indi-viduated selves to pursue private conceptions of self-fulfillment with-out infringing on the capacity of others to do the same. The former, best exemplifed by Aristotle's reflections on the figure of the lawgiver, is more subtle inasmuch as it recognizes that structure, through the medium of habit, shapes the beings who live within it. Yet even so, in the last analysis, Aristotle also misconceives the relationship between conduct and constitution. On his account, the form of action he calls "movement" exhausts its potentialities when its transformative capac-ity is finally and fully realized within a completed structure. As such, it is to be distinguished from those more noble forms that do not aim at ends beyond themselves and so do not find their powers consumed

64. Ibid., p. 73.

within realized embodiments. On the basis of this distinction, Aristotle isolates the quasi-architectural "movement" of the legislator from the political "action" that takes place within the confines he constructs,[65] and so disjoins those who make institutions from those who are made by them.

The insufficiency of this conclusion can be suggested by toying with the ambiguity of the word "design." Simultaneously connoting "purpose," "mode of composition," and "enduring pattern," this term indicates why constitutional conduct and constitutional structure ought not to be categorically distinguished from each other. Granted, "we must not confuse the act of building with the house when built. The latter *is* a means, not a fulfillment. But it is such only because it enters into a new activity which is present not future. Life is continuous. The act of building in time gives way to the acts connected with a domicile."[66] If we are to persist in viewing institutions as "instruments," in other words, we must do so in light of the two senses of instrumentality discussed in Chapter 5. To continue the building metaphor, we must distinguish between "a tool in the external sense, a mere scaffolding to a finished building in which it has no part nor lot, and an immanent tool, as a scaffolding which is an integral part of the very operation of building, and which is set up for the sake of the building-activity which is carried on effectively only with and through a scaffolding. Only in the former case can the scaffolding be considered as a *mere* tool. In the latter case the external scaffolding is *not* the instrumentality; the actual tool is the *action* of erecting the building, and this action involves the scaffolding as a constituent part of itself."[67]

To question the autonomy of constitutional structure from the conduct it informs is to question the unchallengeability that appears to be one of the defining traits of the bureaucratic state; and that, in turn, is the first step toward de-constructing that state. Such deconstruction is a sort of destruction. But "destructive" conduct can sustain its internal connection with the needs that elicit it only when it, in cumulative reenactment at each stage of elaboration, expresses a certain directionality without giving way to the imposition of prior design. If conduct is to remain responsive to experience's indispensable phase of undergoing, explication of the ends guiding it must remain contin-

---

65. See Aristotle, *Nichomachean Ethics*, trans. Terence Irwin (Indianapolis: Hackett, 1985), 1174a14–18; and *Metaphysics*, trans. Richard Hope (Ann Arbor: University of Michigan Press, 1960), 1048b17–46, 104926–36.
66. Dewey, *HNC*, p. 269.
67. Dewey, "The Objects of Thought," in *EEL*, p. 175.

uous with the conduct that unfolds their present meaning. It must take shape not as the de novo imposition of antecedently realized form upon recalcitrant matter, but rather as the resculpting of relational conditions immanent within forms of experience that are already but insufficiently expressive of their significance-making possibilities. To put the same point slightly differently, conduct can demonstrate its sensitivity to the embeddedness of means within the ends they constitute only by showing care for the institutional forms that nurture it. For the participation of such forms in the composition of human powers is a vital "means" of forming or deforming the sense-making capacities of their inhabitants.

As a relational whole whose parts either do or not resonate with one another in sense-making ways, the ability of constitutional structure to make the most of a culture's potential for meaning turns on its capacity to preserve the ambiguity whose presence in nature is a condition of all significant experience. The conditions necessary to any culture's quickened sense of its own significance are not in principle different from those required by each of its members. More specifically, a culture's capacity to foster multiple modes of consummatory experience turns on whether or not its structure remains attuned to the tension between, on the one hand, its thrust toward the assimilation of difference within a more comprehensive unity and, on the other, its need to undermine that thrust so as to keep open the way for sense's unfolding into the future. "There may be many articles in a box, many figures in a single painting, many coins in one pocket, and many documents in a safe. The unity is extraneous and the many are unrelated. The significant point is that unity and manyness are always of this sort or approximate it when the unity of the object or scene is morphological and static. The formula has meaning only when its terms are understood to concern a relation of energies. There is no fullness, no many parts, without distinctive differentiations. But they have esthetic quality, as in the richness of a musical phrase, only when distinctions depend upon reciprocal resistances. There is unity only when the resistances create a suspense that is resolved through coöperative interaction of the opposed energies. The 'one' of the formula is the realization through interacting parts of their respective energies. The 'many' is the manifestation of the defined individualizations due to opposed forces that finally sustain a balance."[68]

68. Dewey, AE, p. 161.

How fully the traits of natural existence are revealed depends on the scope and complexity of the interactions sustained among its diverse elements. By the same token, a constitution's potential for meaning is most adequately realized when its dynamic form, continuously enacted and reenacted, holds in tense equilibrium the greatest variety and scope of opposed parts. To borrow an analogy from another medium, just as a great symphony progressively intensifies its suspensefulness by making diverse but reciprocal voices oppose and answer one another, so too the maximal sense of a constitutional whole requires constant contrapuntal exchange between its centrifugal forces of incorporation and its centripetal powers of dissociation.

VI

When reason's architectonic pretensions are shed, thinking reemerges as one phase of the transformations undergone by experience when it is questioned about the relations sustained among the events and things that appear within it. As such, it neither presupposes nor gives access to a privileged principle of being. "The old center was mind knowing by means of an equipment of powers complete within itself, and merely exercised upon an antecedent external material equally complete in itself. The new center is indefinite interactions taking place within a course of nature which is not fixed and complete, but which is capable of direction to new and different results through the mediation of intentional operations. Neither self nor world, neither soul nor nature (in the sense of something isolated and finished in its isolation) is the center, any more than either earth or sun is the absolute center of a single universal and necessary frame of reference. There is a moving whole of interacting parts; a center emerges wherever there is effort to change them in a particular direction."[69]

Correlatively, when the desire to ground collective order in a fixed center of being is overcome, the possibility of the an-archic mode of experience that bears the adjective "political" (re)appears. Emerging when neither custom nor monologic rule can successfully eliminate struggle over the resources of meaning, the noun "politics" designates one of the many modes of experience in which human beings may partake. It is found in the decentered field wrought out of nature and

69. Dewey, QC, pp. 290–91.

into human being by the transactions sustained among diversely constructed associational forms whose contingent sources of commonality are fully immanent within and articulated by their mutual relations.
Accordingly, whatever authority arises upon that field is a property
that is distributively present within that same complex of relations. To
ascribe that authority to something superior to that constitution—for
instance, to the reason of state, teleocratically construed—is to mistake the apparent for the real by ascribing independent and antecedent existence to what could not be were it not derived from more
immediate forms of experience.[70]

The political art is a mode of conduct dedicated to the cultivation of
such experience. It is a "mediated" activity in the sense that it arises
out of mutual interest in the peculiarly public medium within which
diverse associational forms can flourish. It does not, however, seek to
overcome the particularities of these associations in the construction of
a unified whole. That art is rooted in nothing more sturdy than the
baseless hope that these differences may prove mutually informing
when relocated within a more encompassing construct that nurtures
rather than effaces the qualitatively diverse powers called into being
by their commerce. To hold that this art's conduct presupposes antecedent consensus on the ends common to all of its participants (as
does MacIntyre) is to call for an associational form whose realization
can only make political pragmata disappear. To equate that art with
the exercise of unilinear domination (as does Weber) is to defend a
hierarchical conception of power whose actualization cannot help but
cut against all efforts to sustain those spaces in which the differences
that make politics possible may be displayed and reconciled.

Structuring the play of heterogeneity on behalf of a richer exchange,
the political art is derivative but also distinctive and constitutive. It is
qualitatively different from other less comprehensive kinds because its
conduct cannot proceed apart from a vital sense of the more inclusive

70. In Marx's "Critique of Hegel's Doctrine of the State," in *Early Writings*, trans.
Rodney Livingstone and Gregor Benton (New York: Vintage Books, 1975), he defends
what he calls the "constitution of democracy" in quite similar terms. See especially pp.
87–89: "Democracy is the solution to the *riddle* of every constitution. In it we find the
constitution founded on its true ground: *real human beings* and the *real people*; not merely
implicitly and in essence, but in *existence* and in reality. . . . In a democracy the constitution, the law, i.e., the political state, is itself only a self-determination of the people and a
determinate content of the people." I would add, though, that Marx imports into his
account much more of a subjectivist ontology than I find appropriate. Hence his claim
that the "constitution is thus posited as the people's *own* creation. The constitution is in
appearance what it is in reality: the free creation of man" (p. 87).

web of relations within which partial collectivities, bound together by locality, religious conviction, history, moral agreement, and the like, continually uncover and nurture the terrain upon which they come together and apart. Looking beyond the relations internal to any given part, as well as the relations between several but not all of the parts of such a whole, political art's concern is with parts and the larger constitutional whole to which they belong. To use the metaphor of the body politic, its concern is neither the relations internal to each organ nor the relations sustained between several organs, but rather the relations between one or more organs in their situation as member(s) of the body politic in its organic entirety.

The art of constitutional politics is a matter of separating and recrafting the relations among various modes of collective being in light of some more comprehensive understanding of the sense deficiencies engendered by the patterns into which they are presently resolved. The late liberal state, to the degree that it relies on bureaucratic rationality, cannot give rise to a sense of such a constitutional whole because it cuts its cultural material into so many autonomous realms, each of which relates to all others in mechanical fashion. Doing so, it closes off worlds of meaning that might otherwise become apparent. "Potentiality signifies a certain limitation of present powers, due to the limited number of conditions with which they are in interaction plus the fact of the manifestation of the new powers under different conditions."[71] Lived experience is effectively denied the resources of its own significance when it is unambiguously partitioned into the discrete spheres of work, family, politics, and so on. "Recurring units as such call attention to themselves as isolated parts, and thus away from the whole. Recurring *relationships* serve to define and delimit parts, giving them individuality of their own. But they also connect; the individual entities they mark off demand, *because* of the relations, association and interaction with other individuals. Thus the parts vitally serve in the construction of an expanded whole."[72]

Only when various modes of experience are grasped as parts whose relations within a moving whole are constitutive of their identity can conduct secure a sense of how its present import might be made still fuller. In tacking back and forth between part and whole, however, that art does not strive to subdue the distinguishing qualities that

71. Dewey, "The Subject-Matter of Metaphysical Inquiry," in *ENF*, p. 220.
72. Dewey, *AE*, p. 166.

make different ways of relating individuals what they are; it does not, for example, seek to overcome the dissimilarities between the modes of being we call "familial" and "economic." Rather, and following the example of Solon, it asks how the web of everyday circumstance might be rewoven in ways that more adequately disclose matters of general concern and consequence, that is, of qualitatively inclusive pragmata.

Correlatively, the political art does not seek to establish the primacy of its peculiar mode of experience over all others. Granted, this art does reject liberalism's representation of the state as a mere instrument designed to maximize the end specific to another mode of experience: the economic. But to offer this criticism is not to ascribe to some sovereign institutional center proprietary title over determination and realization of something approximating Rousseau's general will. Rather, to stay with the *oikos-polis* relationship, it is to argue that the most comprehensive set of constitutional relations giving experience its present shape *are* those that accord it its political quality; that economic affairs are one part of this larger whole; that the political qualities sustained by economic matters become open to question when we ask about their contribution to the cause of significant experience within this larger whole; and that those things may become concerns of the political art to the degree that they detract from the potentialities of that cause. To call for a restoration of the political, accordingly, is to call for actualization of conduct that refashions the constitutional relations between persons through reference to some understanding of the way in which those relations, in their totality, give and deny access to the "means" of crafting significance from experienced affairs.

To be deemed intelligent, any particular actualization of the political art need not presuppose global comprehension of the constitutional structure into which it enters. Such a requirement may perhaps be met by God, but it is unavailable to human beings who always think from within the confines of circumscribed situations. Nor is political thinking to be judged true or false according to whether or not its claims accurately mirror a given constitutional whole. Rather, it is to be deemed more or less thoughtful according to the degree to which individuals appreciate the complex manifold of relations that permeate that structure and, in light of this appreciation, fashion from experience the conditions of consummatory experience. Correlatively, constitutional structure reveals *its* "intelligence" to the degree that it solicits individual mind (as opposed to the mind in individuals). For that structure's capacity to nourish experience's sense-giving possibilities is the best single indicator of the truthfulness of its form.

As with all things drawn out of nature's affairs and into human experience, the rhythmic tempos sustained among the moving relations of constitutional structure account for the appearance and disappearance of any collectivity's specifically political pragmata. All constitutional structure is simultaneously constraining and enabling. It encourages certain kinds of conduct while discouraging others, and so it opens experience to some things while closing it to others. For example, with the exception of the extraordinary act of revolution, conventional liberal discourse largely identifies politics with governmental activity taking place within the boundaries of a sovereign state. Predicated on a strict demarcation of the private from the public, classical liberalism is at least nominally committed to the view that the central purpose of government is to minimize what Hobbes called "external impediments to motion," whether erected by individuals or by government itself. That dualism in turn renders suspect any suggestion that political issues are immediately implicated in the structuring of activity within other formally nonpolitical spheres of cultural and economic life. It is not surprising, therefore, to find that the present's reduction of politics to a distant parade of abstract symbols has been accompanied by increasing unreceptivity to the political qualities of everyday experience.

From the perspective suggested in this chapter, it is liberalism's constitutional malformation that accounts for this widespread occlusion of unrefined political pragmata and so makes possible their monopolization by a state that defines their "solution" as its special business. The liberal veiling of ordinary experience's political dimensions, in other words, expresses and reinforces the power of a more enduring rationalistic tradition that construes politics not as a qualitatively distinct mode of experience, but rather as a determinate field of objects whose manipulation is reserved to those who have certified their mastery of its expert imperatives. Political affairs are effectively rendered invisible by institutionalized ways of thinking that shift our sense of reality from concrete things, as they are entangled in ordinary experience, to an intellectualized grasp of reason's refined objects. Reconstructed as so many "problems," the political qualities of everyday experience suffer a loss of ontological stature and so come to appear less real than the objects manufactured by the state's reifying discourses. The distinctive issues of this particular mode of experience thus receive hypostatized form as so many powers alienated from and now looming over their original holders. Participation in matters political is thereby reduced to the simple act of voting, that is, to selecting those who are to occupy a state committed by its very existence to maintaining a salutary distance between itself and those whose conduct calls political things into being.

When it is understood, however, that constitutional structure is an expression of the relations sustained among various associational forms, it then becomes possible to acknowledge that everyday life necessarily elicits *res publicae*. Simply in virtue of its participation in constitutional relations, ordinary experience bears a political quality, albeit one that exists for the most part as an unrealized potentiality. To conduct oneself in a way that reproduces that structure of relations is to find one's life implicated in a collectivity's constitution. Its form, even when not an object of artful refashioning, is internal and essential to those whose habits sustain it in time. Hence its fate is an immediate affair of all, and all have a stake in the shape it is now assuming.[73] Its concerns can become democratically apparent as so many tangible affairs, though, only when deliberately incorporated within conduct aimed at refashioning the medium of its own practice.

If indeed the state is the primary vehicle through which everyday life is presently deprived of its political quality, then the perpetuation of its pseudopolitics is inconsistent with the democratic appearance of political things. If the term "state" refers to that locus of public power which, standing formally independent of the governed, constitutes the supreme source of legitimate authority within a defined territory, then the recovery of political experience requires that its stranglehold on this form of being be broken. A step in that direction is taken when we recall that prior to the sixteenth century the term "status" was used

---

73. The indebtedness of these remarks to Marx's "Critique of Hegel's Doctrine of the State" should be apparent to anyone familiar with that work. See especially p. 187: "The general concerns of the state are political concerns, the state as a *real concern*. Deliberation and decision are the means by which the state becomes *effective* as a real concern. It therefore appears to be self-evident that all the members of the state have a *relation* to the state: it is a matter of *real concern* to them. The very concept 'member of the state' implies that they are a *part* of the state, that the state regards them as a part of itself. However, if they are a *part* of the state, it is obvious that their very *social existence* already constitutes their *real participation* in it. Not only do they share in the state, but the state is *their* share. To be a conscious part of a thing means to take part of it and to take part in it consciously. Without this consciousness the member of the state would be an animal." I take exception to Marx's remarks only insofar as they appear to assume that social existence, simply in virtue of being social, is political in character.

to refer either to the condition in which a specific ruler found himself or to the general circumstances of the realm (a sense preserved in the U.S. president's annual "State of the Union" address). In this larger sense, the term "state" refers to the body politic, that is, to the informed matter within which constitutional relations are embedded. Correspondingly, the phrase "reason of state" may be taken to refer to perpetual articulation and rearticulation of the meaning of this association of associations. So construed, "the problem of discovering the state is not a problem for theoretical inquirers engaged solely in surveying institutions which already exist. It is a practical problem of human beings living in association with one another."[74] A democratic constitutional medium, in other words, can reaffirm its capacity to regulate the conditions of its own association only through so many acts of refounding, each of which breaks to some degree our collective dependence on and addiction to the current state.

The agencies of such withdrawals and reconstitution may, for our purposes, be called "publics." Whenever individuals-in-relation jointly engage in critical conduct regarding the constitutional relations in which they participate, a public is called into being. So defined, publics can exist in varying degrees of actuality. When some partial association is unwittingly affected by the conduct of others, that is, when two or more associations are relationally joined to one another as parts within a larger whole whose effects are felt but not known, then the members of these various associations may be said to constitute a potential public. When the members of such a whole come to be aware of the connections joining the fate of each to that of all others, there emerges an inchoate public. Finally, when those relations become the objects of artful conduct aimed at eliciting a more complete sense of the meaning of the whole in which they are mutually situated, that public becomes fully political.

To think of the constitution of publics in this way is to appreciate the ambiguous character of all associations. For the same association can be both political and nonpolitical at one and the same time, depending on the location of experiencers in different spatial and temporal situations. The nuclear family, for example, is not itself a form of political association. Nor do the ties of acquaintance that join one family to another engender a political association. The political dimensions of familial association become tangibly apparent, however, when this

74. Dewey, *PP*, p. 32.

particular way of relating individuals to one another becomes interwoven with other ways (for example, that of the large business corporation or the welfare state), and so poses constitutional questions
regarding the relationships that bind them together within a larger
whole. Thus, to stay with this example, when it becomes apparent
that the internal organization of the nuclear family is reproduced
within the hierarchical organization of the corporation and recon-
firmed by the patriarchal rationale offered in justification of many
welfare benefits; when it becomes apparent that this homology creates
an interwoven structure of domination that denies some the opportunities to engage in the forms of conduct that generate tangible sense
from the matters presented within experience; and when it becomes
apparent that many of the effects generated by that structure of overlapping powers are rendered more or less invisible by our penchant
for separating and isolating the spheres of family, corporation, and
state, then the relations essential to the nuclear family become a political affair.

If the "state" is the comprehensive association constituted by so
many overlapping publics, each of which is itself called into being by a
felt need to tend to matters that concern them jointly, then there can be
no a priori specification of the good state. The variability and diversity
of political things render them especially ill suited to the cognitional
aspirations of traditional philosophy. In formal terms, though, it is
possible to suggest that a constitution is or is not democratic according
to the degree to which its latent publics realize their potential in
apprehending and caring for distinctively political matters. The democratic quality of a constitutional form, in other words, is indicated by
its capacity to assure the continuing appearance of the political things
wrought from its experience and to cultivate the publics that answer
the call of such things. An indication of a constitution's deficiency,
correlatively, is its inability to expand the field of political appearances.
When all, or most, publics remain merely potential, a constitution
loses its structure and so slips into a condition of political formlessness
(and hence senselessness).

A politics of the sort recommended here is not readily labeled either
reformist or revolutionary. "That the state should be to some a deity
and to others a devil is another evidence of the defects of the premises
from which discussion sets out. One theory is as indiscriminate as the
other."[75] Because any constitution is both medium and outcome of the

75. Ibid., p. 26.

relations it comprises, it is at once a barrier to conduct and an invitation to explore its untapped possibilities. The late liberal state is in that sense a highly ambiguous achievement. On the one hand, the history of the contemporary welfare state out of the parliamentary republic is the history of the penetration of civil society by instrumental rationality and its institutional objectifications. As our most concentrated expression of rationalization's drive to master the world, that state has ever more thoroughly appropriated the resources once exercised within extended households, local communities, voluntary associations, and the like. On the other hand, the history of the late liberal state is also one of partial extension of legal protections within certain ostensibly private associational forms, formal expansion of suffrage to all competent adults, and in limited respects acknowledgment that certain kinds of "private" conduct (for instance, reproduction and labor-management bargaining) have a political dimension. Ironically, then, at the very moment that liberalism's strict segregation of private from public matters is collapsing in on itself, the distance separating the state's formal structure from the complex associational forms it "manages" is growing ever greater.

In any event, it is out of these ambiguous materials that there must emerge any effort to fashion new forms of democratic constitutional structure. Overcoming the present emergency cannot help but take on the character of an emergence from the past. Accordingly, the "aim" of political conduct must be to stimulate and give some measure of shape to our inchoate sense that something is lacking in a politics whose highest aspirations are expressible in terms of the gross national product. It is only out of such dis-ease that we can begin to tease some anticipatory intimation of a politics that is more than merely objectified theatrics palmed off on so many subjectified selves.

If the politics recommended here is appropriately deemed reformist in this sense, it is radical in several others. The institutionalized ways of relating that articulate a constitutional medium's structure prove suspect to the extent that they obstruct the emergence of new publics. "By its very nature, a state is ever something to be scrutinized, investigated, searched for. Almost as soon as its form is stabilized, it needs to be remade. And since conditions of action and of inquiry and knowledge are always changing, the experiment must always be retried; the State must always be rediscovered."[76] The rigidity of the late liberal state, blocking such rediscovery, denies the temporality of constitu-

76. Ibid., pp. 31–32, 34.

tional form. For just as there is no way to furnish an a priori enumeration of the political affairs that may emerge within collective experience, so too there is no way to antecedently delimit the boundaries of the wholes within which those affairs may appear.

It follows that the notion of sovereignty that is now so intimately bound up with our understanding of what constitutes a state must be rejected as an antipolitical expression of the teleocratic conception of action that classical philosophy crafted out of its desire to preserve the formal attributes of Zeus's rule while shedding its mythical foundation. There is no good reason to assume that political pragmata or the potential publics they engender will remain neatly enclosed within the administrative borders set by any given sovereign state. There may be many publics within the boundaries of what we now call a "state," as well as many publics whose affairs cross over into several such entities. Indeed, given the recent appearance of politically charged emergents at both the sub or supra state levels (for example, pollution, terrorism, reproductive rights), it would appear that their tangible relocation entails recognizing that the state's definition of political issues in terms of determinate spatial confines comes at the expense of that which time brings into the world.

There is still another sense in which the politics defended here entails a kind of radicalism. In Book III of Cicero's *Commonwealth*, the following exchange takes place between Scipio and Laelius:

> SCIPIO: What, I ask, was the affair of the Athenians when, at the close of their great war with Sparta, the city was ruled by the Thirty Tyrants in utter defiance of law? Did the ancient renown of the state, or the celebrated beauty of the city, its theater, its gymnasi, its porticoes, its splended propylaea, its citadel, the marvelous creations of Phidias, or its magnificent harbor at Piraeus—did all these make it a commonwealth?
>
> LAELIUS: By no means, for there was no affair of the people [*populi res*].
>
> SCIPIO: Again, what was the case at Rome, when the decemvirs, in that notorious third year, allowed no appeal to the people from their decisions, because there was then no such thing as liberty?
>
> LAELIUS: There was no affair of the people; on the contrary, the people took steps to recover their affair.

This dialogue suggests that ontological rehabilitation of the sensible particulars that constitute political things turns, at least in part, on the achievement of a particular sort of equality.[77] Recall that distinctively political matters first emerged within the Greek city-state when customary hierarchies collapsed and traditional legitimations of rule's authority proved suspect. While neither the appearance of a sphere of political significance nor the formation of a public to care for it was contingent on the existence of a specific set of institutional arrangements, both proved possible only because the resources of effective power were now more or less equitably distributed.

Power is implicated in the constitution of collective existence. It is not a thing, but rather a property of the relations that give experience its distinctive shape. To be powerless, to be embedded in a constitutional structure that fixes relations of subordination and domination, is to be deprived of the opportunity to engage in the transformative conduct that elicits the sense of experience. To be powerful is to be invited by situated affairs to partake of the resources—that is, the means—of meaning, and so to conduct the doings and sufferings that nurture significance. To take part in specifically political power is to engage with others in collaborative elicitation of a world capable of bearing its identity through time. So construed, expansion of the capacities of ordinary women and men is a corollary of freedom and hence of democracy. For "liberty is that secure release and fulfillment of personal potentialities which takes place only in rich and manifold association with others: the power to be an individualized self making a distinctive contribution and enjoying in its own way the fruits of association. A society which makes provision for participation in its good of all its members on equal terms and which secures flexible readjustment of its institutions through interactions of the different forms of associated life is in so far democratic."[78]

Only when there exists a rough equilibrium of effective power can all come not merely to see, but also to taste, feel, and hear the potentialities lurking in present experience. The possibility of meaning's expansion is inseparable from the capacity of constitutional form to engender the premonition that what is presently in experience is not

---

77. In *Economy and Society*, vol. 2, Weber makes much the same point when he asks: "In view of the growing indispensability of the state bureaucracy and its corresponding increase in power, how can there by any guarantee that any powers will remain which can check and effectively control the tremendous influence of this stratum? How will democracy even in this limited sense be *at all possible*?" (p. 1403).

78. Dewey, *DE*, p. 99; *PP*, p. 150.

all it might be. That sense remains absent unless persons are related in ways that bid them to acknowledge the *res novae* emergent in temporally qualified experience, and so to engage in the critical conduct through which such partly knowns come to assume more sensible form. Hence the achievement of democratic constitutional form, as the sine qua non of its susceptibility to incessant reformation, is indivisible from the cause of meaning. For we discover our significant being most fully in those domains where subject and object are synthesized, without being dissolved, in the exercise of transformative power.

This last point suggests the final and perhaps the deepest sense in which the politics sketched here is radical in import. The cause of democracy is not well identified with establishment of the juridical mechanisms through which conflict is adjudicated, or with the creation of common identities among those who might otherwise remain unknown to one another (although both are certainly parts of any complete account of democratic politics). Incarnate in the conduct that elucidates the means of its ideal as well as what that ideal means, the cause of democratic politics is better identified with its capacity to embed within collective life an ongoing attunement to experience's contingency. The fashioning of new meanings, and so expansion of experience's capacity to bear a sense of itself, involves the unsettling of established routines, the contestation of customary meanings, and the challenging of established boundaries between different spheres of collective experience. Only a robust democratic politics, sustaining a tense balance between its centering and decentering drives, can remind human beings of the partialities, incompletions, and ambiguities implicit in how the what of experience is now given encultured form.

Postscript /
On Pragmatism's Cash-Value

"It is silly to deny that there has been gain to the masses accompanying the change of masters. But to glorify these gains and to give no attention to the brutalities and inequities, the regimentation and suppression, the war, open and covert, that attend the present system is intellectual and moral hypocrisy. Distortion and stultification of human personality by the existing regime give the lie to the claim that the present social system is one of freedom."[1]

Although the cure for the ailments of democracy is indeed more democracy, the effort to explicate the present meaning of that prescription is handicapped by the undemocratic character of the constitutional orders now called "democratic." "Nothing is gained by attempts to minimize the novelty of the democratic order, nor the scope of the change it requires in old and long cherished traditions."[2] To a significant degree, contemporary political life in the West is defined by rationalized institutions that structure conduct along hierarchical lines, by inegalitarian distribution of the material resources needed to refashion those institutions, and by internalization of meanings that

1. John Dewey, "Democracy Is Radical," in *Common Sense* (Jan. 1937), 10.
2. Dewey, *FC*, p. 163.

persuade the disenfranchised to acquiesce in their own disempowerment. Moreover, these forms of power simultaneously constrain and
enable one another in ways such that no single form can be reconstituted unless correlative transformations are effected within each of
the others to which it is linked. Hence the struggle for democracy must
proceed on as many fronts as there are modes of experience.

But the tale I have told here offers little comfort to those who wish
to believe that democratically inclined energies are now straining to
break through the eviscerated meanings of a rationalized order. "Revolutions in the formal organization of human relationships are much
easier to effect than revolutions in the hearts and minds of men. Those
who have from infancy drawn their intellectual and moral sustenance
from the institutional conditions into which they were born and by the
necessities of the case have not known any other do not change their
desires and convictions when governments topple and new laws are
enacted. Habituations to the old persist long after the old has changed
its form. Ways of observing, of communicating, of prizing and disap-
proving are engrained in character and are neither thrown off nor
greatly modified by what are deemed revolutions by those who record
the course of history."[3] The vision of a wholesale leap into a wholly
new future must therefore be repudiated as yet another fantasy of the
epistemological ego, as must the hubristic claim to know either *the* root
cause of current unhappiness or *the* privileged agent of progressive
historical change. "A mind that has opened itself to experience and
that has ripened through its discipline knows its own littleness and
impotencies. It knows that its wishes and acknowledgements are not
final measures of the universe whether in knowledge or in conduct,
and hence are, in the end, transient."[4]

By no means are these the only obstacles that thwart deeper realization of the potentialities of democratic experience. New to human
history, the twentieth century has witnessed the rise of totalitarian
regimes claiming to derive authority from the will of their subjects.
The production of that consent derives from the development of technological instrumentalities that have "put at the disposal of dictators
means of controlling opinion and sentiment of a potency which reduces to a mere shadow all previous agencies at the command of
despotic rulers. For negative censorship it has substituted means of

3. Dewey, "Experience and Nature: A Re-introduction," in *LW*, vol. 1, p. 336.
4. Dewey, *EN*, p. 420.

propaganda of ideas and alleged information on a scale that reaches every individual, reiterated day after day by every organ of publicity and communication, old and new."[5] The power of such regimes reminds us why the form of conduct endorsed in these pages may well prove too feeble to forestall additional encroachments by those same instrumentalities. Because the immanent unity of means and ends is critical to its integrity, the "goal" of democratic conduct can only be attained by measures that can in time cohere as parts within the realized whole to which they constitutively contribute. It cannot, consequently, appeal to some contemporary incarnation of the theoretically informed classical legislator (for example, the dictatorship of the proletariat) to supply the knowledge that is to replace the ignorance of the powerless.

"The word democracy has become so intimately associated with a particular political order, that of general suffrage and elective officials, which does not work very satisfactorily, that it may be impossible to recover its basic moral and ideal meaning."[6] The recovery of democratic experience is additionally disabled because it points not to the achievement of some determinate state, but rather to the cultivation of forms of conduct that can secure no final close until experience itself comes to an end. The ideal informing that conduct is not a constant that can be passed on to future generations in its original purity; its meaning must always be reworked in light of the pressing needs and possibilities of the present. As such, it entails repudiation of the comforts otherwise furnished by antecedent specification of unambiguous purposes, precisely articulated strategies guaranteed to manufacture them, and unequivocally demarcated agents necessarily bound to their realization. Furthermore, in the absence of those comforts, democratic conduct must acknowledge the necessarily tragic dimension of its own practice. No longer convinced that the ends of enlightened freedom are rooted in the divinely sanctioned order of a benevolent nature, we must now grant that even the attainment of democracy's purposes will open up some valued forms of being while disabling others.

What, therefore, shall we expect from the future, especially in the land where the "pragmatic" temper finds its native home? On one scenario, the directionless flux of surface politics leaves the essential

5. Dewey, *FC*, p. 131.
6. Dewey, "Mediocrity and Individuality," in *MW*, vol. 13, p. 297.

parameters of existing institutional arrangements more or less unchanged. Persons are "moved primarily by the ills which are easily
seen to be those from which they and the country at large are suffering. Since the evils are attributed more or less to the action of the party
in power, there is a succession of swings back and forward as the
relative impotency of this and that party and of this and that line of
policy to regulate economic conditions, sufficiently to prevent widespread disaster, becomes clear."[7] As reminders of the qualitative peculiarities of democratic experience become ever fainter, it proves ever
more difficult to criticize the present by pointing to its betrayal of a
promise whose terms can no longer be recalled. Spread of the behavioral techniques definitive of what Foucault calls the "carceral"
society thereby renders ever more insignificant the electoral mechanisms whose formalistic perpetuation preserves whatever semblance
of popular consent is needed to ensure domestic contentedness. The
present thus lapses into a "soulless and heartless materialism, com-
pensated for by soulful but futile and unnatural idealism and spiritual-
ism."[8]

On a second scenario, which extrapolates the first into a probable
future, the inability of the bureaucratic state to satisfy the collective
quest for certainty invites redirection of that search toward a less
abstract but equally misplaced object. "Difficulties in the way of effective action by law-making bodies in meeting actual conditions are
increased by the general belief that they, with the courts and with
administrative bodies, are favorable to special interests, by association
and by education and at times by corruption. Distrust gives both the
rabble-rouser and the would-be dictator their opportunities. The former speaks in words for the oppressed mass against oppression; in
historic fact he has usually been an agent, willing or unknowing, of a
new form of oppression. As Huey Long is reported to have said,
Fascism would come in this country under the name of protecting

7. Dewey, FC, p. 60. The similarity between this line of argument and that advanced
by Marx in his "Critical Notes on the 'King of Prussia,'" in *Early Writings*, ed. Quintin
Hoare (New York: Vintage Books, 1975), should be apparent. See especially p. 406: "In
so far as the English bourgeoisie regards pauperism as the *fault of politics* the Whigs put
the blame on the Tories and the Tories put it on the Whigs. According to the Whigs the
chief cause of pauperism is to be discovered in the monopoly of landed property and in
the laws prohibiting the import of grain. In the Tory view the source of the trouble lies in
liberalism, in competition and the excesses of the factory system. Neither party discovers the explanation in politics itself but only in the politics of the other party."
8. Dewey, "Body and Mind," PC, p. 305.

democracy from its enemies."[9] As those presently empowered tighten their grip on established institutions, those who feel they have little to gain from disorder ally themselves with those who are sure they have much to lose. The will to security, although experienced in very different ways depending on class position, effectively unites those who wish to counter the disconcerting effects produced by whatever residue of democratic politics still persists. Unable to stall the sense-depriving drive of a reason that equates its final end with perfect subsumption of all experience beneath the imperatives of managerial science, the present spawns a future whose "mechanized petrification," to use Weber's language, is redeemed only by the affectations of a charismatic figurehead, bloated with "convulsive self-importance."[10]

These two scenarios are twins masquerading as opposites. Each has its roots not in the threat of foreign domination, but rather in the gradual insinuation on the domestic front of anxieties very much like those that have sustained the antipolitics of totalitarianism elsewhere. Should such insecurities continue to chip away at the impulse to consequential political conduct, then the United States and its Soviet alter ego may unwittingly stumble across the unsettling commonalities that mock their ideological differences. "Neither theory nor practical experience has as yet shown that state socialism will be essentially different from state capitalism."[11]

On a third scenario, the future anticipated by the first two is mitigated by recovery, however partial, of the constitutional conditions of vital democratic experience. In light of the external impediments to and internal disabilities of such a project, it is difficult to hear with uncynical ears the claim that critical thinking may yet become an immanent moment within crafty conduct that contests what is. To that

9. Dewey, *FC*, p. 68.
10. Max Weber, *The Protestant Ethic and the Spirit of Capitalism* (New York: Scribner, 1958), p. 182.
11. Dewey, *FC*, p. 71. For Weber's claim to much the same effect, see *Economy and Society*, vol. 2, p. 1453: "What then would be a democracy without any parliamentarism in the German political order with its authoritarian bureaucracy? Such a merely *passive democratization* would be a wholly pure form of *uncontrolled bureaucratic domination*, so familiar to us, which would call itself a 'monarchic regiment.' Or, if we relate this democratization to the economic reconstruction that these 'socialists' hope for, it would be a modern rational counterpart of the ancient liturgical state. Interest groups legitimized and 'allegedly' controlled by the state bureaucracy would be actively the agents of corporate self-administration, and passively they would be the carriers of the public burdens. The civil servants would then be supervised by these profit-oriented associations, but neither by the monarch who would be quite incapable of doing it, nor by the citizen who would lack all representation."

cynicism, I offer two responses. First, "we have every right to point to the long non-democratic and anti-democratic course of human history and to the recentness of democracy in order to protect ourselves from the pessimism that comes from taking a short-span temporal view of events."[12] While the Greeks of antiquity may have been the first to disclose nature's potentiality for specifically political affairs, that experience was confined to a tiny fraction of the city-state's population and so was democratic in import more than in actual fact. The contention that the experience of power is essential to the sense of all persons, regardless of the particularistic qualities that distinguish one from another, is a peculiarly modern claim. As intimated by events in Eastern Europe during 1989 and 1990, to assert that the cause of democracy cannot be more adequately realized in the future is to forget that time always reopens the possibility of the unforeseen.

Second and more important, we should remember that "every thinker puts some portion of an apparently stable world in peril and no one can wholly predict what will emerge in its place."[13] To grasp the import of this claim, recall the central argument of this work. We are the disenchanted legatees of a reason whose internally complex history is unified by its profound impiety toward the prosaic affairs of everyday life as well as their ceaseless struggle to sustain some sense of their own significance. To restore some measure of dignity to that experience and hence to those who have it, we need something this work cannot and does not pretend to provide.

What this project requires is an unending stream of agile undertakings aimed at overcoming the numbness that now blocks our feeling for the concrete, the particular, and the parochial. This, it should be clear, is not to call for a reinvigoration of the forms of political participation most commonly studied by mainstream political science. Those forms—for example, voting, lobbying, campaigning for office—are essentially defined and so malformed by the imperatives of a state that heeds only those who speak the certified discourses of institutionalized expertise. Nor is it to call for a grand insurrection undertaken by those whose ability to engage in principled revolt turns on their universally shared, theoretically articulable, and systematic knowledge of the present crisis's root causes. To advance this latter

---

12. Dewey, FC, p. 176.
13. Dewey, EN, p. 222. The material of the following several paragraphs shows my considerable indebtedness to James Scott's *Weapons of the Weak: Everyday Forms of Peasant Resistance* (New Haven: Yale University Press, 1985), esp. pp. 340–50.

claim is to fall prey to the epistemological illusion that commonality presupposes identity of cognitive vision, that is, uniform apprehension of self-identical representations. It is to demonstrate a failure of confidence in the capacity of politics to effect a reconciliation of the differences it brings into the space of public appearances. It is to substitute the pretensions of the intellectual and the illusions of the propagandist for the palpable immediacies of situated problematic conduct. Finally, it is to presuppose a distinction between *real* revolutionary practice and action that, by way of comparison, is "insignificant" because it is unorganized, oriented to the "trivial" needs of the current incident, and uninformed by a determinate grasp of the goals it seeks to secure.

If the arguments of the preceding chapters are sound, the invidious dualism between reform and revolution must itself be rejected. Besides reinstating the teleological rationality criticized in this work, that disjunction simply confirms disrespect for conduct that is solidly rooted in the commonplace needs of the present moment. In his "What Makes a Life Significant," William James writes: "But if, after all that I have said, any of you expect that they will make any *genuine vital difference*, on a large scale, to the lives of our descendants, you will have missed the significance of my entire lecture. The solid meaning of life is always the same eternal thing—the marriage, namely, of some unhabitual ideal, however special, with some fidelity, courage, and endurance; with some man's or woman's pains."[14] The conduct articulated in these pages is manifest in so many "petty" efforts to affirm the dignity of the ordinary by contesting the manifestations of its disempowerment. Exemplars of such affirmation include women who find the strength to challenge the impoverishment of lives restricted to the domestic sphere, workers who muster the courage to demand greater flexibility in the conditions of their employment, students who no longer tolerate pedagogies that leave unsatisfied their desire to tease sense from the matters of daily experience, consumers who come to recognize the characteristic qualities of goods whose acquisition can only aggravate the hollow sensationalism of late capitalism, academics who prove willing to spurn received criteria of professional advancement, welfare recipients who reject regulations aimed at tightening the bonds of their dependence on a disciplinary state.

14. James, quoted in Cornel West, *The American Evasion of Philosophy* (Madison: University of Wisconsin Press, 1989), p. 60.

"Realistic" in means and modest in ends, such efforts take shape as so many persistent and irreducible struggles, by individuals alone and in association, to chip away at the situations in which the experience of dispossession is immediately and imminently *had*. The impersonal forces that systematically expropriate the resources of mundane meaning are never experienced as such. They are always experienced as they are presently carried into and borne by my current situation; and it is to that particularity that I must respond. My foes are neither the institutionalized imperatives of late monopoly capitalism nor the abstraction known as "the bureaucratic state." Were I to experience either of these abstractions per se, there is little doubt that I would quickly capitulate before their appearance of awesome inexorability. Rather, my foes are those particular persons whom I regard not as structuralism's blank bearers of prefigured roles, but as agencies who are to be held responsible for their complicity in reproducing the institutional forms within which we are commonly bound. My conduct thus takes its departure from the invariably partial (but not for that reason erroneous) sense sprouting from the ground on which I now stand. It is animated by some as yet inarticulate feeling that matters must change, that the future's possibilities have yet to be exhausted, that the losses I (or we) presently endure might be alleviated, that the indignities inflicted on me (or us) by present circumstances are not given in the nature of this world's things.

The common but indeterminate project of such spatially and temporally delimited struggles, whether taking the form of active resistance or less obtrusive forms of noncompliance, is to resecure the contextualized resources of meaningful life. Such actions need not be formally coordinated for their cumulative effects to be felt in time. To hold otherwise is to permit the bureaucratized conception of collective action that expresses the core of teleocratic reason to define what counts as significant resistance. It is enough if such acts, although undertaken by very different persons in a multiplicity of qualitatively distinct situations, manifest a common practical import. As such, they require no leadership, no fixed point of origination, and no singular organizational structure. Indeed, it is precisely these absences that account for conduct's capacity to remain democratically responsive to the peculiarities of particular situations, each of which is changing its essential contours moment by moment.

Whether such simultaneous but unconcerted actions may in time concatenate in a way that poses a vital challenge to a state-centered constitutional order is something that cannot be known until after it is done. To hope that they may do so is to hold to a faith whose tenets James expresses as follows:

> I am against bigness and greatness in all their forms, and with the invisible molecular forces that work from individual to individual, stealing in through the crannies of the world like so many soft rootlets, or like the capillary oozing of water, and yet rending the hardest monuments of man's pride, if you give them time, the bigger the unit you deal with, the hollower, the more brutal, the more mendacious is the life displayed. So I am against all big organizations as such, national ones first and foremost; against all big successes and big results; and in favor of the eternal forces of truth which always work in the individual and immediately unsuccessful way, under-dogs always, till history comes, after they are long dead, and puts them on the top.[15]

It is always tempting to abandon such faith by dismissing out of hand the possibility of a revolution that slowly works its way through the intestines of the body politic. But the hubris of that dismissal is readily exposed by noting its implicit affirmation of privileged insight into a future no one can see clearly.

In these pages I have attempted to think, that is, to engage in "criticism of the influential beliefs that underlie culture; a criticism which traces the beliefs to their generating conditions as far as may be, which tracks them to their results, which considers the mutual compatibility of the elements of the total structure of beliefs. Such an examination terminates, whether so intended or not, in a projection of them into a new perspective which leads to new surveys of possibilities."[16] Yet as I have noted in several places, that perspective is only a perspective; it offers neither precise answers nor concrete programs of reform. As to the question of this perspective's "utility," I neither can nor should respond. Its confirmation cannot be self-contained, for no general orientation is ever self-translating in its application to particular events. What that perspective really signifies can only be known by making apparent its bearing on this or that situation.

Whether I have adequately indicated how conduct may bear the qualitative fruits of enhanced insight into embodied meaning without recourse to the architectonic pretensions of teleocratic reason can only be answered if and when that indication finds itself regrounded in the

---

15. Ibid., p. 59.
16. Dewey, "Context and Thought," in *ENF*, p. 107.

everyday. The much less telling ambition of this work has been to show, first, why making sense of the quality of contemporary experience is impossible as long as that effort is disconnected from an appreciation of the emergence and history of what we take to be reason; and, second, why recovering political affairs from the institutionalized clutches of such rationalism is inseparable from a critique that, from the standpoint of the present, must appear without reason.

Index

Library of Congress Cataloging-in-Publication Data
Kaufman-Osborn, Timothy V. (Timothy Vance), 1953–
    Politics/sense/experience: a pragmatic inquiry into the promise
of democracy / Timothy V. Kaufman-Osborn.
        p. cm.
    Includes bibliographical references and index.
    ISBN 0-8014-2504-2 (alk. paper)
    1. Democracy.   2. Pragmatism.   3. Reason.   4. Experience.
I. Title.
JC423.K35   1991
321.8—dc20   91-6325